Econometrics and Economic Theory

Publisher's Note

Two further volumes of ESSAYS IN HONOUR OF JAN TINBERGEN, also edited by Willy Sellekaerts, are published simultaneously: INTERNATIONAL TRADE AND FINANCE and ECONOMIC DEVELOPMENT AND PLANNING.

Jan Tinbergen

Econometrics and Economic Theory

Essays in Honour of Jan Tinbergen

Edited by

Willy Sellekaerts

International Arts and Sciences Press, Inc.
White Plains, New York

Published in Great Britain by
The Macmillan Press Ltd.

First U.S. edition published in 1974 by
International Arts and Sciences Press, Inc.
901 North Broadway, White Plains, N.Y. 10603

Library of Congress Catalog Card Number: 73-92709

International Standard Book Number: 0-87332-056-5

Printed in Great Britain

Contents

Preface

In 1969 Ragnar Frisch and Jan Tinbergen were selected to share the first Nobel Prize in Economics. As former students of Professor Tinbergen my wife and I decided to honour him by compiling and editing a collection of previously unpublished articles, written by leading economists. In order to create a lasting monument to Jan Tinbergen we decided to use the royalties from the volume to create a scholarship fund from which outstanding Dutch students in economics will receive financial assistance during their first year of study in the North American university of their choice. Further details will later be arranged with the Netherlands School of Economics in Rotterdam.

Several North American and European economists were invited to write a paper, preferably focusing on Tinbergen's pathbreaking work in international trade, economic development and planning, econometrics and economic theory. Most invited economists readily accepted the invitation. I thank all the contributors for their continuous interest and spontaneous co-operation during the two years between the mailing of the invitations and the completion of the manuscript.

Although a Nobel Prizewinner does not need to be introduced to the scholars of his discipline, I decided to include in this collection of essays a paper written by Bent Hansen, in which he not only skilfully appraises Professor Tinbergen's contributions to economics, but also pictures Tinbergen the man as a humanitarian idealist, a worthy candidate for the Nobel Peace Prize. I thank the *Swedish Journal of Economics*, and in particular Peter Bohm, for giving me permission to reprint Bent Hansen's paper. As an appendix to each of the three volumes of this Festschrift, a *selected* bibliography of Jan Tinbergen's contributions to economics has been included.

In addition to the contributors, many persons have helped to make the publication of this collection of essays in honour of Jan Tinbergen possible. I thank Professor Dole Anderson, Director of the Institute for International Business and Economic Development of Michigan State University, who supported my idea and made the facilities of the Institute available to invite the contributors. The Faculty of Social Sciences of the University of Ottawa also contributed to the success of this volume. I thank Patrick Meany of The Macmillan Company of Canada for his assistance in the publication of the Festschrift. Above all, my wife, Brigitte made the publication of this Festschrift feasible, by providing invaluable technical and editorial assistance.

WILLY SELLEKAERTS

Ottawa,
November 1971

PART I ECONOMETRICS

1 An Adjusted Maximum Likelihood Estimator of Autocorrelation in Disturbances

BY CLIFFORD HILDRETH AND WARREN T. DENT*

1. Maximum Likelihood Estimates

ALTHOUGH it has been shown [9] that the maximum likelihood (M.L.) estimator of the autocorrelation coefficient in linear models with autoregressive disturbances is asymptotically unbiased, several Monte Carlo studies [8], [6], [15] suggest that finite sample bias is usually large enough to be of some concern. In the next section an approximation to the bias is developed and used to obtain an adjusted estimator with substantial smaller bias. Section 3 presents the results of applying the adjusted M.L. estimator, the unadjusted M.L., and two other estimators to Monte Carlo data. Some interpretations and conjectures comprise Section 4 and computing procedures are discussed in Section 5. The remainder of this section contains a brief sketch of maximum likelihood estimation.

The model is a normal linear regression model in which the disturbance (or error term) is assumed to be generated by a

* The University of Minnesota and the University of Iowa. This research was supported by National Science Foundation grants GS2268 and GS3317 to the University of Minnesota. The authors are indebted to the RAND Corporation for permission to use the results and the data tapes from the Hildreth–Lu study reported in [8]. The development in Section 2 of an approximate mean of the maxium likelihood estimator is a condensation of the development presented in Dent's thesis [4]. The thesis also contains preliminary studies of other properties of the distribution of $\hat{\rho}$. Applications of these to statistical inference, especially testing, will be reported later.

stationary first-order autoregressive process,

$$y_t = \sum_{k=1}^{K} x_{tk}\beta_k + u_t \qquad (t = 1, 2, \ldots, T) \tag{1}$$

$$u_t = \rho u_{t-1} + v_t \qquad (t = 2, \ldots, T) \tag{2a}$$

$$u_1 = (1 - \rho^2)^{-1/2} v_1 \tag{2b}$$

where y_t is an observed value of a dependent variable, x_{tk} is an observed value of the kth independent variable (treated as non-random), β_k is an unknown constant to be estimated, and u_t is a value taken by an unobserved random disturbance. ρ is an unknown coefficient with $|\rho| < 1$. The u_t are normal with mean zero and common variance denoted by $\nu/(1 - \rho^2)$. The v_t are normal, independent, identical with variance ν.

Alternatively, one may write

$$\mathbf{y} = \mathbf{X}\boldsymbol{\beta} + \mathbf{u} \tag{1*}$$

where $\mathbf{y}$ is a vector of order T and $\mathbf{u}$ is a drawing from a multivariate normal population with mean 0 and variance $\nu\mathbf{A}$ where

$$a_{st} = (1 - \rho^2)^{-1}\rho^{|t-s|} \qquad (s, t = 1, 2, \ldots, T) \tag{3}$$

The log-likelihood function is then

$$\begin{aligned} L(\boldsymbol{\beta}, \rho, \nu) &= \text{const} - \tfrac{1}{2}T \log \nu - \tfrac{1}{2} \log |\mathbf{A}| \\ &\quad - \frac{1}{2\nu}(\mathbf{y} - \mathbf{X}\boldsymbol{\beta})'\mathbf{A}^{-1}(\mathbf{y} - \mathbf{X}\boldsymbol{\beta}) \\ &= \text{const} - \tfrac{1}{2}T \log \nu + \tfrac{1}{2} \log (1 - \rho^2) \\ &\quad - \frac{1}{2\nu}(\mathbf{y} - \mathbf{X}\boldsymbol{\beta})'\mathbf{B}(\mathbf{y} - \mathbf{X}\boldsymbol{\beta}) \end{aligned} \tag{4}$$

where $\mathbf{B} = \mathbf{A}^{-1}$. It may be verified that $\mathbf{B} = \mathbf{I} + \rho^2\mathbf{I}^* - 2\rho\mathbf{H}$ where $\mathbf{I}$ is an identity of order T, $\mathbf{I}^*$ equals $\mathbf{I}$ except that the first element of the first row and last element of the last row of $\mathbf{I}^*$ are zero. $\mathbf{H}$ has elements each equal to $\tfrac{1}{2}$ in the $2(T - 1)$ positions immediately adjacent to the main diagonal and zeros elsewhere. $|\mathbf{B}| = 1 - \rho^2$. Partial derivatives of L with respect to the unknown parameters are

$$\frac{\partial L}{\partial \beta} = \frac{1}{\nu} \mathbf{X}'\mathbf{B}(\mathbf{y} - \mathbf{X}\boldsymbol{\beta}) \tag{5}$$

$$\frac{\partial L}{\partial \rho} = \frac{-2\rho}{1-\rho^2} - \frac{1}{\nu}(\mathbf{y} - \mathbf{X}\boldsymbol{\beta})'(\rho\mathbf{I}^* - \mathbf{H})(\mathbf{y} - \mathbf{X}\boldsymbol{\beta}) \tag{6}$$

$$\frac{\partial L}{\partial \nu} = \frac{-T}{2\nu} + \frac{1}{2\nu^2}(\mathbf{y} - \mathbf{X}\boldsymbol{\beta})'\mathbf{B}(\mathbf{y} - \mathbf{X}\boldsymbol{\beta}) \tag{7}$$

The normal equations obtained by equating these derivatives to zero are highly non-linear so it has generally been found expedient to obtain maximum likelihood estimates by iterative procedures.

The normal equations may be written

$$\hat{\boldsymbol{\beta}} = (\mathbf{X}'\hat{\mathbf{B}}\mathbf{X})^{-1}\mathbf{X}'\hat{\mathbf{B}}\mathbf{y} \tag{8}$$

$$-\hat{\rho}\hat{\nu} - (1-\hat{\rho}^2)(\mathbf{y} - \mathbf{X}\hat{\boldsymbol{\beta}})'(\hat{\rho}\mathbf{I}^* - \mathbf{H})(\mathbf{y} - \mathbf{X}\hat{\boldsymbol{\beta}}) = 0 \tag{9}$$

$$\hat{\nu} = \frac{1}{T}(\mathbf{y} - \mathbf{X}\hat{\boldsymbol{\beta}})'\hat{\mathbf{B}}(\mathbf{y} - \mathbf{X}\hat{\boldsymbol{\beta}}) \tag{10}$$

where $\hat{\mathbf{B}} = \mathbf{I} + \hat{\rho}^2\mathbf{I}^* - 2\hat{\rho}\mathbf{H}$.

If $\hat{\rho}$ were somehow obtained, calculation of $\hat{\beta}$, $\hat{\nu}$ from (8), (10) would correspond to well-known generalised least squares procedures. Equations analogous to (8), (10), say

$$\boldsymbol{\beta}_\rho = (\mathbf{X}'\mathbf{B}_\rho\mathbf{X})^{-1}\mathbf{X}'\mathbf{B}_\rho\mathbf{y} \tag{8*}$$

$$\nu_\rho = \frac{1}{T}(\mathbf{y} - \mathbf{X}\boldsymbol{\beta}_\rho)'\mathbf{B}_\rho(\mathbf{y} - \mathbf{X}\boldsymbol{\beta}_\rho) \tag{10*}$$

could be used to compute the maximum of L corresponding to any assumed value of ρ. The procedure used in this study (more fully explained in Section 5) is to substitute $\boldsymbol{\beta}_\rho$, ν_ρ for $\boldsymbol{\beta}$, ν in (4) obtaining a concentrated likelihood function

$$L^*(\rho) = \text{const} - \tfrac{1}{2}T \log \nu_\rho + \tfrac{1}{2}\log(1-\rho^2) \tag{11}$$

which is then maximised with respect to ρ. This maximising value[1] is the M.L. estimator $\hat{\rho}$ of ρ and may then be used in

[1] The likelihood function may have multiple maxima though these have rarely occurred in practice. The scanning procedure described in Section 5 is designed to give substantial protection against the possibility of being led to a local maximum that is not global.

(8), (10) or (8*), (10*) to obtain $\hat{\boldsymbol{\beta}} = \boldsymbol{\beta}_{\hat{\rho}}$, $\hat{\nu} = \nu_{\hat{\rho}}$. It was found convenient to note that L^* is a monotonic decreasing function of

$$S(\rho) = (1 - \rho^2)^{-1/T}(\mathbf{y} - \mathbf{X}\boldsymbol{\beta}_\rho)'\mathbf{B}_\rho(\mathbf{y} - \mathbf{X}\boldsymbol{\beta}_\rho) \qquad (12)$$

so $\hat{\rho}$ may be found by minimising $S(\rho)$.[2]

Under mild assumptions about the behaviour of $\mathbf{X}$ as T increases [9, p. 584] it has been shown that the M.L. estimators $\hat{\beta}$, $\hat{\rho}$, $\hat{\nu}$ are asymptotically independent and their joint asymptotic distribution is multivariate normal with means equal to the true parameter values and respective variances $(\mathbf{X}'\mathbf{B}\mathbf{X})^{-1}$, $(1 - \rho^2)/T$, $2\nu^2/T$.

An extensive Monte Carlo study [8] was undertaken to compare M.L. estimators with others and to obtain hints about which properties of the asymptotic distribution might be approximately realised in moderate-sized samples ($T = 30$ and 100 were considered). The results for $\hat{\rho}$ along with some subsequent trials are reported in Section 3. Although M.L. estimators compared favourably with the others considered, $\hat{\rho}$ did seem to be generally biased (see Table 3) and this suggested the possibility that if an approximation to the bias could be found it might be used to construct a more accurate estimator. In the absence of a specific utility function, mean square error has been used as the indicator of accuracy.

2. The Adjusted Estimator

Finding a useful approximation to the bias means finding an approximate mean of $\hat{\rho}$ that is substantially closer than the asymptotic mean for sample sizes commonly encountered. The approximation to $E\hat{\rho}$ developed below involves a succession of simplifying alterations whose effects are not checked individually but whose combined effects are checked by using the approximation to adjust the M.L. estimator and then checking the

[2] The likelihood function and the resulting estimators differ slightly according to the assumption made about the distribution of the initial observation y_1. See Zellner and Tiao [17] for a discussion of this point. In their 1960 study of demand relations [10], Hildreth and Lu treated y_1 as a fixed number. In [8], the method described in this section was applied though the expression for $S(\rho)$ was incorrectly stated. The factor $(1 - \rho^2)^{-1/T}$ was omitted [8, p. 35, Equation (13)]. However, the correct form was used in making calculations.

effect of the adjustment on calculations from Monte Carlo data. It is seen from Table 1.2 that about two-thirds of the bias in $\hat{\rho}$ was removed by this adjustment.

To examine the adjustment, consider Equation (9), re-written as

$$\frac{-\hat{\rho}}{(1-\hat{\rho}^2)T}(\hat{\mathbf{u}}'\hat{\mathbf{u}} + \hat{\rho}^2\hat{\mathbf{u}}'\mathbf{I}^*\hat{\mathbf{u}} - 2\hat{\rho}\hat{\mathbf{u}}'\mathbf{H}\hat{\mathbf{u}}) - \hat{\rho}\hat{\mathbf{u}}'\mathbf{I}^*\hat{\mathbf{u}} + \hat{\mathbf{u}}\mathbf{H}\hat{\mathbf{u}} = 0 \quad (9^*)$$

where $\mathbf{y} - \mathbf{X}\hat{\boldsymbol{\beta}}$ has been written $\hat{\mathbf{u}}$ and the value of $\hat{\nu}$ given in Equation (10) has been substituted. Some simplification is achieved by approximating $\hat{\mathbf{u}}'\mathbf{I}^*\hat{\mathbf{u}} = \sum_{t=2}^{T-1} \hat{u}_t^2$ by $\hat{\mathbf{u}}'\hat{\mathbf{u}} = \sum_{t=1}^{T} \hat{u}_t^2$, yielding

$$\frac{-\hat{\rho}}{T(1-\hat{\rho}^2)}[(1+\hat{\rho}^2)\hat{\mathbf{u}}'\hat{\mathbf{u}} - 2\hat{\rho}\hat{\mathbf{u}}'\mathbf{H}\hat{\mathbf{u}}] - \hat{\rho}\hat{\mathbf{u}}'\hat{\mathbf{u}} + \hat{\mathbf{u}}'\mathbf{H}\hat{\mathbf{u}} \simeq 0 \quad (13)$$

where '$\simeq$' is read 'may be approximately equal to'.

As T grows large, the term with the factor $1/T$ grows less important and $\hat{\rho}$ is determined primarily by the two latter terms. This can be made more apparent by rewriting the approximation

$$\hat{\rho} \simeq \frac{\hat{\mathbf{u}}'\mathbf{H}\hat{\mathbf{u}}}{\hat{\mathbf{u}}'\hat{\mathbf{u}}} + \frac{2\hat{\rho}^2}{T(1-\hat{\rho}^2)}\frac{\hat{\mathbf{u}}'\mathbf{H}\hat{\mathbf{u}}}{\hat{\mathbf{u}}'\hat{\mathbf{u}}} - \frac{\hat{\rho}(1+\hat{\rho}^2)}{T(1-\hat{\rho}^2)} \quad (14)$$

or

$$\hat{\rho}\left(1 + \frac{1+\hat{\rho}^2}{T(1-\hat{\rho}^2)}\right) \simeq \frac{\hat{\mathbf{u}}'\mathbf{H}\hat{\mathbf{u}}}{\hat{\mathbf{u}}'\hat{\mathbf{u}}}\left(1 + \frac{2\hat{\rho}^2}{T(1-\hat{\rho}^2)}\right) \quad (15)$$

which may be restated

$$\hat{\rho} \simeq \frac{\hat{\mathbf{u}}'\mathbf{H}\hat{\mathbf{u}}}{\hat{\mathbf{u}}'\hat{\mathbf{u}}}\left(\frac{T(1-\hat{\rho}^2) + 2\hat{\rho}^2}{T(1-\hat{\rho}^2) + 1 + \hat{\rho}^2}\right) \quad (16)$$

For $-1 < \hat{\rho} < 1$, the factor in brackets lies between $T/(T+1)$ and 1. The minimum of the factor is attained at $\hat{\rho} = 0$ and, for moderate or large T, the value of this factor remains close to $T/(T+1)$ over much of the interval $(-1, 1)$. For example, if $\hat{\rho} = \pm 0{\cdot}6$ the factor is $(T + 1 \,.\, 12)/(T + 1 \,.\, 12 + 1)$. In general, it is $(T+\alpha)/(T+\alpha+1)$ where $\alpha = 2\hat{\rho}^2/(1-\hat{\rho}^2)$.

It thus seems reasonable to make a further approximation by setting this factor equal to $T/(T+1)$. Let $\mathbf{G} = T/(T+1)\mathbf{H}$.

Then

$$\hat{\rho} \simeq \frac{\hat{\mathbf{u}}'\mathbf{G}\hat{\mathbf{u}}}{\hat{\mathbf{u}}'\hat{\mathbf{u}}} \tag{17}$$

Approximation (17) represents considerable simplification, but it appears that direct evaluation of the mean of $\hat{\mathbf{u}}'\mathbf{G}\hat{\mathbf{u}}/\hat{\mathbf{u}}'\hat{\mathbf{u}}$ would be difficult because little is known about the distribution of $\hat{\mathbf{u}}$. A further approximation is suggested by considering the coefficient estimator and residual vector for an autoregressive model with known ρ.

Let

$$\tilde{\boldsymbol{\beta}} = (\mathbf{X}'\mathbf{B}\mathbf{X})^{-1}\mathbf{X}'\mathbf{B}\mathbf{y} \tag{18}$$

be the M.L. estimator (also generalised least squares and best unbiased) for the case of known ρ. Then the residual vector

$$\tilde{\mathbf{u}} = \mathbf{y} - \mathbf{X}\tilde{\boldsymbol{\beta}} = \mathbf{M}\mathbf{y} = \mathbf{M}\mathbf{u} \tag{19}$$

is distributed according to the (singular) multivariate normal law with mean zero and variance

$$E\tilde{\mathbf{u}}\tilde{\mathbf{u}}' = \nu\mathbf{M}\mathbf{A}\mathbf{M}' = \nu\mathbf{M}\mathbf{A} = \nu(\mathbf{A} - \mathbf{X}(\mathbf{X}'\mathbf{B}\mathbf{X})^{-1}\mathbf{X}') \tag{20}$$

where

$$\mathbf{M} = \mathbf{I} - \mathbf{X}(\mathbf{X}'\mathbf{B}\mathbf{X})^{-1}\mathbf{X}'\mathbf{B} \tag{21}$$

In connection with the proof that $\hat{\boldsymbol{\beta}}$ has the same asymptotic distributions as $\tilde{\boldsymbol{\beta}}$, it was conjectured [9, Section 5] that the distributions of these vectors tend to be approximately equal for moderate sample sizes and this tended to be confirmed by subsequent Monte Carlo trials [8, p. 26]. Thus one might hope that $\hat{\mathbf{u}} = \mathbf{y} - \mathbf{X}\hat{\boldsymbol{\beta}}$ is distributed not too differently from $\tilde{\mathbf{u}} = \mathbf{y} - \mathbf{X}\tilde{\boldsymbol{\beta}}$, or at least that

$$E\frac{\hat{\mathbf{u}}'\mathbf{G}\hat{\mathbf{u}}}{\hat{\mathbf{u}}'\hat{\mathbf{u}}} \simeq E\frac{\tilde{\mathbf{u}}'\mathbf{G}\tilde{\mathbf{u}}}{\tilde{\mathbf{u}}'\tilde{\mathbf{u}}} \tag{22}$$

To investigate the expectation on the right, let $\mathbf{R}$ be an orthogonal matrix that diagonalises $\mathbf{MA}$. For convenience, suppose the rows of $\mathbf{R}$ are chosen so that

$$\mathbf{RMAR} = \begin{pmatrix} \mathbf{P} & \mathbf{0} \\ \mathbf{0} & \mathbf{0} \end{pmatrix} \tag{23}$$

where $\mathbf{P}$ is a matrix of order $T - K$ with positive diagonal elements, $p_1, p_2, \ldots, p_{T-k}$ ($\mathbf{RMAR}'$ is known to be of rank

$T - K$ since $\mathbf{A}$ is non-singular and $\mathbf{M}$ can readily be shown to be of rank $T - K$). Define

$$\mathbf{z} = \mathbf{R}\tilde{\mathbf{u}} = \begin{pmatrix} \mathbf{R}_1 \\ \mathbf{R}_2 \end{pmatrix} \tilde{\mathbf{u}} = \begin{pmatrix} \mathbf{z}_1 \\ \mathbf{z}_2 \end{pmatrix} \tag{24}$$

where $\mathbf{R}_1$ comprises the first $T - K$ rows of $\mathbf{R}$. It follows that $\mathbf{z}_1$ is multivariate normal with mean zero, variance $\nu\mathbf{P}$; $\mathbf{z}_2 = 0$; $\tilde{\mathbf{u}}'\tilde{\mathbf{u}} = \mathbf{z}'\mathbf{R}\mathbf{R}'\mathbf{z} = \mathbf{z}'\mathbf{z} = \mathbf{z}_1'\mathbf{z}_1$; $\tilde{\mathbf{u}}'\mathbf{G}\tilde{\mathbf{u}} = \mathbf{z}'\mathbf{R}\mathbf{G}\mathbf{R}'\mathbf{z} = \mathbf{z}_1'\mathbf{R}_1\mathbf{G}\mathbf{R}_1'\mathbf{z}_1$. Therefore

$$\frac{\tilde{\mathbf{u}}'\mathbf{G}\tilde{\mathbf{u}}}{\tilde{\mathbf{u}}'\tilde{\mathbf{u}}} = \frac{\mathbf{z}_1'\mathbf{R}_1\mathbf{G}\mathbf{R}_1'\mathbf{z}_1}{\mathbf{z}_1'\mathbf{z}_1} \tag{25}$$

Now consider

$$\mathbf{w} = \nu^{-1/2}\mathbf{P}^{-1/2}\mathbf{z}_1 \tag{26}$$

$\mathbf{w}$ is standard multivariate normal and

$$\frac{\tilde{\mathbf{u}}'\mathbf{G}\tilde{\mathbf{u}}}{\tilde{\mathbf{u}}'\tilde{\mathbf{u}}} = \frac{\mathbf{w}'\mathbf{P}^{1/2}\mathbf{R}_1\mathbf{G}\mathbf{R}_1'\mathbf{P}^{1/2}\mathbf{w}}{\mathbf{w}'\mathbf{P}\mathbf{w}} = \frac{\mathbf{w}'\mathbf{C}\mathbf{w}}{\mathbf{w}'\mathbf{P}\mathbf{w}} \tag{27}$$

where $\mathbf{C}$ is defined by the second equality. Let $\gamma_{st} = w_s w_t / \sum_{r=1}^{T-k} p_r w_r^2$ for $s, t = 1, 2, \ldots, T - K$. Then

$$E\frac{\mathbf{w}'\mathbf{C}\mathbf{w}}{\mathbf{w}'\mathbf{P}\mathbf{w}} = E\sum_{t=1}^{T-K}\sum_{s=1}^{T-K} c_{st}\gamma_{st} = \sum_{t=1}^{T-K} c_{tt}E\gamma_{tt} \tag{28}$$

where the second equality follows from the fact that the density of γ_{st} for $s \neq t$ is symmetric about zero and therefore has mean zero.

To evaluate $E\gamma_{tt}$, write

$$\gamma_{tt} = \frac{w_t^2}{\sum_{r=1}^{T-K} p_r w_r^2} = \frac{k_1}{k_2} \tag{29}$$

Let

$$\psi(h_1, h_2) = Ee^{h_1k_1 + h_2k_2} = \prod_{r=1}^{T-K}(1 - h_1\delta_{tr} - h_2 p_r)^{-1/2} \tag{30}$$

be the joint moment generating function of k_1 and k_2 where δ_{tr} is the Kronecker delta.

By a theorem of Anderson and Anderson [1, p. 77]

$$E\frac{k_1}{k_2} = \int_{-\infty}^{0}\left[\frac{\partial\psi}{\partial h_1}\bigg|_{h_1=0}\right]dh_2 = \tfrac{1}{2}\int_{-\infty}^{0}(1 - p_t h)^{-1}\prod_{r=1}^{T-K}(1 - p_r h)^{-1/2}\,dh \tag{31}$$

This is a difficult integral and obtaining the p_r can also involve substantial computation. Both tasks can be greatly simplified at the cost of still another approximation. Suppose the average of the p_r, call it p, is substituted for each individual element.[3] Then $p = 1/(1 - K)\,\text{tr}\,\mathbf{MA}$ and

$$E\gamma_{tt} = E\frac{k_1}{k_2} \simeq \tfrac{1}{2}\int_0^\infty (1 - ph)^{-(T-K+2)/2}\,dh = \frac{1}{p(T-K)} \tag{32}$$

Substitution in (27), (26) yields

$$E\frac{\tilde{\mathbf{u}}'\mathbf{G}\tilde{\mathbf{u}}}{\tilde{\mathbf{u}}'\tilde{\mathbf{u}}} = E\frac{\mathbf{w}'\mathbf{C}\mathbf{w}}{\mathbf{w}'\mathbf{P}\mathbf{w}} \simeq \sum_{t=1}^{T-K}\frac{c_{tt}}{p(T-K)} = \frac{\text{tr}\,\mathbf{C}}{\text{tr}\,\mathbf{MA}} \tag{33}$$

which can be readily calculated for any value of ρ. Let $(\text{tr}\,\mathbf{C})/(\text{tr}\,\mathbf{MA}) = \varphi(\rho)$. If the various approximations sketched are not too gross, then it will be true that

$$E(\hat{\rho}) \simeq \frac{\text{tr}\,\mathbf{C}}{\text{tr}\,\mathbf{MA}} = \varphi(\rho) \tag{34}$$

It is seen in Section 4 that $\varphi(\rho)$ is approximately linear. Thus, if $E\hat{\rho}$ is sufficiently well approximated by $\varphi(\rho)$, then $\overset{*}{\rho} = \varphi^{-1}(\hat{\rho})$ will have smaller bias than $\hat{\rho}$. For the structures considered in the next section $\overset{*}{\rho}$ tends to have about one-third the bias of $\hat{\rho}$ though this varies substantially from one structure to another. Unfortunately, the variance of $\overset{*}{\rho}$ is typically larger than the variance of $\hat{\rho}$ so $\overset{*}{\rho}$ does not always have lower mean square error. These comparisons and possible improvements are discussed after the results have been presented. In Section 5 it is explained how calculation of $\overset{*}{\rho}$ may be conveniently combined with calculation of $\hat{\rho}$.

3. The Monte Carlo Trials

Because of formidable mathematical difficulties in determining properties of the distributions of various estimators that have been used with the autoregressive disturbance model, it was

[3] Dent [4, pp. 34–6] has also considered the possibility of making the p_r equal in pairs. Finding the mean of the ratio then involves finding the eigenvalues of MA. This should provide a somewhat more accurate approximation to the mean of $\hat{\rho}$, but at the cost of substantially heavier computations.

decided to compare the behaviour of the adjusted maximum likelihood (A.M.L.) estimator with the M.L. estimator and others when applied to artificially generated samples with known parameters.

To make the hints furnished by such comparisons as useful as possible, a number of structures were chosen, twenty-two in all, representing a variety of circumstances that might be encountered in applications. To enhance the statistical reliability of the results a relatively large number, 300, of samples were generated for each structure.

Four estimates of ρ were computed for each sample. These included M.L., A.M.L., an estimator developed by Theil and Nagar [16] denoted in this report by T.N., and an estimator suggested by Durbin [5] denoted D.[4]

The T.N. estimator is

$$\rho_{\text{TN}} = \frac{T^2(1 - \frac{1}{2}d) + K^2}{T^2 - K^2} \tag{35}$$

where $d = \sum_{t=2}^{T} (\bar{u}_t - \bar{u}_{t-1})^2 / \sum_{t=1}^{T} \bar{u}_t^2$ is the Durbin–Watson (DW) statistic calculated for least squares residuals $\bar{u}_t$ of the regression of $\mathbf{y}$ on $\mathbf{X}$. The Durbin estimator is the coefficient of the lagged endogenous variable y_{t-1} in the least squares regression of y_t on y_{t-1}; x_{tk} $(k = 1, 2, \ldots, K)$ and $x_{(t-1)k}$ $(k = 2, 3, \ldots, K)$ where it is assumed that $x_{t1} = 1$ $(t = 1, 2, \ldots, T)$.

A structure is specified by choosing a design matrix $\mathbf{X}$ of observed values of independent variables and specific values for the parameters ρ, β, ν. Table 1.1 shows some properties of the structures used in this study. $x_{t1} = 1$ $(t = 1, 2, \ldots, T)$ for every structure; thus β_1 is the constant term in each case. Structures 1 to 8 were used by Hildreth and Lu [8] and 9–12 were obtained by modifying some parts of these structures. In all of these $\beta_1 = 0$, $\beta_k = 1$ for $k \neq 1$, $\nu = 1$. Other characteristics are shown in Table 1.1(a). Each independent variable for structures 1–3 was generated by adding a random component to a harmonic term of low frequency. For structures

[4] [8] also considered the approximate Bayes estimator suggested by Zellner and Tiao [17, p. 776]. It turned out to be numerically very close to M.L. and to have, on the average, slightly larger mean square error so it was omitted from the present study.

TABLE 1.1(*a*) *Some Characteristics of Structures 1–12**

Properties of independent variables

Structure number	ρ	T	Means x_{t2}	Means x_{t3}	Means x_{t4}	Variances x_{t2}	Variances x_{t3}	Variances x_{t4}	Correlation coefficients $x_{t2}x_{t3}$	Correlation coefficients $x_{t2}x_{t4}$	Correlation coefficients $x_{t3}x_{t4}$
1	0·3	30	0·064	0·015	0·015	0·466	0·711	0·460	0·113	0·026	0·048
2	0	30	−0.061	−0·024	−0·024	0·539	0·616	0·477	0·131	−0·153	0·089
3	−0·7	100	0·006	−0·007	−0·007	0·553	0·578	0·606	0·028	−0·040	0·089
4	0·7	30	0·000	0·025	0·025	0·750	0·727	0·736	0·010	−0·349	0·218
5	0·3	100	0·000	0·020	0·020	0·750	0·750	0·750	0·015	0·012	−0·025
6	0	100	0·000	0·020	0·020	0·750	0·750	0·750	0·015	0·012	−0·025
7	0·5	30	0·000	0·000	0·000	0·750	0·750	0·750	0·937	0·698	0·704
8	0·9	100	0·000	0·001	0·000	0·750	0·748	0·750	0·798	0·293	0·108
9	−0·9	60	0·100	0·000	−0·020	0·577	0·590	0.597	0·063	−0·143	0·157
10	−0·5	60	0·245	−0·012	−0·155	0·690	0·616	0·555	0·048	0·028	−0·058
11	0·4	60	−0·124	−0·130	0·045	0·932	0·563	0·797	−0·125	−0·220	−0·168
12	0·6	60	0·157	0·026	−0·504	0·526	0·572	0·623	−0·045	−0·014	−0·021

* For all of these structures $\beta_1 = 0$, $\beta_2 = \beta_3 = \beta_4 = 1$, $\nu = 1$.

4–6, sums of several harmonic terms including terms of high frequency were employed. Further details are given in [8, pp. 3–6, pp. 33–4]. This arrangement should make structures 1–3 relatively favourable for least squares estimation of β and for tests based on the Durbin–Watson upper limits [2].

Observations of independent variables for structure 9 were obtained by taking the last sixty observations of corresponding variables for structure 3. Observations for structure 12 are the first sixty observations for structure 3. The design matrix for structure 10 was obtained by adding small random terms to the first 50 rows of the matrix for structure 5 (except for the first column which has unit elements in all structures) and multiplying the sum by a constant designed to approximately preserve sample variances. The design matrix for structure 11 was obtained similarly except that the last sixty rows of the matrix for structure 5 were used. The independent variables for structures 7 and 8 are series for the United States wholesale price index, numbers of immigrants to the United States, and exports of foodstuffs from the United States for the years 1928–57 (7) and 1858–1957 (8). The series were coded to produce zero means and sample variances less than unity.

The purpose of using observed series for structures 7 and 8 was to ensure that properties which might be encountered in applications would be reflected in the structures used for Monte Carlo trials. This notion was carried further in choosing structures 13–22. Structures 13 and 14 use observations of independent variables from Prest's [14] study of demand for textiles. The data are tabulated in Theil and Nagar [16, p. 805]. For structure 13, β, σ, ν are one-digit approximations to the M.L. estimates. For structure 14, a different value of ρ was used.

Similarly, structures 15 and 16 come from Hoos and Shear [11], and structures 17 and 18 from Lindstrom and King [13]. The Hoos and Shear data are tabulated in Henshaw [7] and the Lindstrom–King data in Hildreth and Lu [10, p. 70].[5]

Structures 19 and 20 are based on Klein's [12, p. 135] simplified consumption function and structures 21 and 22 use the data for a wage-rate equation in the Federal Reserve-M.I.T.

[5] There are errors in the Hoos–Shear data presented in [10]. These have been corrected in [7].

TABLE 1.1(*b*) *Some Characteristics*

Structure number	Coefficients								Moments of independent Means			
	ρ	ν	T	β_1	β_2	β_3	β_4	β_5	x_{t2}	x_{t3}	x_{t4}	x_{t5}
13	−0·5	0·0002	17	1·4	1·1	−0·8			0·699	0·626		
14	−0·1											
15	0	0·03	16	−0·009	−0·02	0·03	0·8	−0·02	79·875	36·125	89·625	0·000
16	0·4											
17	−0·8	0·08	17	−4·6	−0·06	1·1			422·765	68·912		
18	−0·4											
19	0·3	1·7	22	15·7	0·3	0·8			16·700	41·005		
20	0·6											
21	0·7	0·0001	56	−0·09	0·2	0·09	0·2		0·219	1·023	0·016	
22	0·9											

Econometric Model.[6] In all cases observed values of independent variables were used with approximate M.L. estimates of β, ν. Two structures were specified from each study by using the approximate M.L. estimate of ρ for one structure and a value chosen to help ensure wide selection for the other. Some characteristics of structures 13–22 are shown in Table 1.1(*b*).

For each structure described above, 300 samples were generated by drawing values of v_t from a table of random numbers and then calculating u_t, y_t from Equations (1), (2a), (2b). For each sample, estimates of ρ were computed by each of the four procedures – T.N., D., M.L., A.M.L.

The main results are summarised in Table 1.2. Each cell, corresponding to a particular structure and estimator, contains three series. The first is the calculated bias of the estimator when applied to the indicated structure. It is obtained by subtracting the true value of ρ from the mean of the 300 values estimated by the indicated procedure. The second entry is the sample variance of the estimator for the 300 trials and the third is the calculated mean square error (bias^2 + variance). Structures are arranged according to increasing values of the autocorrelation coefficient since this simplifies examination of properties sensitive to the coefficient.

4. Examination of Results

Looking first at the results for bias, it is seen that the adjustment was surprisingly successful considering the crudeness of some of

[6] The equation is no. 96 in the Appendix to reports by de Leeuw and Gramlich. See [3, p. 266].

Structures 13–22

ariables

ructure umber	Variances x_{t2}	x_{t3}	x_{t4}	x_{t5}	Correlations $x_{t2}x_{t3}$	$x_{t2}x_{t4}$	$x_{t2}x_{t5}$	$x_{t3}x_{t4}$	$x_{t3}x_{t5}$	$x_{t4}x_{t5}$
13	0·0001	0·0025			0·232					
14										
15	316·86	137·61	185·73	85·00	0·618	0·613	−0·526	0·688	−0·154	−0·299
16										
17	54839·95	144·75			0·367					
18										
19	16·953	56·667			0·655					
20										
21	0·0042	0·0053	0·0007		−0·242	0·359		−0·440		
22										

the approximations on which it is based. A.M.L. bias is lowest (in absolute value) among the four estimators in twenty of the twenty-two structures (15 and 17 are the exceptions). It is lower than M.L. bias in all structures except structure 17. For the twelve structures with positive ρ, A.M.L. bias is less than one-third of M.L. bias in ten.

Among the three unadjusted estimators, T.N. tends to have the lowest bias if ρ is zero or a small positive fraction; M.L. tends to have the smallest bias if $|\rho|$ is large. M.L. seems to improve relative to T.N. as sample size increases. D. is frequently in between.

Results of approximate tests for bias are given in Table 1.3. Consider testing the null hypothesis that a particular estimator, call it $\tilde{\rho}$, for a chosen structure is unbiased, i.e. $H_0:E\tilde{\rho} = \rho$. Let $\tilde{\rho}_\alpha$ be the estimate obtained by the method in question from the αth sample. Let

$$\tilde{\rho}_{\mathrm{M}} = \tfrac{1}{300}\sum_{\alpha=1}^{300}\tilde{\rho}_\alpha$$
$$\tilde{\rho}_{\mathrm{V}} = \tfrac{1}{300}\sum_{\alpha=1}^{300}(\tilde{\rho}_\alpha - \tilde{\rho}_{\mathrm{M}})^2 \qquad (36)$$

be the sample mean and variance. From the central limit theorem, the distribution of the statistic

$$\zeta = (\tilde{\rho}_{\mathrm{M}} - \rho)\tilde{\rho}_V^{-1/2}(300)^{1/2} \qquad (37)$$

approaches the standard normal. The value of this statistic for each structure-estimator combination is the upper entry in the appropriate cell of Table 1.3. The lower entry is the marginal

TABLE 1.2 *Monte Carlo Bias, Variance and Mean Square Error, for Various Estimators of* ρ

Structural characteristics				Estimators			
Structure number	True ρ	K	T	T.N.	D	M.L.	A.M.L.
				0·0340	0·0239	0·0244	−0·0018
9	−0·9	4	60	0·0051	0·0047	0·0039	0·0045
				0·0062	0·0053	0·0045	0·0045
				0·2348	0·0266	0·0101	−0·0638
17	−0·8	3	17	0·0248	0·0302	0·0151	0·0280
				0·0799	0·0309	0·0152	0·0320
				0·0285	0·0058	0·0042	0·0022
3	−0·7	4	100	0·0059	0·0058	0·0055	0·0062
				0·0067	0·0058	0·0055	0·0062
				0·0820	−0·0630	−0·0470	−0·0246
13	−0·5	3	17	0·0481	0·0491	0·0411	0·0789
				0·0548	0·0531	0·0433	0·0795
				0·0279	0·0084	−0·0062	0·0055
10	−0·5	4	60	0·0124	0·0127	0·0117	0·0135
				0·0132	0·0127	0·0117	0·0135
				0·0978	−0·0432	−0·0625	−0·0290
18	−0·4	3	17	0·0384	0·0485	0·0432	0·0694
				0·0480	0·0503	0·0471	0·0702
				−0·0280	−0·1775	−0·1419	−0·0046
14	−0·1	3	17	0·0467	0·0608	0·0526	0·0964
				0·0475	0·0923	0·0728	0·0964
				−0·0150	−0·1325	−0·2112	−0·1061
15	0	5	16	0·0707	0·0816	0·0875	0·1487
				0·0707	0·0991	0·1324	0·1600
				−0·0618	−0·1360	−0·1199	−0·0252
2	0	4	30	0·0341	0·0369	0·0388	0·0479
				0·0379	0·0554	0·0532	0·0486
				−0·0264	−0·0341	−0·0389	−0·0106
6	0	4	100	0·0088	0·0095	0·0098	0·0103
				0·0095	0·0106	0·0113	0·0104
				−0·1364	−0·2142	−0·1802	−0·0287
19	0·3	3	22	0·0407	0·0558	0·0491	0·0606
				0·0593	0·1017	0·0816	0·0614
				−0·1063	−0·1920	−0·1472	−0·0260
1	0·3	4	30	0·0348	0·0419	0·0406	0·0443
				0·0461	0·0787	0·0622	0·0450
				−0·0369	−0·0359	−0·0298	0·0017
5	0·3	4	100	0·0104	0·0106	0·0119	0·0119
				0·0118	0·0119	0·0128	0·0119
				−0·1687	−0·3320	−0·3349	−0·1534
16	0·4	5	16	0·0627	0·0768	0·0912	0·1415
				0·0912	0·1870	0·2033	0·1650
				−0·0778	−0·0621	−0·0391	−0·0039
11	0·4	4	60	0·0147	0·0157	0·0172	0·0174
				0·0207	0·0196	0·0187	0·0174
				−0·1909	−0·2337	−0·2024	−0·0622
7	0·5	4	30	0·0320	0·0484	0·0423	0·0480
				0·0684	0·1030	0·0833	0·0518
				−0·2455	−0·3194	−0·2652	−0·1022
20	0·6	3	22	0·0485	0·0655	0·0616	0·0680
				0·1088	0·1676	0·1319	0·0784

TABLE 1·2 (*contd.*)

Structural characteristics				Estimators			
Structure number	True ρ	K	T	T.N.	D	M.L.	A.M.L.
				−0·1168	−0·1146	−0·0859	−0·0199
12	0·6	4	60	0·0150	0·0143	0·0156	0·0147
				0·0286	0·0275	0·0230	0·0151
				−0·1881	−0·1454	−0·0874	−0·0107
4	0·7	4	30	0·0264	0·0363	0·0322	0·0403
				0·0617	0·0574	0·0398	0·0404
				−0·1008	−0·1177	−0·0813	−0·0117
21	0·7	4	56	0·0143	0·0187	0·0162	0·0157
				0·0244	0·0325	0·0228	0·0159
				−0·1229	−0·1182	−0·0826	−0·0152
22	0·9	4	56	0·0108	0·0138	0·0103	0·0102
				0·0259	0·0277	0·0171	0·0104
				−0·1033	−0·0774	−0·0304	0·0081
8	0·9	4	100	0·0053	0·0050	0·0048	0·0047
				0·0160	0·0110	0·0057	0·0048

significance level, the approximate probability under the null hypothesis that a random value of the statistic will differ from zero by more than the calculated value.

The test emphatically (significance level 0·005) rejects the hypothesis of unbiasedness of T.N. for all structures and of D. for all structures except 3 and 10. For the M.L. estimator, marginal significance levels above 0·005 are obtained for structures 3, 10, 13, 17. These are all cases in which the true value of ρ is in the vicinity of −0·6 and it will be seen from Table 1.4 and Figure 1.1 that, for all of the structures considered here, $\varphi(\rho)$ tends to be close to ρ in this region.

The marginal significance level for A.M.L. is above 0·005 for all structures except 20 and above 0·05 for fourteen of the twenty-two structures. This tends to confirm the impression obtained from Table 1.2 that the adjustment applied here removes much, but not all, of the bias in the M.L. estimator.

Variance is another matter. T.N. variance is lowest in fourteen of the twenty-two cases including nine of twelve in structures with positive ρ. This suggests that it may be worth while to study the distribution of the T.N. estimator more carefully. An adjustment that would reduce T.N. bias without materially increasing variance might produce typically smaller mean square error than other available estimators. M.L. tends to have lower variances than T.N. and D. when $|\rho|$ is large and again shows relative improvement for large T.

TABLE 1.3 *Test Statistics and Marginal Significance Levels for Tests of Bias*

Structure	True ρ	T	T.N.	D.	M.L.	A.M.L.
9	−0·9	60	8·24	6·03	6·75	0·40
			*	*	*	0·69
17	−0·8	17	25·77	2·65	1·42	−6·60
			*	0·01	0·16	*
3	−0·7	100	6·41	1·33	0·98	0·48
			*	0·18	0·33	0·63
13	−0·5	17	6·17	−3·91	−2·64	1·64
			*	*	0·03	0·10
10	−0·5	60	4·34	1·29	−0·99	0·87
			*	0·20	0·32	0·38
18	−0·4	17	8·63	−3·39	−5·20	−1·90
			*	*	*	0·06
14	−0·1	17	−6·82	−10·73	−11·01	−0·30
			*	*	*	0·76
15	0·0	16	−0·97	−8·02	−12·38	−4·76
			0·33	*	*	*
2	0·0	30	−5·79	−12·24	−10·52	−1·99
			*	*	*	0·05
6	0·0	100	−4·87	−6·06	−6·79	−1·81
			*	*	*	0·07
19	0·3	22	−11·69	−15·68	−14·07	−2·02
			*	*	*	0·04
1	0·3	30	−9·84	−16·23	−12·64	−2·14
			*	*	*	0·03
5	0·3	100	−6·25	−6·02	−4·73	0·27
			*	*	*	0·78
16	0·4	16	−11·65	−20·72	−19·18	−7·06
			*	*	*	*
11	0·4	60	−11·10	−8·58	−5·15	−0·51
			*	*	*	0·61
7	0·5	30	−18·46	−18·36	−17·01	−4·91
			*	*	*	*
20	0·6	22	−19·26	−21·57	−18·48	−6·78
			*	*	*	*
12	0·6	60	−16.52	−16·56	−11·88	−2·84
			*	*	*	0·01
4	0·7	30	−20·04	−13·20	−8·43	−0·98
			*	*	*	0·33
21	0·7	56	−14·59	−14·90	−11·06	−1·62
			*	*	*	0·11
22	0·9	56	−20·48	−17·43	−14·11	−2·61
			*	*	*	0·01
8	0·9	100	−24·48	−18·91	−7·58	1·75
			*	*	*	0·08

* indicates a marginal significance level below 0·005.

TABLE 1.4 *Some Properties of* $\varphi(\rho)$ *for Alternative Structures*

Structure number	T	Fixed point	Extreme difference Abscissa	Extreme difference difference	Ordinates and slopes for selected values of ρ −0·9	−0·6	−0·3	0·0	0·3	0·6	0·9
1	30	−0·662	0·400	−0·130	−0·855	−0·612	−0·364	−0·106	0·171	0·475	0·783
					0·80	0·81	0·84	0·89	0·97	1·04	0·94
2	30	−0·650	0·300	−0·121	−0·855	−0·612	−0·363	−0·103	0·179	0·487	0·786
					0·80	0·81	0·84	0·90	0·98	1·04	0·91
3	100	−0·660	0·350	−0·043	−0·886	−0·604	−0·320	−0·034	0·258	0·561	0·865
					0·94	0·94	0·95	0·96	0·98	1·02	0·97
4	30	−0·630	0·990	−0·122	−0·856	−0·604	−0·330	−0·035	0·262	0·539	0·795
					0·60	0·87	0·95	1·00	0·96	0·88	0.82
5, 6	100	−0·657	0·990	−0·042	−0·886	−0·604	−0·318	−0·029	0·268	0·571	0·866
					0·73	0·94	0·95	0·98	1·00	1·00	0·96
7	30	−0·662	0·720	−0·155	−0·855	−0·612	−0·364	−0·105	0·166	0·448	0·755
					0·80	0·81	0·84	0·88	0·92	0·96	1·08
8	100	−0·660	0·460	−0·047	−0·886	−0·604	−0·321	−0·035	0·255	0·555	0·863
					0·73	0·94	0·94	0·95	0·98	1·01	1·00
9	60	−0·496	0·390	−0·073	−0·872	−0·600	−0·301	−0·058	0·230	0·534	0·838
					0·93	0·92	0·91	0·85	0·97	1·03	0·97
10	60	−0·615	0·990	−0·065	−0·875	−0·604	−0·327	−0·036	0·264	0·560	0·843
					0·90	0·92	0·94	0·97	1·00	0·99	0·91
11	60	−0·615	0·990	−0·065	−0·878	−0·603	−0·328	−0·034	0·268	0·561	0·844
					0·90	0·92	0·94	0·98	1·00	0·98	0·91
12	60	−0·650	0·350	−0·072	−0·876	−0·608	−0·340	−0·058	0·231	0·532	0·838
					0·89	0·90	0·91	0·96	0·97	1·04	0·95
13, 14	17	−0·605	0·586	−0·277	−0·816	−0·600	−0·387	−0·170	0·058	0·323	0·628
					0·72	0·72	0·72	0·73	0·77	0·96	1·09
15, 16	16	−0·559	0·680	−0·261	−0·815	−0·584	−0·359	−0·137	0·093	0·342	0·655
					0·67	0·80	0·74	0·74	0·77	0·88	1·23
17, 18	17	−0·588	0·990	−0·220	−0·815	−0·595	−0·369	−0·121	0·145	0·423	0·694
					0·72	0·74	0·78	0·84	0·90	0·94	0·82
19, 20	22	−0·611	0·480	−0·175	−0·833	−0·597	−0·366	−0·122	0·136	0·426	0·743
					0·78	0·78	0·79	0·82	0·88	1·02	0·93
21, 22	56	−0·673	0·390	−0·074	−0·873	−0·603	−0·336	−0·058	0·230	0·527	0·833
					0·90	0·90	0·91	0·93	0·97	1·01	0·98

For reasons that will become clearer after Table 1.4 and Figure 1.1 are inspected, variance of the A.M.L. estimator is usually larger than that of M.L. (eighteen of twenty-two structures).

Turning to relations among mean square errors of the various estimators, the true value of ρ makes a striking differ-

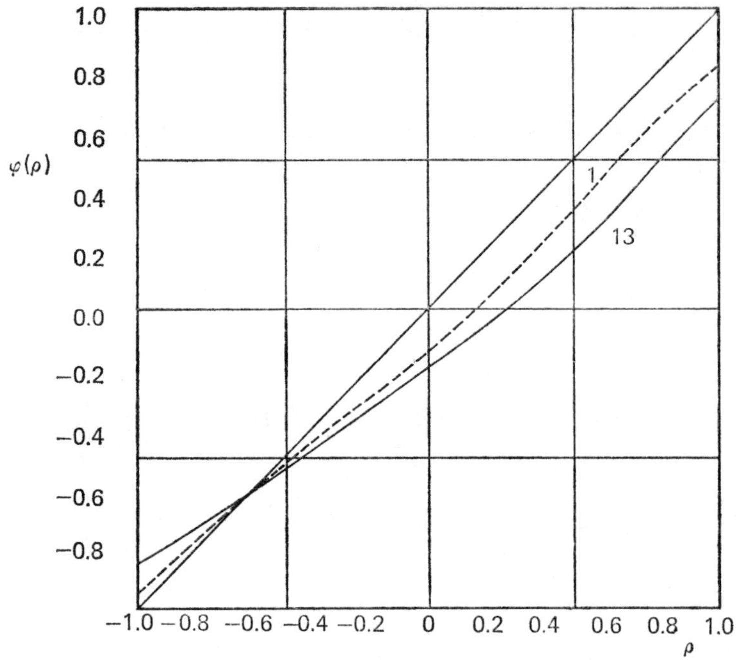

FIG. 1.1. $\varphi(\rho)$ *for Structures 1 and 13*

ence. M.L. has lowest mean square error for the six structures with $\rho < -0{\cdot}1$. T.N. is lowest for seven of the nine structures for which $-0{\cdot}1 \leq \rho \leq 0{\cdot}4$. A.M.L. is lowest for six of the seven structures for which $\rho > 0{\cdot}4$ and eight of twelve where ρ is positive.

Comparing mean square error for A.M.L. and M.L. shows that the adjustment fails to improve the mean square error in every case in which $\rho < 0$ and does improve the estimator for eleven of the twelve structures for which $\rho > 0$. Various comparisons that have been made between A.M.L. and M.L. can usefully be related to the typical behaviour of the approximate mean $\varphi(\rho)$.

Some properties of $\varphi(\rho)$ for each structure are given in Table 1.4 and graphs for two illustrative cases are presented in Figure 1.1. Certain common features are apparent.

For each structure, $\varphi(\rho)$ has a fixed point ($\varphi(\rho) = \rho$) between $-0{\cdot}710$ and $-0{\cdot}560$. $\varphi(\rho) > \rho$ (indicating probably positive bias) to the left of the fixed point and $\varphi(\rho) < \rho$ to the right of the fixed point. $\varphi'(\rho)$ is predominantly, but not universally, less than 1 and tends to increase with ρ, but not monotonically.

The most striking difference among functions determined by different structures is an approximate scale factor that may roughly be associated with the extreme difference between $\varphi(\rho)$ and ρ. Define the extreme difference as $\varphi(\rho_0) - \rho_0$ where $-0{\cdot}99 \leq \rho_0 \leq 0{\cdot}99$ and ρ_0 maximises $|\varphi(\rho) - \rho|$ in the interval $[-0{\cdot}99, 0{\cdot}99]$. Extreme differences are tabulated in the fourth column of Table 3 along with the values at which the extrema occur.

Extreme difference is clearly associated with sample size. Let Δ represent the extreme difference. Then the following hold for these trials

$$-0.281 \leq \Delta \leq -0.200 \quad \text{for} \quad 16 \leq T \leq 22$$

$$-0.160 \leq \Delta \leq -0.121 \quad \text{for} \quad T = 30$$

$$-0.090 \leq \Delta \leq -0.053 \quad \text{for} \quad T = 56 \text{ or } 60$$

$$-0.052 \leq \Delta \leq -0.040 \quad \text{for} \quad T = 100$$

Consider a linear approximation, $a + b\rho$, to $\varphi(\rho)$ in the vicinity of a M.L. estimate $\hat{\rho}$. Then the corresponding A.M.L. estimate, $\overset{*}{\rho} = \varphi^{-1}(\rho)$, is approximately $-(a/b) + (1/b)\hat{\rho}$ and Var $\overset{*}{\rho}$ is approximately $1/b^2$ Var $\hat{\rho}$. Since b is approximately $\varphi'(\rho)$ and the latter is typically less than unity, it is to be expected that Var $\overset{*}{\rho}$ is typically greater than Var $\hat{\rho}$.

From Table 1.4 and Figure 1.1 it is seen that the bias of $\hat{\rho}$ is relatively small when $\rho < 0$ and the discrepancy between Var $\overset{*}{\rho}$ and Var $\hat{\rho}$ is relatively large since $\varphi'(\rho)$ is typically smaller than when $\rho > 0$. These relations both tend to make the mean square error of $\hat{\rho}$ small relative to that of $\overset{*}{\rho}$ when $\rho < 0$ and the opposite tendencies usually prevail when $\rho > 0$. This suggests a possible rule of using M.L. when prior knowledge and/or tests indicate negative autocorrelation and A.M.L. when positive autocorrelation is indicated. Of course, it is hoped that further study will, in time, provide superior alternatives.

For developing better estimators, two principal avenues seem to be suggested by the trials reported here. One is to study the distribution of the T.N. estimator with the prospect that an adjusted estimator might be found which might have substantially smaller mean square error. The second avenue is continued study of the M.L. estimator. Since the adjustment obtained by concentrating on bias typically increased the variance of the estimator, a more refined adjustment involving lower mean square error seems possible.

5. Computations for Maximum Likelihood and Adjusted Maximum Likelihood Estimation

From Equation (12) the maximum likelihood estimator of ρ is found as that value of ρ which minimises the function

$$S(\rho) = (1 - \rho^2)^{-1/T}(\mathbf{y} - \mathbf{X}\boldsymbol{\beta}_\rho)'\mathbf{B}_\rho(\mathbf{y} - \mathbf{X}\boldsymbol{\beta}_\rho) \qquad (12)$$

The differences between the stationary and non-stationary versions of the linear model have been noted earlier. The scanning technique for the non-stationary model [10, Appendix C, p. 55] has been incorporated in some software computer packages, e.g. The Econometric Software Package, available from the University of Chicago, and the Econometric Pack for the C.D.C. 6600 at the University of Minnesota (and elsewhere). For small T, this method may yield a substantially different numerical value for the maximum likelihood estimator than the scanning procedure set forth in [8, Appendix C, p. 35]. As an example, using Hildreth and Lu's data on the demand for California pears [10, Equation (13), p. 65, 7, p. 652], the earlier scanning procedure yields an estimate of 0·30 for ρ, while the later technique yields a value of 0·39. A brief outline of the computational procedure for the stationary model is given below. From (8*)

$$\boldsymbol{\beta}_\rho = (\mathbf{X}'\mathbf{B}_\rho\mathbf{X})^{-1}\mathbf{X}'\mathbf{B}_\rho\mathbf{y}$$

so that substituting in (12) yields

$$\begin{aligned} S(\rho) &= (1-\rho^2)^{-1/T}\mathbf{y}'\{\mathbf{I}-\mathbf{X}(\mathbf{X}'\mathbf{B}_\rho\mathbf{X})^{-1}\mathbf{X}'\mathbf{B}_\rho\}' \\ &\quad \times \mathbf{B}_\rho\{\mathbf{I}-\mathbf{X}(\mathbf{X}'\mathbf{B}_\rho\mathbf{X})^{-1}\mathbf{X}'\mathbf{B}_\rho\}\mathbf{y} \\ &= (1-\rho^2)^{-1/T}\mathbf{y}'\{\mathbf{B}_\rho - \mathbf{B}_\rho\mathbf{X}(\mathbf{X}'\mathbf{B}\mathbf{X})^{-1}\mathbf{X}'\mathbf{B}_\rho\}\mathbf{y} \qquad (38) \end{aligned}$$

In computer evaluations, it is convenient to store the $K \times 1$ vector $(\mathbf{X}'\mathbf{B}_\rho\mathbf{X})^{-1}\mathbf{X}'\mathbf{B}_\rho\mathbf{y}$, since this is used eventually for least squares and maximum likelihood estimates of β. Further, $S(\rho) \times (1-\rho^2)^{1/T}/T$ yields the appropriate estimate of ν for $\rho = 0$ and $\rho = \hat{\rho}$ (the M.L. estimate) and the second factor in the last relation above should be evaluated independently. To check for multiple minima, it is suggested that $S(\rho)$ be evaluated at values of ρ: $-0{\cdot}9$ $(0{\cdot}1)$ $0{\cdot}9$. If the sign of successive first differences changes only once, one has reasonable assurance that the minimum is unique.

When scanning the range of ρ in this manner, it is convenient to compute and store the approximation to $E(\hat{\rho})$ given in (33). This may be written

$$E(\hat{\rho}_\rho) = \frac{T(T-1)\rho - (T+1)(1-\rho^2)\,\mathrm{tr}\,\mathbf{X}'\mathbf{H}\mathbf{X}(\mathbf{X}'\mathbf{B}_\rho\mathbf{X})^{-1}}{T(T+1) - (T+1)(1-\rho^2)\,\mathrm{tr}\,\mathbf{X}'\mathbf{X}(\mathbf{X}'\mathbf{B}_\rho\mathbf{X})^{-1}} \qquad (39)$$

For this computation one needs $\mathbf{X}'\mathbf{H}\mathbf{X}$ and $\mathbf{X}'\mathbf{X}$, the latter being most conveniently found as $\mathbf{X}'\mathbf{B}_0\mathbf{X}$. In this initial scan, suppose the minimum value of $S(\rho)$ occurs at $\rho = \rho_0^1$, and no evidence of multiple minima is found. The numerical search for the minimum value of $S(\rho)$ is then carried out as follows:

(1) Evaluate $S(\rho)$ at $\rho_1 = \rho_0^i - d_i$ (i corresponds to an iteration index; $i = 1, \ldots, 10$ and $d_1 = 0{\cdot}05$), and $\rho_2 = \rho_0^i + d_i$;
(2) choose ρ_0^{i+1} as that value of ρ yielding the minimum of $S(\rho_0)$, $S(\rho_1)$, $S(\rho_2)$;
(3) set $d_{i+1} = \frac{1}{2}d_i$ and repeat the process.

After ten iterations, the final value of ρ emerging from step (2) is taken as the maximum likelihood estimator, and is denoted as ρ_3.

To find the adjusted maximum likelihood estimator, two values of ρ, ρ_4 and $\rho_5 = \rho_4 + 0{\cdot}1$ are determined to satisfy

$E(\hat{\rho}_{\rho_4}) \leq \rho_3 < E(\hat{\rho}_{\rho_5})$. The technique used here is to approximate the function $\varphi(\rho)$ by a straight line segment about the point $\overset{*}{\rho}$ for which $\varphi(\overset{*}{\rho}) = \hat{\rho}$. While the interval of approximation could be made as small as possible it has been found convenient to use intervals of length 0·1 with values of $E(\hat{\rho}_\rho)$ calculated using Equation (39) in the initial scan. The points ρ_4 and ρ_5 are the end points of such an interval. The adjusted maximum likelihood estimator ρ_6 is then computed, using linear interpolation, as

$$\rho_6 = \rho_4 + \frac{\rho_3 - E(\hat{\rho}_{\rho_4})}{10[E(\hat{\rho}_{\rho_5}) - E(\hat{\rho}_{\rho_4})]} \tag{40}$$

A FORTRAN subroutine for the calculation of the maximum likelihood and adjusted maximum likelihood estimates is available, upon request, from the second author.

References

[1] ANDERSON, R. L. and ANDERSON, T. W., The Distribution of the Circular Serial Correlation Coefficient for Residuals from a fitted Fourier Series, *Annals of Mathematical Statistics*, XXI (1950) 50–81.

[2] CHIPMAN, JOHN S., The Problem of Testing for Serial Correlation in Regression Analysis, *Technical Report 4*, Department of Economics, University of Minnesota, 1965.

[3] DE LEEUW, FRANK and GRAMLICH, EDWARD, The Channels of Monetary Policy: a Further Report on the Federal Reserve-M.I.T. Model, *The Journal of Finance*, XXIV (1969) 265–90.

[4] DENT, WARREN T., The Distribution of the Maximum Likelihood Estimator of the Autocorrelation Coefficient in a Linear model with Autoregressive Disturbances, Unpublished Ph.D. Thesis, University of Minnesota, 1971.

[5] DURBIN, J., Estimation of Parameters in Time-Series Regression Models, *Journal of the Royal Statistical Society, Series B*, XXII (1960) 139–53.

[6] GRILICHES, ZVI and RAO, P., Small-Sample Properties of Several Two-Stage Regression Methods in the Context of Autocorrelated Errors, *Journal of the American Statistical Association*, LXIV (1969) 253–72.

[7] Henshaw, R. C., Jr., Testing Single-Equation Least-Squares Regression Models for Autocorrelated Disturbances, *Econometrica*, xxxiv (1966) 646–60.

[8] Hildreth, Clifford and Lu, John Y., A Monte Carlo Study of the Regression Model with Autoregressive Disturbances, Rand Memorandum RM5728PR, Santa Monica, 1969.

[9] Hildreth, Clifford, Asymptotic Distribution of Maximum Likelihood Estimators in a Linear Model with Autoregressive Disturbances, *Annals of Mathematical Statistics*, xl (1969) 583–94.

[10] Hildreth, Clifford and Lu, John Y., Demand Relations with Auto-Correlated Disturbances, Technical Bulletin 276 of the Michigan State University Agricultural Experiment Station, East Lansing, 1960.

[11] Hoos, S., and Shear, S. W., Relation Between Auction Prices and Supplies of California Fresh Bartlett Pears, *Hilgardia*, xiv, California Agricultural Experiment Station, 1942.

[12] Klein, Lawrence R., *Economic Fluctuations in the United States, 1921–41.* New York: John Wiley and Sons, 1950.

[13] Linstrom, I., and King, Richard A., The Demand for North Carolina Slicing Cucumbers and Green Peppers, North Carolina State College, A. E. Information Series, No. 49, 1956.

[14] Prest, A. R., Some Experiments in Demand Analysis, *The Review of Economics and Statistics*, xxxi (1949) 33–49.

[15] Reilly, D. P., Evaluation of the Small Sample Properties of Five Alternative Estimation Methods when the Errors are Correlated; Discussion Paper No. 87, Department of Economics, University of Pennsylvania, 1968.

[16] Theil, Henri and Nagar, A. L., Testing the Independence of Regression Disturbances, *Journal of the American Statistical Association*, lvi (1961) 793–806.

[17] Zellner, Arnold and Tiao, G. C., Bayesian Analysis of the Regression Model with Autocorrelated Errors, *Journal of the American Statistical Association*, lix (1964) 763–78.

2 Estimation and Prediction in Dynamic Econometric Models

BY H. N. JOHNSTON, L. R. KLEIN, AND K. SHINJO*

1. Statement of the Problem

THE PRESENCE of lags and other dynamic operators in the equation systems of economics is known to be a complicating factor in many aspects of estimation theory, but accepted practice is to follow the 'comforting' asymptotic result of Mann and Wald [6] that maximum likelihood estimates of linear difference equation systems are based on the specification that lagged variables may be formally treated like exogenous variables. Mann and Wald required dynamic stability, normality of error, stability of the distribution, and other assumptions that are usually made.

The Mann–Wald result led to the expansion of the concept of 'exogenous' or 'independent' variables in economic systems to the wider term 'predetermined' variable. This latter concept includes genuine exogenous variables and lagged endogenous variables. In general practice, the whole set of predetermined variables in a model are treated as though they are purely exogenous variables. Franklin Fisher [4], in other contexts, has shown that lagged variables may not be useful predetermined variables in a causal sense if there is serial correlation of error, or if there is strong collinearity among the several lag variables of a simultaneous equations model.

In using models for dynamic application involving prediction into an unknown future or general multiperiod simulation, it is well known that lagged values are not predetermined; they

* University of Pennsylvania.

are estimated in the dynamic application. Let us consider the dynamic linear system.

$$A(\mathbf{L})\mathbf{y}_t + \mathbf{Bx}_t = \mathbf{e}_t$$

where $A(\mathbf{L})$ is a matrix polynomial of pth order in the lag operator $\mathbf{L}$.

$$\mathbf{L}^i\mathbf{y}_t = \mathbf{y}_{t-i}$$

The sample period will be denoted as $t = 1, 2, \ldots, T$. For prediction into the future beyond the end of the sample, all lag values may be predetermined and known without error for estimating $\mathbf{y}_{T+1}$. This value will depend on $\mathbf{y}_T, \ldots, \mathbf{y}_{T-p+1}$ and $\mathbf{x}_{T+1}$. In order to estimate $\mathbf{y}_{T+2}$, however, values of $\mathbf{y}_{T+1}$ must be used, together with $\mathbf{y}_T, \mathbf{y}_{T-1}, \ldots, \mathbf{y}_{T-p+2}$ and $\mathbf{x}_{T+2}$. The value of $\mathbf{y}_{T+1}$ is not error-free. In genuine prediction, its true value is not known. Similarly, $\mathbf{y}_{T+2}$ and $\mathbf{y}_{T+1}$ must be used as stochastic inputs for estimating $\mathbf{y}_{T+3}$, etc.

In estimation theory, lags are treated as predetermined. In prediction theory, only initial conditions are predetermined. Other lag values are developed by the stochastic system over the future time horizon. The purpose of the present paper is to investigate whether common practice in estimation procedures can be improved upon so as to produce systems that give better predictions. The general approach will be to see whether a closer correspondence between assumptions and conditions in the prediction and estimation situations can lead to parameter estimates that improve predictions.

There are two special cases where there can be no improvement and where accepted practice is undoubtedly correct.

(1) *Static Systems:* In this case, the linear model is

$$\mathbf{Ay}_t + \mathbf{Bx}_t = \mathbf{e}_t$$

Best estimates of $\mathbf{A}$ and $\mathbf{B}$ should lead to best predictions over any horizon. The assumed inputs for prediction are $\mathbf{x}_{T+1}$, $\mathbf{x}_{T+2}, \mathbf{x}_{T+3}, \ldots$. These are non-stochastic variables, even though they are not known with certainty over the future horizon.

(2) *Uni-period prediction:* If the dynamic system

$$A(\mathbf{L})\mathbf{y}_t + \mathbf{Bx}_t = \mathbf{e}_t$$

is to be projected, at any future time point, only one period beyond observations, then it is quite correct to treat lag values like exogenous variables in the estimation of the parameters.

The general application, however, is multi-period prediction or path prediction. In this case, the estimated model must be solved for several periods, given observed initial conditions. Haavelmo [5] has proved the following important result: the optimum prediction formulas in $T + 1$ and $T + 2$ for the process

$$y_t = \alpha y_{t-1} + e_t$$

obtained by minimising the quadratic loss function

$$W_{11}e^2_{T+1} + 2W_{12}e_{T+1}e_{T+2} + W_{22}e^2_{T+2}$$

subject to

$$y_{T+1} = \alpha y_T + e_{T+1}$$

$$y_{T+2} = \alpha y_{T+1} + e_{T+2}$$

are given by

$$y_{T+1} = \alpha y_T$$

$$y_{T+2} = \alpha^2 y_T$$

The weights in the loss function are chosen so as to make the quadratic expression positive definite.

The importance of this result is that the maximum likelihood estimate of α ($\hat{\alpha}$) provides a maximum likelihood estimate of α^2 ($\hat{\alpha}^2$) as well as of α ($\hat{\alpha}$). This is a well-known property of maximum likelihood estimates that their properties are preserved under continuous single-valued transformation. The Mann–Wald results indicate that the maximum likelihood estimate of α is obtained by regressing y_t on y_{t-1}, i.e. by minimising

$$\sum_{t=1}^{T} e_t^2 = \sum_{t=1}^{T} (y_t - \alpha y_{t-1})^2$$

with respect to α. This is an asymptotic result.

A similar result can be obtained for the general linear model:

$$A(\mathbf{L})\mathbf{y}_t + \mathbf{x}_t = \mathbf{e}_t$$

Let $Q(\mathbf{e}_{T+1}, \ldots, \mathbf{e}_{T+n})$ be a positive definite quadratic loss function of the prediction errors conditional on values of $\mathbf{y}_t$ up to time T. The generalisation of Haavelmo's result then states that the predictor which minimises the expected value of Q is the linear least squares predictor.[1] For the general linear model this is the predictor obtained by assuming the residuals are zero and successively generating $\mathbf{y}_{T+1}, \ldots, \mathbf{y}_{T+n}$. Because $A(\mathbf{L})$ is a linear operator the asymptotic prediction efficiency of the maximum likelihood estimator also follows. The issue before us is whether it can be improved upon in small samples.

From the general linear model the solution may be written as:

$$\mathbf{y}_t = \mathbf{K}\boldsymbol{\lambda}^t - [A(\mathbf{L})]^{-1}\mathbf{B}\mathbf{x}_t + [A(\mathbf{L})]^{-1}\mathbf{e}_t$$

where $\mathbf{K}$ is an $n \times np$ matrix of constants depending on the initial conditions of the system and $\boldsymbol{\lambda}$ is an np-element vector of characteristic roots associated with the homogeneous equation

$$det.\ A(\mathbf{L})\mathbf{y}_{it} = \mathbf{0}$$

The error over a dynamic solution path is $A(\mathbf{L})^{-1}\mathbf{e}_t$, which is a lag distribution in $\mathbf{e}_t$. This error will, in general, be serially correlated. From time to time in the econometric literature, investigators have considered minimising the sum of squares of elements of $A(\mathbf{L})^{-1}\mathbf{e}_t$. One could suggest the minimisation of the trace of

$$\sum_{t=1}^{T} [\{A(\mathbf{L})\}^{-1}\mathbf{e}_t][\{A(\mathbf{L})\}^{-1}\mathbf{e}_t]'$$

or some weighted function of trace elements with respect to the parameters. Indeed, this is what many model builders do nowadays. They test an estimated system for dynamic simulation error and keep changing specifications and estimates of individual equations until they generate simulation paths with small errors.

The drawback to minimising the trace or other properties of the covariance matrix

$$\sum_{t=1}^{T} [\{A(\mathbf{L})\}^{-1}\mathbf{e}_t][\{A(\mathbf{L})\}^{-1}\mathbf{e}_t]'$$

[1] Proof of this result follows simply with the application of the concept of certainty equivalence. Certainty equivalence holds because of the constraints based on Q. See Whittle [9, p. 137 for a statement and proof of the relevant certainty equivalence theorem.

is the serial correlation properties of $[A(\mathbf{L})]^{-1}\mathbf{e}_t$. Since the solution equation is derived from fixed initial conditions and the path of $\mathbf{x}_t$, however, the assumptions of the model from which estimates are made are completely consistent with the assumptions of the model from which predictions are made. Predictions for $T+1$, $T+2$, etc. from the linear dynamic model would be given by

$$\mathbf{y}_t = \mathbf{K}\boldsymbol{\lambda}^t - [A(\mathbf{L})]^{-1}\mathbf{B}\mathbf{x}_t \qquad (t = T+1, T+2, \ldots$$

this is the analogue of Haavelmo's prediction formula with $\mathbf{K}\boldsymbol{\lambda}^t$ replacing $\alpha^t y_0$. He has no exogenous variables in his system.

The estimation problem posed here for dynamic systems is a difficult non-linear calculation, as are maximum likelihood calculations for the static case. For some small single equation models in sampling experiments, we shall indicate below the extent to which gains in predictive efficiency might be made through use of an estimator that is alternative to the time honoured method of ordinary least squares (O.L.S.). Usual practice, however, in econometric model building, especially for large-scale systems is to use T.S.L.S. or some variant of it. The variants that are mainly used are techniques of choosing instruments to get round the problems of shortage of degrees of freedom or multicollinearity, both of which cause singularity in the basic moment matrices used in the first stage of T.S.L.S.

In the present paper, a different variant of T.S.L.S. (I.T.S.L.S.) will be explored, namely iteration of the method that makes better use of full system identifying restrictions and the simulation of error in predetermined variables that are lagged values of dependent variables.

As will be explained below, a system estimated by T.S.L.S. (or some single equation variant of it) has a restricted reduced form, which is to be distinguished from the unrestricted reduced form used in the first stage of T.S.L.S. Instrumental variables can be computed from the restricted reduced forms and used again in another round of single equation estimates. If the values computed from the restricted reduced forms are used as instrumental variables in single equation estimation of each equation in the system, the resulting estimates (I.T.S.L.S.) have the same asymptotic efficiency as T.S.L.S. If the values computed from the restricted reduced forms are used as *regressors* in each single equation estimate the resulting estimates cannot necessarily be ranked as to asymptotic efficiency, but they are consistent, as are the estimates in the instrumental variable case. The iterations could be repeated, but their convergence properties have not been fully explored. In a closely related iteration, Theil [8] and Nagar [7] found cases of non-convergence.

Our problem will be to see whether in small samples (sixty-six observations), I.T.S.L.S. estimates of the Wharton model improve its forecasting efficiency. Since forecast error depends on the errors associated with parameter estimates, improved efficiency in parameter estimation should lead to improved forecast precision.

The I.T.S.L.S. method has been developed for the static case, where all lag values are treated like other predetermined variables, but it can be readily extended to the dynamic case by generating computed values of lagged variables as well as computed values of contemporaneous dependent variables. This is to say, the restricted reduced forms are solved dynamically from given initial conditions. This means that the final single equation regressions in I.T.S.L.S. are best fitting relationships, given only initial values and exogenous values. This is precisely what is wanted in prediction.

The econometrician wants a single flexible model that is capable of doing many things at once – capable of estimating many different variables efficiently over both single- and multi-period horizons. It may turn out, however, that best single-period forecasts are made from one set of estimates of a system; that best two-period point forecasts are made from another estimated system; that best three-period point forecasts are made from another estimated system, and so forth. We shall consider the efficiency of different range predictions from I.T.S.L.S. systems that generate only contemporaneous dependent variables from restricted reduced forms; that generate both contemporaneous and one-period lagged dependent variables from restricted reduced forms; and so forth. Our null hypothesis will be that systems using up to pth order generated lag values as instruments or regressors will perform best in p period point predictions.

The residual error in prediction equations will be estimates of

$$[A(\mathbf{L})]^{-1}\mathbf{e}_t$$

apart from the error contribution of parameter estimation. In static methods of estimation, the residual errors will be estimates of $\mathbf{e}_t$. Many investigators that have close fitting relationships, judged by the size of elements in

$$\sum_{t=1}^{T} \mathbf{e}_t\mathbf{e}_t'$$

are led to overstate their precision in multiperiod prediction. The errors involved in fitting equations by the dynamic versions of the I.T.S.L.S. method, however, give a more realistic notion of their expected forecast precision. The high correlations obtained in autoregression are not indicative of the residual variance in multiperiod extrapolation because observed lag values are used in fitting the autoregressive relationship. If dynamically generated values of lags are used in fitting, the residual variance will be closer to the values that will be obtained in multiperiod extrapolation. The dynamic methods that are being proposed guard against one's giving exaggerated importance to goodness of fit using lagged dependent variables.

The properties of the solution of a dynamic system and its estimation by I.T.S.L.S. methods are known for the linear case. Closed form expressions can be developed, but applications will frequently be made for non-linear systems. If such systems are linear in parameters, but not in variables, the T.S.L.S. estimates and the I.T.S.L.S. estimates can all be computed by using (approximate) numerical solutions to dynamic systems, but the full probability properties are not known. Predictions for an application of I.T.S.L.S. can, however, be made and compared with other methods for an actual non-linear system.

2. Small sample experiments with estimation and prediction of simple autoregressive processes

The following experiments examine the relative performance in small samples of O.L.S. and the non-linear estimator suggested above minimising

$$\mathrm{tr} \sum_{t=1}^{T} (A(\mathbf{L})^{-1}\mathbf{e}_t)(A(\mathbf{L})^{-1}\mathbf{e}_t)'$$

For the three cases of simple autoregressive process examined below the latter estimator has a simple non-linear form and since it can be seen to minimise the sum of squares of dynamic solution errors it will be referred to as the dynamic least squares (D.L.S.) estimator.

2.1 *Experimental design*

Given a sample of observations of length n on a first-order autoregressive process

$$y_t = \alpha y_{t-1} + e_t \tag{1}$$

the dynamic estimation procedure minimises $\sum_{j=1}^{n} (y_j - y_0\alpha^j)^2$ with respect to α and since a closed form expression for this estimator is not available, a sample search procedure must be utilised. However, in the experiments below, instead of searching through all values of α in [0, 1] to find the one which minimises the objective function, a search was made on a grid of mesh size 0·05, centred on the true value of α restricted to the region $(\alpha \pm 0{\cdot}25)$ with the additional constraint that $|\alpha| \leq 1$.

The properties of this estimator are examined by generating artificial samples according to particular experimental specifications. For example, one experiment specifies that a set of twenty hypothetical realisations, each of length 60 can be generated assuming the initial value of y is $y_0 = 200$ and the standard deviation of the residual error is 6·0. Successive observations of each realisation are generated iteratively using a random Gaussian generator to provide disturbance values. In this particular experiment the first fifty observations are then used to calculate both the O.L.S. and D.L.S. estimates. The estimated coefficients and true coefficient values are then used to predict the next ten values to compare their prediction efficiency.

Each experiment consists of twenty replications, and four factors are varied to provide a total number of sixty experiments. These are:

(1) The initial value used to generate the series is varied from 0, to 1 to 200;
(2) the autoregressive parameter α is given the values of 0·856, 0·614, 0·397, 0·153;
(3) for some experiments the first twenty observations are thrown away, while for others they are kept;
(4) for each of the cases in (3) three sample sizes are generated to give sample sizes of 10, 20 and 50.

It should be noted that throwing away the first twenty observations has a similar effect to generating a series with a stochastic initial value. In our case even for $\alpha = 0{\cdot}856$ the mean expected initial value is then close to zero.[2]

TABLE 2.1 *Mean Values of the O.L.S. Estimator (First-order Autoregressive Process)*

		Value of α	Initial value = 0 $\sigma = 1$	Initial value = 1 $\sigma = 1$	Initial value = 200 $\sigma = 6$
Discard first twenty observations (stochastic initial value)	Sample length = 50	0·856	0·8422	0·8421	0·8351
		0·614	0·6145	0·6145	0·6145
		0·397	0·4086	0·4085	0·4136
		0·153	0·1737	0·1737	0·1759
	Sample length = 20	0·856	0·8246	0·8246	0·8196
		0·614	0·6359	0·6359	0·6359
		0·397	0·4801	0·4801	0·4588
		0·153	0·2162	0·2162	0·2395
No observations discarded (fixed initial value)	Sample length = 50	0·856	0·8297	0·8289	0·8512
		0·614	0·6053	0·6058	0·6130
		0·397	0·4016	0·4023	0·4000
		0·153	0·1657	0·1661	0·1663
	Sample length = 20	0·856	0·7768	0·7648	0·8514
		0·614	0·5284	0·5287	0·6105
		0·397	0·3150	0·3179	0·3817
		0·153	0·0894	0·0907	0·1285
Discard first twenty observations	Sample length = 10	0·856	0·8148	0·8152	0·8120
		0·614	0·5697	0·5697	0·5697
		0·397	0·3684	0·3684	0·3684
		0·153	0·1713	0·1713	0·1713

[2] Since the mean expected value after twenty periods is given by $\alpha^{20}y_0$ and since $(0{\cdot}86)^{20} = 0{\cdot}05$, this implies a mean expected value of 10 for a prior initial value of 200. This falls further to 0·01 for $\alpha = 0{\cdot}614$.

TABLE 2.2 *Mean Values of the D.L.S. Estimator (First-order Autoregressive Process)*

		Value of α	Initial value = 0 $\sigma = 1$	Initial value = 1 $\sigma = 1$	Initial value = 200 $\sigma = 6$
Discard first twenty observations (stochastic initial value)	Sample length = 50	0·856	0·8543	0·8569	0·8652
		0·614	0·6465	0·6465	0·6465
		0·397	0·4145	0·4145	0·3945
		0·153	0·1830	0·1530	0·1755
	Sample length = 20	0·856	0·8583	0·8583	0·8388
		0·614	0·6415	0·6415	0·6415
		0·397	0·4145	0·4145	0·3945
		0·153	0·1530	0·1530	0·1755
No observations discarded (fixed initial value)	Sample length = 50	0·856	Method breaks down	0·8068	0·8560
		0·614		0·5965	0·6115
		0·397		0·4295	0·3995
		0·153		0·1955	0·1555
	Sample length = 20	0·856	Method breaks down	0·7793	0·8560
		0·614		0·5940	0·6115
		0·397		0·4295	0·3995
		0·153		0·1955	0·1555
Discard first twenty observations	Sample length = 10	0·856	0·8502	0·8541	0·8452
		0·614	0·6640	0·6640	0·6640
		0·397	0·4195	0·4195	0·4195
		0·153	0·1530	0·1530	0·1530

Table 2.1 presents the results on the means of the O.L.S. estimator.

Table 2.2 presents the results for D.L.S. over the same samples except for those with fixed initial value of zero where this method breaks down since y_0 is zero and $(y_0\hat{\alpha}^j)$ must be zero for all values of $\hat{\alpha}$ and j.[3] Table 2.3 summarises the variances of the estimators for a subset of the experiments, that is those with initial value 200 and sample lengths twenty and fifty periods, and Table 2.4 summarises the prediction efficiency of the estimators, as measured by the mean square prediction

[3] In this instance the estimator could have been generalised to

$$\min_{\alpha} \sum_{T=0}^{n-m} \sum_{j=1}^{m} (y_{t+j} - y_t\alpha^j)^2 \qquad \text{where} \qquad m < n$$

This estimator can of course be used for non-zero y_0 and more recent work indicates that it may in fact dominate the estimator used in this study.

TABLE 2.3 *Variances for the Two Estimators* (First-order Autoregressive Process)*

		Value of α	O.L.S.	D.L.S.
Discard first twenty observations (stochastic initial value)	Sample length = 50	0·856	0·0050	0·0194
		0·614	0·0126	0·0371
		0·397	0·0232	0·0480
		0·153	0·0124	0·0417
	Sample length = 20	0·856	0·0068	0·0146
		0·614	0·0126	0·0344
		0·397	0·0194	0·0449
		0·153	0·0313	0·0459
No observations discarded (fixed initial value)	Sample length = 50	0·856	0·0003	0·0000
		0·614	0·0011	0·0009
		0·397	0·0032	0·0011
		0·153	0·0082	0·0014
	Sample length = 20	0·856	0·0001	0·0000
		0·614	0·0011	0·0009
		0·397	0·0038	0·0011
		0·153	0·0177	0·0014

* For all experiments the initial value was 200 and the variance of the disturbance term was 36.

error, averaged over the twenty replications of each experiment. Where samples of size 50 are used to estimate the coefficients, the estimated coefficients are compared over a prediction horizon of ten periods, and correspondingly for samples of size 20, the prediction horizon is five periods.

An extension of this dynamic estimation procedure makes it applicable to first-order mixed autoregressive processes of the form

$$y_t = \alpha y_{t-1} + \beta x_t + e_t \tag{2}$$

In this case the estimator becomes

$$\min_{\alpha,\beta} \sum_{j=1}^{n} \left(y_j - \alpha^j y_0 - \sum_{i=1}^{j} \alpha^{j-i} \beta x_i \right)^2$$

A comparison of this estimator was made with O.L.S. also. The D.L.S. estimator is again calculated using a search procedure, but this time it is over a two-dimensional grid around the three parameter values. The grid is of mesh size 0·05 and covers the region of ±0·25 around the true parameter values and is again restricted by the condition $|\hat{\alpha}| \leq 1$.

TABLE 2.4 *Mean Square Prediction Error for the Two Estimators* (First-Order Autoregressive Process)*

		Value of α	O.L.S.	D.L.S.	Prediction using the true value α
Discard first twenty observations (stochastic initial value)	Sample length = 50	0·856	2·0310	2·2663	2·0220
		0·614	1·2054	1·2723	1·2102
	Prediction length = 10	0·397	0·9989	1·0120	1·0467
		0·153	0·9170	0·9196	0·9137
	Sample length = 20	0·856	0·5772	0·5768	0·5170
		0·614	0·3593	0·3564	0·3384
	Prediction length = 5	0·397	0·2810	0·2663	0·2714
		0·153	0·2429	0·2391	0·2392
No observations discarded (fixed initial value)	Sample length = 50	0·856	2·5127	2·4977	2·4977
		0·614	1·2829	1·2814	1·2819
	Prediction length = 10	0·397	0·9628	0·9622	0·9618
		0·153	0·8368	0·8354	0·8349
	Sample length = 20	0·856	0·2144	0·2152	0·2142
		0·614	0·1446	0·1442	0·1444
	Prediction length = 5	0·397	0·1162	0·1157	0·1163
		0·153	0·1019	0·1010	0·1040

* For all experiments the initial value was 200 and the variance of the disturbance term was 36. The figure presented for each experiment is the average mean square error of prediction for the twenty replications divided by 1000.

In these experiments quarterly government expenditure is used as the exogenous variable. All experiments have a single initial value of 200·0 for y_0 and 36·0 for the variance of the residual, the first twenty observations are always discarded and fifty replications are made of each experiment. Five different experiments are generated by:

(1) Detrending the exogenous variable of some experiments;
(2) having two sets of (α, β); (0·614, 0·56) and (−0·50, 0·65);
(3) varying the sample length for estimation between twenty and forty observations and the corresponding prediction period between five and ten periods.

Table 2.5 presents means and ranges of estimators for each experiment and Table 2.6 the mean square error of prediction averaged over the fifty replications of each experiment.

TABLE 2.5 *Means and Ranges of Coefficient Estimates (First-order Mixed Autoregressive Process)*

		Coefficient values	O.L.S.	D.L.S.
Exogenous variable with trend	Sample length = 40	$\alpha = 0{\cdot}614$	0·5627 (0·3487, 0·7700)	0·5870 (0·4640, 0·7140)
		$\beta = 0{\cdot}560$	0·6361 (0·3316, 0·9438)	0·6020 (0·4100, 0·8100)
	Sample length = 20	$\alpha = 0{\cdot}614$	0·5178 (0·1421, 0·7467)	0·5600 (0·4640, 0·7140)
		$\beta = 0{\cdot}560$	0·7023 (0·2640, 1·2617)	0·6410 (0·4100, 0·8100)
Exogenous variable without trend	Sample length = 40	$\alpha = -0{\cdot}500$	−0·5119 (−0·7899, −0·1753)	−0·5040 (−0·2500, −0·6500)
		$\beta = 0{\cdot}650$	0·6773 (0·4797, 0·9362)	0·6810 (0·5000, 0·9000)
	Sample length = 40	$\alpha = 0{\cdot}614$	0·5628 (0·3350, 0·7742)	0·6020 (0·4640, 0·8140)
		$\beta = 0{\cdot}560$	0·6529 (0·3466, 0·9721)	0·6000 (0·4100, 0·8100)
	Sample length = 20	$\alpha = 0{\cdot}614$	0·5295 (0·2150, 0·7937)	0·5890 (0·4640, 0·7640)
		$\beta = 0{\cdot}560$	0·7062 (0·3728, 1·3412)	0·6220 (0·4100, 0·8100)

TABLE 2.6 *Mean Square Prediction Error of the Two Estimators (First-order Mixed Autoregressive Process)**

		Coefficient values	O.L.S.	D.L.S.	Prediction using true parameters
Sample length = 40 Prediction horizon = 10	Exogenous variable with trend	$\alpha = 0{\cdot}614$ $\beta = 0{\cdot}560$	1·3637	1·3864	1·1814
	Exogenous variable without trend	$\alpha = -0{\cdot}50$ $\beta = 0{\cdot}65$	1·0491	1·0513	1·0314
		$\alpha = 0{\cdot}614$ $\beta = 0{\cdot}560$	1·2765	1·2490	1·1814
Sample length = 20 Prediction horizon = 5	Exogenous variable with trend	$\alpha = 0{\cdot}614$ $\beta = 0{\cdot}560$	0·2058	0·2145	0·1692
	Exogenous variable without trend	$\alpha = 0{\cdot}614$ $\beta = 0{\cdot}560$	0·1735	0·1704	0·1692

* The figure presented for each experiment is the average mean square error of prediction over the fifty replications divided by 1000.

A further extension of this procedure can be applied to the pure second-order autoregressive process of the form

$$y_t = \alpha y_{t-1} + \beta y_{t-2} + e_t \qquad (3)$$

In this case the D.L.S. estimator used is that which minimises $\sum_{j=1}^{n} (y_j - \hat{y}_j)^2$ where the $\hat{y}_j$ are generated successively from the initial values assuming the error term is zero. Again this estimator is obtained via numerical methods using a two-dimensional grid around the true parameter values. A mesh size of 0·05 is used and the range examined restricted to ±0·25 around the true values. For comparison purposes the O.L.S. estimator is again calculated.

TABLE 2.7 *Means and Variances of Coefficient Estimates (Second-order Autoregressive Process)*

		Coefficient values	O.L.S.	D.L.S.
Standard deviation = 0·001	Sample length = 50	$\alpha = 0·6140$	0·6006 (0·0172)	0·5950 (0·0062)
		$\beta = 0·5130$	0·5205 (0·0196)	0·5170 (0·0068)
	Sample length = 20	$\alpha = 0·6140$	0·6488 (0·0464)	0·6040 (0·0047)
		$\beta = 0·5130$	0·4317 (0·0523)	0·5040 (0·0106)
Standard deviation = 6·0	Sample length = 40	$\alpha = 0·3940$	0·3831 (0·0158)	0·3870 (0·0220)
		$\beta = 0·4560$	0·4495 (0·0156)	0·4550 (0·0179)
		$\alpha = 1·2000$	1·1736 (0.0239)	1·2850 (0.0254)
		$\beta = -0·5000$	−0·4675 (0·0229)	−0·5600 (0·0183)
	Sample length = 20	$\alpha = 0·3940$	0·4581 (0·0447)	0·3880 (0·0211)
		$\beta = 0·4560$	0·3817 (0·0376)	0·4700 (0·0171)
		$\alpha = 1·2000$	1·1734 (0·0349)	1·2710 (0·0264)
		$\beta = -0·5000$	−0·4988 (0·0311)	−0·5470 (0·0220)

Three examples of this process were examined. The first two with parameter specification (α, β, σ, y_{-1}, y_{-2}) given by (0·3940, 0·4560, 6·0, 175·0, 200·0) and (1·2, −0·5, 6·0, 175·0, 200·0) are stable processes while the third given by (0·614, 0·513, 0·001, 0·0018, 0·0020) is unstable. Each of these examples in turn generates two experiments by changing the (sample length, prediction horizon) from (40, 10) to (20, 5). In all cases these

TABLE 2.8 *Mean Square Prediction Error of the Two Estimators* (Second-order Autoregressive Process)*

		Coefficient values	O.L.S.	D.L.S.	Prediction using true parameters
Standard deviation = 6.0	Sample length = 40 Prediction horizon = 10	$\alpha = 0{\cdot}3940$ $\beta = 0{\cdot}4560$	0·0360	0·0370	0·0329
		$\alpha = 1{\cdot}2000$ $\beta = -0{\cdot}5000$	0·0587	0·0792	0·0557
	Sample length = 20 Prediction horizon = 5	$\alpha = 0.3940$ $\beta = 0.4560$	0.0091	0.0090	0.0087
		$\alpha = 1{\cdot}2000$ $\beta = -0{\cdot}5000$	0·0174	0·0201	0·0161

* The figure presented for each experiment is the average mean square error of prediction over the fifty replications divided by 1000.

samples are obtained after throwing away the first twenty observations and each experiment is replicated fifty times.

Table 2.7 presents means and variances of estimates for each experiment and Table 2.8 mean square error of prediction averaged over the replications of each experiment. Results are not presented for the unstable process on prediction error since the variance of the residual is so small that mean square prediction error is insignificant for both O.L.S. and D.L.S. The variance and initial value for y_t were both low in this case to ensure manageable samples.

2.2 *Discussion of results*

Prediction efficiency is closely associated with parameter, estimation efficiency. Possible determinants of prediction efficiency in addition to the residual error variance are:

(*a*) the bias in parameter estimation.
(*b*) the variance in parameter estimation.[4]
(*c*) the length of the prediction period and the consequential build up in error due to the disturbance.

Tables 2.4, 2.6 and 2.8 clearly illustrate the build-up in prediction error as the horizon increases. Table 2.4 also indicates, as one would expect, a larger prediction error the larger α. Examination of Table 2.4, however, will show that the number of replications has not been large enough to bring out the clear superiority of knowledge of the true parameter value. Such an estimator must be superior since it can only contribute to prediction error through (*c*) above, while the other estimators will have that contribution plus those of (*a*) and (*b*).

It should also be noted that use of a grid in the search for the D.L.S. estimator has sometimes meant an overstatement of the efficiency of the D.L.S. estimator. For example, if a search over a continuous range yields an estimate $\hat{\alpha}$, then a search over the grid will put it at the true value α. Thus, the estimator in Table 2.3 of 0·856 for fixed initial value of 200 has a variance of zero.

Comparison of the tables delineates the contribution of (*a*) and (*b*) to prediction efficiency; that is, as bias and variance fall, so prediction efficiency increases. There is, however, no clear relationship between O.L.S. and D.L.S. in their means and variances. However, the results suggest the conjecture that the relative prediction efficiency of D.L.S. to O.L.S. improves and may dominate as the sample size falls. This result is clearest in Table 2.4 for the pure first-order autoregressive process where D.L.S. generally dominates the O.L.S. estimator. It also

[4] When more than one parameter is involved the covariance structure will be important also, as will the higher moments of the sampling distribution. However, the statistics compiled for this Monte Carlo study enable us to examine only the effects of the mean and variance of the sampling distribution.

dominates in some of the experiments in Tables 2.6 and 2.8 and in those cases where it does not, the relative efficiency does approach that for O.L.S. as the sample size falls.

The results also suggest the conjecture that the efficiency of D.L.S. improves the more the variation in the sample. This result is illustrated in the case of the first order autoregression in Table 2.4 for fixed initial value of 200, where the effect of the initial value is sizeable throughout the sample. That is, given the residual variance, the greater the variation in the realisation the better D.L.S. approximates the coefficient value.

3. Iterated T.S.L.S. in the Dynamic Case

3.1 *Description of estimator*

As explained in the introductory section, I.T.S.L.S. may be an improved method of estimation because it takes into account endogeneity of the lagged dependent variable in parameter estimation, i.e. parameters are estimated consistently with the assumption of the model and goals of prediction.

Consider the standard linear model

$$\sum_{i=0}^{P} \mathbf{A}_i \mathbf{y}_{t-i} + \mathbf{B}\mathbf{x}_t = \mathbf{e}_t \qquad (t = 1, \ldots, T)$$

We start by estimating parameters of this model ($\mathbf{A}_i$, $\mathbf{B}$) by the usual T.S.L.S. method, using principal components or some other data reduction method for the exogenous instruments, on the assumption that the number of predetermined variables is large relative to the number of data points. Having the estimated system

$$\sum_{i=0}^{P} \hat{\mathbf{A}}_i \mathbf{y}_{t-i} + \hat{\mathbf{B}}\mathbf{x}_t = \mathbf{0} \qquad (t = 1, \ldots, T)$$

we obtain solutions for the dependent variables, denoted as $\hat{\hat{\mathbf{y}}}_t$. The notation $\hat{\hat{\mathbf{y}}}_t$ is used here to distinguish these computed values from the second-stage instruments of the usual T.S.L.S. procedure $\hat{\mathbf{y}}_t$, which are computed from unrestricted reduced form regressions.

We may solve the system dynamically for the whole sample period without reinitialising, but in general we are interested in predicting over a certain time horizon, say F periods ahead, where F is much shorter than the sample period T. In that case, we would obtain complete system solutions for F periods $\hat{\hat{\mathbf{y}}}_{1,t}, \hat{\hat{\mathbf{y}}}_{2,t}, \ldots, \hat{\hat{\mathbf{y}}}_{F,t}$, based on the initial values for $\mathbf{y}_{t-1}, \mathbf{y}_{t-2}, \ldots, \mathbf{y}_{t-p}$, shifting the starting point (t) one period forward each time, over the whole sample period. The second subscript $\hat{\hat{\mathbf{y}}}_{j,t}$ indicates the particular period in which the solution starts, while the first subscript indicates the number of periods ahead for which the solution is made.

In the F-period prediction case, t goes from 1 to $(T - F + 1)$, i.e. F periods before the end of the sample period.

Having obtained the $\hat{\hat{\mathbf{y}}}_{j,t}$, the complete set of equations are now re-estimated, equation by equation, by O.L.S., using appropriate elements of $\hat{\hat{\mathbf{y}}}_{j,t}$ as regressors or as instruments to replace $\hat{\mathbf{y}}_t$.

To form these final stage regressions let us rewrite the above system as

$$\mathbf{y}_t = -\mathbf{A}_0^*\mathbf{y}_t - \sum_{t=1}^{P} \mathbf{A}_i\mathbf{y}_{t-i} - \mathbf{B}\mathbf{x}_t + \mathbf{e}_t, \qquad \alpha_{0ij}^* = 0$$

which expresses each element of $\mathbf{y}_t$ as a linear function of other elements in $\mathbf{y}_t$, lagged values $\mathbf{y}_{t-i}$ $(i = 1, 2, \ldots, p)$ and exogenous variables $\mathbf{x}_t$. Then we form one single regression for each element of $\mathbf{y}_t$ on

$$\hat{\hat{\mathbf{y}}}_{F,t-F+1}, \hat{\hat{\mathbf{y}}}_{F-1,\ t-F+1}, \ldots, \hat{\hat{\mathbf{y}}}_{1,t-F+1}, \mathbf{y}_{t-F}, \ldots, \mathbf{y}_{t-p}$$

and $\mathbf{x}_t$ for the sample period from F to T, and obtain a new set of parameter estimates for $\mathbf{A}_i$ and $\mathbf{B}$ denoted as $\hat{\hat{\mathbf{A}}}_i$, $\hat{\hat{\mathbf{B}}}$, respectively. Thus, the re-estimated system would be

$$\sum_{i=0}^{P} \hat{\hat{\mathbf{A}}}_i\mathbf{y}_{t-i} + \hat{\hat{\mathbf{B}}}\mathbf{x}_t = \mathbf{0}$$

This re-estimation process may be continued until changes in $\hat{\hat{\mathbf{A}}}_i$, $\hat{\hat{\mathbf{B}}}$ in each iteration satisfy a certain criterion of convergence.

The statistical theory for this class of estimator, however, has not yet been fully worked out. In a recent unpublished paper, P. Dhrymes and V. Pandit [2] showed that in the case where the prediction length F is equal to one the first iterate of the iterated T.S.L.S. estimator is consistent, but its asymptotic efficiency relative to T.S.L.S. cannot be uniformly ranked, i.e. it depends upon the nature of the matrix of coefficients of the jointly dependent variables as well as the covariance matrix of the systems disturbances.[5]

Further, Dhrymes [1] showed that if the $\hat{\hat{\mathbf{y}}}_t$ are used as instruments instead of regressors, I.T.S.L.S. has the same asymptotic efficiency as T.S.L.S. The major differences between the I.T.S.L.S. estimator and the usual T.S.L.S. estimator lie in the fact that the former takes into account all the *a priori* restrictions on the system in using $\hat{\hat{\mathbf{y}}}_{jt}$ in the final stage regressions, while the latter merely uses those imposed on the particular single equation under consideration, for $\hat{\mathbf{y}}_t$ does not carry information on the system as a whole, except to use all the predetermined variables in the system as regressors. In that sense, the I.T.S.L.S. method may be regarded as a variant to the full-information class of estimation, but intercorrelation of errors between different equations is not taken into consideration.

In addition, the I.T.S.L.S., extended in the dynamic case, does not make the usual assumption that $\mathbf{y}_{t-i}$ $(i \leq F - 1)$ are predetermined at period t in the final stage regressions. In the case illustrated above, $\hat{\hat{\mathbf{A}}}_i$, $\hat{\hat{\mathbf{B}}}$ are estimated so as to minimise the error in each equation in forecasting F periods ahead with system solutions of the other dependent variables. Thus, there is no inconsistency between estimation and prediction, as is usually the case for T.S.L.S. when it is used in multi-period prediction.

Our concern is, as stated in the first section, to see whether, or how much, these different aspects of the I.T.S.L.S. estimator will improve the predictive efficiency in small samples.

So far we have been considering linear systems in which case the statistical interpretation of this estimation procedure is straightforward. For, if the system is linear, each element of $\mathbf{y}_t$ can be expressed as a linear function of exogenous variables, initial conditions and an additive weighted average of random errors, and therefore, the probability limit of $\mathbf{y}_t$ is a linear function of predetermined variables and initial conditions.

[5] This result is subject to the condition that the original coefficients are estimated consistently by the usual T.S.L.S. method.

However, this does not hold for non-linear systems. In solving non-linear systems, we cannot assert that the solution splits into two additive and independent components – one a systematic part composed of exogenous variables and initial conditions and the other a function of random errors. Therefore, such solutions are not necessarily the probability limit of $\mathbf{y}_t$, and the statistical interpretation for non-linear systems is not clear, but there is little problem in carrying out the indicated calculations.

Since a macroeconometric model, to be realistic, is likely to be non-linear, and if we are interested in testing this estimation method in a realistic context, we necessarily have to deal with a non-linear system.

In the next section, we present the results of our experiments with the Wharton model.

3.2 *Results with the Wharton model*

The version of the Wharton model used for this study is the one published in the second edition of *The Wharton Econometric Forecasting Model* [3], with the two-equation monetary sector. This model contains forty-seven stochastic equations and was estimated for the sample period 1948·3 to 1964·4 using the two-stage least squares method with principal components.

Before presenting the results, procedures followed in solving this model may need some explanation. Since the sample period includes the Korean war, a period of major economic disturbance, the equation system had to be handled by adjusting constant terms of relevant equations. The idea here is not to add fine-tuning operations to the model, but to generate economically meaningful solutions (e.g. a positive unemployment rate) no matter at which period the model may be started. In this connection, adjustments were made in the downward direction with respect to non-farm investment expenditure and non-farm inventory investment and total labour force was adjusted upward. All these were during the Korean war period. In addition, there were similar adjustments needed for import and export equations to take care of such external disturbances as the sterling devaluation in late 1949 and also the stockpiling of basic materials during the Korean war.

There are no other adjustments to the model equations after 1953·2 except to take into account changes in tax-transfer equations during periods of varying tax laws. Another subtle problem concerns data revision, which occurred after the original model had been estimated. We used data that included revisions of the July 1967 national income accounts, while the model was estimated with data revised through July 1965 only. Thus, most of the 1963 and 1964 data are slightly changed and a few series were even revised for earlier years. We considered these data revisions not so crucial as to affect our basic results, and carried on calculations based on the recent data.[6]

Following the procedures discussed above, we re-estimated the whole set of equations of the Wharton Model and investigated its forecasting properties in comparison with the original system. We tested four cases, each assuming a different prediction length (F), from 1 to 4 quarters; i.e. we had four different re-estimated systems, called Model 1 to Model 4 corresponding to each prediction length in F.[7]

Re-estimation resulted in changing coefficients in the direction of shifting weights from endogenous variables (including lagged variables if solution values were substituted for them) to lagged endogenous variables and exogenous variables. As the prediction interval is lengthened; i.e. as more lagged endogenous variables are replaced by computed solutions, there are changes in signs of coefficients in some equations.

To deal with this problem, when coefficients turned out to be of wrong sign on the basis of *a priori* economic reasoning, we modified the system by dropping that particular variable from the equation.[8] This improved the predictive ability in most cases; so we selected the modified system in all except the one-period prediction case in testing predictive performance.

[6] We are now engaged in testing the effect of data revision on the estimated coefficients and predictive ability of the original model.

[7] We initially started from the long-run prediction case, i.e. $F = T$ (sample period), but the re-estimated system did not generate convergent solutions.

[8] This rule was not followed strictly because sometimes the modified system which eliminates all the wrong signs turned out to be non-convergent in the three- and four-period prediction case. Then we made a compromise to get convergent solutions by leaving some insignificant coefficients of wrong sign in the system.

To illustrate how coefficients have changed in re-estimation, the estimated coefficients of the consumption and inventory investment equations are shown as examples in Tables 2.9 and 2.10 respectively. In Table 2.10 it is observed that the sign of the coefficient of ΔX_m which is presumably poorly predicted, changes as the prediction period is lengthened. The asterisk shows which set of coefficients was chosen for testing.

TABLE 2.9 *Coefficients of Equation No. 1 C_{ns}/y*

Original $$\frac{C_{ns}}{y} = 0{\cdot}2273 - 0{\cdot}4590\left[\left(\frac{\Delta y}{y}\right) + 0{\cdot}75\left(\frac{\Delta y}{y}\right)_{-1} + 0{\cdot}50\left(\frac{\Delta y}{y}\right)_{-2} + 0{\cdot}25\left(\frac{\Delta y}{y}\right)_{-3}\right] + 0{\cdot}7232 \times \frac{1}{4}\sum_{i=1}^{4}\left(\frac{C_{ns}}{y}\right)_{-i}$$

Model 1	0·2297	− 0·2835	0·7154
Model 2	0·2608	− 0·2774	0·6764
Model 3	0·1218	− 0·3019	0·8534
Model 4	0·2159	− 0·3123	0·7335

Notation: C_{ns}: Purchases of consumer non-durables and services, billions of 1958 dollars
y: Personal disposable income, billions of 1958 dollars

Each of the four re-estimated systems was tested for its forecasting properties by examining the behaviour of seventeen key variables agreed upon for the Income and Wealth Conference on the cyclical content of econometric models, for each of the prediction intervals of 1 to 4 quarters.[9] The same sample period (1948·3–1964·4) was used for re-estimation, but the simulation was extended to 1968·1 to test the predictive ability beyond the sample period.

We present the simulation results with the Wharton model within the sample period followed by the post-sample simulation results.

[9] The seventeen variables are: short-term interest rate, long-term interest rate, non-farm investment in plant and equipment, implicit G.N.P. deflator, unfilled orders, investment in non-farm residential construction, personal income, corporate income before taxes, G.N.P. in current dollars, G.N.P. in constant dollars, unemployment rate, total consumption, inventory investment, Balance of Payments, employment, hours worked, and wage rate.

TABLE 2.10 *Coefficients of Equation No. 9* ΔI_{in}

Original model ΔI_{in} =	$-14{\cdot}94$	$+ 0{\cdot}0668(S_n)_{-1}$	$- 0{\cdot}1173(I_{in})_{-2}$	$+ 0{\cdot}2180(C_d)_{-1}$	$+ 0{\cdot}3325(\Delta X_m)$	$+ 40{\cdot}43(P_m - (P_m)_{-2})$
Model 1	−20·7172	0·0890	−0·1726	0·3406	0·0217	10·9094
Model 2	−22·0348	0·1221	−0·1386	0·1538	−0·0027	33·8069
*Model 2 (Modified)	−22·1193	0·1226	−0·1392	0·1543		33·7551
Model 3	−14·6122	0·0788	−0·0410	0·0440	−0·0694	92·6030
*Model 3 (Modified)	−14·4688	0·0743	−0·0488	0·0741		82·8930
Model 4	−18·0992	0·1032	−0·0758	0·0587		101·0880

Notation I_{in}: stock of non-manufacturing, non-farm inventories, billions of 1958 dollars
S_n: sales originating in non-manufacturing, non-farm private sector
C_d: purchases of consumer durables
X_m: gross output originating in the manufacturing sector
P_m: implicit deflator for gross output originating in the manufacturing sector

(i) *Within sample case*

Table 2.11 shows the root mean squared error (R.M.S.E.) for real G.N.P. predictions by each of the four re-estimated systems as compared with the original model. The improvement of predictive ability turned out to be quite sizeable. In forecasting one quarter ahead, Model 1 gave rise to R.M.S.E. of 4·557 in billions of 1958 dollars compared with 7·343 by the original model. Model 2 and Model 3 had also smaller R.M.S.E. than the original model.

TABLE 2.11 *R.M.S.E. in Real G.N.P. Prediction (Billions of 1958 Dollars)*

	Quarters ahead			
	1	2	3	4
Within sample (1948·3–1964·4)				
Original model	7·343	8·796	9·036	10·209
Model 1	4·557	5·709	7·083	7·963
Model 2	5·631	6·212	6·194	7·261
Model 3	6·424	6·345	6·334	7·782
	(9·093)	(9·065)	(6·342)	7·872
Model 4	9·646	10·526	6·412	7·704
Post sample (1965·1–1968·1)				
Original model	17·694	15·174	10·534	12·448
Model 1	15·924	21·595	28·457	15·561
Model 2	16·259	20·028	18·560	15·558
Model 3	30·087	34·903	27·753	24·293
	(16·902)	(20·516)	(20·206)	(18·856)
Model 4	19·017	22·914	23·136	21·995

In forecasting two quarters ahead, Model 1 had the smallest R.M.S.E., and Model 2 and Model 3 again predicted better than the original model by more than \$2 billion. In the case of three and four quarters prediction, re-estimation by the I.T.S.LS again reduced R.M.S.E. by more than \$2 billion.

It may be worth pointing out that Model 3 and Model 4 did not accumulate error as the prediction period lengthened as did the original Model, Model 1 and 2. Model 3 and Model 4 both predicted the third quarter best. It was conjectured in the introduction that each re-estimated model may show its best performance at the particular prediction period that is assumed for re-estimation. That is to say, a model that generates instruments for pth period lagged variables, should perform best in predictions p periods ahead. The result here, however, is not fully consistent with the conjecture, but this is not unexpected because as the prediction period for re-estimation becomes longer, the more wrong information due to possible mis-specification in the original model is likely to be embodied

TABLE 2.12 *Total Consumption* (*C*) (*Billions of 1958 Dollars*)

	Quarters ahead			
	1	2	3	4
Within sample				
Original	5·006	5·442	5·419	5·719
Model 1	3·581	4·120	4·560	5·155
Model 2	3·921	4·034	4·264	4·825
Model 3	4·200	4·157	4·415	5·080
	(5·237)	(4·842)	(4·290)	(5·011)
Model 4	4·900	5·386	4·693	5·530
Post-sample				
Original	12·870	9·479	7·334	7·359
Model 1	14·065	13·826	11·906	9·247
Model 2	13·686	13·370	11·586	9·424
Model 3	25·584	24·892	20·396	17·821
	(15·754)	(16·102)	(15·078)	(13·718)
Model 4	16·589	17·114	16·420	15·418

TABLE 2.13 *Unemployment rate* (*UN*) (per cent)

	Quarters ahead			
	1	2	3	4
Within sample				
Original	1·564	1·605	1·456	1·563
Model 1	1·392	1·199	1·156	1·232
Model 2	1·680	1·567	1·287	1·397
Model 3	2·172	1·982	1·794	1·898
	(2·621)	(2·239)	(1·315)	(1·623)
Model 4	3·087	2·935	1·541	1·849
Post-sample				
Original	0·982	1·191	0·956	1·328
Model 1	0·745	0·515	0·892	1·664
Model 2	0·971	0·865	1·281	2·054
Model 3	2·929	2·963	1·413	1·223
	(1·502)	(1·412)	(1·800)	(2·432)
Model 4	1·660	1·434	1·846	2·563

TABLE 2.14 *G.N.P. Deflator (p) (1958:1·00)*

	Quarters ahead			
	1	2	3	4
Within sample				
Original	0·005	0·007	0·009	0·010
Model 1	0·003	0·006	0·007	0·009
Model 2	0·004	0·006	0·008	0·010
Model 3	0·004	0·007	0·009	0·011
	(0·004)	(0·007)	(0·009)	(0·011)
Model 4	0·005	0·008	0·011	0·013
Post-sample				
Original	0·005	0·015	0·020	0·022
Model 1	0·002	0·007	0·011	0·015
Model 2	0·002	0·005	0·009	0·012
Model 3	0·002	0·007	0·011	0·013
	(0·002)	(0·004)	(0·006)	(0·008)
Model 4	0·002	0·004	0·006	0·008

in the solution value, which in turn leads to distorted re-estimated coefficients.

Prediction errors for some other key variables such as total consumption (Table 2.12), unemployment (Table 2.13), G.N.P. deflator (Table 2.14), inventory investment (Table 2.15), personal income (Table 2.16), are similarly summarised in the

TABLE 2.15 *Investment in Non-farm Inventories (I_{in}) (Billions of 1958 Dollars)*

	Quarters ahead			
	1	2	3	4
Within sample				
Original	3·442	3·490	3·733	3·864
Model 1	2·207	2·447	2·770	3·037
Model 2	2·632	2·739	2·892	3·235
Model 3	3·057	3·094	3·296	3·677
	(4·276)	(4·536)	(3·287)	(3·655)
Model 4	5·403	5·725	3·342	3·788
Post-sample				
Original	8·993	7·700	4·855	5·070
Model 1	3·114	6·137	6·373	5·946
Model 2	3·506	5·413	5·711	5·632
Model 3	4·265	7·462	5·101	5·187
	(3·813)	(3·997)	(4·397)	(4·690)
Model 4	3·646	4·316	4·708	4·903

TABLE 2.16 *Personal Income (PI) (Billions of 1958 Dollars)*

	Quarters ahead			
	1	2	3	4
Within sample				
Original	5·640	6·313	5·887	5·668
Model 1	3·512	3·928	4·436	4·996
Model 2	4·249	4·362	4·576	5·098
Model 3	5·589	5·422	5·570	6·096
	(6·138)	(5·683)	(4·936)	(5·694)
Model 4	6·848	6·764	5·097	5·602
Post-sample				
Original	36·163	34·206	29·185	27·036
Model 1	28·060	31·639	30·886	27·355
Model 2	27·861	30·680	29·687	26·414
Model 3	45·103	47·189	40·751	36·554
	(26·323)	(28·621)	(27·779)	(25·204)
Model 4	27·472	29·435	28·334	25·515

accompanying tables. Each table indicates that there is the same general tendency with respect to the distribution of R.M.S.E. over different prediction periods.

Reduction in R.M.S.E. is most distinct in the short-run prediction by Model 1, and as the prediction period is made longer, the gain from re-estimation is reduced. In order to evaluate the overall predictive performance of each model, we standardised R.M.S.E. by dividing by the standard error (S.E.) for each of seventeen variables and then formed the average of them.[10] The result is shown in Table 2.17.

[10] The formula is

$$\frac{1}{17}\sum_{i=1}^{17}\frac{(\text{R.M.S.E.})_i}{(\text{S.E.})_i}$$

where

$$(\text{R.M.S.E.})_i = \left(\frac{1}{P}\sum_{t=1}^{P}(Y_{it} - \hat{Y}_{it})^2\right)^{1/2}$$

$$(\text{S.E.})_i = \left(\frac{1}{P}\sum_{t=1}^{P}(Y_{it} - \bar{Y}_{it})^2\right)^{1/2}$$

This measure is the degree of correlation of observed values about the 45° line in the prediction-realisation diagram.

TABLE 2.17 *Average Standardised R.M.S.E.*

	Quarters ahead			
	1	2	3	4
Within sample				
Original	0·322	0·350	0·366	0·399
Model 1	0·279	0·304	0·327	0·361
Model 2	0·320	0·344	0·346	0·382
Model 3	0·364	0·374	0·380	0·416
	(0·412)	(0·428)	(0·368)	(0·414)
Model 4	0·461	0·493	0·391	0·436
Post-sample				
Original	1·224	1·302	1·238	1·343
Model 1	0·844	1·002	1·111	1·214
Model 2	0·852	0·961	1·057	1·170
Model 3	1·499	1·642	1·295	1·237
	(0·956)	(1·016)	(1·113)	(1·221)
Model 4	1·013	1·058	1·157	1·260

We may conclude from these results that as far as the sample period prediction is concerned, the improvement in the short-run predictive accuracy gained by I.T.S.L.S. is found to be considerable.

(ii) *The post-sample prediction case*

The results of the post-sample prediction case (1965·1–1968·1) for the same six variables out of seventeen are reported in the preceding tables (bottom half of Tables 2.11 to 2.16). They show that beyond the sample period, reduction in R.M.S.E. gained from re-estimation becomes less pronounced and less uniform. Particularly, real G.N.P. was poorly predicted in most cases (Table 2.11), mainly as a result of poor consumption prediction (Table 2.12). As regards other variables, too, reduction of prediction error was distinct only in short run prediction e.g. unemployment, inventory investment, and personal income, with a possible exception of the G.N.P. deflator whose R.M.S.E. was reduced much more in post-sample prediction than within-sample prediction.

It is also observed that in the post-sample prediction case, error builds up relatively faster than the original model, and error in predicting one quarter ahead is the smallest in most cases. This is particularly true for Model 4. However, as shown in Table 2.17 the overall predictive ability as measured by the average standardised R.M.S.E. was again found to be uniformly improved by the I.T.S.L.'s estimation procedure in every case but Model 3.[11]

Besides variables explicitly presented in these tables, sizeable improvement in predictive accuracy was observed with respect to such variables as unfilled orders, corporate profits before taxes and balance of payments which contributed to improve the overall performance in the post-sample predictions.

4. Some Tentative Conclusions

The sampling experiments indicate that O.L.S. is a difficult method to beat, even in predictive accuracy over several time periods, but we have managed to isolate some instances in which the structure favours a method of estimation that is more directly tied to prediction accuracy.

The experiments with actual data and a living model are encouraging. They show, first, that it is definitely possible to find a set of sample estimates by a systematic method that improves on accepted T.S.L.S. estimates as far as dynamic simulation performance is concerned. Within the sample period, the dynamic extensions of T.S.L.S. do not improve dynamic simulation performance, but the dynamic extensions, together with the static version of I.T.S.L.S. all do better than the original set of coefficients.

Outside the sample period, the main problem with the forecasts of G.N.P. and other overall variables seems to be

[11] It should also be noted that simulation performance of the re-estimated model was greatly improved by renormalising (i.e. choosing a different left-hand dependent variable) the manufacturing production function in calculating new coefficients. In re-estimating the production function (of Cobb–Douglas type), which is expressed as a labour requirement equation in the model, we renormalised in terms of man-hour input with the constraint of constant returns to scale. In Model 3, however, it was estimated only with constant returns to scale condition without renormalisation because renormalisation led to a wrong sign for the capital input coefficient. Figures in the parentheses under Model 3 show the results if the renormalised production function was used. Renormalisation made little difference to within sample results, but markedly improved the post sample results of the re-estimated systems, while it did not affect the original system.

narrowed to poor performance of a small block of equations. In a situation like this, at least as much effort should go into improvement of the specification and estimation of the block of equations as into more refined methods of estimation for the whole system. Yet, the comprehensive measure of forecast error does show that there is some gain to iteration of T.S.L.S. and to the dynamic extension of it.

In the difficult and challenging problem of economic prediction, all gains, no matter how small, are to be valued highly. The evidence so far suggests that some form of iterating T.S.L.S. may indeed provide a small gain in predictive performance.

References

[1] P. J. Dhrymes, A Simplified Structural Estimator for Large Scale Econometric Models, April, 1970, Discussion Paper No. 162, University of Pennsylvania.

[2] P. J. Dhrymes and V. Pandit, Asymptotic Properties of an Iterate of the Two Stage Least Squares Estimator, February, 1970, Discussion Paper No. 154, University of Pennsylvania.

[3] M. K. Evans and L. R. Klein, *The Wharton Econometric Forecasting Model*, 2nd ed. (Philadelphia: University of Pennsylvania, 1968).

[4] F. Fisher, The Choice of Instrumental Variables in the Estimation of Economy-Wide Econometric Models, *International Economic Review*, vi (September 1965) 245–74.

[5] T. Haavelmo, The Probability Approach in Econometrics, *Econometrica*, xii (July 1944) supplement.

[6] H. B. Mann and A. Wald, On the Statistical Treatment of Linear Stochastic Difference Equations, *Econometrica*, xi (July–October 1943) 173–220.

[7] A. L. Nagar, *Statistical Estimation of Simultaneous Economic Relationships*, Ph.D. Thesis, Rotterdam, 1959.

[8] H. Theil, *Economic Forecasts and Policy*, (Amsterdam: North-Holland, 1958).

[9] P. Whittle, *Prediction and Regulation by Linear Least-Squares Method*, (New York: D. Van Nostrand Company, Inc., 1963).

3 An Essay on Aggregation Theory and Practice

BY EDWIN KUH*

1. Introduction

One perplexing problem in the design of econometric research that remains largely unsolved is how estimation is affected by aggregation. The main purpose of this paper will be to show not only that aggregation gains exist, but how to provide practical estimates of their extent.

A volume dedicated to Jan Tinbergen is one highly natural place to analyse aggregation, since his famous League of Nations business cycle study [25] initiated the modern era of large-scale macroeconomic models. While statistical procedures have advanced in the interim, the model which he constructed has a truly modern flavour in many respects. In terms of detail, for instance, his model covered agriculture, finance, supply equations and prices, as well as the standard demand equations. Tinbergen's systematic attention to sectoral detail has only been matched or extended in the past decade, in constrast to what we now believe to be excessively aggregative Keynesian models of the 1940s and 1950s.

Theil's aggregation theorems [24] show that population regression coefficients must be nearly identical for all members of a universe if estimates from aggregated data are to reflect meaningful behaviour. The limitations of using aggregative data as seen from Theil's work have recently been reinforced by Orcutt, Watts and Edwards [17]. Their simulation results show that estimates from aggregate data generated by one particular simplified macroeconomic model can be inefficient as well as inconsistent, even when the micro parameters are

* Massachusetts Institute of Technology.

identical. They conclude '. . . that the loss of effective estimation and testing power, incurred through aggregation carried all the way up to the national level, can be extremely great' [17, p. 773]. Interesting further extensions of their analysis appear in E. B. Edwards and G. H. Orcutt [4], [5]. There exists a contrary position that favours greater aggregation. First, Griliches and Grunfeld [8] showed that error variances for aggregate regression equations will be less than the sum of the micro variances if negative error covariance terms are sufficiently large; furthermore, costs are normally less for estimates based on macro data. They restricted themselves to the important statistical problem of forecasting, but did not, as we shall here, consider efficiency of estimation in terms of parameter estimator variances. Second, there is a metaphysical view most vigorously espoused by Friedman and Meiselman [7] that the relevant behaviour of the economy can best be represented by a simple aggregated model: 'truth will out', even or especially in the aggregates, since complex, disaggregated models of behaviour are ineffectual vehicles for testing macroeconomic propositions. The third pragmatic view, of perhaps a majority of practising econometricians, is that micro data probably are better. However, micro data are either unavailable or excessively expensive, so that for practical purposes, aggregates must be used.

From a somewhat different aspect, many cross-sectional studies based on micro data (firms, families or individuals) have proven so disappointing that many researchers prefer to avoid this data source. The major failure is the prevalence of low correlations. Even though the statistical tests of significance may be highly affirmative in the sense of decisively rejecting the no-relationship hypothesis, it is exceedingly cold comfort to find a 'very significant' multiple correlation in a large sample which may explain no more than 5 or 10 per cent of the dependent variable's fluctuations.[1]

Finally, as with Goldilocks, something that seems 'just right' can sometimes be found in subaggregates such as two-digit

[1] If all micro-data were available, consistent estimates (see [18]) can be obtained by ordinary least squares. But more often than not, only aggregates can be obtained, so that measuring the benefits from using aggregates, by examining the relation between macro-parameter and micro-coefficient estimates, appears to be a sensible procedure.

industries, or subcategories of the labour force broken down by age, sex and skill. While the last remark is mere *obiter dictum* at this juncture, some analytical basis for it will soon be provided. I shall attempt to show that 'proper' aggregation is not merely neutral, nor just a major cost saving (which it usually is), but proper aggregation causes major reductions in the parameter estimator variances, relative to the underlying individual error variances. In addition, operational guidance to expected aggregation gain can be obtained from information present in the size distribution of the explanatory variables.

My perspective extends recent work of Theil [23] and Zellner [27], who have also used the random coefficient regression model as an appropriate stochastic assumption in the context of aggregating micro relations.

We will demonstrate that, on reasonable assumptions, the variances of the macro coefficients decrease as the number of individuals in the aggregate increases.[2] At first glance, this result might appear counterintuitive, since the variance of the sum tends to infinity even though the variance of their average tends to zero. However, given the random coefficients assumption, the aggregates can be interpreted as averages of random samples, which is a sensible intuitive way to understand what is happening here.

How all this comes about is sketched next in a simple example. More general asymptotic proofs are presented in Section 3. From the structure of the general proofs, it is possible to construct an approximate measure of aggregation gain that has practical relevance for empirical work. Simple economic assumptions about relations between aggregation weights and aggregation gain received substantial support in an investigation of four samples of data reported on later in this paper.

2. One Resolution: A Sketched Proof

The basic analytical tools are twofold. The first is the random coefficient model that was brought to the attention of

[2] This result applies to variance originating with the random coefficients in the structural estimating form of the macro equation. In the next section we take up the additional problems that arise, in the context of estimation and from the additive error term.

practising econometricians by Klein [12] in the context of cross-section models.[3] The complex maximum likelihood estimator proposed by Klein discouraged subsequent application. Nevertheless, the random coefficient model itself has much to recommend it. An aggregate relation may include heterogeneous micro parameters which nevertheless can be conceived of as random drawings from a population with a stable mean.[4] The random coefficient model also helps to rationalise the dilemma posed by the extremely low explanation of variance of most cross-section analysis. The basic economic behaviour *is* explicable on the average through time, even though it is not in one given time slice when the variances of the individual coefficients are large.[5] In this section, I shall indicate the main line of argument by means of a simple illustration of a regression equation with two explanatory variables.[6]

C. R. Rao [18] has shown that ordinary least squares is a consistent estimator in the random coefficient case when micro data are used. Theil's aggregation theory [24], the second analytical device on which this paper depends, has been translated into compact matrix notation by Kloek [13].

We will suppose that there are N individual behavioural equations of the form

$$\tilde{\mathbf{y}}_i = \tilde{\beta}_{i1}\mathbf{x}_{i1} + \tilde{\beta}_{i2}\mathbf{x}_{i2} + \tilde{\boldsymbol{\epsilon}}_i \qquad (1)$$

where $\tilde{\mathbf{y}}_i$ is a column vector of the dependent variable with T

[3] H. Rubin [19] had earlier presented a similar model in a somewhat less accessible formulation.

[4] As an alternative which will not be pursued here, casual introspection (the kind in which most of us excel) suggests that in making our own individual consumer expenditure decisions, we do not go through an exact calculation involving many relative prices and income, and then tack on a random error to this painstaking effort; rather, we often buy haphazardly, on impulse, even though 'on average' our purchases reflect more basic consumer preferences and economic parameters. This sort of behaviour is more compatible with a random coefficient model than it is with the standard shock model.

[5] Indeed, a related alternative explanation is the errors-in-variable model, where the argument has been made that cross-sectional consumption and income data contain error components which will bias least squares estimates.

[6] For ease of exposition, I have suppressed the intercept term, which does not affect the substance of the analysis in any significant way.

rows for the ith individual; $\mathbf{x}_{i1}$ and $\mathbf{x}_{i2}$ are $T \times 1$ column vectors of exogenous variables for the ith individual and $\tilde{\boldsymbol{\epsilon}}_i$ is a $T \times 1$ column vector of errors for the ith individual with $E(\tilde{\boldsymbol{\epsilon}}_i) = 0$. We distinguish a random variable from a value assumed by it with a tilde; e.g. the random variable $\tilde{z}$ assumes the value z. Lower-case bold-face characters represent vectors, while upper-case capital bold-face characters denote matrices.

In the random coefficients model the $\tilde{\beta}$ are random variables. The specific assumptions adopted for this paper are the following

$$\tilde{\beta}_{i1} = \xi_1 + \tilde{\delta}_{i1}, \qquad \tilde{\beta}_{i2} = \xi_2 + \tilde{\delta}_{i2} \tag{2}$$

$\tilde{\delta}_{i1}$ and $\tilde{\delta}_{i2}$ $(i = 1, 2, \ldots, N)$ have zero mean and are mutually independent random variables identically distributed across individuals.

The assumption that $\tilde{\beta}_{i1}$ has mean ξ_1 and $\tilde{\beta}_{i2}$ has mean ξ_2 is not, of course, a demand imposed by the random coefficient model itself but is a basic requirement of the aggregation approach used in this paper. The corresponding aggregative variables are, for $t = 1, 2, \ldots, T$

$$\tilde{Y}_t = \sum_{i=1}^{N} \tilde{y}_{it}, \qquad X_{t1} = \sum_{i=1}^{N} x_{it1}, \qquad X_{t2} = \sum_{i=1}^{N} x_{it2} \tag{3}$$

$$\tilde{\mathbf{Y}} = \begin{bmatrix} \tilde{Y}_1 \\ \cdot \\ \cdot \\ \cdot \\ \tilde{Y}_T \end{bmatrix}, \qquad \mathbf{X}_1 = \begin{bmatrix} X_{11} \\ \cdot \\ \cdot \\ \cdot \\ X_{T1} \end{bmatrix}, \qquad \mathbf{X}_2 = \begin{bmatrix} X_{12} \\ \cdot \\ \cdot \\ \cdot \\ X_{T2} \end{bmatrix} \tag{4}$$

The least squares estimator for the aggregative variables is then defined in (5).

$$\begin{bmatrix} \tilde{b}_1 \\ \tilde{b}_2 \end{bmatrix} = \{[\mathbf{X}_1\ \mathbf{X}_2]'[\mathbf{X}_1\ \mathbf{X}_2]\}^{-1}[\mathbf{X}_1\ \mathbf{X}_2]'\tilde{\mathbf{Y}} \tag{5}$$

Provided the expected values exist, we can then define macro parameters as the expected value of the estimator in (5)

$$\begin{bmatrix} \beta_1 \\ \beta_2 \end{bmatrix} = E\begin{bmatrix} \tilde{b}_1 \\ \tilde{b}_2 \end{bmatrix} \tag{6}$$

Before going further it is convenient to introduce Theil's concept of auxiliary regressions which enables us to express the micro explanatory variables as a function of the aggregates. When each micro series for each exogenous variable is regressed on all the macro exogenous variables (a useful step essential to a clear interpretation of the macro parameters in terms of the micro parameters), the resulting regression coefficients denoted by W will be called the aggregation weights. The auxiliary equation also contains a residual vector $\mathbf{u}_i$. Setting $\begin{bmatrix}1\\ \cdot\\ \cdot\\ \cdot\\ 1\end{bmatrix} = \mathbf{1}$

$$\mathbf{x}_{i1} = W_{i1}^{(1)}\mathbf{X}_1 + W_{i1}^{(2)}\mathbf{X}_2 + W_{1}^{(0)}\mathbf{1} + \mathbf{u}_{i1} \tag{7a}$$

$$\mathbf{x}_{i2} = W_{i2}^{(1)}\mathbf{X}_1 + W_{i2}^{(2)}\mathbf{X}_2 + W_{i2}^{(0)}\mathbf{1} + \mathbf{u}_{i2} \tag{7b}$$

The aggregation weights W satisfy the following conditions as a direct implication of least squares estimation

$$\sum_{i=1}^{N} W_{ip}^{(l)} \begin{cases} = 1 & \text{for} \quad p = l \quad \text{(corresponding } W\text{-weights)} \\ = 0 & \text{for} \quad p \neq l \quad \text{(non-corresponding } W\text{-weights)} \end{cases} \tag{8}$$

Thus, the weights for corresponding parameters sum to unity, and sum to zero for non-corresponding parameters.

When the right-hand sides of (7a) and (7b) respectively are substituted for $\mathbf{x}_{i1}$ and $\mathbf{x}_{i2}$ in (1), we have

$$\begin{aligned}\tilde{\mathbf{Y}}_i &= \tilde{\beta}_{i1}(W_{i1}^{(1)}\mathbf{X}_1 + W_{i1}^{(2)}\mathbf{X}_2) + \tilde{\beta}_{i2}(W_{i2}^{(1)}\mathbf{X}_1 + W_{i2}^{(2)}\mathbf{X}_2) \\ &\quad + \tilde{\beta}_{i1}(W_{i1}^{(0)}\mathbf{1} + \mathbf{u}_{i1}) + \tilde{\beta}_{i2}(W_{i2}^{(0)}\mathbf{1} + \mathbf{u}_{i2}) + \tilde{\boldsymbol{\epsilon}}_i \\ &= (\tilde{\beta}_{i1}W_{i1}^{(1)} + \tilde{\beta}_{i2}W_{i2}^{(1)})\mathbf{X}_1 + (\tilde{\beta}_{i1}W_{i1}^{(2)} + \tilde{\beta}_{i2}W_{i2}^{(2)})\mathbf{X}_2 \\ &\quad + \tilde{\beta}_{i1}(W_{i1}^{(0)}\mathbf{1} + \mathbf{u}_{i1}) + \tilde{\beta}_{i2}(W_{i2}^{(0)}\mathbf{1} + \mathbf{u}_{i2}) + \tilde{\boldsymbol{\epsilon}}_i\end{aligned} \tag{9}$$

When (9) is summed over all i individuals in the sample, (10) results

$$\begin{aligned}\tilde{\mathbf{Y}} &= \left[\sum_{i=1}^{N}(\tilde{\beta}_{i1}W_{i1}^{(1)} + \tilde{\beta}_{i2}W_{i2}^{(1)})\right]\mathbf{X}_1 + \left[\sum_{i=1}^{N}(\tilde{\beta}_{i1}W_{i1}^{(2)} + \tilde{\beta}_{i2}W_{i2}^{(2)})\right]\mathbf{X}_2 \\ &\quad + \sum_{i=1}^{N}(\tilde{\beta}_{i1}W_{i1}^{(0)} + \tilde{\beta}_{i2}W_{i2}^{(0)})\mathbf{1} + \tilde{\boldsymbol{\epsilon}}\end{aligned} \tag{10}$$

where the macro equation residual $\tilde{\boldsymbol{\epsilon}}$ satisfies

$$\tilde{\boldsymbol{\epsilon}} = \sum_{i=1}^{N} (\tilde{\beta}_{i1}\mathbf{u}_{i1} + \tilde{\beta}_{i2}\mathbf{u}_{i2} + \tilde{\boldsymbol{\epsilon}}_i) \tag{11}$$

The expectations of b_1 and b_2 which define the macro parameters can now be derived in terms of the aggregation weights as follows. Recalling the aggregation weight rules,

$$\sum_{i=1}^{N} W_{i1}^{(1)} = \sum_{i=1}^{N} W_{i2}^{(2)} = 1 \qquad \text{and} \qquad \sum_{=1}^{N} W_{i2}^{(1)} = \sum_{i=1}^{N} W_{i1}^{(2)} = 0$$

$$E\begin{bmatrix} \tilde{b}_1 \\ \tilde{b}_2 \end{bmatrix} = E(\{[\mathbf{X}_1\ \mathbf{X}_2]'[\mathbf{X}_1\ \mathbf{X}_2]\}^{-1}[\mathbf{X}_1\ \mathbf{X}_2]'\tilde{\mathbf{Y}}) \tag{12}$$

Upon expanding $E(\tilde{\mathbf{Y}})$ in (12)

$$\begin{aligned} E(\tilde{\mathbf{Y}}) &= \left\{\sum_{i=1}^{N} [E(\tilde{\beta}_{i1})W_{i1}^{(1)} + E(\tilde{\beta}_{i2})W_{i2}^{(1)}]\right\}\mathbf{X}_1 \\ &\quad + \left\{\sum_{i=1}^{N} [E(\tilde{\beta}_{i1})W_{i1}^{(2)} + E(\tilde{\beta}_{i2})W_{i2}^{(2)}]\right\}\mathbf{X}_2 + E(\tilde{\boldsymbol{\epsilon}}) \\ &= \left[E(\tilde{\beta}_{i1})\sum_{i=1}^{N} W_{i1}^{(1)} + E(\tilde{\beta}_{i2})\sum_{i=1}^{N} W_{i2}^{(1)}\right]\mathbf{X}_1 \\ &\quad + \left[E(\tilde{\beta}_{i1})\sum_{i=1}^{N} W_{i1}^{(2)} + E(\tilde{\beta}_{i2})\sum_{i=1}^{N} W_{i2}^{(2)}\right]\mathbf{X}_2 + E(\tilde{\boldsymbol{\epsilon}}) \\ &= E(\beta_{i1})\mathbf{X}_1 + E(\beta_{i2})\mathbf{X}_2 + E(\tilde{\boldsymbol{\epsilon}}) \\ &= \xi_1\mathbf{X}_1 + \xi_2\mathbf{X}_2 + E(\tilde{\boldsymbol{\epsilon}}) \end{aligned} \tag{13}$$

Finally, substituting the last line of (13) into (12) yields

$$\begin{aligned} E\begin{bmatrix} \tilde{b}_1 \\ \tilde{b}_2 \end{bmatrix} &= \{[\mathbf{X}_1\ \mathbf{X}_2]'[\mathbf{X}_1\ \mathbf{X}_2]\}^{-1}[\mathbf{X}_1\ \mathbf{X}_2]'[\mathbf{X}_1\ \mathbf{X}_2]\begin{bmatrix} \xi_1 \\ \xi_2 \end{bmatrix} \\ &\quad + \{[\mathbf{X}_1\ \mathbf{X}_2]'[\mathbf{X}_1\ \mathbf{X}_2]\}^{-1}[\mathbf{X}_1\ \mathbf{X}_2]' \\ &\quad \times \sum_{i=1}^{N} \{\xi_1\mathbf{u}_{i1} + \xi_2\mathbf{u}_{i2} + E(\tilde{\boldsymbol{\epsilon}}_i)\} \\ &= \begin{bmatrix} \xi_1 \\ \xi_2 \end{bmatrix} = \begin{bmatrix} \beta_1 \\ \beta_2 \end{bmatrix} \end{aligned} \tag{14}$$

The terms in $E(\bar{\boldsymbol{\varepsilon}})$ involving $\mathbf{u}_{i1}$ and $\mathbf{u}_{i2}$ vanish since these residual vectors are orthogonal to the macro variables $\mathbf{X}_1$ and $\mathbf{X}_2$; remaining terms in $\bar{\boldsymbol{\varepsilon}}_1$ have an expected value of zero. Hence, the expected value of the macroparameter estimate is the mean of the micro-coefficient parameter vector.

The assumption that $E(\beta_{i1}) = \xi_1$ and $E(\beta_{i2}) = \xi_2$ can be conceived of in two different ways. The treatment adopted here is to view ξ_1 as defining the mean of a frequency distribution across individuals with different regression coefficients. By selecting N individuals randomly from this frequency distribution, it is permissible to view the regression coefficients as random departures from their mean, ξ_i. Note that random departures are cross-sectional in this context, i.e. they occur once and for all when the sample is drawn, rather than at each time period.

In a related context, Theil [23] has indicated how critical the assumption is that the *x*s are fixed variates:

> These results indicate that there are no problems of aggregation bias if one works with a random-coefficients micro-model. In fact, the macro coefficients, contrary to the micro coefficients, are not random at all when N is sufficiently large. Note, however, that the assumption of non-stochastic *x*s is not at all innocuous. If we select households at random, not only their βs but also their *x*s become stochastic. This does not mean that we cannot treat the *x*s as if they are fixed. But this does mean that if we do so, we operate conditionally on the *x*s and we assume implicitly that the conditional distribution of the βs given the *x*s is independent of these *x*s. Thus the analysis is based on the condition that over the set of individuals who are aggregated, there is stochastic independence between the factors determining their behavior (the *x*s) and the way in which they react given these factors (the βs).

The assumption that the explanatory variables are distributed independently of their coefficients is not trivial, but it seems no more offensive than the same kind of assumption made about error terms and exogenous variables in the standard regression model. Every random process ultimately involves untestable assumptions of this sort. Some econometricians feel less secure about this assumption than the more usual case. Yet if non-linearities are not severe, and in most empirical situations this appears to be true, the assumption seems equally valid. The great convenience of the random coefficients model in the aggregation context (initially recognised by Zellner [26]), is that it allows individual parameters to be different which seems realistic, yet to possess a common average.

The variance of $\tilde{b}_1$ can be written by inspection of the random coefficient terms in (10) as

$$V_N(\tilde{b}_1) = \left[\sum_{i=1}^{N}(W_{i1}^{(1)})^2\right]\sigma_1^2 + \left[\sum_{i=1}^{N}(W_{i2}^{(1)})^2\right]\sigma_2^2 + 2\left[\sum_{i=1}^{N}W_{i1}^{(1)}W_{i2}^{(1)}\right]\sigma_{12} \tag{15}$$

where σ_1^2 is the variance of the first micro parameter, σ_2^2 is the variance of the second micro parameter, and σ_{12} their covariance, provided that the micro parameters are assumed to be identically and independently distributed for all N individuals.

We must now evaluate the nature of the W-weights more closely, for it is their behaviour that basically determines what happens to the variance of the macro-parameter as N increases.[7] While it is true, as Theil and Kloek have emphasised, that these weights are arbitrary, it is nevertheless reasonable to suppose under a wide variety of circumstances that the $W_{i1}^{(1)}$ will be approximately the proportion of $\mathbf{X}_1$ that originates with x_{i1}, and similarly for x_{i2} and $\mathbf{x}_2$. Furthermore, one would suppose that the $W_{i2}^{(1)}$ non-corresponding weights would tend to be much smaller than the $W_{i1}^{(1)}$. The arbitrary nature of the entire auxiliary equation estimation procedure for the Ws leads one to expect that the net regression coefficient of x_{i1} on $\mathbf{X}_2$ will be small, term by term. Furthermore, we know that $\sum_{i=1}^{N} W_{i1}^{(1)} = 1$ and $\sum_{i=1}^{N} W_{i2}^{(1)} = 0$.

From these assumptions about the relation of W-weights to each other and to proportions, the following significant and straightforward assertion emerges: the share of each component in an aggregate will remain unchanged or decrease when the aggregate increases through the inclusion of more elements,

[7] The least squares *estimator* variance includes an additional term which reflects the additive error terms in the micro equations, a complicating factor that will be discussed in the next section.

and the corresponding W-weights will behave in corresponding fashion. The sum of squares, $\sum_{i=1}^{N}(W_{i1}^{(1)})^2$ will thus gradually decline as the squared fractions and their sum decrease, and so will the coefficient variance.

Consider the purely illustrative case where the following simplified conditions are assumed to hold:

(*a*) The $W_{i1}^{(1)}$ weights represent shares divided equally among members in the aggregate.

(*b*) The $W_{i2}^{(1)}$ are individually negligible or the variance σ_2^2 of $\tilde{\beta}_{i2}$ is negligible relative to that $\tilde{\beta}_{i1}$ and similarly for the covariance σ_{i2} among the micro-parameter estimates, $\tilde{\beta}_{i1}$ and $\tilde{\beta}_{i2}$.

Then

$$V_N(\tilde{b}_1) \cong \left[\sum_{i=1}^{N}(W_{i1}^{(1)})^2\right]\sigma_{\beta i1}^2 = \left[\sum_{i=1}^{N}\left(\frac{1}{N}\right)^2\right]\sigma_{\beta i1}^2 = \frac{1}{N}\,\sigma_{\beta i1}^2 \qquad (16)$$

In this situation, the variance of the macro-parameter approximately obeys the law of large numbers, decreasing as $1/N$, i.e. it is as if we were averaging parameters of individually distributed variables, rather than taking weighted sums of independent random variables. The more unequal the weight distribution, the more slowly does the variance of the macro-parameter decrease. Empirical results confirm that, even with skewed size distributions that exist in many manufacturing industries, the sums of the squared shares, to which corresponding W-weights are close analogues, tend rapidly to small magnitudes in most four-digit industries.

3. General Proof

Symbol definitions

Symbol	Dimension	Description
Micro equations		
$\tilde{\boldsymbol{\beta}}_i$	$K \times 1$	Column vector of micro-parameters for ith equation
$\mathbf{X}_i$	$T \times K$	Matrix of explanatory variable observations for ith equation
$\tilde{\mathbf{y}}_i$	$T \times 1$	Column vector of dependent variable for ith equation
$\tilde{\boldsymbol{\epsilon}}_i$	$T \times 1$	Column vector of disturbances for ith equation

$\boldsymbol{\xi}$	$K \times 1$	Column vector of mean parameter values common to all equations
$\tilde{\boldsymbol{\delta}}$	$K \times 1$	Column vector of random components for micro parameters in ith equation

Macro equations

$\tilde{\mathbf{b}}$	$K \times 1$	Least squares estimator of macro coefficients
$\boldsymbol{\beta}$	$K \times 1$	Column vector of macro parameter expected values
$\mathbf{X}$	$T \times K$	Matrix of explanatory variable observations in macro equation
$\tilde{\mathbf{Y}}$	$T \times 1$	Column vector of dependent variable in macro equation
$\tilde{\boldsymbol{\epsilon}}$	$T \times 1$	Column vector of disturbances for macro equation

Auxiliary equations

$\mathbf{W}_i^{(l)}$	$1 \times K$	Row vector of least squares regression coefficients in lth auxiliary equation for the ith individual
$\mathbf{W}$	$K \times KN$	Matrix of all W-weights, i.e. regression coefficients in auxiliary equations
$\mathbf{u}_i^{(l)}$	$T \times 1$	Column vector of residuals in lth auxiliary equation for ith individual
$\mathbf{U}_i$	$T \times K$	Matrix of all auxiliary equation residuals for ith individual

Relationship Definitions

Micro equations corresponds to

(17) $$\tilde{\mathbf{y}}_i = \mathbf{X}_i\tilde{\boldsymbol{\beta}}_i + \tilde{\boldsymbol{\epsilon}}_i$$ (1)

(18) $$\tilde{\boldsymbol{\beta}}_i = \boldsymbol{\xi} + \tilde{\boldsymbol{\delta}}_i$$ (2)

Macro equations

(*a*) Structural macro equation

(19) $$\mathbf{X} = \sum_{i=1}^{N} \mathbf{X}_i, \qquad \mathbf{Y} = \sum_{i=1}^{N} \tilde{\mathbf{y}}_i$$ (3) and (4)

(20) $$\tilde{\mathbf{b}} \equiv (\mathbf{X}'\mathbf{X})^{-1}\mathbf{X}'\tilde{\mathbf{Y}} \qquad (5)$$

(21) $$\boldsymbol{\beta} \equiv E(\tilde{\mathbf{b}}) \qquad (6)$$

(22) $$\tilde{\mathbf{b}} \equiv (\tilde{\mathbf{b}}_1\ \tilde{\mathbf{b}}_2 \cdots \tilde{\mathbf{b}}_K)'$$

(23) $$\tilde{\mathbf{Y}} = \mathbf{XW}\begin{bmatrix} \tilde{\boldsymbol{\beta}}_1 \\ \cdot \\ \cdot \\ \cdot \\ \tilde{\boldsymbol{\beta}}_N \end{bmatrix} + \tilde{\boldsymbol{\epsilon}} \qquad (10)$$

(24) $$\tilde{\boldsymbol{\epsilon}} = [\mathbf{u}_1\tilde{\boldsymbol{\beta}}_1 + \tilde{\boldsymbol{\epsilon}}_1 + \mathbf{u}_2\tilde{\boldsymbol{\beta}}_2 + \tilde{\boldsymbol{\epsilon}}_2 + \cdots + \mathbf{u}_N\tilde{\boldsymbol{\beta}}_N + \tilde{\boldsymbol{\epsilon}}_N] \qquad (11)$$

(25) $$\tilde{\mathbf{b}}_l = \sum_{i=1}^{N} \mathbf{W}_i^{(l)}\tilde{\boldsymbol{\beta}}_i$$

(*b*) Estimated macro equation

(26) $$\mathbf{Y} = \mathbf{Xb} + \mathbf{e}$$

Auxiliary equations and aggregation weights

(27) $$\mathbf{x}_i^{(l)} = \mathbf{XW}_i^{(l)\prime} + \mathbf{u}_i^{(l)} \qquad \text{(7a) and (7b)}$$

(28) $$\mathbf{W}_i^{(l)\prime} = (\mathbf{X}'\mathbf{X})^{-1}\mathbf{X}'\mathbf{x}_i^{(l)}$$

(29) $$\mathbf{W}_i^{(l)} = [W_{i1}^{(l)}\ W_{i2}^{(l)} \cdots W_{iK}^{(l)}]$$

(30) $$\mathbf{U}_i = [\mathbf{u}_i^{(1)}\ \mathbf{u}_i^{(2)} \cdots \mathbf{u}_i^{(K)}]$$

(31) $$\mathbf{W} = \begin{bmatrix} \mathbf{W}_1^{(1)} & \mathbf{W}_2^{(1)} & \cdots & \mathbf{W}_N^{(1)} \\ \cdot & & & \cdot \\ \cdot & & & \cdot \\ \cdot & & & \cdot \\ \mathbf{W}_1^{(K)} & \mathbf{W}_2^{(K)} & \cdots & \mathbf{W}_N^{(K)} \end{bmatrix}$$

We make the following

Assumptions. Given $\boldsymbol{\xi}, \tilde{\boldsymbol{\beta}}_i = \boldsymbol{\xi} + \tilde{\boldsymbol{\delta}}_i (i = 1, 2, \ldots, N)$ is a sequence of mutually independent identically distributed $(K \times 1)$ random variables, with mean vector $\boldsymbol{\xi}$ and positive definite symmetric covariance matrix $\boldsymbol{\Omega}$.[8] And $\{\tilde{\boldsymbol{\epsilon}}_i\}$ $(i = 1, 2,$

[8] The task of also proving that the limiting variances are zero when the individual parameter variance matrices are correlated has not been attempted. One may conjecture that when the tedious algebra is done, the basic results obtained here will not be altered. Highly complex product chains of fractions under the assumptions I have used throughout seem likely to converge to zero in the limit.

$\ldots, N$) is also a sequence of mutually independent identically distributed random variables with mean $\mathbf{0}$ and variance matrix $\sigma^2\mathbf{I}$. Also, the sequences $\{\tilde{\boldsymbol{\delta}}_i\}$ and $\{\tilde{\boldsymbol{\epsilon}}_i\}$ are mutually independent.

Theorem 1. The ordinary least squares estimate of $\tilde{\mathbf{b}}$ is an unbiased estimate of the common micro regression vector $\boldsymbol{\xi}$.

Proof[9]

$$E(\tilde{\mathbf{b}}) \equiv \boldsymbol{\beta} = E\{(\mathbf{X}'\mathbf{X})^{-1}\mathbf{X}'\mathbf{Y}\}$$

$$= E\left\{(\mathbf{X}'\mathbf{X})^{-1}\mathbf{X}'\mathbf{X}\mathbf{W}\begin{bmatrix}\tilde{\boldsymbol{\beta}}_1\\ \cdot\\ \cdot\\ \cdot\\ \tilde{\boldsymbol{\beta}}_N\end{bmatrix} + (\mathbf{X}'\mathbf{X})^{-1}\mathbf{X}'\tilde{\boldsymbol{\epsilon}}\right\}$$

$$= \mathbf{W}[\boldsymbol{\xi}_1' \cdots \boldsymbol{\xi}_N'] = \boldsymbol{\xi} \qquad \text{Q.E.D.} \quad (32)$$

The next step is to explore the variance properties of the least-squares estimator of $\tilde{\mathbf{b}}$ which is of even greater interest for our purposes. It is convenient to define two further symbols: $\mathbf{G} = (\mathbf{X}'\mathbf{X})^{-1}\mathbf{X}'$ and $\sum_{i=1}^{N} \tilde{\boldsymbol{\epsilon}}_i = \tilde{\mathbf{e}}$.

When the micro equations $\tilde{\mathbf{y}}_i$ from (17) are substituted into the estimator (20) we have

$$\tilde{\mathbf{b}} = \mathbf{G}\sum_{i=1}^{N}(\mathbf{X}_i\tilde{\boldsymbol{\beta}}_i + \tilde{\boldsymbol{\epsilon}}_i) \qquad (33)$$

$$\text{var}\,(\tilde{\mathbf{b}}) = E[\tilde{\mathbf{b}} - E(\tilde{\mathbf{b}})][\tilde{\mathbf{b}} - E(\tilde{\mathbf{b}})]' = E(\tilde{\mathbf{b}} - \boldsymbol{\xi})(\tilde{\mathbf{b}} - \boldsymbol{\xi})' \qquad (34)$$

Now $\tilde{\mathbf{b}}$ differs from $\boldsymbol{\xi}$ because of random variation in $\tilde{\boldsymbol{\beta}}_i$ measured by $\tilde{\boldsymbol{\delta}}_i$ and from random variation arising from the micro equation errors, the $\tilde{\boldsymbol{\epsilon}}_i$.

$$(\mathbf{b} - \boldsymbol{\xi}) = \mathbf{G}\sum_{i=1}^{N}(\mathbf{X}_i\tilde{\boldsymbol{\delta}}_i + \tilde{\boldsymbol{\epsilon}}_i) \qquad (35)$$

[9] This is equivalent to Zellner's proof [26], although unlike his result, mine explicitly introduces aggregation weights. This proof is a straightforward extension of the bivariate case where (see Equation (14) and discussion). Orthogonality of $\mathbf{X}$ with $\mathbf{u}_i$ together with $E(\epsilon_i) = 0$ causes the right-hand term of the second equality to vanish, leading to the final result.

But $\mathbf{GX}_i = \mathbf{W}_i$ so that

$$(\mathbf{b} - \boldsymbol{\xi}) = \mathbf{W}\begin{bmatrix} \tilde{\boldsymbol{\delta}}_1 \\ \cdot \\ \cdot \\ \cdot \\ \tilde{\boldsymbol{\delta}}_N \end{bmatrix} + \mathbf{G}\tilde{\mathbf{e}} \tag{36}$$

$$\mathbf{V}_N(\tilde{\mathbf{b}}) = E(\mathbf{b} - \boldsymbol{\xi})(\mathbf{b} - \boldsymbol{\xi})'$$

$$= \mathbf{W}\begin{bmatrix} \boldsymbol{\Omega}_1 & & & & \mathbf{0} \\ & \boldsymbol{\Omega}_2 & & & \\ & & \cdot & & \\ & & & \cdot & \\ & & & & \cdot \\ \mathbf{0}' & & & & \boldsymbol{\Omega}_N \end{bmatrix}\mathbf{W}' + \sigma^2_{\tilde{\mathbf{e}}}(\mathbf{X}'\mathbf{X})^{-1}_N \tag{37}$$

The central question is what happens to each of these terms as N becomes large.[10] We will show under plausible assumptions that the first expression on the right-hand side of (37) tends to zero as $N \to \infty$ and, by a different route, that the second expression on the right-hand side of (37) will do the same. A generic diagonal of $\mathbf{V}_N(\tilde{\mathbf{b}})$ in (37) can be written as

$$\mathbf{V}_N(\tilde{\mathbf{b}}_l) = \sum_{i=1}^{N} \mathbf{W}_i^{(l)}\boldsymbol{\Omega}_i\mathbf{W}_i^{(l)\prime} + \sigma^2_{\tilde{\mathbf{e}}_N}[\mathbf{X}'\mathbf{X}]^{-1}_{ll}$$

$$= \operatorname{tr}\sum_{i=1}^{N} \boldsymbol{\Omega}_i\mathbf{W}_i^{(l)\prime}\mathbf{W}_i^{(l)} + \sigma^2_{\tilde{\mathbf{e}}_N}[\mathbf{X}'\mathbf{X}]^{-1}_{ll}$$

$$= \mathbf{V}_N(\tilde{\mathbf{b}}_l \mid \boldsymbol{\delta}) + \mathbf{V}_N(\tilde{\mathbf{b}}_l \mid \tilde{\mathbf{e}}_N) \tag{38}$$

Theorem 2. Under conditions to be stated

$$\lim_{N\to\infty} \mathbf{V}_N(\tilde{\mathbf{b}}) = 0$$

Part A – Random coefficient variance component

Proof that

$$\lim_{N\to\infty} \mathbf{W}\begin{bmatrix} \boldsymbol{\Omega}_1 & & & & \mathbf{0} \\ & \boldsymbol{\Omega}_2 & & & \\ & & \cdot & & \\ & & & \cdot & \\ & & & & \cdot \\ \mathbf{0}' & & & & \boldsymbol{\Omega}_N \end{bmatrix}\mathbf{W}' = \mathbf{0}$$

[10] It should be noted when variances in (36) are calculated that $\sigma^2_{\tilde{\varepsilon}} = N\sigma^2_{\tilde{\varepsilon}_i}$ since matrix multiplication involving terms in $\mathbf{V}_i\boldsymbol{\beta}_i$ (which appear in (23)) and $(\mathbf{X}'\mathbf{X})\mathbf{X}' = \mathbf{G}$ vanish identically in the quadratic form (37).

It must now be shown what restrictions on the W-weights will lead to a decrease in the macro parameter variances as the aggregate population grows. A lemma concerning a sequence of fractions which sum to unity is needed at this point.

Lemma. For $i = 1, 2, \ldots, N$ and $N = 1, 2, \ldots,$ let $\{p_{iN}\}$ be such that $-1 \leq p_{iN} < 1$ and $\sum_{i=1}^{N} p_{iN} = 1$. If $\sum_{i=1}^{N} |p_{iN}| \leq M$ where M is finite and $\lim_{N} \rho_N \to 0$ where $\rho_N \equiv \max \{|p_{iN}|, i = 1, 2, \ldots, N\}$ then $\lim_{N\to\infty} \sum_{i=1}^{N} p_{iN}^2 = 0$.[11]

Corollary. For $i = 1, 2, \ldots, N$ and $N = 1, 2, \ldots,$ let $\{p_{iN}\}$ be such that $0 \leq p_{iN} < 1$ and $\sum_{i=1}^{N} p_{iN} = 1$. Then a necessary and sufficient condition that $\lim_{N\to\infty} \sum_{i=1}^{N} p_{iN} = 0$ is that $\lim \rho_N \to 0$ where $\rho_N \equiv \max \{p_{iN}, i = 1, 2, \ldots, N\}$.

[11] *Proof.* Examine the sum

$$\sum_{i=1}^{N} \left(p_{iN}^2 - \frac{1}{N^2}\right) = \sum_{i=1}^{N} \left(p_{iN} + \frac{1}{N}\right)\left(p_{iN} - \frac{1}{N}\right)$$

Clearly, $\rho_N \geq |p_{iN}| - (1/N)$ for each i, so

$$\sum_{i=1}^{N} \left(p_{iN}^2 - \frac{1}{N^2}\right) \leq \rho_N \sum_{i=1}^{N} \left(|p_{iN}| + \frac{1}{N}\right) \leq (1 + M)\rho_N$$

By hypothesis $\lim \rho_N \to 0$ so that

$$\lim_{N\to\infty} \sum_{i=1}^{N} \left(\rho_{iN}^2 - \frac{1}{N^2}\right) = \lim_{N\to\infty} \left[\left(\sum_{i=1}^{N} p_{iN}^2\right) - \frac{1}{N}\right] \leq 0$$

But the minimum value of $\sum_{i=1}^{N} p_{iN}^2$ is $1/N$ implying for each N that

$$\lim_{N\to\infty} \left[\left(\sum_{i=1}^{N} p_{iN}^2\right) - \frac{1}{N}\right] \geq 0$$

thus

$$\lim_{N\to\infty} \left[\left(\sum_{i=1}^{N} p_{iN}^2\right) - \frac{1}{N}\right] = 0$$

whereupon

$$\lim_{N\to\infty} \sum_{i=1}^{N} p_{iN}^2 = \lim_{N\to\infty} \frac{1}{N} = 0.$$

Proof. Necessity is obvious. To prove sufficiently, from the previous lemma all that is needed is to show that there exists an M such that $\sum_{i=1}^{N} |p_{iN}| \leq M$.

But

$$\sum_{i=1}^{N} |p_{iN}| = \sum_{i=1}^{N} p_{iN} = 1$$

Assumptions for Part A of Theorem

(1) $|W_{il}^{(l)}| < 1$, and $\sum_{i=1}^{N} |W_{il}^{(l)}| \leq M$

(2) When $j \neq l$, $|W_{ij}^{(l)}| \leq |W_{il}^{(l)}|$

(3) $\lim_{N \to \infty} \max |W_{il}^{(l)}| = 0 \ (i = 1, 2, \ldots, N)$

Proof. Let $\Omega_{rc,i}$ be a generic element of $\mathbf{\Omega}_i$ and $\theta_{rc} = \max \{\Omega_{rc,i}; i = 1, 2, \ldots, N\}$. By setting $\mathbf{\Xi} = [\theta_{rc}]$ and $\sum_{i=1}^{N} \mathbf{W}_i^{(l)\prime}\mathbf{W}_i^{(l)} = \mathbf{\Phi}_N^{(l)}$, we have

$$V_N(\tilde{\mathbf{b}}_l \mid \boldsymbol{\delta}) \leq \text{tr}\, \mathbf{\Xi}\mathbf{\Phi}_N^{(l)} \tag{39}$$

That $\lim_{N \to \infty} \sum_{i=1}^{N} [W_{il}^{(l)}]^2 = 0$ follows from condition (3) and the lemma.

Since $|W_{ij}^{(l)}| \leq |W_{il}^{(l)}|$ implies that $\sum_{i=1}^{N} [W_{ij}^{(l)}]^2 \leq \sum_{i=1}^{N} [W_{il}^{(l)}]^2$, convergence of the right-hand side of the inequality to zero as $N \to \infty$ implies that all diagonal terms in $\mathbf{\Phi}_N^{(l)}$ converge to zero as $N \to \infty$. By Cauchy–Schwarz inequality, convergence of all diagonal terms in $\mathbf{\Phi}_N^{(l)}$ to zero as $N \to \infty$ implies that $\lim_{N \to \infty} \mathbf{\Phi}_N^{(l)} = \mathbf{0}$. Hence, $V_N(\tilde{\mathbf{b}}_l) \to 0$ as $N \to \infty$, since elements of $\mathbf{\Xi}$ are bounded as well. For each N, $\mathbf{V}(\tilde{\mathbf{b}})$ is positive definite symmetric, so that $\lim_{N \to \infty} \mathbf{V}_N(\tilde{\mathbf{b}}_l) = \mathbf{0}$ for $l = 1, 2, \ldots, K$ implies that $\lim_{N \to \infty} \mathbf{V}_N(\tilde{\mathbf{b}}) = \mathbf{0}$. Q.E.D.

A problem with the second term in (38) is that $\lim \sigma_{\tilde{\mathbf{e}}}^2 \to \infty$ because $\sigma_{\tilde{\mathbf{e}}}^2 = N\sigma_{\boldsymbol{\varepsilon}_i}^2$. Hence, we must show under what conditions $N[\mathbf{X}'\mathbf{X}]^{-1} \to 0$ since $\sigma_{\boldsymbol{\varepsilon}_i}^2$ is simply a scalar.

Part B – Additive component of variance

Proof that $\lim_{N \to \infty} \sigma_{\boldsymbol{\varepsilon}_i}^2 N[\mathbf{X}'\mathbf{X}]^{-1} = 0$

Some further definitions are required to develop this particular proof. These are

Symbol	Dimension	Description
$\mathbf{1} = \begin{bmatrix} 1 \\ \cdot \\ \cdot \\ \cdot \\ 1 \end{bmatrix}$	$T \times 1$	Column vector of ones
$\mathbf{X}_0 = \begin{bmatrix} N \\ \cdot \\ \cdot \\ \cdot \\ N \end{bmatrix}$	$T \times 1$	Column vector for intercept variable in macro equation
$[\mathbf{X}_1\, \mathbf{X}_2 \cdots \mathbf{X}_{K-1}]$	$T \times (K-1)$	Data matrix for ordinary explanatory variables in macro equation
$\mathbf{X} = [\mathbf{X}_0\, \mathbf{X}_1 \cdots \mathbf{X}_{K-1}]$	$T \times K$	Data matrix for all explanatory variables in macro equation
ρ_{lm}		Simple correlation between macro explanatory variables X_l and X_m.
σ_l		Standard deviation of macro variable X_l
V_l		Coefficient of variation of macro variable X_l
$\sigma^2_{l.}$		Error variance for regression of X_l on remaining explanatory macro variables
$R_{l..}$		Multiple correlation of macro variable X_l with remaining $(K-2)$ macro explanatory variables
$\mathbf{C}$	$(K-1) \times (K-1)$	Correlation matrix of explanatory variables $X_l (l = 1, 2, \ldots, K-1)$
$\mathbf{D} = \mathbf{C}^{-1}$	$(K-1) \times (K-1)$	Definition of inverse of $\mathbf{C}$

Theorem 2. Part A.

Provided that, for $l = 1, 2, \ldots, K-1$,

(1) $\lim\limits_{N\to\infty} \sum_{t=1}^{T} \dfrac{(X_{lt} - \bar{X}_l)^2}{N} \to \infty$

(2) $R_{l..} < \delta_l < 1$

(3) $\left|\dfrac{\bar{X}_l}{N}\right| < M_l < \infty$

then $\lim\limits_{N\to\infty} N[\mathbf{X}'\mathbf{X}]^{-1} = \mathbf{0}.$

Proof

Now,

$$
\mathbf{X}'\mathbf{X} = \begin{bmatrix} N^2T & \mathbf{X}_0'\mathbf{X}_1 & \cdots & \mathbf{X}_0'\mathbf{X}_{K-1} \\ \mathbf{X}_0'\mathbf{X}_1 & \mathbf{X}_1'\mathbf{X}_1 & \cdots & \cdot \\ \cdot & \cdot & \cdot & \cdot \\ \cdot & \cdot & \cdot & \cdot \\ \cdot & \cdot & \cdot & \\ \mathbf{X}_0'\mathbf{X}_{K-1} & & \cdots & \mathbf{X}_{K-1}'\mathbf{X}_{K-1} \end{bmatrix} \tag{40}
$$

By elementary row and column operations $\mathbf{X}'\mathbf{X}$ can be transformed into a partitioned matrix whose lower right-hand partition is the correlation matrix $\mathbf{C}$

$$
\mathbf{X}'\mathbf{X} = \mathbf{F}\mathbf{G}\left[\begin{array}{c|cccc} N & 1/V_1 & 1/V_2 & \cdots & 1/V_{K-1} \\ \hline 0 & 1 & \rho_{12} & \cdots & \rho_{1,K-1} \\ & \rho_{12} & 1 & & \\ \cdot & \cdot & & \cdot & \cdot \\ \cdot & \cdot & & \cdot & \cdot \\ \cdot & \cdot & & \cdot & \cdot \\ 0 & \rho_{1,K-1} & & \cdots & 1 \end{array}\right]\mathbf{G}
$$

$$
= \mathbf{F}\mathbf{G}\left[\begin{array}{c|ccc} N & 1/V_1 & \cdots & 1/V_{K-1} \\ \hline 0 & & & \\ \cdot & & \mathbf{C} & \\ \cdot & & & \\ \cdot & & & \end{array}\right]\mathbf{G} \tag{41}
$$

where

$$
\mathbf{F} = \begin{bmatrix} NT & & & & \mathbf{0} \\ \mathbf{1X}_1 & T & & & \\ \mathbf{1X}_2 & 0 & T & & \\ \cdot & & & \cdot & \\ \cdot & & & & \cdot \\ \cdot & & & & \cdot \\ \mathbf{1X}_{K-1} & 0 & & \cdots & T \end{bmatrix} \tag{42}
$$

subsumes elementary row operations that reverse the subtraction of means from second moments about the origin and

$$\mathbf{G} = \begin{bmatrix} 1 & & & & & & \mathbf{0} \\ & \sigma_1 & & & & & \\ & & \sigma_2 & & & & \\ & & & \cdot & & & \\ & & & & \cdot & & \\ & & & & & \cdot & \\ \mathbf{0}' & & & & & & \sigma_{K-1} \end{bmatrix} \tag{43}$$

is used for elementary row and column operations to reverse the conversion of centred moments into correlations. Then

$$(\mathbf{X}'\mathbf{X})^{-1} = \mathbf{G}^{-1} \left[\begin{array}{c|cccc} 1/N & \alpha_1 & \alpha_2 & \cdots & \alpha_{K-1} \\ \hline 0 & & & & \\ \cdot & & & & \\ \cdot & & & \mathbf{D} & \\ \cdot & & & & \\ 0 & & & & \end{array}\right] \mathbf{G}^{-1}\mathbf{F}^{-1} \tag{44}$$

where

$$\mathbf{F}^{-1} = \begin{bmatrix} 1/NT & & & & \\ -\dfrac{\mathbf{1X}_1}{NT^2} & 1/T & & \mathbf{0} & \\ -\dfrac{\mathbf{1X}_2}{NT^2} & 0 & 1/T & & \\ \cdot & & & \cdot & \\ \cdot & & & & \cdot \\ \cdot & & & & \cdot \\ -\dfrac{\mathbf{1X}_{K-1}}{NT^2} & 0 & \cdots & 0 & \cdots & 1/T \end{bmatrix} \tag{45}$$

and

$$\alpha_l = -\frac{1}{N}\left[\frac{D_{1l}}{V_1} + \frac{D_{2l}}{V_2} + \cdots + \frac{D_{K-1,l}}{V_{K-1}}\right] \tag{46}$$

The matrix **C** is now in the form of a correlation matrix from whose inverse **D** the multiple correlation $R_{l..}$ can be evaluated as

$$R^2_{l..} = 1 - \frac{1}{D_{ll}} = 1 - \frac{\sigma^2_{l..}}{\sigma^2_l} \text{[12]} \tag{47}$$

[12] See Paul S. Dwyer [3a] who cites P. Horst [10a] for the earliest derivation of this result.

Hence

$$D_{ll} = \frac{\sigma_l^2}{\sigma_{l..}^2} \tag{48}$$

From this we can evaluate the diagonal elements of $(\mathbf{X}'\mathbf{X})^{-1}$ by reversing our operations with the elementary matrices **F** and **G** to establish that

$$(\mathbf{X}'\mathbf{X})_{ll}^{-1} = \frac{D_{ll}}{\sigma_l^2 T} = 1/TR_{l..}^2 \qquad (l = 1, 2, \ldots, K-1) \tag{49}$$

and

$$\begin{aligned}(\mathbf{X}'\mathbf{X})_{00}^{-1} &= \frac{1}{N^2T} - \frac{1}{NT}\left(\frac{\alpha_1}{V_1} + \frac{\alpha_2}{V_2} + \cdots + \frac{\alpha_{K-1}}{V_{K-1}}\right)\\ &= \frac{1}{NT}\left\{\frac{1}{N} - \left(\frac{\alpha_1}{V_1} + \frac{\alpha_2}{V_2} + \cdots + \frac{\alpha_{K-1}}{V_{K-1}}\right)\right\}\end{aligned} \tag{50}$$

To establish that the previous conditions are sufficient for $\lim_{N\to\infty} N(\mathbf{X}'\mathbf{X})^{-1} = \mathbf{0}$, we need only examine the diagonal terms since, by the Schwarz inequality, the off-diagonal terms will tend to zero if the diagonal terms do so for a positive definite symmetric matrix.

$$\begin{aligned}N(\mathbf{X}'\mathbf{X})_{ll}^{-1} &= \frac{N}{T\sigma_l^2(1 - R_{l..}^2)}\\ &= \left[\frac{1}{N}(\mathbf{X}_l - \bar{\mathbf{X}}_l)'(\mathbf{X}_l - \bar{\mathbf{X}}_l)(1 - R_{l..}^2)\right]^{-1}\end{aligned} \tag{51}$$

Hence, provided

$$\begin{aligned}&(a)\ \lim_{N\to\infty} \sum_{t=1}^{T} \frac{(X_t - \bar{X})^2}{N} \to \infty\\ &(b)\ 1 - R_{l..}^2 > \delta_l > 0\end{aligned} \tag{52}$$

$$\lim_{N\to\infty} N(\mathbf{X}'\mathbf{X})_{ll}^{-1} = 0 \qquad (l = 1, 2, \ldots, K-1)$$

Finally, looking at the intercept term,

$$N(\mathbf{X}'\mathbf{X})_{00}^{-1} = \frac{1}{T}\left\{\frac{1}{N} - \left(\frac{\alpha_1}{V_1} + \cdots + \frac{\alpha_{K-1}}{V_K}\right)\right\} \tag{53}$$

Recalling from (46),

$$\alpha_l = -\frac{1}{N}\left(\frac{D_{1l}}{V_1} + \frac{D_{2l}}{V_2} + \cdots + \frac{D_{K-1,l}}{V_{K-1}}\right)$$

a typical term in (53) becomes

$$\frac{1}{T}\frac{\alpha_l}{V_l} = -\frac{1}{TN}\left(\frac{D_{1l}}{V_1 V_l} + \frac{D_{2l}}{V_2 V_l} + \cdots + \frac{D_{K-1,l}}{V_{K-1,}V_l}\right) \tag{54}$$

Examine

$$\frac{D_{ll}}{TV_l^2 N} = \frac{D_{ll}}{NT\sigma_l^2}\bar{X}_l^2 = \frac{ND_{ll}}{T\sigma_l^2} \times \frac{\bar{X}_l^2}{N^2} \tag{55}$$

Using the result from the previous section that $\lim_{N\to\infty} ND_{ll}/T\sigma_l^2 = 0$ and proviso 3, that

$$\left|\frac{\bar{X}_l}{N}\right| < M_l < \infty \qquad (l = 1, 2, \ldots, K-1)$$

where M_l is an arbitrary upper bound,

$$\lim_{N\to\infty} \frac{D_{ll}}{TV_l^2 N} = 0 \tag{56}$$

Next consider a typical off-diagonal term in **D** which also appears in (54), $(1/TN)(D_{jl}/V_j V_l)$.

From the Schwarz inequality,

$$(\mathbf{X'X})^{-1}_{rs} \leq \sqrt{(\mathbf{X'X})^{-1}_{rr}}\sqrt{(\mathbf{X'X})^{-1}_{ss}}) \tag{57}$$

since $(\mathbf{X'X})^{-1}$ is a positive definite symmetric covariance matrix. Thus,

$$\begin{aligned}\frac{1}{TN}\frac{D_{jl}}{V_j V_l} &= \frac{D_{jl}}{\sigma_j \sigma_l} \times \frac{\bar{X}_j \bar{X}_l}{TN} \\ &= \frac{1}{N}(\mathbf{X'X})^{-1}_{jl}\bar{X}_j \bar{X}_l \\ &\leq \frac{1}{N^2}\sqrt{N(\mathbf{X'X})^{-1}_{jj}}\sqrt{N(\mathbf{X'X})^{-1}_{ll}}\;\bar{X}_j \bar{X}_l \end{aligned} \tag{58}$$

since $\lim_{N\to\infty} N(\mathbf{X'X})^{-1}_{jj} = 0$, and $\lim_{N\to\infty} N(\mathbf{X'X})^{-1}_{ll} = 0$ it is still a sufficient condition (see 3 above) to have $\bar{X}_{l/N}$ bounded away from infinity for all these terms to zero in the limit. Hence, all $\lim_{N\to\infty} \alpha_l/V_l = 0$ as does the first term of (53) in curly brackets, $1/N$, so, under the three stated conditions

$$\lim_{N\to\infty} N(\mathbf{X}'\mathbf{X})^{-1} = \mathbf{0} \qquad \text{Q.E.D.}$$

Corollary. If

$$\lim_{N\to\infty} \sum_{t=1}^{T} \frac{(X_{lt} - \bar{X}_l)^2}{N} = J_{1l}$$

an arbitrary constant, and $\lim_{N\to\infty} (\bar{X}_l/N) = J_{2l}$, another arbitrary constant, while similarly $\lim_{N\to\infty} R^2_{l..} \to \bar{R}^2_{l..} < \delta_l < 1$ (for $l = 1, 2, \ldots, K-1$), then $\lim \sigma^2_{\varepsilon_i} N(\mathbf{X}\,\mathbf{X})^{-1} = \mathbf{\Sigma}$, a constant matrix. The proof follows directly from these modified assumptions applied to (51) and (53).

Some few comments may be in order on conditions 1–3 of part A of Theorem 2. Much of their motivation has already been provided, and empirical support will be forthcoming in subsequent sections. That all W-weights are less than 1 in absolute value follows from the generally proportion-like character of the corresponding W-weights. The corollary to the lemma provides a more powerful result when the W-weights are positive fractions (though not necessarily proportions).

While the example in Section 2 and much of the discussion were motivated in terms of proportions, so that positive fractional W-weights are assumed to exist, the principal statistical results require only that the sum be bounded and the weights be fractions.[13] However, if W-weights are approximately like proportions, it then becomes possible to obtain estimates of aggregation gain from individual size distribution data, provided also that non-corresponding W-weights are small relative to corresponding W-weights. In fact, all corresponding W-weights estimated in this paper (210 altogether) were fractions. $\sum_{i=1}^{N} W_{ii}^{(l)} = 1$ follows identically from the least squares restriction, so that the corollary to the lemma applies directly.

[13] The modified lemma does not even make these requirements, but their retention is desirable. Subsequent interpretation of aggregation gain is based on proportions and assumptions about their behaviour.

The second condition, that non-corresponding W-weights be smaller than corresponding W-weights, is an implication of the greater systematic correspondence that $x_{1\iota}$ has with X_ι than with X_j. Available empirical evidence supports this presumption most of the time. The last and most critical assumption for the lemma, and hence for the proof, depends on how increasingly large aggregates are made up. Suppose that the $W_{ii}^{(\iota)}$ *are* proportions; then, by construction, the addition of another amount decreases the proportional share of every single antecedent member of the aggregate. Unless the aggregate happened to be constructed systematically to make the Nth member a larger fraction than the largest preceding one, the condition will be satisfied. Aggregates are usually built up in two ways: by combining various sub-populations (e.g. two-digit into one-digit industries) or by expanding a given sample. In the first case, one can only suppose that the share of U.S. Steel in total manufacturing is less than it is in the steel industry as a whole. In the second case, supposing sampling to be random, the share of each member can be expected to halve, if the sample is doubled, irrespective of the shape of the underlying population. In general, then, we suppose that the W-weights will behave in similar fashion and that this condition will hold in the vast majority of cases.

Part B of Theorem 2 holds under three conditions. The first condition, that $T\sigma_\iota^2/N$ tend to infinity as N tends to infinity, is reasonable under a wide variety of circumstances, although not universally. Consider the behaviour of its reciprocal, $N/T\sigma_\iota^2$ as a function of the micro variables which are included in the aggregate variable X_ι. In the case of a single explanatory variable we require that $\lim_{N\to\infty} N(\mathbf{X}_\iota'\mathbf{X}_\iota)^{-1} = \mathbf{0}$ and, with means removed, this becomes simply $\lim_{N\to\infty}(N/T\sigma_\iota^2) = 0$ which is evidently equivalent to the formulation of the more general problem.

Upon defining the average variance among micro variables by S and the average simple correlation among micro variables by r, $N/T\sigma_\iota^2$ can be expressed as:

$$\frac{N}{T\sigma_\iota^2} = \frac{1}{TS^2\{1 + (N-1)r\}} \tag{59}$$

where

$$S^2 = \frac{1}{N}\sum_{i=1}^{N}\frac{1}{T}\sum_{t=1}^{T}(X_{ilt} - \bar{X}_{il})^2$$

and

$$r = \frac{1}{N(N-1)}\sum_{i<j}^{N}\frac{1}{T}\sum_{t=1}^{T}\frac{(X_{ilt} - \bar{X}_{il})(X_{jlt} - \bar{X}_{jl})}{S^2}$$

If $S^2 > 0$ (which it will always be in any case of interest), $r > 0$ is a sufficient condition for $\lim_{N\to\infty} N/T\sigma_l^2 = 0$ so that this variance term will tend to zero in the limit. We would normally expect the average correlation for the same micro variable to be positive. A meaningful aggregate usually consists of firms with similar customers producing similar products and using similar production methods. In some short run a given quantity of market demand might result in one firm's sales gain becoming another's loss, thus creating some negative correlation. In general, fluctuations in market demand will be shared in some manner roughly proportional to each firm's productive capacity. This expected positive correlation will be attenuated by declining firms (in a period of growing market demand) or 'growth' firms (in a period of falling market demand), but these negative covariances are most unlikely to dominate.[14]

The second condition, that $R_{l..}^2 < \delta_l < 1$ is the familiar one that linear dependence among the explanatory macro variables must be avoided. Apart from aggregation, this is a necessary condition for invertibility of $\mathbf{X'X}$ to obtain estimates of the macro-parameters and their standard errors. It is interesting to note, however, that the usual desiderata for low correlation among explanatory variables is reinforced in the context of aggregation, since aggregation gain will be greater, *ceteris paribus*, the more orthogonal the explanatory variables are to each other.

Finally, it is required that $\bar{X}_l/N$ be bounded as $N \to \infty$. But this magnitude, which can be rewritten as $\sum_{t=1}^{T}\sum_{i=1}^{N} X_{ilt}/TN$ is

[14] Another sufficient condition is less likely to prevail, namely, that $r_2 < 0$ and $S^2 \to \infty$, since it is implausible to suppose that the average variance S^2 will, in fact, tend to infinity under most conceivable circumstances.

nothing more than the average share of the aggregate per individual over the time period to which the data pertain. This average is surely bounded so that this condition will always be satisfied.

The corollary to part B of the theorem is an interesting alternative to the main theorem since, under these economically weaker assumptions (which are more stringent from a mathematical viewpoint), the macro parameter variances will remain finite irrespective of the magnitude of N. Since, in fact, we normally observe non-negligible parameter variances even for very large aggregates, the possibility exists that the conditions of the corollary are the most realistic.

Genuine aggregation and/or specification errors doubtless contribute to observed variances as well. Furthermore, the manner in which aggregates are formed from macro variables and the related problem of speed of convergence needs further empirical investigation. Monte Carlo experiments on the properties of macro parameter variances as functions of varying conditions for the three assumptions adduced in connection with the additive error term as well as study of actual data will be important, since no such convenient links to population distributions such as the relation between aggregation weights and proportions exist here. Subsequent empirical material shows that aggregation weights resemble proportions and that approximations based on the aggregation weight properties in part A of the theorem can often be used to obtain sensible predictions about aggregation gain irrespective of the additive variance component properties. Thus, despite the different characterisation of limiting properties for the two variance components, the aggregation weights can still provide valuable insights into the statistical behaviour of regression estimates obtained from aggregate data.

4. Empirical Evidence: Firm Investment Relations

Manufacturing investment equations will provide some empirical evidence on the underlying assumptions and the aggregation properties contained in Theorem 2. I have chosen investment behaviour for several reasons, not the least of which is an earlier interest in its substantive aspects, as well as its aggregation characteristics [15]. In addition, the earliest empirical study of aggregation theory was that of Boot and De Wit [2], using a similar model of investment behaviour and based on a study by Grunfeld [9]. Among recent contributions to testing alternative models of investment behaviour, the research of Jorgenson and Siebert [11] places heavy reliance on individual firm investment equations. In nearly all the studies cited, a basic equation form was the simple Chenery-Koyck distributed lag [3] [14], in which investment is a linear function of sales or output and the lagged capital stock.

Since my present aim is to study aggregation, I shall adopt the Chenery-Koyck formulation without theoretical motivation (available, however, in the sources cited) and without a detailed critique of its merits. The basic data have similar origins to the previous firm studies, except that here none of the series on gross investment, sales and gross fixed assets were price-corrected. The cost of rectifying the data did not seem warranted in light of my predominantly methodological purpose. There is little reason to suppose that failure to correct for price level variations will seriously affect the aggregation characteristics of the underlying series, although comparability with previous studies is diminished.

The raw data came from the COMPUSTAT tape which contains financial information from 868 companies listed on the New York Stock Exchange, the American Stock Exchange, and, in a few instances, regional exchanges or those with securities traded over the counter.[15] From this larger universe, several

[15] While in most cases, the numbers are identical with corporate records, some disparities exist. According to the COMPUSTAT manual:

> Differences will frequently occur between the financial statistics included in COMPUSTAT and those in Corporation records. These differences may be due to one of the following considerations:
>
> (*a*) Some restatement of company-recorded information has been made in COMPUSTAT in accordance with the definitions outlined in this manual for the purpose of increasing comparability, both within a single company and within a single industry.
>
> (*b*) COMPUSTAT includes some material taken from SEC and outside sources · · ·
>
> Although almost any item of information in COMPUSTAT may differ from that in the Annual Reports in accordance with the definitions

industries were selected whose aggregation properties will be reported. These were chosen on the basis of size and relative internal homogeneity, as well as different production characteristics between industries. In order to limit costs within reasonable bounds, calculations were restricted to four moderate-sized industries (Table 3.1).

TABLE *3.1 Sample composition*

Industry	Years	Firms	Observations
Steel	1949–1967 (19)	23	437
Retail	1949–1966 (18)	19	342
Petroleum	1950–1967 (18)	22	396
Machinery	1950–1967 (18)	41	738
	Total	105	1913

We thus have data beginning in 1949 or 1950, and ending in 1966 or 1967 for 105 firms. A total of 1913 observations on gross investment are to be explained by corresponding data vectors for sales and gross fixed assets.

A. *Model Assumptions: W-weights and Proportions*

A basic assumption of the aggregation gain approximation is that *W*-weights resemble proportions. Proportions, calculated as the sample period sum of each firm's sales or assets divided by the corresponding sample aggregate sum, will be compared with estimated *W*-weights. Table 3.2(*a*) presents a comprehensive comparison, which is the simple regression of the *W*-weights on proportions, with and without intercept. Since the basic hypothesis is homogeneous, the most pertinent regression for each industry pair is the one that has been forced through the origin.

given, a few specific notes are listed below in some of the most frequently used statistics in the system · · ·

(*a*) Annual data in COMPUSTAT for years prior to a merger are not stated on a pro forma basis. Both pro forma and reported data are normally given in Corporation Records.

(*b*) Employment and capital expenditure data may vary slightly because of differing sources of information · · ·

TABLE 3.2 (*a*) *Regression of W-weight on proportion*

Industry		Sales Slope	Sales Intercept	Assets Slope	Assets Intercept
Steel	Coefficient	1·0575	−0·0025	0.8356	0·0071
	t-statistic	(31·8271)	(−0·9767)	(31·3322)	(3·0041)
	Coefficient	1·0391	forced through origin	0·8747	forced through origin
	t-statistic	(37·9362)		(32·1531)	
Retail	Coefficient	−0·3114	0·0690	0·6174	0·0201
	t-statistic	(−1·1032)	(2·7318)	(2·0663)	(0·8785)
	Coefficient	0·1421	forced through origin	0·7974	forced through origin
	t-statistic	(0·5339)		(3·6911)	
Petroleum	Coefficient	−0·1220	0·0510	1·4166	−0·0189
	t-statistic	(−0·7194)	(4·2623)	(15·4912)	(−3·1438)
	Coefficient	0·3439	forced through origin	1·2182	forced through origin
	t-statistic	(1·9665)		(15·4298)	
Machinery	Coefficient	0·3136	0·0167	1·0240	−0·0006
	t-statistic	(1·6463)	(2·1568)	(11·0235)	(−0·1426)
	Coefficient	0·5596	forced through origin	1·0168	forced through origin
	t-statistic	(3·5102)		(13·2754)	

Note: There are as many observations in each regression as there are firms in each industry, as reported in Table 3.1

The regressions for asset parameters are very close to or within plausible range of the slope value of unity required by the hypothesis in every case, although the hypothesis of unit slope is refuted for each sales coefficient except for steel. Considering the extent of collinearity in all but steel (on which a table will be presented shortly), the net outcome is mixed, but not unsatisfactory. We have tested the strongest possible hypothesis – that corresponding *W*-weights are proportions – although a weaker hypothesis that a significant linear dependence exists between the two would lend support to the present analysis. Starting from the initial extreme proposition that *no* economic content can be read into the auxiliary regression equation parameters, we have come a long way.

Table 3.2(*b*) reports summary information bearing on another basic assumption for the theorems, as well as the aggregation gain approximation, which is that corresponding *W*-weights are large relative to non-corresponding *W*-weights. For the steel industry, the assumption held up in all the asset auxiliary regressions and for nineteen out of twenty-three sales auxiliary regressions. The machinery industry had eight and nine failures to confirm, or success on the order of 80 per cent. A similar average success rate prevails in petroleum, while retail had less

TABLE 3.2(*b*) *Comparison of W-weights with non-corresponding W-weights and proportions*

Industry	Frequency with which corresponding exceeds non-corresponding *W*-weights Sales	Assets	Mean absolute difference between proportions and corresponding *W*-weights Sales	Assets	Mean relative difference between corresponding *W*-weights and proportions Sales	Assets
Steel	21/23	23/23	0·0069	0·0083	zero	−0·15
Retail	7/19	6/19	0·0468	0·0518	−0·19	−0·54
Petroleum	19/22	16/22	0·0190	0·0168	−0·37	0·18
Machinery	33/41	32/41	0·0194	0·0116	−0·20	0·16

than 50 per cent support for the hypothesis about *W*-weight magnitude within the auxiliary regressions. As might have been expected, every single corresponding and non-corresponding *W*-weight was a fraction, so the basic assumption of the lemma has been validated.

Once again, with the exception of retailing, the average discrepancy between proportions and corresponding *W*-weights is comparatively small in absolute magnitude, according to Table 3.2(*b*). In the case of steel, the differences are negligible, while in petroleum and machinery, the absolute differences range from 0·01 to 0·02. Average relative differences, with the exception of the petroleum sales parameters, are order of magnitude one-fifth.

A comparison of relative statistical significance between corresponding and non-corresponding *W*-weights in Table 3.3

TABLE 3.3 *Frequency with which absolute value of t-statistic for corresponding W-weight exceeds absolute value of t-statistic for non-corresponding W-weight*

Industry	Sales	Assets
Steel	18/23	23/23
Retail	10/19	13/19
Petroleum	19/22	18/22
Machinery	35/41	29/41

reinforces the impression obtained by simply comparing magnitudes. Retail once more excepted, corresponding *W*-weights have the greater statistical significance most of the time, overwhelmingly so for steel and petroleum with somewhat less, though clearly evident, superiority in machinery.

There appears to be a definite relation to collinearity. The quality of the results is inverse to the extent of linear dependence among explanatory variables: when there is not excessive correlation among the explanatory variables, the assumptions of the statistical aggregation model are more nearly validated. Furthermore, this is exactly what the conditions of part B of the theorem would lead us to expect. The correlation between the two macro explanatory variables appears in Table 3.4.

TABLE *3.4 Correlation between sales and assets for aggregate industry data: post-war annual time series*

Industry	Aggregate variables
Steel	0·8378
Retail	0·9978
Petroleum	0·9902
Machinery	0·9696

In summarising this section, we have found qualified support for the assumptions relating corresponding *W*-weights to proportions, and the magnitudes of corresponding and non-corresponding *W*-weights. When there is excessive collinearity among the explanatory variables, however, the assumptions tend to break down. Yet under this particular circumstance, it is exceedingly difficult to obtain sensible macro estimates anyway. In short, when estimation feasibility breaks down most, so does the aggregation assumption.

B. Model Predictions: Micro Variances, Macro Variances and Aggregation Gain

An innovation of this paper is to predict how aggregation gain can be expected to occur, and its magnitude. That there is *any* aggregation gain whatsoever would have been a puzzling result of itself until recently. Table 3.5 reports the most revealing empirical results about this central feature.

TABLE 3.5 *Summary table on industry aggregation*

	Steel		Retail		Petroleum		Machinery	
	Sales	Assets	Sales	Assets	Sales	Assets	Sales	Assets
Coefficients								
1. Mean of micro	0·08417	0·02094	0·03314	−0·03773	0·30074	−0·08810	0·07345	−0·05550
2. Macro	0·13407	0·00858	0·07539	−0·16308	0·39543	−0·16154	0·10657	−0·11744
Variances								
3. Micro-variance*	0·01558	0·00703	0·00128	0·01585	0·09233	0·02372	0·00414	0·01238
4. Macro-variance	0·00200	0·00047	0·00137	0·02169	0·00168	0·00070	0·00015	0·00085
Sum of squared weights								
5. *H* index	0·13634	0·18295	0·15219	0·11187	0·10946	0·09546	0·06806	0·08044
6. Sum of squared *W*-weights	0·14947	0·14296	0·19717	0·16510	0·08325	0·15416	0·09050	0·10204
Theoretical aggregation gain								
7. from proportions†	7·33458	5·46534	6·57088	8·93919	9·15383	10·47594	14·69215	12·43115
8. from *W*-weights‡	6·69025	6·99507	5·07180	6·05694	12·01257	6·48672	11·04968	9·80046
Actual aggregation gain§								
9. $\frac{\text{micro-variance}}{\text{macro-variance}}$	7·77511	15·03620	0·94166	0·73086	55·11301	33·77803	27·07858	14·52785

* Calculated as var β_{il}, where b_{il} is the lth coefficient for the ith firm in a given industry.
† Reciprocal of line 5.
‡ Reciprocal of line 6.
§ Line 3 divided by line 4.

Aggregation gain is here measured by the reduction of the estimated regression coefficient variances. This is a valid procedure if the macro coefficient equals the mean of the micro coefficients, which it will on the average on the assumptions employed throughout this paper.

Aggregation gain is defined as the reduction in macro parameter variances relative to the microparameter variance. We expect both components of the parameter variances to tend to zero in the limit, but we only have observable information about the variance-decreasing effects of aggregation for the variance component arising from the random coefficients, either the aggregation weights themselves which are only available in a methodological study such as this, or estimates of them obtained from proportions, most relevant to empirical work because of their greater accessibility. Hence, predictions of aggregation gain can only be inferred for this component of variance. Since the second variance-decreasing component can be expected to respond to aggregation in similar fashion, though we cannot demonstrate that it behaves identically, the behaviour of aggregation weights (or proportions) will be used as an index to predict overall aggregation gain. If the predicted gains for the sample industries approximate the actual gains reasonably well, we will have tentatively established both the existence and approximate magnitude of aggregation gain.

In measuring the expected reduction in the macro relative to the micro estimates, the approximate theoretical gain can be calculated in two ways. It is an approximation because information from non-corresponding W-weights is neglected. First, assuming that proportions are good approximations to the corresponding W-weights, their squared sum designated as H (for reasons given in the next section) shows the expected reduction in the macro variance as a consequence of aggregation. Its reciprocal is therefore termed the aggregation gain. Second, and in parallel fashion, the sum of squared corresponding W-weights and its reciprocal provides another relevant estimate of potential aggregation gain. Since the postulated empirical relation between the two measures has already been considered at length, it is encouraging although not surprising that the two sums of squares turn out to be so similar (see lines 5 and 6 of Table 3.5).

The revelant empirical micro coefficient variance is essentially cross-sectional. Assuming that the micro equation estimates are close to the true micro coefficients, the best estimate is simply obtained by calculating the variance where each observation is a firm's estimated coefficient. This, divided by the macro coefficient estimated coefficient variance, provides the actual estimate of aggregation gain for these data. The closer line 7 or line 8 (theoretical gain) is to line 9 (actual gain), the more effective is this approach as a device for estimating aggregation gains.

The results in Table 3.5 are mixed. Retail acted perversely as usual, as it conforms least to the assumptions of the basic model; aggregation gain was predicted and aggregation loss occurred. The three other industries all showed aggregation gain. In the case of petroleum the gain was much greater than the theoretical predictions. Steel and machinery had actual gains very close to those predicted for one coefficient and twice as great as predicted for another coefficient. From this I conclude, first, that the theoretical gain has some predictive value, but that it has a downward bias, and second, that substantial aggregation gains are likely to occur in practice.[16]

[16] When the micro variance is defined as the average of the least squares microvariance

$$\text{est } V(\mathbf{b}_i) = \frac{\sum_{i=1}^{N} \hat{\sigma}^2_{\varepsilon_i}(X_i'X_i)^{-1}}{N}$$

the predicted and actual gain are much closer than shown by Table 3.5, perhaps suggesting that a time-series oriented interpretation of the error process is preferable to a cross-sectional interpretation. For the sake of comparison line 9(a), based on this calculation, is produced below:

	Steel		Retail	
Actual Aggregation Gain	Sales	Assets	Sales	Assets
9(a) $\dfrac{\text{Mean of micro variance}}{\text{Macro variance}}$	3·71689	6·85962	0·83455	0·75629
	Petroleum		Machinery	
	Sales	Assets	Sales	Assets
	8·54690	6·80369	8·01489	10·24131

5. Empirical Evidence: All Manufacturing H Indexes

According to the previously developed theory, a finite sample approximation of aggregation gain can be calculated from information contained in the number of elements in the aggregate and their size distribution, provided corresponding *W*-weights resemble proportions and non-corresponding *W*-weights are relatively small. We shall explore the implications for manufacturing industries by reference to share information. In the previous section, the sum of squared corresponding *W*-weights closely resembled the sum of squared proportions which encourages further pursuit of this point. Maximum aggregation gain arises when all elements (corresponding *W*-weights) are the same size. This is evident, since the variances of proportions will be zero when all shares are identical and the correlative fact that the sum of squared proportions (or variances) is nearly one for very skewed shares. The sum of squares for equal shares is $1/N$.

Data on the sum of squared shares exist for manufacturing industries because this market parameter has begun to acquire descriptive and analytical significance in the study of industrial organisation. It has been named the *H* concentration measure or index after the two originators who independently promoted it, O. C. Herfindahl and A. P. Hirschman.[17]

Since its introduction into industrial organisation literature by Herfindahl [10], the *H* index has been calculated for various firm attributes for four- (and some five-) digit industries in a 1963 volume on concentration in manufacturing by Ralph L. Nelson [16] and reproduced here in Table 3.6. Resort to four-digit industries is stringent but useful. It is stringent in the sense that such a fine subdivision has comparatively few firms in it, useful because one might reasonably expect that substantial homogeneity of markets and production methods will prevail

[17] The most interesting interpretation is that of M. A. Adelman [1], who shows that the *H* index can be viewed as the weighted average slope of the cumulative concentration curve. In a second interpretation, suppose that there were *N* equal-sized firms in an industry; then *N* turns out to be equal to $1/H$. Adelman suggests that the reciprocal of *H* can properly be viewed as a 'numbers equivalent'.

TABLE *3.6 H Indexes for shipments of four-digit industries in 1947, company basis*

Industry	*H* Index	Industry	*H* Index	Industry	*H* Index
3352	*	3842	0·1223	2295	0·0490
3583	*	3261	0·1220	3585	0·0489
3612	*	3613	0·1197	3564	0·0489
3651	*	3691	0·1181	3579	0·0483
3664	*	3614	0·1158	3589	0·0475
3511	0·2997	3312	0·1129	3322	0·0460
3272	0·2971	3351	0·1112	3943	0·0417
3021	0·2843	2092	0·1096	2234	0·0394
2829	0·2837	3576	0·1090	3241	0·0357
2141	0·2628	3742	0·1085	3561	0·0348
2111	0·2461	3262	0·1040	3554	0·0330
3411	0·2447	3333	0·1004	3399	0·0328
3615	0·2102	3359	0·1001	2041	0·0322
3692	0·2059	3253	0·0998	2834	0·0317
3861	0·2013	3565	0·0949	2031	0·0308
2052	0·1941	3721	0·0936	3661	0·0267
2825	0·1847	3229	0·0934	3611	0·0261
3572	0·1800	3491	0·0860	3141	0·0257
3562	0·1794	2522	0·0853	2893	0·0251
2062	0·1775	3631	0·0795	3566	0·0246
3011	0·1746	2271	0·0777	2033	0·0242
3571	0·1745	2011	0·0733	3323	0·0231
3221	0·1736	2823	0·0731	3542	0·0227
3717	0·1692	3392	0·0710	2432	0·0221
2043	0·1609	3264	0·0699	3591	0·0220
3715	0·1603	3751	0·0687	3391	0·0218
3722	0·1584	3493	0·0651	3494	0·0184
3662	0·1583	2952	0·0630	3489	0·0171
2073	0·1520	3581	0·0629	3541	0·0171
2812	0·1518	3263	0·0627	3531	0·0169
2085	0·1514	2661	0·0602	2082	0·0160
3641	0·1488	2045	0·0598	2671	0·0140
2063	0·1472	3871	0·0597	3463	0·0127
3425	0·1391	3293	0·0594	2071	0·0111
3593	0·1362	2911	0·0556	3321	0·0109
3292	0·1329	3621	0·0550	2261	0·0093
3914	0·1326	2121	0·0515	2252	0·0078
3275	0·1309	3431	0·0503		

* *H* Index withheld to avoid disclosing figures for individual companies.

at this classification level, in contrast to the more common econometric category of two-digit aggregates.

H indexes in manufacturing four-digit industries have a median value of 0·09 in Table 3.6. Translated into our approach to aggregation, the gain in terms of variance reduction from aggregation is twelve-fold for the median value. Even at the first quartile mark, a seven-fold gain will occur from using aggregated data instead of micro information directly. At the third quartile, an *H* index of just under 0·04 implies that a 28-fold aggregation gain may be expected.

6. Heterogeneous Parameters and Research Strategy

A complementary statistical aggregation approach starts with the assumption of heterogeneity, but concludes that structural simplification through clustering of similar objects can lead to increased understanding and manageability, although at some cost in precision. Walter Fisher [6] provides operational solutions to this problem through statistical decision theory.

When the *W*-weights for corresponding parameters resemble proportions, and non-corresponding parameter aggregation weights are negligible term-by-term, ordinary least squares parameter estimates of macro relations will have desirable properties, even when the micro parameters are different. In this exposition, my debt to Theil should be evident, even though it is my inclination to emphasise the economic substance of *W*-weights and, hence, the feasibility of using appropriate macro relations effectively to predict and study behaviour.

Assume the following conditions hold:

(1) Corresponding W_{il} weights are proportions, i.e. $W_{il} = x_{il}/X_l \equiv P_{il}$.

(2) Non-corresponding *W*-weights are zero. Then

$$\tilde{\beta}_l = \sum_{i=1}^{N} P_{il}\tilde{\beta}_{il} \qquad (60$$

The macro-predictions will then be

$$\hat{Y} = \sum_{l=1}^{K} \tilde{\beta}_l X_l$$

$$\hat{Y} = \left(\frac{x_{11}}{X_1}\tilde{\beta}_{11} + \cdots + \frac{x_{N1}}{X_1}\tilde{\beta}_{N1}\right)X_1 + \cdots$$
$$+ \left(\frac{x_{1K}}{X_K}\tilde{\beta}_{1K} + \cdots + \frac{x_{NK}}{X_K}\tilde{\beta}_{NK}\right)X_K \qquad (61)$$

$$\hat{Y} = \sum_{i=1}^{N} \tilde{\beta}_{i1}x_{i1} + \cdots + \sum_{i=1}^{N} \tilde{\beta}_{iK}x_{iK}$$

In these circumstances, the micro-predictions and macro predictions are the same. Theil characterises this outcome as one where no contradiction exists between the micro relation and the macro-relation. The forecasting benefits from relying on macro equations are evident, even when these conditions hold only approximately. Much interest thus attaches to the stability of shares through time for members of economic populations. The law of proportional growth analysed by Simon and Bonini [20] suggests that stability in shares is not implausible among economic populations.

Furthermore, the optimal properties of least squares estimation apply to the auxiliary equation parameter estimate as an estimator of proportions under the conditions stated above. When shares are changing, ordinary least squares provide an efficient estimate of the average proportion over the sample period.

Efficient predictions can be obtained when shares are stable and parameters differ or when parameters are similar, even when shares are not. Often one, the other, or both sets of conditions will hold; this explains much of the modest success that highly aggregative macro-models have had. The ideal situation, of course, prevails when underlying behaviour is relatively homogeneous so that compositional aspects of the data universe become secondary. But macro model-building strategy can and should proceed on several fronts simultaneously, relying on aggregates (and hence share stability) more heavily in the short term, while searching for significant behavioural homogeneities in the longer run. When the disaggregated data can be obtained, it becomes possible to weigh aggregation gains arising from grouping similar behaviour units against the losses from subsuming too much disparate behaviour in one relationship, and the perils or benefits inherent in shifting or stable shares and, more generally, aggregation weights.

When parameters are heterogeneous, Griliches and Grunfeld [8] have recommended a comparison between the error variance properties of the aggregate equation and the error variance properties of the summed error (across firms, at each time period) derived from micro equations. If the combined error variance thus obtained from the micro equations is large relative to the aggregate equation error variance, aggregation gain has occurred because of additional negative covariance terms in the aggregate equation, and additional aggregation benefits therefore will have accrued. Results in the case of our four industries, which will be reported in terms of (relative) error sum of squares, are, according to Table 3.7, decidedly mixed.

TABLE *3.7 Ratio of combined to aggregate error sum of squares*

Steel	0·985
Retail	0·938
Petroleum	1·285
Machinery	1·440

Modest to severe aggregation losses according to the Griliches – Grunfeld criterion occur in petroleum and machinery. There is a stand-off in steel, while negligible aggregation gains do in fact arise in retail. Their analysis in the end seems unilluminating.

Material in Section 4 was fragmentary. Some of the empirical propositions held up well, others less so. While clear advantages accrue from proper aggregation (i.e. aggregation over homogeneous behaviour parameters), one noticeable instance that failed especially badly was retail trade. The main reason seemed to be extreme multi-collinearity. In this case, no aggregation gain occurred. There were actual aggregation losses. Where collinearity is pervasive, we may speculate that the only possibility for successful estimation is to rely more heavily on disaggregated data. This is neither necessary nor sufficient to assure success. It is a conjecture based partly on this study and on other econometric work with micro data.

Another reason why micro data should be analysed is fundamental to understanding how much heterogeneity exists within an aggregate. Thus, sensible research strategy requires simultaneous exploration of micro and macro data for statistical efficiency in appropriate circumstances, and as a way of holding down expenses to tolerable levels.

Intensive analysis of aggregation was restricted to manufacturing, using some concocted two-digit industries from COMPUSTAT for which all possible parameters were calculated that bear on the theory, and also 'real' four-digit census data using the sum of squared shares, or H index as a direct indicator of aggregation gains that can be expected from such industries in future investigations. It seems likely that H indexes are smaller for personal income (income is more evenly distributed than are firm sizes in most industries), so that potential aggregation gain is even greater in the study of consumption than for most industry studies.

7. Related Literature and Acknowledgements

Zellner [26] was first to point out that the random coefficient model provided a natural approach to the problem of consistent aggregation. He demonstrated the unbiasedness of least squares estimation in the random coefficient case where data had been aggregated.

Zellner [26] and Theil [23] postulated a random coefficient model with similar properties to those we have adopted. In the regression equation

$$\bar{y}_t = \frac{\sum_{i=1}^{N} \tilde{\beta}_{i1t} x_{i1t}}{\sum_{i=1}^{N} x_{i1t}} \bar{x}_{1t} + \cdots + \frac{\sum_{i=1}^{N} \tilde{\beta}_{iKt} x_{iKt}}{\sum_{i=1}^{N} x_{iKt}} \bar{x}_{Kt} + \frac{1}{N} \sum_{i=1}^{N} \tilde{\varepsilon}_{it} \qquad (62)$$

the typical aggregate coefficient is a function of time and

sample size

$$\tilde{\beta}_{lt} = \frac{\sum_{i=1}^{N} \tilde{\beta}_{ilt} x_{ilt}}{\sum_{i=1}^{N} x_{ilt}} \tag{63}$$

Then Theil shows that the covariance of macro coefficient $\tilde{\beta}_l$ with $\tilde{\beta}_h$ can be written as follows

$$\frac{\sigma_{hl}}{N} l + \frac{\frac{1}{N}\sum_{i=1}^{N}(x_{hit} - \bar{x}_{ht})(x_{lit} - \bar{x}_{lt})}{\bar{x}_{ht}\bar{x}_{lt}} \tag{64}$$

where σ_{hl} is the covariance among micro parameters $\tilde{\beta}_{li}$ and $\tilde{\beta}_{hi}$. The variance of β_l can thus be written

$$\{\sigma^2_{\beta ilt}(1 + c^2_{lt}\}/N \tag{65}$$

where c^2_{lt} is the squared coefficient of variation of x_l during the tth period.

Theil was the first to show by this demonstration (together with the assumption that c_{lt} converges to a finite non-zero limit as N tends to infinity) that, as the numbers in the aggregate N increase, the variance of the macro parameters tends to zero. An advantage of my treatment, in addition to its being directly related to standard least squares estimation, is that the macro parameters variance is closely though approximately related to important – and often available – information on size distribution of firms, individuals, or incomes, for example. The relative stability of these distributions and their properties provide genuine insight into when, and how much, aggregation gain can arise from enlarging the population aggregate. Coefficients of variation do not seem to have the same intuitive significance, are less readily available and we know less of their stability over time. It is reassuring, however, that two rather different approaches using similar assumptions, arrive at the same basic conclusion.

Charles Revier, with some help from Dan Luria and Joe Steuart, provided admirable research assistance, relying heavily on M.I.T. computational facilities. Zvi Griliches, T. N. Srinivasan and Arnold Zellner made useful comments. Support by the National Science Foundation is gratefully acknowledged.

My colleagues, Gordon Kaufman and Roy Welsch supplied generous assistance. They devised the lemma in a more ingenious form than I had contemplated, as well as helping to set up and prove the main theorem in its full generality. Gregory Chow's careful reading of an earlier draft led to essential clarification of the underlying assumptions and structure of the statistical model. I retain the onus for remaining errors.

References

[1] ADELMAN, M. A., 'Comment on the 'H' Concentration Measure as a Numbers-Equivalent', *Review of Economics and Statistics*, LI (February 1969) 99–101.

[2] BOOT, J. C. G. and DE WIT, G. M., 'Investment Demand: An Empirical Contribution to the Aggregation Problem', *International Economic Review*, X (February 1969) 3–30.

[3] CHENERY, H., 'Overcapacity and the Acceleration Principle', *Econometrica*, XX (January 1952) 1–28.

[3a] DWYER, P. S., 'Recent Developments in Correlation Technique', *Journal of the American Statistical Association*, XXXVII (December 1942) 441–60.

[4] EDWARDS, E. B. and ORCUTT, G. H., 'Should Aggregation Prior to Estimation be the Rule?', *Review of Economics and Statistics*, XV (November 1969) 409–20.

[5] EDWARDS, E. B. and ORCUTT, G. H., 'The Reliability of Statistical Indicators of Forecasting Ability', unpublished manuscript, September 1969.

[6] FISHER, W. D., *Clustering and Aggregation in Economics*, (Baltimore, Maryland: Johns Hopkins University Press, 1969).

[7] FRIEDMAN, M., and MEISELMAN, D., 'The Relative Stability of Monetary Velocity and the Investment Multiplier in the United States, 1897–1958', in *Stabilization Policies*, by E. C. Brown *et al.* (Englewood Cliffs, N.J.: Prentice-Hall, 1964).

[8] GRILICHES, ZVI and GRUNFELD, Y., 'Is Aggregation Necessarily Bad?', *Review of Economics and Statistics*, XLII (February 1960) 1–13.

[9] GRUNFELD, Y., *The Determinants of Corporate Investment*, unpublished Ph.D. Thesis (Chicago, 1958).

[10] HERFINDAHL, O. C., *Three Studies in Mineral Economics*, (Baltimore, Maryland: Johns Hopkins University Press, 1961).

[10a] HORST, P., 'A General Method of Evaluating Multiple Regression Constants', *Journal of the American Statistical Association*, XXVII (September 1932) 270–78.

[11] JORGENSON, D. W. and SIEBERT, C. D., 'A Comparison of Alternative Theories of Corporate Investment Behavior', *American Economic Review*, LVIII (September 1968) 681–712.

[12] KLEIN, L. R., *A Textbook of Econometrics*, (New York: Harper and Row, 1953).

[13] KLOEK, T., 'Note on a Convenient Notation in Multivariate Statistical Analysis and in the Theory of Linear Aggregation', *International Economic Review*, II (September 1961) 351-60.

[14] KOYCK, L. M., *Distributed Lags and Investment Analysis*, (Amsterdam: North-Holland Publishing Company, 1954).

[15] KUH, E., *Capital Stock Growth: A Micro-Econometric Approach*, (Amsterdam, North-Holland Publishing Company, 1963).

[16] NELSON, R. L., *Concentration in Manufacturing Industries of the United States, a Midcentury Report*, (New Haven, Yale University Press, 1963).

[17] ORCUTT, G. H., WATTS, H. W. and EDWARDS, E. B., 'Data Aggregation and Information Loss', *American Economic Review*, LVIII (September 1968) 773–87.

[18] RAO, C. R., 'The Theory of Least Squares when the Parameters are Stochastic and Its Application to the Analysis of Growth', *Biometrika*, (1965), parts 3 and 4, 447–58.

[19] RUBIN, H., 'Note on Random Coefficients in Statistical Inference', in *Statistical Inference in Dynamic Economic Models*, ed. T. C. Koopmans. (New York and London: J. Wiley and Sons, 1950).

[20] SIMON, H. A. and BONINI, C. P., 'The Size Distribution of Business Firms', *American Economic Review*, XLVIII (September 1958) 607–17.

[21] Standard Statistics Company, Inc., *Compustat Information Manual*, 1967.

[22] SWAMY, P. A. V. B., 'Statistical Inference in Random Coefficient Regression Models Using Panel Data', S.S.R.I., University of Wisconsin, Systems Formulation Methodology and Policy Workshop Paper 6701, (January 18, 1967), mimeo.

[23] THEIL, H., 'Consistent Aggregation of Micromodels with Random Coefficients'. Chicago, Center for Mathematical Studies in Business and Economy, April 1968. (A more accessible and somewhat more extensive treatment can be found in H. Theil, *Principles of Econometrics*, New York: John Wiley and Sons, 1971).

[24] THEIL, H., *Linear Aggregation of Economic Relations*, (Amsterdam: North-Holland Publishing Company, 1954).

[25] TINBERGEN, J., *Les Cycles économiques aux États-Unis d'Amérique*, Vol. II. (Geneva: League of Nations, 1939).

[26] ZELLNER, A., 'On the Aggregation Problem: A New Approach to a Troublesome Problem', Unpublished manuscript (October 1966), to appear in a forthcoming volume honouring Gerhard Tintner, edited by Karl Fox.

[27] ZELLNER, A., 'An Efficient Method of Estimating Seemingly Unrelated Regressions and Tests for Aggregation Bias', *Journal of the American Statistical Association*, LVII (June 1962) 348–68.

4 Specification Bias in Seemingly Unrelated Regressions

BY POTLURI RAO*

MULTIPLE regression analysis specifies a linear relation between a dependent variable and a set of independent variables. When the independent variables are non-stochastic, and the error terms are homoscedastic and serially independent, the ordinary least squares estimation of the parameters yields the best linear unbiased estimates. But when there is a set of linear regression equations whose error terms are contemporaneously correlated, then the ordinary least squares estimation of each of the equations separately is not the 'best' estimation procedure. When the parameters of contemporaneous correlation are known then it is possible to obtain unbiased estimates with smaller variance than the corresponding ordinary least squares estimates by estimating all the regression equations jointly using the Aitken's generalised least squares.[1] In the absence of information on these parameters Professor Zellner [5] suggested the use of estimates of these parameters from residuals of the ordinary least squares. This procedure is called the 'seemingly unrelated regression equations' (SURE) procedure.

The theoretical properties of the SURE estimation procedure have been investigated extensively under the assumption that the estimations are the true relations.[2] In econometric research, however, one can never be certain that the estimated equations are the true specifications. Often we leave out some variables

* This paper was prepared when the author was visiting the University of Washington, Seattle. The author is grateful to Professors Zvi Griliches, Jan Kmenta and Lester Telser for their helpful comments.

[1] For a discussion on the Aitken's generalised least squares procedure in the context of a set of linear regression equations, see [4].

[2] A brief survey of the literature may be found in [1].

in estimation either because we are not aware of their relevance in the true model, or that data are not available on some variables. In such situations we may want to choose an estimator that is less sensitive to mis-specification even though it may not be the 'best' estimator under the ideal set of assumptions. With this objective in mind we investigate the consequences of left out variables on the ordinary least squares and SURE estimation procedures. The consequences of mis-specification on the ordinary least squares estimates were analysed in detail elsewhere [2]. In this paper we concentrate mainly on the consequences of a left-out variable in the SURE estimation procedure and compare these results with that of the ordinary least squares.

The Model

For our analysis we shall concentrate on a simple case with two linear regression equations. Let the true model be

$$\begin{aligned} x_{4t} &= \alpha_1 x_{1t} + x_{3t} + \eta_{1t} \\ x_{5t} &= \alpha_2 x_{2t} + \beta x_{3t} + \eta_{2t} \end{aligned} \qquad (t = 1, \ldots, T) \qquad (1)$$

In this model all the variables are measured from their respective means, hence the constant terms are implicit. The independent variables x_1, x_2 and x_3 are assumed to be non-stochastic; that is, held constant in repeated samples. Since we are interested in isolating the consequences of mis-specification we shall assume that in the true model, error terms (ηs) are contemporaneously uncorrelated. As in the classical linear regression model we shall assume that the error terms (ηs) are homoscedastic and serially independent. The independent variable x_3 is measured in units such that its coefficient in the first equation of (1) is unity. This simplifies discussion without loss of generality. Whenever there is no ambiguity we shall delete the subscript t and use $\mathbf{x}_i$ to denote a vector of T observations on the variable x_i.

Let us suppose that instead of the true model (1) the following mis-specified model is used for estimation

$$\begin{aligned} \mathbf{x}_4 &= \alpha_1 \mathbf{x}_1 + \mathbf{u}_1 \\ \mathbf{x}_5 &= \alpha_2 \mathbf{x}_2 + \mathbf{u} \end{aligned} \qquad (2)$$

The estimated model may also be written in matrix notation as

$$\mathbf{Y} = \mathbf{X}\boldsymbol{\alpha} + \mathbf{U} \tag{3}$$

where

$$\mathbf{X} = \begin{bmatrix} \mathbf{x}_1 & \mathbf{0} \\ \mathbf{0} & \mathbf{x}_2 \end{bmatrix}$$

$$\mathbf{Y} = \begin{bmatrix} \mathbf{x}_4 \\ \mathbf{x}_5 \end{bmatrix}$$

$$\boldsymbol{\alpha} = \begin{bmatrix} \alpha_1 \\ \alpha_2 \end{bmatrix}$$

$$\mathbf{U} = \begin{bmatrix} \mathbf{u}_1 \\ \mathbf{u}_2 \end{bmatrix}$$

Even though the true error terms (ηs) are contemporaneously uncorrelated, error terms in the estimated model (**u**s) are because the same variable is left out in both equations. This kind of problem is common in empirical research. For example, in an investment study, error terms in the investment functions of the General Electric and Westinghouse [5] would be contemporaneously correlated when a common variable, namely the business fluctuation, is left out from both the equations.

The variance-covariance matrix of error terms in the estimated model is

$$E(\mathbf{UU}') = \boldsymbol{\Sigma} = \begin{bmatrix} \sigma^2_{x_3} + \sigma^2_{\eta_1} & \beta\sigma^2_{x_3} \\ \beta\sigma^2_{x_3} & \beta^2\sigma^2_{x_3} + \sigma^2_{\eta_2} \end{bmatrix} \otimes \mathbf{I}_T \tag{4}$$

where $\mathbf{I}_T$ is an identity matrix of order T.

Ordinary least squares estimation of the equations of model (2) separately yields the following estimates for the αs

$$\begin{aligned} \hat{\alpha}_1 &= (\mathbf{x}_1'\mathbf{x}_1)^{-1}\mathbf{x}_1'\mathbf{x}_4 \\ \hat{\alpha}_2 &= (\mathbf{x}_2'\mathbf{x}_2)^{-1}\mathbf{x}_2'\mathbf{x}_5 \end{aligned} \tag{5}$$

These estimates may also be expressed in matrix form as

$$\hat{\boldsymbol{\alpha}} = (\mathbf{X}'\mathbf{X})^{-1}\mathbf{X}'\mathbf{Y} \tag{6}$$

When the variance-covariance matrix of error terms in the estimated model ($\boldsymbol{\Sigma}$) is known, then the generalised least squares estimates of the αs may be obtained as

$$\tilde{\boldsymbol{\alpha}} = (\mathbf{X}'\boldsymbol{\Sigma}^{-1}\mathbf{X})^{-1}\mathbf{X}'\boldsymbol{\Sigma}^{-1}\mathbf{Y} \tag{7}$$

The generalised least squares estimates are not attainable because the matrix $\boldsymbol{\Sigma}$ is a function of the unknown parameters. However, this variance-covariance matrix may be estimated from residuals of the ordinary least squares defined as

$$\begin{aligned} \mathbf{e}_1 &= \mathbf{x}_4 - \hat{\alpha}_1\mathbf{x}_1 \\ \mathbf{e}_2 &= \mathbf{x}_5 - \hat{\alpha}_2\mathbf{x}_2 \end{aligned} \tag{8}$$

An estimate of the variance-covariance matrix is

$$\hat{\boldsymbol{\Sigma}} = T^{-1}\begin{bmatrix} \mathbf{e}_1'\mathbf{e}_1 & \mathbf{e}_1'\mathbf{e}_2 \\ \mathbf{e}_2'\mathbf{e}_1 & \mathbf{e}_2'\mathbf{e}_2 \end{bmatrix} \otimes \mathbf{I}_T \tag{9}$$

SURE estimates of the parameters α may be obtained by using the estimate $\hat{\boldsymbol{\Sigma}}$ instead of the true matrix $\boldsymbol{\Sigma}$ as

$$\boldsymbol{\alpha}^* = (\mathbf{X}'\hat{\boldsymbol{\Sigma}}^{-1}\mathbf{X})^{-1}\mathbf{X}'\hat{\boldsymbol{\Sigma}}^{-1}\mathbf{Y} \tag{10}$$

Now we have two sets of estimates for the αs, the ordinary least squares estimates $\hat{\boldsymbol{\alpha}}$ and the SURE estimates $\boldsymbol{\alpha}^*$. Both these sets are obtained from the mis-specified model (2) and hence may have a certain amount of 'sin'. The question is now: Which of these two estimation procedures has the least sin? *If* we knew that the set of equations of model (1) were the true relations, and *If* we had data for the variable x_3, then of course, there would be no need to resort to these sinful estimation procedures. But these two *Ifs* have a capital I. We shall measure the extent of sin of these estimation procedures in the units of bias and variance of the estimators. In our study we shall concentrate on variance and asymptotic bias of these two alternative estimation procedures and see how they compare.

In order to simplify the algebra involved we shall adopt the following notation

$$\begin{aligned} x_{ij} &= \mathbf{x}_i'\mathbf{x}_j \\ e_{ij} &= \mathbf{e}_i'\mathbf{e}_j \\ b_{ij} &= (\mathbf{x}_j'\mathbf{x}_j)^{-1}\mathbf{x}_j'\mathbf{x}_i \end{aligned} \tag{11}$$

These bs are used only as a shorthand notation and need not have any causal interpretation. Our analysis also needs a statistic γ defined as

$$\gamma = (e_{22})^{-1}e_{21} \tag{12}$$

By substituting equations (1), (5) and (8) in equation (12) it may be seen that

$$\text{plim}\,(\gamma) = \gamma^* = \frac{\beta\sigma^2_{x_3}}{\beta^2\sigma^2_{x_3} + \beta^2 b^2_{32} + \sigma^2_{\eta_2}} \tag{13}$$

In our analysis we do not use this complete expression for γ^*. We only use the property that γ^* and β have the same sign.

The Nature of Asymptotic Bias

The ordinary least squares estimates of the parameters α are given by Equation (5). Since the true relations are given by Equation (1), by substituting for the variables x_4 and x_5 we obtain

$$\begin{aligned} \hat{\alpha}_1 &= b_{41} = \alpha_1 + b_{31} + (\mathbf{x}_1'\mathbf{x}_1)^{-1}\mathbf{x}_1'\eta_1 \\ \hat{\alpha}_2 &= b_{52} = \alpha_2 + \beta b_{32} + (\mathbf{x}_2'\mathbf{x}_2)^{-1}\mathbf{x}_2'\eta_2 \end{aligned} \tag{14}$$

Since the results of this investigation are symmetric we shall concentrate on only one of the estimates, namely the $\hat{\alpha}_1$. The expected value of the $\hat{\alpha}_1$ is

$$E(\hat{\alpha}_1) = \alpha_1 + b_{31} \tag{15}$$

The ordinary least squares estimate of the parameter α_1 is a biased estimate, unless the left-out variable $\mathbf{x}_3$ is orthogonal to the included variable $\mathbf{x}_1$.

SURE estimates of the αs are obtained as

$$\boldsymbol{\alpha}^* = (\mathbf{X}'\hat{\boldsymbol{\Sigma}}^{-1}\mathbf{X})^{-1}\mathbf{X}'\hat{\boldsymbol{\Sigma}}^{-1}\mathbf{Y} \tag{16}$$

where $\hat{\boldsymbol{\Sigma}}$ is an estimate of the variance-covariance matrix $\boldsymbol{\Sigma}$ obtained from the residuals as given in Equation (9). The expressions in Equation (16) may be evaluated as follows[3]

[3] In the following section we take this direct approach to evaluate these expressions because the compact matrix notation simplifies the algebra at the expense of insight into the problem.

$$\hat{\boldsymbol{\Sigma}} = T^{-1}\begin{bmatrix} e_{11} & e_{12} \\ e_{12} & e_{22} \end{bmatrix} \otimes \mathbf{I}_T \tag{17}$$

$$\hat{\boldsymbol{\Sigma}}^{-1} = \frac{T}{e_{11}e_{22} - e_{12}e_{12}}\begin{bmatrix} e_{22} & -e_{12} \\ -e_{12} & e_{11} \end{bmatrix} \otimes \mathbf{I}_T \tag{18}$$

$$\mathbf{X}'\hat{\boldsymbol{\Sigma}}^{-1}\mathbf{X} = \begin{bmatrix} \mathbf{x}_1' & \mathbf{0} \\ \mathbf{0} & \mathbf{x}_2' \end{bmatrix} \hat{\boldsymbol{\Sigma}}^{-1} \begin{bmatrix} \mathbf{x}_1 & \mathbf{0} \\ \mathbf{0} & \mathbf{x}_2 \end{bmatrix}$$

$$= \frac{T}{e_{11}e_{22} - e_{12}e_{12}}\begin{bmatrix} e_{22}x_{11} & -e_{12}x_{12} \\ -e_{12}x_{12} & e_{11}x_{22} \end{bmatrix} \tag{19}$$

$$(\mathbf{X}'\hat{\boldsymbol{\Sigma}}^{-1}\mathbf{X})^{-1} = \frac{e_{11}e_{22} - e_{12}e_{12}}{T(e_{11}e_{22}x_{11}x_{22} - e_{12}e_{12}x_{12}x_{12})}\begin{bmatrix} e_{11}x_{22} & e_{12}x_{12} \\ e_{12}x_{12} & e_{22}x_{11} \end{bmatrix} \tag{20}$$

$$\mathbf{X}'\hat{\boldsymbol{\Sigma}}^{-1}\mathbf{Y} = \begin{bmatrix} \mathbf{x}_1' & \mathbf{0} \\ \mathbf{0} & \mathbf{x}_2' \end{bmatrix} \hat{\boldsymbol{\Sigma}}^{-1} \begin{bmatrix} \mathbf{x}_4 \\ \mathbf{x}_5 \end{bmatrix}$$

$$= \frac{T}{e_{11}e_{22} - e_{12}e_{12}}\begin{bmatrix} e_{22}x_{14} - e_{12}x_{15} \\ e_{11}x_{25} - e_{12}x_{24} \end{bmatrix} \tag{21}$$

Hence

$$\alpha_1^* = \frac{e_{11}x_{22}e_{22}x_{14} - e_{11}x_{22}e_{12}x_{15} + e_{12}x_{12}e_{11}x_{25} - e_{12}e_{12}x_{12}x_{24}}{e_{11}e_{22}x_{11}x_{22} - e_{12}e_{12}x_{12}x_{12}} \tag{22}$$

By taking out the expression $(e_{11}e_{22}x_{11}x_{22})$ as a common factor we obtain

$$\alpha_1^* = \frac{b_{41} - \gamma b_{51} + \gamma b_{21}b_{52} - r^2_{e_1e_2}b_{21}b_{42}}{1 - r^2_{x_1x_2}r^2_{e_1e_2}} \tag{23}$$

where r is the correlation coefficient.

Since the true model is given by Equation (1), by substituting for the variables x_4 and x_5 in Equation (23) we obtain

$$\alpha_1^* = \alpha_1 + \frac{b_{31} - \gamma\beta(b_{32} - b_{31}) - r^2_{e_1e_2}b_{21}b_{32}}{1 - r^2_{x_1x_2}r^2_{e_1e_2}} + f(X'\eta) \tag{24}$$

where $f(\mathbf{X}'\eta)$ stands for the terms containing $\mathbf{X}'\eta$, and $\text{plim}\,[f(\mathbf{X}'\eta)] = 0$.

For large samples we obtain

$$\text{plim}\,(\alpha_1^*) = \alpha_1 + \frac{b_{31} - \gamma^*\beta(b_{32} - b_{31}) - P^2 b_{21}b_{32}}{1 - P^2 r^2_{x_1x_2}} \tag{25}$$

where $P^2 = \text{plim}\,(r^2_{e_1e_2})$.

In the case of mis-specification in the estimated model, the SURE estimates are also biased estimates, unless the left out variable is orthogonal to all the independent variables of all the equations in the model.

We have shown that when estimated equations have left out variables specified by the true relation, both the estimation procedures, the ordinary least squares and SURE, in general yield biased estimates of the parameters of the model. In order to compare which of these two estimates has larger bias let us consider the following cases.

Case 1

The left-out variable $\mathbf{x}_3$ is orthogonal to the independent variables in both equations. In this case b_{31} and b_{32} are zero. Therefore, both estimates, $\hat{\alpha}_1$ and α_1^* are unbiased. Note that in our analysis we are investigating bias in only one of the estimates, namely $\hat{\alpha}_1$. Similar results follow for the other estimate, except that the ordering of these cases with respect to it would be different.

$$\begin{aligned} E(\hat{\alpha}_1) &= \alpha_1 \\ \text{plim}\,(\alpha_1^*) &= \alpha_1 \end{aligned} \tag{26}$$

Case 2

The left-out variable $\mathbf{x}_3$ is orthogonal to the independent variable $\mathbf{x}_1$ of the first equation (the equation with the parameter we are interested in), but not with that of the second equation. In this case b_{31} is zero, but not b_{32}. Hence the SURE estimate is biased whereas the ordinary least squares estimate is not.

$$E(\hat{\alpha}_1) = \alpha_1$$

$$\text{plim}\,(\alpha_1^*) = \alpha_1 - \frac{\gamma^*\beta b_{32} + P^2 b_{21} b_{32}}{1 - P^2 r^2_{x1x2}} \tag{27}$$

Case 3

The left-out variable $\mathbf{x}_3$ is orthogonal to the independent variable of the second equation, $\mathbf{x}_2$, but not to that of the first equation. In this case both estimates are biased, but the SURE estimate has larger bias than the ordinary least squares estimate.

$$E(\hat{\alpha}_1) = \alpha_1 + b_{31}$$

$$\text{plim}\,(\alpha_1^*) = \alpha_1 + b_{31}\frac{1 + \gamma^*\beta}{1 - P^2 r^2_{x_1 x_2}} \qquad (28)$$

As we have already shown in Equation (13), γ^* and β are of the same sign. Since the correlation coefficients are fractions, it follows that the bias in the SURE estimate α_1^* is larger in magnitude than the bias in the ordinary least squares estimate $\hat{\alpha}_1$.

Case 4

The left-out variable $\mathbf{x}_3$ is not orthogonal to either of the independent variables $\mathbf{x}_1$ or $\mathbf{x}_2$. In this case both estimates are biased. It is not obvious which one has the smaller bias. When b_{31} and b_{32} are of the same order of magnitude, the bias in the ordinary least squares and SURE procedures are approximately equal. When $\mathbf{x}_1$ and $\mathbf{x}_2$ are the same variable these estimates, α_1^* and $\hat{\alpha}_1$, are identical[4] and hence have the same bias. Bias in the SURE procedure depends on the magnitude of b_{31} relative to b_{32}. One should keep in mind that we are also estimating the parameter α_2 in the SURE procedure. If one were to choose values of b_{31} and b_{32} so as to reduce bias in the estimate α_1^* one would be increasing bias in the estimate α_2^*.

Our analysis leads to the conclusion that when the estimated model is mis-specified both the ordinary least squares and SURE estimates are asymptotically biased and the bias of the SURE estimator is generally larger than the bias of the ordinary least squares estimator. Asymptotic bias of these estimators is a consequence of systematic relation between the left-out variable and independent variables of the estimated model. In many practical situations, however, it may be reasonable to believe that the left-out variable is orthogonal to the included variables (or nearly so), in which case asymptotic bias of these estimators is zero (or nearly zero). In this case the choice of estimation procedure depends crucially on the relative variances.

[4] This point may be seen by substituting $\mathbf{x}_1$ for $\mathbf{x}_2$ in equation (23).

The Relative Efficiency

In order to isolate the consequences of mis-specification on the relative efficiency of the estimators we shall consider the case where both estimators are asymptotically unbiased, that is the left-out variable $\mathbf{x}_3$ is orthogonal to the variables $\mathbf{x}_1$ and $\mathbf{x}_2$. Note that in our model the independent variables are non-stochastic and only the error terms (ηs) change in each of the repeated samples.

As shown in Equation (14) the ordinary least squares estimate $\hat{\alpha}_1$ may be expressed as

$$\hat{\alpha}_1 = \alpha_1 + b_{31} + (\mathbf{x}_1'\mathbf{x}_1)^{-1}\mathbf{x}_1'\eta_1 \tag{29}$$

Since $\mathbf{x}_3$ is orthogonal to $\mathbf{x}_1$ we have

$$\hat{\alpha}_1 = \alpha_1 + (\mathbf{x}_1'\mathbf{x}_1)^{-1}\mathbf{x}_1'\eta_1 \tag{30}$$

Hence the variance of the estimate $\hat{\alpha}_1$ is[5]

$$V(\hat{\alpha}_1) = E[(\mathbf{x}_1'\mathbf{x}_1)^{-1}\mathbf{x}_1'\eta_1\eta_1'\mathbf{x}_1(\mathbf{x}_1'\mathbf{x}_1)^{-1}] \tag{31}$$

Since the **x**s are non-stochastic the variance of the estimate $\hat{\alpha}_1$ reduces to

$$V(\hat{\alpha}_1) = (\mathbf{x}_1'\mathbf{x}_1)^{-1}\sigma^2_{\eta 1} \tag{32}$$

The SURE estimates of α may be expressed as

$$\begin{aligned}\alpha^* &= (\mathbf{X}'\hat{\mathbf{\Sigma}}^{-1}\mathbf{X})^{-1}\mathbf{X}'\hat{\mathbf{\Sigma}}^{-1}\mathbf{Y}\\ &= \alpha + (\mathbf{X}'\hat{\mathbf{\Sigma}}^{-1}\mathbf{X})^{-1}\mathbf{X}'\hat{\mathbf{\Sigma}}^{-1}\eta\end{aligned} \tag{33}$$

because $\mathbf{x}_3$ is orthogonal to $\mathbf{x}_1$ and $\mathbf{x}_2$ by assumption.

The variance-covariance matrix of the SURE estimates is

$$\begin{aligned}V(\alpha^*/\hat{\mathbf{\Sigma}}) &= E[(\mathbf{X}'\hat{\mathbf{\Sigma}}^{-1}\mathbf{X})^{-1}\mathbf{X}'\hat{\mathbf{\Sigma}}^{-1}\eta\eta'\hat{\mathbf{\Sigma}}^{-1}\mathbf{X}(\mathbf{X}'\hat{\mathbf{\Sigma}}^{-1}\mathbf{X})^{-1}]\\ &= (\mathbf{X}'\hat{\mathbf{\Sigma}}^{-1}\mathbf{X})^{-1}\mathbf{X}'\hat{\mathbf{\Sigma}}^{-1}E(\eta\eta')\hat{\mathbf{\Sigma}}^{-1}\mathbf{X}(\mathbf{X}'\hat{\mathbf{\Sigma}}^{-1}\mathbf{X})^{-1}\end{aligned} \tag{34}$$

To be able to compare the variance of the SURE estimate with that of the ordinary least squares estimate let us express the variance of the estimates of the αs from the ordinary least

[5] The estimate $\hat{\alpha}_1$ has the same variance, even when $\mathbf{x}_3$ is not orthogonal to $\mathbf{x}_1$.

squares as

$$V(\hat{\alpha}) = \begin{bmatrix} x_{11} & 0 \\ 0 & x_{22} \end{bmatrix}^{-1} \begin{bmatrix} \sigma_{\eta_1}^2 & 0 \\ 0 & \sigma_{\eta_2}^2 \end{bmatrix} \otimes \mathbf{I}$$

$$= (\mathbf{X}'\mathbf{X})^{-1}E(\eta\eta')$$

$$= (\mathbf{X}'[E(\eta\eta')]^{-1}\mathbf{X})^{-1} \tag{35}$$

Now let us consider a hypothetical seemingly unrelated regression equations model with no mis-specification in the estimated model. Let the true variance-covariance matrix of the errors be $\boldsymbol{\varphi}$. Instead of $\boldsymbol{\varphi}$ another matrix $\hat{\boldsymbol{\Sigma}}(\hat{\boldsymbol{\Sigma}} \neq \boldsymbol{\varphi})$ is used in its place in computing the seemingly unrelated estimates. The variance matrix of the resulting estimates is

$$\mathbf{V} = (\mathbf{X}'\hat{\boldsymbol{\Sigma}}^{-1}\mathbf{X})^{-1}\mathbf{X}'\hat{\boldsymbol{\Sigma}}^{-1}\boldsymbol{\varphi}\hat{\boldsymbol{\Sigma}}^{-1}\mathbf{X}(\mathbf{X}'\hat{\boldsymbol{\Sigma}}^{-1}\mathbf{X})^{-1} \tag{36}$$

The variance matrix of the generalised least squares estimates using the true variance matrix $\boldsymbol{\varphi}$ is

$$\mathbf{V}^* = (\mathbf{X}'\boldsymbol{\varphi}^{-1}\mathbf{X})^{-1} \tag{37}$$

But the generalised least squares estimates are the minimum variance unbiased estimates. Therefore it follows that

$$(\mathbf{X}'\hat{\boldsymbol{\Sigma}}^{-1}\mathbf{X})^{-1}\mathbf{X}'\hat{\boldsymbol{\Sigma}}^{-1}\boldsymbol{\varphi}\hat{\boldsymbol{\Sigma}}^{-1}\mathbf{X}(\mathbf{X}'\hat{\boldsymbol{\Sigma}}^{-1})^{-1} \geq (\mathbf{X}'\boldsymbol{\varphi}^{-1}\mathbf{X})^{-1} \tag{38}$$

This inequality becomes an equality only when $\hat{\boldsymbol{\Sigma}} = \boldsymbol{\varphi}$.

Since the inequality (38) is true for all $\boldsymbol{\varphi}$, it is true for $E(\eta\eta')$ as well. Hence by substituting $E(\eta\eta')$ for $\boldsymbol{\varphi}$ in the inequality (38) *and noting that the inequality is valid for all* $\hat{\boldsymbol{\Sigma}}$ we obtain[6]

$$V(\boldsymbol{\alpha}^*) \geq V(\hat{\boldsymbol{\alpha}}) \tag{39}$$

The SURE estimation procedure leads to less efficient estimates than the ordinary least squares when the contemporaneous correlation in the error terms is caused by mis-specification of the model. When there is no mis-specification in the model, then of course, these results do not hold. Even in the case where the estimated model is the true relation, for small sample sizes the SURE estimates are less efficient than the ordinary least squares. This result is due to Professor Zellner [6].

[6] This inequality holds for any number of equations in a set, and also for any number of independent variables in each equation.

The Nature of Bias in Standard Errors

The results presented in the above section may come as a surprise to researchers who worked with ordinary least squares and SURE estimation. Often standard errors of SURE estimates are smaller than standard errors of corresponding least squares estimates. Many researchers attributed this to the 'true' efficiency of SURE procedure. The true efficiency of an estimator is reflected by its variance and *not* by an estimate of the variance. Even though the ordinary least squares estimator has smaller variance than SURE whenever there is a left-out variable, the estimated variance would be larger for ordinary least squares than for SURE simply because of the way these estimates are computed from the data. As we shall prove below standard errors of the estimates do not reflect the true relative efficiency of these estimators.

The variance of the estimate $\hat{\alpha}_1$ is computed as[7]

$$\hat{V}(\hat{\alpha}_1) = T^{-1}(x_{11})^{-1}e_{11} \tag{40}$$

In Equation (40) the expression $(T^{-1}e_{11})$ is an estimate of the variance u_1 $(= x_3 + \eta_1)$ and not that of η_1. The appropriate expression to compute $\hat{V}(\hat{\alpha}_1)$ is the variance of η_1 and not that of u_1. In the context of left-out variables the standard errors of ordinary least squares estimates are always upward biased [3, pp. 136–8].

On the other hand, the SURE procedure estimates the variance of α_1^* as

$$\hat{V}(\boldsymbol{\alpha}^*) = (\mathbf{X}'\hat{\mathbf{\Sigma}}^{-1}\mathbf{X})^{-1} \tag{41}$$

By using Equation (20) we may obtain the estimate of $\mathbf{V}(\alpha_1^*)$ as

$$\hat{V}(\alpha_1^*) = \frac{e_{11}x_{22}(e_{11}e_{22} - e_{12}e_{12})}{T(e_{11}e_{22}x_{11}x_{22} - e_{12}e_{12}x_{12}x_{12})} \tag{42}$$

which simplifies to

$$\hat{V}(\alpha_1^*) = T^{-1}(x_{11})^{-1}e_{11}\frac{1 - r^2_{e_1e_2}}{1 - r^2_{e_1e_2}r_{x_1x_2}} \tag{43}$$

[7] In this study we are dividing the residual sum of squares by T instead of the number of degrees of freedom merely for simplicity of notation.

A comparison of Equations (40) and (43) reveals that

$$\hat{V}(\alpha_1^*) \leq \hat{V}(\hat{\alpha}_1) \tag{44}$$

Whether the estimated model is a true model or a misspecified one, standard errors of SURE estimates will be smaller than the corresponding ordinary least squares estimates because of the way they are computed. Even in cases where $V(\alpha_1^*) > V(\hat{\alpha}_1)$ the estimates yield the inequality $\hat{V}(\alpha_1^*) \leq \hat{V}(\hat{\alpha}_1)$, in every sample. Therefore the computed standard errors of these estimators do not reflect the true relative efficiency.

Conclusions

Our analysis points out that bias and variance of the ordinary least squares and SURE estimators are sensitive to misspecification caused by a left-out variable, and the SURE procedure is more sensitive than the ordinary least squares. When contemporaneous correlation in a set of regression equations is the result of a common left-out variable, the SURE estimation procedure results in less efficient estimates than ordinary least squares. The true relative efficiency of these estimators is not reflected by the computed standard errors of the estimates.

References

[1] KMENTA, JAN and GILBERT, R., Small Sample Properties of Alternative Estimators of Seemingly Unrelated Regressions, *Journal of the American Statistical Association*, LXIII (December 1968) 1180–1200.

[2] RAO, POTLURI, Some Notes on Misspecification in Multiple Regressions, *The American Statistician*, XXV (December 1971) 37–9.

[3] RAO, POTLURI and MILLER, R. L., *Applied Econometrics*, Belmont: Wadsworth Publishing Co., 1971.

[4] TELSER, LESTER G., Iterative Estimation of a Set of Linear Regression Equations, *Journal of the American Statistical Association*, LIX (September 1964) 845–62.

[5] ZELLNER, ARNOLD, An Efficient Method of Estimating Seemingly Unrelated Regressions and Tests for Aggregation

Bias, *Journal of the American Statistical Association*, LVII (June 1962) 348–68.

[6] ZELLNER, ARNOLD, Estimators for Seemingly Unrelated Regression Equations: Some Exact Finite Sample Results, *Journal of the American Statistical Association*, LVIII (December 1963) 977–92.

5 Economic Policy Simulation in Dynamic Control Models Under Econometric Estimation

BY JATI K. SENGUPTA*

1. Introduction

THE USE of modern control theory in various dynamic economic models has raised a number of interesting issues in the theory of economic policy and its operational applications to problems of economic growth, stabilisation and development planning. Two of these seem to be of great importance: econometric estimation viewed as a part of the decision-making process by a policymaker and the operational linkages between a consistency model without any explicit optimisation criterion and an optimisation model with an explicit objective function defined in a programming framework. In order to compare and evaluate alternative economic policies defined within a dynamic econometric model, these two problems become most relevant and they have to be resolved in some manner. As an example of the first type of problem one may refer to the use of the Brookings quarterly econometric model of the U.S. economy by Fromm and Taubman [1] for evaluation of the relative desirability of a set of monetary and fiscal policy actions. They noted that the

* This work is partly supported by the National Science Foundation Project GS-1810 at the Department of Economics, Iowa State University. Simulation experiments on the world cocoa model were made possible by the courtesy and encouragement of Mr. L. M. Goreux of the International Bank for Reconstruction and Development, Washington, D.C., where the author was a consultant to the Basic Research Center during summer, 1969; needless to say the author alone in his personal capacity is responsible for all the views expressed here. For the other simulation runs the author is indebted to his research students, Gene Gruver and Shyamal Roychowdhury for computational assistance.

method of optimum growth defined in a Ramsay-type framework of maximisation of a utility functional over a horizon is not applicable to cyclical paths; moreover it ignores the disutility of the time path of variances of the arguments (e.g. consumption, etc.) in the utility function. They proposed a utility functional as the sum of two components $u_1(x_1, \ldots, x_n)$ and $u_2(1/\text{var}\, x_1, 1/\text{var}\, x_2, \ldots, 1/\text{var}\, x_n)$ where x_i denotes instrument variables like consumption, government expenditure, etc., with their variances denoted by var x_i. The component $u_1(x)$ has time-discounting and the form of the component $u_2(1/\text{var}\, x)$ implies that utility increases as the variances decrease. Note, however that in this approach the utility functional is not optimised to derive the time paths of the instrument variables as in the Ramsay approach, but the functional is used to provide ranking among alternative policies, particularly when cyclical instability is associated with those policies. Even in recent models of optimum growth based on optimising a social utility functional, different sources of instability and cyclical fluctuations have been mentioned by several authors [2, 3] and Morishima [4] has shown and emphasised in great detail how the oscillations cannot be avoided in realistic economic cases, unless a strong aversion to fluctuations and oscillations is built into the Ramsay-type utility functional itself.

As an example of the second type of problems (i.e. linkages between consistency and optimisation models) one may refer to the methods increasingly used in input-output models [5, 6], where alternative set of forecasts (e.g. of gross output vector given a set of final demands) is prepared to allow for inequality constraints on sectoral capacities or specific policy instruments like the rate of public investment. An important distinction is made in this connection by Stone and his associates [5] between transient (or short-run) and steady-state (or long-run) solutions of the model; whereas steady-state solutions are equilibrium projections made on the assumption that short-run bottlenecks and inequality constraints (e.g. capacity constraints) would work themselves out, the transient solutions have to pay particular attention to the short-run constraints and inequality restrictions and in particular the disequilibrium dynamics (i.e. the method of adjustment following sectoral gaps between demand and supply) become very important. The transient solutions can be viewed as the result of a short-run optimisation process, whereas the steady-state solution is a consistent specification of a long-run tendency, under some assumptions about equilibrium (e.g. equiproportional growth).

So long as the correspondence between the short-run transient solution (optimisation model) and the long-run steady-state solution (consistency model) is not explicitly introduced, the problem of linkage remains unspecified and unresolved. This creates a dichotomy, in my opinion, which persists not only in input-ouput models but in the theory of optimum growth [7]. To illustrate the latter case one may refer to the two-step method of introducing monetary and fiscal instruments by Uzawa [8] in an optimum growth model under a two-sector framework (private and public sectors, each having separate production functions). In the first step one computes a long-run optimum growth solution satisfying the conditions of Pontryagin's maximum principle [9] and this specifies the equilibrium ratios of consumption and two sectoral investments to national income. Denote these ratios by $\alpha(t)$, $\beta_1(t)$ and $\beta_2(t)$ respectively. One asks in the second step: how to use a detailed short-run model to choose instrument variables such as tax rate variation (θ_1), rate of deficit financing (θ_2) and transfer payments (θ_3) such that the short-run values of $\alpha_1(t)$, $\beta_1(t)$ and $\beta_2(t)$ denoted by $\hat{\alpha}_1(t)$, $\hat{\beta}_1(t)$ and $\hat{\beta}_2(t)$ are as close as possible to the long run optimal values? If one restricts to the stationary solution of the optimum system satisfying Pontryagin's maximum principle and thereby determines the long-run equilibrium values α^*, β_2^*, β_1^* (assuming that such a solution exists), then the short-run policy problem is to choose the control variables θ_1, θ_2, θ_3 such that

$$\hat{\alpha}(\theta_1, \theta_2, \theta_3) = \alpha^*$$

$$\hat{\beta}_1(\theta_1, \theta_2, \theta_3) = \beta_1^*$$

$$\hat{\beta}_2(\theta_1, \theta_2, \theta_3) = \beta_2^*$$

where $(\alpha^*, \beta_1^*, \beta_2^*)$ specifies the chosen equilibrium point. Note that this approach allows the flexibility of using detailed econometric models in the short-run in order to determine the controls which should be applied to converge to the desired values $(\alpha^*, \beta_1^*, \beta_2^*)$. It is clear also that unlike the input-output models, the short-run model here is an econometric model emphasising consistency, whereas the long-run model is one of optimisation with an ordinally specified objective function. We should mention, however, that there is an alternative formulation about the linkage between the short and long run in the theory of economic policy under optimal growth and this is due to Arrow and Kurz [10]. In this latter formulation, only the second of the two parts of the maximum principle of Pontryagin (the first part satisfying the canonical or adjoint differential equations and the second part satisfying the condition of maximisation of the current value Hamiltonian with respect to the control variables) is taken to define a short run equilibrium, and the deviations from this level are analysed for stability or otherwise in terms of the slopes of the relevant demand and supply functions (e.g. by testing for the sign of the Hessian determinant). Note that this does not allow the introduction of monetary and fiscal instruments through separate econometric models. Also the short-run equilibrium solutions may be dependent on the appropriate (i.e. optimal) values of the adjoint (or costate) variables in the Pontryagin principle. A slightly different interpretation has been attempted by Gale and Sutherland [11] for the case where prices are given to be optimal in some sense and the short-run equilibrium can be decomposed into consumers' and producers' optimum.

The object of this paper is to explore by simulation methods some aspects of the two problems mentioned above. More specifically we discuss two types of dynamic economic models both econometrically estimated in order to compare the relative stabilising effects of alternative policy instruments. The first is a seven-equation model of world cocoa due to Goreux [12] which is utilised to test the structural stability of those parameters which are critical to the stabilising impact of the instrument variables on the system. The second is a simple multiplier-accelerator model of income determination, where the values of the parameters are so chosen as to conform to a previous simulation study attempted by Naylor *et al.* [13]. In the first case the econometric model was estimated by ordinary least squares (O.L.S.) applied to each single equation separately (except the last one which is an identity) and a simulation study performed by Goreux in order to project the likely effects of certain types of price stabilisation rules. In the second case (i.e. the simulation experiments by Naylor *et al.* [13]) the instrument variable represented by government expenditure was assumed directly proportional to national income and the factor of proportionality (i.e. the coefficient of proportional feedback control) was varied to characterise alternative policies. This case, like the first, did not specify any objective function indicating aversion to fluctuations or oscillation, although policies more stable in terms of average variance measures based on the simulated samples were preferred.

2. A Model of World Cocoa

The econometric model of the world cocoa economy which will be used to illustrate the problem of testing for structural stability was constructed and estimated by Goreux [12a] by O.L.S. applied to each behavioural equation on the basis of annual time series data over 1950–67. This econometric model attempts to predict the behaviour of annual demand and supply and hence prices over time, although the elements of simultaneity were ignored in estimating the model. The complete estimated model is as follows.

Demand in developed countries (D_1)

$$\ln D_{1t} = 2{\cdot}8013 + 0{\cdot}3274 \ln y_{1t}$$

(0·0137) (865·8) (5·73)

$$- 0{\cdot}4182 \ln P_t + 0{\cdot}1817 \ln (P_t/P_{t-1}) \tag{1}$$

(9·58) (5·01)

$$\bar{R}^2 = 0{\cdot}969;\ d = 1{\cdot}63$$

Demand in socialist countries (D_2)

$$\ln D_{2t} = 0{\cdot}763 + 0{\cdot}0636t + 0{\cdot}2760 \ln P_{t-1} \tag{2}$$

(0·0245) (132·0) (43·33) (4·62)

$$\bar{R}^2 = 0{\cdot}994; \quad d = 1{\cdot}541$$

Demand in developing countries (D_3)

$$\ln D_{3t} = 175{\cdot}86 + 6{\cdot}848t - 2{\cdot}836\left(\frac{P_{t-1} + P_{t-2}}{2}\right) \qquad (3)$$

(22·07) (33·81) (5·20) (3·16)

$\bar{R}^2 = 0{\cdot}853; \quad d = 2{\cdot}24$

Demand for stocks (S)

$$\ln (S_t/S_{t-1}) = 0{\cdot}03909 - 0{\cdot}88070 \ln (P_{Nt}/P_{Nt-1}) - 0{\cdot}00312t$$

(0·0171) (9·7) (19·35) (3·8)

$$+ 0{\cdot}1809X + 0{\cdot}2119Y + 0{\cdot}1983Z \qquad (4)$$

(10·5) (12·1) (6·2)

$\bar{R}^2 = 0{\cdot}969; \quad d = 1{\cdot}58$

Feedback between export unit value (P) and New York spot price (P_N)

$$P_t = 0{\cdot}69005P_{Nt} + 0{\cdot}19403P_{Nt-1} \qquad (5)$$

(1·39) (20·4) (5·7)

$\bar{R}^2 = 0{\cdot}976; \quad d = 2{\cdot}45$

Production (Q) response

$$\ln Q_t = 2{\cdot}9025 + 0{\cdot}000\,000\,034P_t^* - 17{\cdot}21(1/P_{t-1}^2) \qquad (6)$$

(0·03106) (396·5) (9·2) (1·3)

$\bar{R}^2 = 0{\cdot}911; \quad d = 3{\cdot}149$

Equilibrium condition (identity)

$$Q_t - D_t = S_t - S_{t-1}, \quad \text{where} \quad D_t = D_{1t} + D_{2t} + D_{3t} \qquad (7)$$

Here the total world demand for grindings (D) is decomposed into three components (D_1, D_2, D_3), of which the demand component (D_1) arising in developed countries is the most important. The exogenous variables in the model are: time in years (t), gross domestic product (deflated) in developed countries (y_1) and the dummy variables (X, Y, Z) in the stock equation. The remaining seven variables (D_1, D_2, D_3, S, P, P_N and Q) are endogenous and can be solved from the seven equations. Note also that the numbers in parentheses immediately below the respective regression coefficients indicate values of the t-ratio, while the standard error of estimates of each dependent variable is indicated in the left hand side of each equation; $\bar{R}^2$ denotes multiple correlation coefficient squared and corrected for degrees of freedom, d denotes Durbin–Watson statistic and P_t^* denotes a long run price factor defined as

$$P_t^* = \sum_{k=1-s}^{t-s} (P_k^2 - \bar{P}^2)C_{k+s-2} \tag{6a}$$

where $\bar{P}$ is the stationary long period price (assumed to equal 22·0 in the estimation period 1950–67) and C_t equals a three-year moving average of world production i.e. $\frac{1}{3}(Q_{t-1} + Q_t + Q_{t+1})$.

The above econometric model seemed to provide a very good fit over the estimation period (1950–67) and it was utilised by Goreux for three types of simulation:

1. To simulate a one-year price forecast, by solving the model for the year 1950 from actual values for 1949 and earlier; then for 1951 from actual values for 1950 and earlier and so on for 1952 and later years up to 1967;
2. to simulate a long-term forecast up to 1967 by assuming all error terms unknown form 1950 to 1967 e.g. the projections for 1967 are based on the projected values from 1966 to 1950 and actual values for 1949 and before;
3. to project a forecast for 1968–2000 (i.e. 33 years) by drawing random numbers assumed normally and independently distributed with zero mean and standard deviation equal to that observed between 1950–67. This experiment based on $33 \times 7 = 231$ random numbers replicated 25 times showed that the structural model did not explode and that the long-term price cycle was basically generated by basic supply and demand factors and not by an auto-regressive process of random disturbances.

It is clear, however that, in spite of the very high degree of predictive efficiency of the model in the estimation period, questions of alternative price stabilisation schemes (e.g. buffer stock) and their impact cannot be discussed in the model, since each equation has been estimated by O.L.S. by ignoring the three basic links of simultaneity: (*a*) the presence of otherwise dependent variables (P_{Nt} and P_t) in the explanatory part of the stock and demand (D_{1t}) equations; (*b*) the equilibrium condition specified by Equation (7) and (*c*) the presence of lagged variables with high intercorrelation with time trend. Note also that the sensitivity of any dynamic control policy (e.g. any price or production support programmes) is dependent very crucially on the demand and supply coefficients identified in this general nonlinear cobweb model. The most important structural coefficients relevant for analysing cyclical fluctuations under control variables are those associated with $\ln P_t$ in Equation (1), $\ln P_{Nt}$ in Equation (4) and P_t^* and $1/P_{t-1}^2$ in Equation (6). But since P_t^* and P_{t-1} are essentially predetermined values, the stability of the generalised cobweb model depends very critically on the elasticity coefficients, θ_1 and θ_2 say, associated with $\ln P_t$ in Equation (1) and $\ln P_{Nt}$ in Equation (4) respectively. Hence, our problem is to re-estimate these coefficients for analysing the structural stability of the model and it is clear that the reduced-form method is inapplicable here due to non-linearities. Three methods are employed here.

Method 1 Test the sensitivity of the estimates of the coefficients θ_1 and θ_2 defined before by adopting an instrument variables method.

Method 2 Re-estimate θ_1 and θ_2 by conditional reduced-form method.

Method 3 Apply a conditional maximum likelihood method to estimate θ_1 and θ_2 under constraints on the size of σ_1^2 and σ_2^2 (i.e. population variances for Equations (1) and (4) respectively).

According to method 1 we re-estimate Equations (1) and (4) of the original model by replacing $\ln P_t$ and $\ln P_{Nt}$ by their estimates $\ln \hat{P}_t$, $\ln \hat{P}_{Nt}$ obtained from other instrument variables. From several alternative forms, the following estimated equation was used for $\hat{P}_{Nt}$

$$\ln \hat{P}_{Nt} = \ln \bar{P}_{-Nt-1} - \underset{(0{\cdot}07249)}{0{\cdot}00058^*} Q_t^F + \underset{(2{\cdot}4315)}{0{\cdot}00027} D_t^F - \underset{(6{\cdot}1298)}{0{\cdot}57694} \ln \frac{S_{t-1}}{D_t^F} \tag{8a}$$

$$\bar{R}^2 = 0{\cdot}727; \quad d = 1{\cdot}676$$

Here the quantity $\bar{P}_{Nt}$ denotes sample average of P_{Nt} over the period 1950–67 and Q_t^F, D_t^F denote respectively the market forecasts of total production and demand prepared by Gill and Dufus and available in Weymar's tables [14]. The feedback relation between P_t and P_{Nt} was derived from (5) as

$$\ln \hat{P}_t = \ln\left(1 + \frac{0{\cdot}19403\bar{P}_{Nt-1}}{0{\cdot}69005\bar{P}_{Nt}}\right) + 0{\cdot}69005 \ln \hat{P}_{Nt} \qquad (8b)$$

Using these estimated series $\hat{P}_t$ and $\hat{P}_{Nt}$ the econometric estimates of Equations (1) and (4) turn out to be as follows

$$\begin{aligned} \ln D_{1t} &= 3{\cdot}4395^* + 0{\cdot}1618 \ln y_{1t} - 0{\cdot}6884^* \ln \hat{P}_t \\ &(0{\cdot}01847) \quad (790{\cdot}96) \quad (1{\cdot}3571) \qquad (5{\cdot}1909) \\ &\qquad + 0{\cdot}1865^*(\ln \hat{P}_t - \ln P_{t-1}) \\ &\qquad (3{\cdot}7332) \end{aligned} \qquad (1a)$$

$$\bar{R}^2 = 0{\cdot}943; \quad d^* = 2{\cdot}081; \quad 0{\cdot}82 \leq d_{\text{theor}} \leq 1{\cdot}75$$

$$\begin{aligned} (\ln (S_t/S_{t-1}) &= 0{\cdot}0250 - 0{\cdot}9982^*(\ln \hat{P}_{Nt} - \ln P_{Nt-1}) - 0{\cdot}0029t \\ &(0{\cdot}0655) \quad (1{\cdot}6213) \quad (4{\cdot}4475) \qquad (0{\cdot}9167) \\ &\quad + 0{\cdot}1289^*X + 0{\cdot}1345^*Y + 0{\cdot}2722^*Z \\ &\quad (2{\cdot}6140) \quad (2{\cdot}2303) \quad (2{\cdot}2160) \end{aligned} \qquad (4a)$$

$$\bar{R}^2 = 0{\cdot}543; \quad d = 2{\cdot}364; \quad 0{\cdot}56 \leq d_{\text{theor}} \leq 2{\cdot}21$$

Here the asterisk against any regression coefficient denotes that it is statistically significant at 5 per cent level. Two important changes are indicated by the two re-estimated Equations (1a) and (4a). First, the Durbin–Watson statistics improve in both cases suggesting that the residuals are not autocorrelated at 5 per cent level (note that in the original equations the *d*-values were in the inconclusive range). Second, the absolute value of the regression coefficients increased in both cases (the coefficient of $\ln P_{Nt}$ is raised from 0·88070 to 0·99819 in Equations (4) and (4a) and that of $\ln P_t$ from −0·2365 to −5·0519 in Equations (1) and (1a) respectively).

According to method 2 (conditional reduced form) we use the estimated values of $\ln \hat{Q}_t$ from Equation (6) to re-estimate the price Equation (5) conditionally as step 1. $\ln (P_{Nt}/P_{Nt-1}) = \hat{\alpha}_{10} - \hat{\alpha}_{11}[\ln \hat{Q}_t - \ln Q_{t-1} - \hat{\alpha}_t]$ where

$$\hat{\alpha}_{10} = (0{\cdot}88070)^{-1}(0{\cdot}03909 - 0{\cdot}00312t + 0{\cdot}18087X + 0{\cdot}21192Y + 0{\cdot}19826Z)$$

$$\hat{\alpha}_t = \ln\left(1 - \frac{\bar{D}_t}{\bar{Q}_t}\right) - \ln\left(1 - \frac{\bar{D}_{t-1}}{\bar{Q}_{t-1}}\right) + \ln\left(1 - \frac{\bar{S}_{t-2}}{\bar{S}_{t-1}}\right) - \ln\left(1 - \frac{\bar{S}_{t-1}}{\bar{S}_t}\right)$$

Step 2. Regress P_t on $\hat{P}_{Nt}$ obtained in step 1

$$\underset{(4{\cdot}7705)}{P_t} = \underset{(4{\cdot}5647)}{0{\cdot}45760^*\, P_{Nt}} + \underset{(3{\cdot}0928)}{0{\cdot}35505^* P_{Nt-1}}$$

$$\bar{R}^2 = 0{\cdot}723; \quad d = 1{\cdot}884$$

Step 3. Re-estimate Equation (1) using the estimated $\hat{P}_t$ from step 2

$$\underset{(0{\cdot}02094)}{\ln D_{1t}} = \underset{(505{\cdot}93)}{2{\cdot}49738^*} + \underset{(4{\cdot}8449)}{0{\cdot}40551^* \ln y_{1t}} - \underset{(5{\cdot}6126)}{0{\cdot}31869^* \ln \hat{P}_t} + \underset{(1{\cdot}9648)}{0{\cdot}13884(\ln \hat{P}_t - \ln P_{t-1})}$$

$$\bar{R}^2 = 0{\cdot}927; \quad d = 1{\cdot}638$$

Note, however, that the d-statistic here is still in the inconclusive range and the coefficient of $\ln (\hat{P}_t/P_{t-1})$ is not statistically significant. From this viewpoint, the re-estimates based on method 1 appear to be far superior.

From a technical viewpoint, method 3 (conditional maximum likelihood) is the most satisfactory, since it allows the simultaneity links in a more basic sense. The conditional M.L. method designed here was intended to test the sensitivity of the original estimates of the two structural coefficients (denoted here by $\hat{\theta}_1^{(1)}$ $\hat{\theta}_2^{(1)}$) of $\ln P_t$ and $\ln P_{Nt}$ in the demand ($\ln D_{1t}$ in (1)) and stock ($\ln S_t$ in (4)) equations, under the assumption that the remaining structural coefficients were unchanged. The method applied here tests the sensitivity of the log-likelihood function when the estimates $\hat{\theta}_1^{(1)}$, $\hat{\theta}_2^{(1)}$ are successively revised by following the method of scoring in the direction of higher maximum of the log-likelihood function. Two sets of computation were performed; the first assumes the standard errors $\hat{\sigma}_1$ = standard error of $\ln D_{1t} = 0{\cdot}0137$, $\hat{\sigma}_2$ = standard error of $\ln (S_t/S_{t-1}) = 0{\cdot}01714$ as in the original seven-equation model and the second increases those values by a multiple of 10 i.e. $\hat{\sigma}_1 = 0{\cdot}137$ and $\hat{\sigma}_2 = 0{\cdot}1714$, thereby increasing the size of the neighbourhood within which the maximum of the log-likelihood function may be searched for. The resulting estimates appeared as follows.

Iteration number k	First set			Second set		
	$-\hat{\theta}_1^{(k)}$	$-\theta_2^{(k)}$	$-\hat{L}^{(k)}$	$-\hat{\theta}_1^{(k)}$	$-\hat{\theta}_2^{(k)}$	$-\hat{L}^{(k)}$
1	0·2365	0·8807	141·91	0·2365	0·8807	56·30
2	0·2773	1·0672	270·39	0·2756	0·8721	56·68
4	0·4147	1·1403	3270·16	0·2684	0·8548	56·27
6	*0·2196*	*1·1711*	*128·30*	0·2680	0·8375	56·19
8	0·2661	1·1872	185·53	0·26805	0·8202	56·12
10	0·3653	1·1965	1754·19	*0·2681*	*0·8030*	56·06
20	0·3698	1·2012	194·03	0·2698	0·8001	56·41

where

$$\hat{L} = T \ln |J| + R_1(\hat{\theta}_1, \hat{\theta}_2) + R_2(\hat{\theta}_1, \hat{\theta}_2)$$

denotes that part of the log-likelihood function which is a function of the two parameters $\hat{\theta}_1$ and $\hat{\theta}_2$ and $|J|$ denotes the Jacobian associated with this method.

Two comments may be added here. First, the maximum M.L. estimates in the two sets show that the maximum values of the pair $(\hat{\theta}_1, \hat{\theta}_2)$ tend to pull in opposite directions (e.g. if the M.L. estimate of $\hat{\theta}_1$ is higher in the second set compared to its original value, 0·2365, then the value of $\hat{\theta}_2$ (= 0·8030) is lower in this set when compared with its original value of 0·8807). Second, the convergence of the log-likelihood function is much more stable in the second set, where the size of the neighbourhood of perturbation was larger. The logic involved in this is that if there is a global maximum of the likelihood function different from the local one, then this method of search is more likely to locate it. Hence, the second set of computations appeared more reasonable and logically more tenable. Note however that the second set of maximum M.L. estimates are very close to the original estimates of the two parameters e.g.

	Original	*Maximum M.L. estimates*
$\hat{\theta}_1$	0·2365	0·2681
$\hat{\theta}_2$	0·8807	0·8030
$\hat{\theta}_1 + \hat{\theta}_2$	1·1172	1·0711

This suggests two very interesting points. First, the single-equation estimates of the coefficients are quite stable against the simultaneous links in the model. Similar econometric results were noted by Fox [15], although in a linear model for a model with U.S. pork production and prices for the period 1922–41. In a linear cobweb model the factors leading to an increase in price response of demand (for consumption and stocks) tend to increase *ceteris paribus* the rate of convergence to equilibrium and hence to a stable level, if the equilibrium is stable. Since the sum of the two coefficients is lower for the M.L. estimates, the revised estimates suggest that the intensity of stabilising effects measured by the rate of convergence to a stable equilibrium is a little lower than that what would be suggested by the single equation O.L.S. estimates.

Having resolved the question of structural stability of the most important coefficients of the model, we now discuss the stability of the deterministic part of the seven-equation model given by Equations (1) through (7). This is necessary to test that the equilibirum solution of the model has certain stability characteristics, so that the policy instruments (e.g. buffer stock) can maintain stabilising tendencies. In order to apply this stability test, we linearise the non-linear model and discuss approximately its stability characteristics around an equilibrium point.

Consider the linear approximation of the first six equations of the original seven-equation econometric model. Denoting by $\bar{x}$ the equilibrium level of x around which Taylor series expansions are made (where x stands for any variable which enters non-linearly), we obtain the aggregate demand-supply model

$$D_t = \bar{D}_{1t}\left(-0{\cdot}2365\frac{P_t}{\bar{P}_t} - 0{\cdot}1817\frac{P_{t-1}}{\bar{P}_{t-1}}\right) + \bar{D}_{2t}\left(0{\cdot}2760\frac{P_{t-1}}{\bar{P}_{t-1}}\right)$$

$$+ \bar{D}_{3t}(-1{\cdot}418P_{t-1} - 1{\cdot}418P_{t-2})$$

$$Q_t = \bar{Q}_t\left(34{\cdot}42\frac{P_{t-1}}{(\bar{P}_{t-1})^3}\right)$$

$$S_t = S_{t-1} + (\bar{S}_t/\bar{P}_{Nt}\{-0{\cdot}88070(P_{Nt} - P_{Nt-1})\}$$

(assuming $\bar{S}_{t-1} = \bar{S}_t$, $\bar{P}_{Nt} = \bar{P}_{Nt-1}$).

Since we are interested in the characteristic roots of this difference equation system for its stability tests, we ignore the intercept terms and use the approximations $\bar{P}_t = \bar{P}_{t-1} = \bar{P}_{Nt} = \bar{P}_{Nt-1}$ to hold in equilibrium and the relation

$$P_t = 0{\cdot}69005P_{Nt} + 0{\cdot}19403P_{Nt-1}$$

Then we obtain a second-order system as follows

$$P_t + r_1P_{t-1} + r_2P_{t-2} = 0 \tag{9}$$

where

$$r_1 = N/D \quad \text{and} \quad r_2 = 1{\cdot}418\bar{D}_{3t}\{(\bar{P}_t)^{-1}(0{\cdot}8807\bar{S}_t + 0{\cdot}2365\bar{D}_{1t})\}^{-1}$$

$$N = -0{\cdot}8807(\bar{S}_t/\bar{P}_t) + 0{\cdot}1817(\bar{D}_{1t}/\bar{P}_t) - 0{\cdot}2760(\bar{D}_{2t}/\bar{P}_t)$$

$$+ 1{\cdot}418\bar{D}_{3t} + 34{\cdot}42\frac{\bar{Q}}{\bar{P}_t^3}$$

$$D = 0{\cdot}8807(\bar{S}_t/\bar{P}_t) + 0{\cdot}2365(\bar{D}_{1t}/\bar{P}_t)$$

So long as the equilibrium values of $\bar{S}_t$, $\bar{D}_{1t}$, $\bar{D}_{2t}$, $\bar{D}_{3t}$ etc., are arbitrary the following cases of characteristic roots may arise from Equation (9).

Case 1. Both roots real, which is possible for the characteristic equation $\lambda^2 + \lambda r_1 + r_2 = 0$ if $(r_1^2 - 4r_2)$ is non-negative.

Case 1(a). If the two roots are real, then since r_2 is positive, both roots must be either positive or negative.

Case 1(b). If the two roots are real and negative, then each is less than unity in absolute value if $0 < |r_1|, |r_2| < 1$;

Case 2. Both roots are complex if $r_1^2 < 4r_2$

If the equilibrium values of $\bar{S}_t$, $\bar{D}_t$, $\bar{P}_t$ are chosen to be the average values over 1950–67, the stabilising tendency implied by case 1(*b*) is most likely to be expected. This is because the simulated projection based on the non-linear model do not diverge; also it is easily shown that the convergence tendency would be more pronounced, if it holds for the equilibrium values that

$$0{\cdot}8807(\bar{S}_t/\bar{P}_t) < 34{\cdot}42(\bar{Q}_t/\bar{P}_t^3)$$

This result is easy to illustrate by a simple linear cobweb model of the following form

$$\begin{aligned} D_t &= -a_1P_t, \qquad Q_t = b_1P_{t-1} \qquad (a_1, b_1, c_1 > 0) \\ S_t &= S_{t-1} - c_1(P_t - P_{t-1}) \qquad (10) \\ S_t - S_{t-1} &= Q_t - D_t \end{aligned}$$

Its solution is obviously

$$P_t = (P^e - P_0)\left(\frac{c_1 - b_1}{a_1 + c_1}\right)^t + P^e$$

where

$$P^e = \text{equilibrium price}$$
$$P_0 = \text{initial price}$$

If there were no separate stock equation so that $Q_t = D_t$ defines the equilibrium, then the characteristic root $\lambda = -b_1/a_1$ would have completely determined the stability of the system. But if λ satisfied the condition $-1 < \lambda < 0$, so that the system converges to equilibrium, then this tendency would be intensified when $(-b_1/a_1)$ is replaced by $(c_1 - b_1)/(a_1 + c_1)$ with $c_1 - b_1 < 0$, $c_1 > 0$ and $-1 < (c_1 - b_1)/(c_1 + a_1) < 0$. In this simplified model with stocks, if we introduce a Nerlove-type adjustment for-stock equation replacing the above stock equation, e.g.

$$S_t = S_{t-1} - c_1P_t^F$$

where the forecast price P_t^F is based on adaptive expectations as

$$P_t^F = P_{t-1}^F + m(P_{t-1} - P_{t-1}^F) \qquad (0 < m < 1)$$

then we get the final equation for prices as

$$P_t + g_1P_{t-1} + g_2P_{t-2} = 0$$

where

$$g_1 = b_1 - a_1 + m(a_1 + c_1)$$
$$g_2 = (m - 1)b_1$$

which has the characteristic equation

$$\lambda^2 + g_1\lambda + g_2 = 0$$

and the solution

$$P_t = P^e + A_1\lambda_1^t + A_2\lambda_2^t$$

where

$$A_1 = (P_1 - P_0\lambda_2 + P^e\lambda_2)/(\lambda_1 - \lambda_2)$$

$$A_2 = (P_0 - P^e\lambda_1 - P_1)/(\lambda_1 - \lambda_2)$$

$$\lambda_1 \neq \lambda_2$$

assumed

$$P_0, P_1 = \text{two initial prices}$$

Note that the role of the adjustment coefficient $m(0 < m < 1)$ is to impart a stabilising tendency by making the coefficients $|g_1|, |g_2|$ fall into the stability zone i.e. $0 < |g_1|, |g_2| < 1$. It is of some interest to note that in the simulation mechanism of Forrester and his associates [16] this type of built-in stabiliser through adjustment coefficients is often used to modify simulated profiles which are to correspond to observed time series which do not explode in real life.

Thus we may conclude that the non-linear econometric model has some stabilising tendencies both in its deterministic and stochastic components around suitable equilibrium values, provided they are so chosen that the linearisation approximation would hold in their neighbourhood. However, this does not rule out destabilising tendencies in other phases where such linear approximations may not hold. Another alternative test would have been to consider the non-linear model as a whole and to approximate its structural solution. Such a method was applied here and the stabilising tendency approximately confirmed but this would not be reported here for reasons of space.

3. A Multiplier-Accelerator Model

It is in some sense more tractable to examine the stability behaviour of a linear stochastic system, since the approximations to non-linearities may here be avoided. As a second example, therefore, we consider a second-order difference equation in national income (y_t) measured as a deviation from some reference level

$$y_t = w_t - a_1 y_{t-1} - a_2 y_{t-2} \tag{11}$$

which may arise from the usual multiplier-accelerator type [17] relations e.g.

$$\begin{aligned} C_t &= c_1 Y_{t-1} + c_2 Y_{t-2} + u_t && \text{(consumption)} \\ I_t &= b(Y_{t-1} - Y_{t-2}) + v_t && \text{(investment)} \\ G_t &= g Y_{t-1} && \text{(government expenditure)} \\ Y_t &= C_t + I_t + G_t && \text{(income identity)} \end{aligned} \tag{12}$$

where $a_1 = -(c_1 + b + g)$, $a_2 = b - c_2$ and $w_t = u_t + v_t$ is the error term assumed to be random. The solution of the reduced form Equation (11) is

$$y_t = k_1 r_1^t + k_2 r_2^t + \sum_{j=0}^{t-2} \lambda_j w_{t-j} \tag{11a}$$

where r_1, r_2 are the characteristic roots of Equation (11), k_1, k_2 are two arbitrary constants of integration determined by two initial conditions and

$$\lambda_j = (r_1^{j+1} - r_2^{j+1})/(r_1 - r_2) \qquad (j = 1, 2) \tag{11b}$$

assuming $r_1 \neq r_2$.

By the assumption that the stochastic term w_t is independently distributed over time with constant mean and finite variance, one could easily compute the variance of y_t from (11)

$$\text{var } y_t = ((1 + a_2)/[(1 - a_2)\{(1 + a_2)^2 - a_1^2\}]) \text{ var } w_t$$

It is clear that for specific values of a_1 (i.e. $a_1 < 0$) one could have the following type of instability

$$\left.\frac{\partial \lambda_j}{\partial a_1}\right|_{\bar{a}_1} < 0 \quad \text{and} \quad \left.\frac{\partial \text{ var } y}{\partial a_1}\right|_{\bar{a}_1} > 0, \qquad \text{if } 0 < \frac{a_1^2}{a_1^2 - 4a_2} < 1$$

which implies [18] that stabilisation policies which increase the stability of the system by reducing the modulus of the characteristic roots may in fact increase the variance of the system. Naylor and his associates [13] used the above model (11) for comparing the stability measured in variance from simulated output series due to alternative feedback policies specified in terms of five pre-assigned values of g, the factor of proportionality in the government expenditure relation in (12). This simulation experiment, however, appeared to be very incomplete in three basic respects. First, comparative evaluation of policies was limited only to the proportional-type feedback controls with no reference to adaptive or optimising control (e.g. the stabilising objective of the government expenditure policy is completely ignored in the simulation tests). Second, the maximal characteristic root of the system (11) and its variance as a function of the parameters a_1, a_2 which indicate an important source of instability in the above model had been completely neglected (e.g. it is clear that for some values of g, the two characteristic roots r_1, r_2 may be less than unity in absolute value but for other values of g, they may exceed unity and hence the model may be explosive). Third, the question of comparing oscillatory time paths of income has not been posed, since the destabilising effects of government expenditure policies not limited to the form specified in (12) are completely ignored in the analysis by Naylor and his associates. The economic models of regulation proposed by Phillips [19] and their extensions [20] suggest, however, that oscillations may in some cases be the rule rather than exceptions. We have already referred to similar results in optimal growth theory.

Our objective, therefore, is to consider a modified version of the model (11) in order to analyse the stability characteristics of alternative policies. The form of this model appears in terms of deviations $y_t = Y_t - Y_t^*$, $\hat{g}_t = G_t - G_t^*$ as:

$$w_t + a_1 y_{t-1} + a_2 y_{t-2} + \hat{g}_t - y_t = 0 \tag{13}$$

where Y_t^*, G^* are desired levels of income and government expenditure, $a_1 = 1{\cdot}525$, $a_2 = -0{\cdot}85$ and w_t is a random term assumed to be normally independently distributed with mean zero and variance 18·53 (e.g. as in Naylor and his associates [13]). The variable $\hat{g}_t$ denoting government expenditure is not limited to the proportional feedback form.

Two methods of analysing instability in this framework will be briefly reported here. The first uses a quadratic objective function to arrive at an optimal control G_t^0 and then we test for the variance of the maximal characteristic root. The objective function used in the form

$$\text{minimise} \sum_{t=0}^{T} E[w_1 y_t^2 + w_2 \hat{g}_t^2]$$

$$E: \text{ expectation} \tag{14a}$$

$$w_1 = w_2 = 0{\cdot}50 \text{ (weights)}$$

is quite conventional in economic stabilisation analysis [21] and also in control theory [22]. In the second method we consider the optimal solutions derived from the first method and estimate by least squares the relation

$$G_t = gY_{t-1} \tag{14b}$$

from the optimal time series of G_t and Y_t values for $T = 10$. Then we use this approximate optimal value of g to simulate its effects and compare them with two other values of g.

Before we apply the first method, we should note that if $\hat{g}_t$ is constant in Equation (13), then, since $a_1^2 = 2{\cdot}32$ is less than $-4a_2 = 3{\cdot}40$, the characteristic roots of the system are complex and, hence, there exist zones of oscillation (e.g. the characteristic roots are $\lambda_i = 0{\cdot}7625 \pm 0{\cdot}5183i$). Now consider the method of optimising (14a) subject to (13) and the two initial conditions (in \$10 billion) $y_{-1} = 1{\cdot}1899$, $y_0 = 1{\cdot}2193$ which correspond roughly to the quarterly U.S. values for 1959 and 1960. The optimising conditions may be easily derived as

$$a_1 y_{t-1} + a_2 y_{t-2} + \hat{g}_t - y_t = 0 \qquad (t = 0, 1, \ldots, T) \tag{15a}$$

$$y_t - a_1 \hat{g}_{t+1} - a_2 \hat{g}_{t+2} + \hat{g}_t = 0 \qquad (t = 0, 1, \ldots, T) \tag{15b}$$

The characteristic equation for this system is

$$-a_2\lambda^4 + (a_1a_2 - a_1)\lambda^3 + (2 + a_1^2 + a_2^2)\lambda^2 + (a_1a_2 - a_1)\lambda - a_2 = 0$$

It is clear that because of the symmetry of the coefficients, the reciprocal of any solution (or root λ_i) will also be a solution of the characteristic equation. Hence the characteristic roots (λ_i) may be found from a second-order system by the substitution $x = \lambda + \lambda^{-1}$, where

$$-a_2x^2 + (a_1a_2 - a_1)x + (2 + a_1^2 + 2a_2 + a_2^2) = 0 \tag{16}$$

The four characteristic roots turn out to be complex numbers as follows

$$\begin{aligned} \lambda_1 &= 1{\cdot}3196 + 1{\cdot}4654i, & \lambda_2 &= 0{\cdot}3399 + 0{\cdot}3770i \\ \lambda_3 &= 0{\cdot}3399 - 0{\cdot}3770i, & \lambda_4 &= 1{\cdot}3196 - 1{\cdot}4654i \end{aligned} \tag{17}$$

Since both λ_1 and λ_4 have absolute values greater than unity, the fourth-order equation derived from (15a) and (15b) will have explosive oscillations as $T \to \infty$, even though the initial second-order Equation (13) with $w_t = 0$ and $\hat{g}_t$ constant had damped oscillations with the same set of values of a_1, a_2.

Also, we can compute the asymptotic standard error of the maximal characteristic root $|\lambda_1|$ in absolute value, by following the method of Neudecker and van de Panne [23], although in this case the computation is a bit laborious, since the root is complex and the associated characteristic vectors have to be normalised. For illustrative purposes we computed the asymptotic standard error of the maximal root $|\lambda_1|$ under the assumption that the coefficient $a_2 = -0{\cdot}85$ is non-random and a_1 is random with expectation and variance equal to 1·525. The asymptotic standard error of $|\lambda_1|$ then turns out to be 1·8596. This shows that the optimal system characterised by (15a) and (15b) is not ordinarily stable in every domain, unless the initial conditions can be so manipulated that the zone of instability becomes infeasible. This numerical illustration shows that the steady-state approximations to the optimal control equations may at times be more explosive and unstable than simple feedback controls; also it is quite essential in policy evaluations to specify in some sense a measure of aversion to oscillation and instability.

According to the second method of testing stability, we consider three values of g in Equation (14b) as follows

Policy 1 $g = 0{\cdot}25$ (Naylor's estimate)

Policy 2 $g = 0{\cdot}194$ (average U.S. ratio in 1960)

Policy 3 $g = 0{\cdot}310$ (regression estimate from method 1)

Using these values we generate simulated output, 200 observations per sample and 50 replications for each policy, assuming the error term to be normal and independent i.e. w_t: $N(0, 18{\cdot}53)$. Denote by x the transformation $x = \ln \hat{\text{var}}\, y$, where $\hat{\text{var}}\, y$ is the sample variance computed from the simulated data, then the relative variabilities of three policies turn out to be as follows

	Mean x	*Variance x*	*Mean* $\lvert y \rvert$
Policy 1	6·62445	0·07658	0·331
Policy 2	6·09800	0·08604	0·187
Policy 3	8·24739	0·12483	5·256

It is clear that if the policies are to be ranked in terms of stability measured by average variance, then policy 2 is to be preferred to policy 1 and policy 1 is to be preferred to policy 3. This is indeed verified by the multiple ranking test proposed by Bachhofer, Dunnett and Sobel [24]; also a separate *F*-test performed on the simulated data shows that the three policies compared here are significantly different in a statistical sense.

These results tend to confirm our earlier result that the optimal control solution (17) derived from mean squared deviation criterion contains sources of instability associated with the maximal characteristic root. Note that the first best policy (i.e. Policy 2) has not only the lowest variance of income ($\hat{\text{var}}\, y$) but also the lowest expected level of income (mean $\lvert y \rvert$), whereas the third best policy (i.e. Policy 3 derived from the optimal control model) has the highest variance and highest expected level of income. It is clear that control models even in the simpler form considered here show a high degree of sensitivity to variations in either the structural parameters or the distribution characteristics of the random process underlying the system. If anything, this suggests a note of caution to applying dynamic control policies within an infinite-horizon model without performing any comparative stability tests.

4. Concluding Remarks

The sensitivity analyses applied here to two different econometric models, one linear and the other non-linear, show very clearly two points of contrast. First, the non-linear model estimated by single-equation least squares appears to be quite stable in its two structural coefficients that determine the convergence of the cobweb-type cycles, even when the simultaneity links are introduced; the linear model, however, contains zones of explosive oscillations and instability, unless the initial conditions of the system could be so determined and manipulated that one switches from one stable zone to another. Second, the design of economic policy must consider the terms of trade between short-run and long-run fluctuations in the model, particularly when optimal controls are solved for in the model. This is shown by the non-linear model which never explodes, since to a large measure the price fluctuations in the model are geared around the long-run stationary price determined outside the model; the linear multiplier-accelerator model, however, is not geared to any such long-run stationary income levels. It seems that the problem of linkage between short-run and long-run policy models is yet to be explored in the theory of optimum economic policy. Until then there would be no satisfactory empirical way of testing the prescriptions of optimal growth and stabilisation theories.

References

[1] FROMM, G. and P. J. TAUBMAN, *Policy Simulations with an Econometric Model*, (Amsterdam: North-Holland/ Washington, D.C.: Brookings Institution, 1968).

[2] KURZ, M., 'The General Instability of a Class of Competitive Growth Processes', *Review of Economic Studies*, XXXV (1968) 155–74.

[3] LIVIATAN, N. and SAMUELSON, P. A., 'Notes on Turnpikes: Stable and Unstable', *Journal of Economic Theory*, I (1969) 454–75.

[4] MORISHIMA, M., *The Theory of Economic Growth*, (Oxford: Clarendon Press, 1969).

[5] STONE, R., ed., *A Programme for Growth*, Vol. V: The Model and its Environment, (Cambridge, Mass.: M.I.T. Press, 1964).

[6] SENGUPTA, J. K. and THORBECKE, E., 'Employment Response in an Input-Output Framework under Technological Change', Paper presented at the Fifth International Conference on Input-Output Techniques held in Geneva, 11–15 January 1971.

[7] SENGUPTA, J. K., *Adaptive Control in Models of Optimum Economic Growth*, Unpublished manuscript, 1970.

[8] UZAWA, H., 'An Optimal Fiscal Policy in an Aggregative Model of Economic Growth', in *The Theory and Design of Economic Development*, ed. I. Adelman and E. Thorbecke, (Baltimore: Johns Hopkins Press, 1966).

[9] PONTRYAGIN, L. S., *et al.*, *The Mathematical Theory of Optimal Processes*, (New York: Interscience Publishers, 1962).

[10] ARROW, K. J. and KURZ, M., *The Public Investment, the Rate of Return and Optimal Fiscal Policy*, (Baltimore: Johns Hopkins Press, 1970).

[11] GALE, D. and SUTHERLAND, W. R., 'Analysis of a One-good Model of Economic Development', in *Mathematics of the Decision Sciences*, Part 2, ed. G. B. Dantzig and A. F. Veinott, (Providence, R.I.: American Mathematical Society, 1968).

[12a] GOREUX, L. M., *Cocoa: Simulation of Stabilization Policies*, Unpublished manuscript. I.B.R.D., 11 February 1969.

[12b] GOREUX, L. M., *Price Stabilization Policies in World Markets for Primary Commodities: an Application to Cocoa*, Paper presented to the Conference of the International Association of Agricultural Economists, Summer, 1970.

[13] NAYLOR, T. H., WERTZ, K. and WONNACOTT, T., 'Some Methods for evaluating the Effects of Economic Policies using Simulation Experiments', *Review of International Statistical Institute*, XXXVI (1968) 184–200.

[14] WEYMAR, H., *The Dynamics of the World Cocoa Market*, (Cambridge, Mass.: M.I.T. Press, 1969).

[15] FOX, K. A., *Econometric Analysis for Public Policy*, (Ames, Iowa: Iowa State University Press, 1958).

[16a] FORRESTER, J. E., *Industrial Dynamics*, (Cambridge, Mass.: M.I.T. Press, 1961).

[16b] MEADOWS, D. L., *The Dynamics of Commodity Production Cycles: a Dynamic Cobweb Theorem*, Unpublished Ph.D. Dissertation, Sloane School, M.I.T., Cambridge, 1969.

[17] HICKS, J. R., *A Contribution to the Theory of the Trade Cycle*, (Oxford: Clarendon Press, 1950).

[18] HOWREY, E. P., 'Stabilization Policy in Linear Stochastic Systems', Mimeo report, Econometric Research Program, Princeton University, 1966.

[19] PHILLIPS, A. W., 'Stabilization Policy in a Closed Economy', *Economic Journal*, LXIX (1954), 290–323.

[20] SENGUPTA, J. K., 'Optimal Stabilization Policy with a Quadratic Criterion Function', *Review of Economic Studies*, XXXVII (1970) 127–45.

[21] THEIL, H., *Optimal Decision Rules for Government and Industry*, (Amsterdam: North-Holland, 1964).

[22] AOKI, M., *Optimization of Stochastic Systems*, (New York: Academic Press, 1967).

[23] NEUDECKER, H. and VAN DE PANNE, C., 'Note on the Asymptotic Standard Errors of Latent Roots of Econometric Equation Systems', *Review of International Statistical Institute*, XXXIV (1966) 43–7.

[24] BECHOFER, R. E., DUNNETT, C. W. and SOBEL, M., 'A Two-Sample Multiple Decision Procedure for ranking Means of Normal Populations with a Common Unknown Variance', *Biometrika*, XLI (1954) 170–6.

6 A Macro Model of the Economy for the Explanation of Trend and Business Cycle with Applications to India

BY GERHARD TINTNER,
GOPAL KADEKODI AND
M. V. RAMA SASTRY*

This is in a sense a continuation of some work undertaken some years ago in an effort to explain both the trend and the business cycle in the United States.[1] We propose to construct a dynamic model for this purpose.

Let us consider the following dynamic system

$$\mathbf{y}_t = \mathbf{A}\mathbf{y}_{t-1} + \mathbf{B}\mathbf{z}_t + \mathbf{C}\mathbf{z}_{t-1} + \mathbf{u}_t$$

where $\mathbf{y}_t$, $\mathbf{z}_t$ are column vectors with n and m components; $\mathbf{A}$ is a constant $n \times n$ matrix; $\mathbf{B}$ and $\mathbf{C}$ are $n \times m$ matrices. The column vector $\mathbf{u}_t$ of order n represents disturbances with the following properties

$$E(\mathbf{u}_t) = 0, \qquad E(\mathbf{u}_t'\mathbf{u}_t) = \Sigma, \qquad E(\mathbf{u}_s'\mathbf{u}_t) = 0 \quad (t \neq s)$$

This system might be interpreted as a simple version of reduced form equations.[2]

* Gerhard Tintner, Institut für Oekonometrie, Technische Hochscule, Wien; Gopal Kadekodi, Institute of Economic Growth, Dehli University; M. V. Rama Sastry, School of Business, Chico State College, Chico, California. Research was supported by the National Science Foundation, Washington, D.C.

[1] See: Tintner [27], [28] and [29]. See also: Baumol [4].

[2] See: Basmann [3], Christ [6], Fisher [8], Fisk [9], Goldberger [12], Gruber [14], Hood and Koopmans [15], Johnston [16], Klein [18], Leser [19], Malinvaud [20], Menges [22], Tinbergen [26], Tintner [30] and Wold and Jureen [31].

Defining

$$\mathbf{x}_t = \begin{bmatrix} \mathbf{y}_{t-1} \\ \mathbf{z}_t \\ \mathbf{z}_{t-1} \end{bmatrix}$$

$$\mathbf{M} = [\mathbf{A}\ \mathbf{B}\ \mathbf{C}]$$

we can write our system as

$$\mathbf{y}_t = \mathbf{M}\mathbf{x}_t + \mathbf{u}_t$$

Maximum likelihood methods or, alternatively, the method of least squares [21] give the following estimates [2] [17]. Define

$$\mathbf{U} = \mathbf{y}_t\mathbf{x}_t'$$

$$\mathbf{V} = \mathbf{x}_t\mathbf{x}_t'$$

We derive for our estimate

$$\hat{\mathbf{M}} = [\hat{\mathbf{A}}\ \hat{\mathbf{B}}\ \hat{\mathbf{C}}] = \mathbf{U}\mathbf{V}^{-1}$$

The variance-covariance matrix of the disturbances is estimated by

$$\hat{\mathbf{\Sigma}} = (1/n)(\mathbf{y}_t - \hat{\mathbf{M}}\mathbf{x}_t)(\mathbf{y}_t - \hat{\mathbf{M}}\mathbf{x}_t)' = (1/n)(\mathbf{y}_t\mathbf{y}_t' - \hat{\mathbf{M}}\mathbf{V}\hat{\mathbf{M}}')$$

The variances and covariances of the estimates $\hat{\mathbf{M}}$ are given by:

$$\mathbf{\Sigma} \otimes \mathbf{V}^{-1}$$

where $\otimes$ is the Kronecker product [17] [12].

Stability of the system exists, if all the latent roots of $\mathbf{A}$ are in the unit circle. Consider the determinantal equation

$$|\mathbf{A} - L\mathbf{I}| = 0$$

where $\mathbf{I}$ is the unit matrix. Real roots of this equation give rise to exponential trends, complex roots to sinusoidal fluctuations, i.e. business cycles [1] [5] [11] [13] [23] [32].

Following Theil and Boot [25], we consider the case where the latent root is complex

$$L_k = p_k + iq_k$$

The variance of the absolute value of L_k is given by[3]

$$\sigma^2_{|L_k|} = \mathbf{K}'\mathbf{W}\mathbf{K}$$

[3] See also Anderson [2], Girshik [10], Narashimham [23], and Zellner and Theil [32].

Here

$$\mathbf{F} = \mathbf{A} - L_k\mathbf{I} = \mathbf{F}^* + \mathrm{i}\mathbf{F}^{**}$$

$$r = p/\sqrt{(p^2 + q^2)}, \qquad s = F/\sqrt{(p^2 + q^2)}$$

$$g_{hk} = \frac{(\sum F^*_{hh})F^*_{hk} + (\sum F^{**}_{hh})(F^{**}_{hk})}{(\sum F^*_{hh})^2 + (\sum F^{**}_{hh})^2}$$

$$h_{hk} = \frac{-(\sum F^{**}_{hh})(F^*_{hk}) + (\sum F^*_{hh})F^{**}_{hk}}{(\sum F^*_{hh})^2 + (\sum F^{**}_{hh})^2}$$

Subscripts denote cofactors of the matrices involved, and **W** is the covariance matrix of the estimate **M**, i.e. a partition of $\mathbf{\Sigma} \otimes \mathbf{V}^{-1}$.

$$\mathbf{K} = r\mathbf{G} + s\mathbf{H}$$

$$q = 0, \qquad \mathbf{K} = \mathbf{G}$$

We have applied the foregoing theory to some Indian data. We have been using yearly data from the period 1954–66. All data are converted into index numbers, 1954 = 100. Let X_{1t} be an index of agricultural production, real per capita. X_{2t} is the index of industrial production, real per capita. X_{3t} is the index of employment in manufacturing industry, per capita. X_{4t} is the index of government expenditure, real per capita. X_{5t} is the index of net imports, real per capita.

We find empirically the following linear dynamic relations between our variables

$$X_{1t} = \underset{}{448{\cdot}557} + \underset{(0{\cdot}322)}{0{\cdot}196X_{1t-1}} + \underset{(0{\cdot}270)}{0{\cdot}244X_{2t-1}} - \underset{(1{\cdot}827)}{4{\cdot}303X_{3t-1}}$$

$$+ \underset{(0{\cdot}186)}{0{\cdot}397X_{4t-1}} + \underset{(0{\cdot}016)}{0{\cdot}009X_{5t-1}}$$

$$R^2 = 0{\cdot}587$$

$$X_{2t} = 132{\cdot}860 + \underset{(0{\cdot}143)}{0{\cdot}322X_{1t-1}} + \underset{(0{\cdot}119)}{1{\cdot}261X_{2t-1}} - \underset{(0{\cdot}809)}{1{\cdot}930X_{3t-1}}$$

$$+ \underset{(0{\cdot}082)}{0{\cdot}112X_{4t-1}} - \underset{(0{\cdot}007)}{0{\cdot}006X_{5t-1}}$$

$$R^2 = 0{\cdot}994$$

$$X_{3t} = 97{\cdot}651 + \underset{(0\cdot119)}{0{\cdot}170X_{1t-1}} + \underset{(0\cdot100)}{0{\cdot}150X_{2t-1}} - \underset{(0\cdot675)}{0{\cdot}344X_{3t-1}}$$

$$+ \underset{(0\cdot069)}{0{\cdot}089X_{4t-1}} - \underset{(0\cdot006)}{0{\cdot}006X_{5t-1}}$$

$$R^2 = 0{\cdot}910$$

The variance-covariance matrix of the errors between the regression equations is given by

$$\mathbf{\Sigma} = \begin{bmatrix} 36{\cdot}460 & 2{\cdot}084 & 0{\cdot}384 \\ & 7{\cdot}154 & -0{\cdot}159 \\ & & 4{\cdot}972 \end{bmatrix}$$

The matrix:

$$\mathbf{A} = \begin{bmatrix} 0{\cdot}196 & 0{\cdot}244 & -4{\cdot}303 \\ 0{\cdot}322 & 1{\cdot}261 & -1{\cdot}929 \\ 0{\cdot}170 & 0{\cdot}150 & -0{\cdot}344 \end{bmatrix}$$

will evidently determine the dynamics of the system. Its largest latent root or characteristic value is

$$L_1 = 1{\cdot}0373$$

This is connected with an exponential trend increasing about 4 per cent each year. In order to test the absolute value of the root we construct the matrix

$$\mathbf{A} - L_1\mathbf{I} = \begin{bmatrix} -0{\cdot}841 & 0{\cdot}244 & -4{\cdot}303 \\ 0{\cdot}323 & 0{\cdot}224 & -1{\cdot}929 \\ 0{\cdot}170 & 0{\cdot}150 & -1{\cdot}381 \end{bmatrix}$$

The matrix of the cofactors of this matrix is

$$\mathbf{F} = \begin{bmatrix} -0{\cdot}020 & 0{\cdot}118 & 0{\cdot}010 \\ -0{\cdot}308 & 1{\cdot}893 & 0{\cdot}168 \\ 0{\cdot}493 & -3{\cdot}012 & -0{\cdot}267 \end{bmatrix}$$

Noting that the sum of the diagonal elements of this matrix is 1·606 we construct the matrix

$$\mathbf{G} = \begin{bmatrix} -0{\cdot}012 & 0{\cdot}073 & 0{\cdot}006 \\ -0{\cdot}192 & 1{\cdot}179 & 0{\cdot}105 \\ 0{\cdot}307 & -1{\cdot}875 & -0{\cdot}166 \end{bmatrix}$$

We find the variance of the absolute value of our largest root

$$\sigma^2_{L_1} = 0{\cdot}347$$

This corresponds to a standard error of 0·589. Hence the approximate 95 per cent limits of the root are 2·192 and −0·117.

The remaining roots of our matrix **A** are

$$L_2 = 0{\cdot}038 + 0{\cdot}780\mathrm{i}$$

and the corresponding conjugate root. This corresponds to a cycle length 7·95 years, which, however, is damped; the root can also be written as

$$L_2 = 0{\cdot}781(\cos 0{\cdot}780 + \mathrm{i} \sin 0{\cdot}780)$$

which shows that the amplitude of the fluctuations decreases by 21 per cent each year. We want to test again the modulus of the second root which is

$$|L_2| = 0{\cdot}781$$

From our data we find $r = 0{\cdot}048$, $s = 0{\cdot}999$. We have

$$\mathbf{A} - L_2\mathbf{I} = \begin{bmatrix} 0{\cdot}158 + 0{\cdot}79\mathrm{i} & 0{\cdot}244 & -4{\cdot}303 \\ 0{\cdot}322 & 1{\cdot}223 + 0{\cdot}79\mathrm{i} & -1{\cdot}929 \\ 0{\cdot}170 & 0{\cdot}150 & -0{\cdot}382 + 0{\cdot}79\mathrm{i} \end{bmatrix}$$

We write the matrix of cofactors of this last matrix as

$$\mathbf{F} = \mathbf{F}^* + \mathrm{i}\,\mathbf{F}^{**}$$

and derive the following matrices

$$\mathbf{F}^* = \begin{bmatrix} -1{\cdot}091 & -0{\cdot}203 & -0{\cdot}160 \\ -0{\cdot}552 & -0{\cdot}684 & 0{\cdot}018 \\ -5{\cdot}733 & -1{\cdot}081 & 0{\cdot}115 \end{bmatrix}$$

Note that the sum of the diagonal elements of this matrix is −1·660.

By the formulae given above we derive the matrices **G** and **H**

$$\mathbf{G} = \begin{bmatrix} 0{\cdot}644 & 0{\cdot}071 & 0{\cdot}080 \\ 0{\cdot}320 & 0{\cdot}310 & -0{\cdot}023 \\ 2{\cdot}995 & 0{\cdot}790 & 0{\cdot}046 \end{bmatrix}$$

$$\mathbf{H} = \begin{bmatrix} -0{\cdot}630 & -0{\cdot}166 & -0{\cdot}107 \\ -0{\cdot}342 & -0{\cdot}489 & -0{\cdot}002 \\ -3{\cdot}702 & -0{\cdot}473 & 0{\cdot}181 \end{bmatrix}$$

$$\mathbf{K} = \begin{bmatrix} -0{\cdot}601 & -0{\cdot}162 & -0{\cdot}103 \\ -0{\cdot}327 & -0{\cdot}477 & -0{\cdot}003 \\ 3{\cdot}555 & -0{\cdot}435 & 0{\cdot}183 \end{bmatrix}$$

The variance of the absolute value of our second root $|L_2| = 0{\cdot}791$ is given by

$$\sigma^2_{L_2} = 4{\cdot}292$$

hence its standard error is 2·071 and the approximate upper 95 per cent limit of the absolute value is 4·85. Again, instability cannot be ruled out.

References

[1] ADELMAN, I. and ADELMAN, F. L., 'The Dynamic Properties of the Klein-Goldberger Model', *Econometrica*, XXVII (October 1959) 596–625.

[2] ANDERSON, T. W., *An Introduction to Multivariate Statistical Analysis*, (New York: Wiley, 1958).

[3] BASMANN, R. L., 'A Generalized Classical Method of Linear Estimation of Coefficients in a Structural Equation', *Econometrica*, XXV (January 1957) 77–83.

[4] BAUMOL, W., *Economic Dynamics*, 2nd ed. (New York: Macmillan, 1959).

[5] BELLMAN, R. E., *Introduction to Matrix Analysis*, (New York: McGraw-Hill, 1960).

[6] CHRIST, C. F., *Econometric Models and Methods*, (New York: Wiley, 1966).

[7] CONLISK, J., 'The Equilibrium Covariance Matrix of Dynamic Econometric Models', *Journal of the American Statistical Association*, LXIV (March 1969) 277–9.

[8] FISHER, F. M., *The Identification Problem in Econometrics*, (New York: McGraw-Hill 1966).

[9] FISK, P. R., *Stochastically Dependent Equations*, (New York: Hafner, 1967).

[10] GIRSHIK, A. M., 'On the Sampling Theory of Roots of Determinental Equations', *Annals of Mathematical Statistics*, X (1939) 203–24.

[11] GOLDBERGER, A. S., *Impact Multipliers and Dynamic Properties of the Klein-Goldberger Model*, (Amsterdam: North-Holland, 1959).

[12] GOLDBERGER, A. S., *Econometric Theory*, (New York: Wiley, 1964).

[13] GOLDBERGER, A. S., NAGAR, A. L. and ODEH, H. S., 'The Covariance Matrices of Reduced-Form Coefficients and of Forecasts for a Structural Econometric Model', *Econometrica*, XXIX (1961) 556–73.

[14] GRUBER, J., *Oekonometrische Modelle des Cowles-Commission Typs: Bau und Interpretation*, (Hamburg: Parey, 1968).

[15] HOOD, W. C. and KOOPMANS, T. C., ed. *Studies in Econometric Methods*, (New York: Wiley, 1953).

[16] JOHNSTON, J., *Econometric Methods*, (New York: McGraw-Hill 1963).

[17] KENDALL, M. G. and STUART, A., *The Advanced Theory of Statistics*, (New York: Hafner, 1966) III.

[18] KLEIN, L. R., *An Introduction to Econometrics*, (Englewood Cliffs, N.J.: Prentice-Hall, 1962).

[19] LESER, C. E. V., *Econometric Techniques and Problems*, (New York: Hafner, 1966).

[20] MALINVAUD, E., *Statistical Methods in Econometrics*, (Amsterdam: North-Holland, 1966).

[21] MANN, H. B. and WALD, A., 'On the Statistical Treatment of Linear Stochastic Difference Equations', *Econometrica*, XI (1943) 173–230.

[22] MENGES, G., *Oekonometrie*, (Wiesbaden: Betriebs-Wirtschaflicher Verlag, 1961).

[23] NARASHIMHAM, G. V. L., 'The Asymptotic Theory of Certain Characteristic Roots of Econometric Equation Systems', *Econometrica*, XXXVI (Supplement, 1968), 95–7.

[24] THEIL, H., *Economic Forecasts and Policy*, 2nd ed. (Amsterdam, North Holland, 1961).

[25] THEIL, H. and BOOT, J. C. G., 'The Final Form of Econometric Equation Systems', *Review of the International Statistical Institute*, XXX (1962) 136–52.

[26] TINBERGEN, J., *Econometrics*, (Philadelphia: Blakiston, 1951).

[27] TINTNER, G., 'A Simple Theory of Business Fluctuations', *Econometrica*, X (July–October 1942) 317–20.

[28] TINTNER, G., 'The Simple Theory of Business Fluctuations: A Tentative Verification', *Review of Economics and Statistics*, XXVI (1944) 148–57.

[29] TINTNER, G., 'Une Theorie 'Simple' des Fluctuations Economiques', *Revue d'économie politique*, LVII (1947), 209–15.

[30] TINTNER, G., *Econometrics*, (New York: Wiley, 1952).

[31] WOLD, H. O. and JUREEN, L., *Demand Analysis*, (New York: Wiley, 1953).

[32] ZELLNER, A. and THEIL, H., 'Three-Stage Least Squares', *Econometrica*, XXX (1962) 54–78.

7 The Quality of Quantitative Economic Policy-making when Targets and Costs of Change are Mis-specified

BY ARNOLD ZELLNER*

1. Introduction

In a series of well-known works [3], [4], [5], [6], Tinbergen has made pioneering and outstanding contributions to the theory and application of quantitative economic policy-making (Q.E.P.). Tinbergen's approach to Q.E.P. involves the following elements: (*a*) a criterion or welfare function that depends on certain economic variables, (*b*) a classification of variables into categories, target and non-target endogenous variables and instrumental and non-instrumental exogenous variables, (*c*) an econometric model involving relationships for variables and (*d*) boundary conditions for selected variables. Within this framework, which resembles closely the framework of modern control theory, Tinbergen provided simple, operational procedures for solving for values of policy instrument variables at a time when modern control theory was in its infancy.

In addition to structuring and providing solutions to Q.E.P. problems, Tinbergen's work importantly involves consideration of the sensitivity of policy solutions to possible errors in

* Research financed in part by the National Science Foundation under grant GS-2347 and by income from the H. G. B. Alexander Fund, Graduate School of Business, University of Chicago. This paper was written when the author was Visiting Ford Research Professor in the Department of Economics, University of California at Berkeley. Some of the material in this paper was presented to the Econometrics Seminar, Stanford University. Several comments of T. W. Anderson were particularly helpful.

formulating welfare functions and economic models. He is quite aware of the many difficulties in formulating satisfactory welfare functions to be used in Q.E.P. With regard to the relation of welfare functions of individuals and of policy-makers, he writes, '. . . there may be a certain degree of similarity between individual welfare functions and that of the policy-maker. The more democratic is the community, the more will the citizens be able to further this similarity. . . .' [5, p. 14]. Also, he recognises possible inconsistencies between short-run and long-run targets, mentions a possible reconciliation by instrument differentiation, and then states, 'If, however, no differentiation is possible, the only possibility is a 'weighing of targets' or, in practical terms, a compromise' [5, p. 137]. Further, in a pragmatic fashion, he writes, 'For practical purposes it will often be desirable and sometimes possible to specify the mathematical form of the utility functions in such a way as to make them workable. For modest ranges of the relevant variables simple mathematical forms will always be acceptable as approximations. . . .' [3, p. 52]. He goes on to discuss the use of a quadratic approximation. As regards errors associated with econometric models, he explicitly considers errors in estimated parameter values and in functional forms of relationships [4, pp. 59–63]. Taken together, these considerations constitute a remarkable contribution to the problem of assessing the *robustness* of Q.E.P., a vital subject that has not received much attention in the literature.

In the present paper, attention is focused on several problems in which there is uncertainty about the values of parameters in a quadratic criterion function. That there may be uncertainty about the values of such parameters is emphasised by van Eijk and Sandee, who write:

> In principle, the coefficients of a welfare function can be estimated only by interviewing the policy-makers. They would have to answer a series of questions about the marginal rates of substitution for all target variables and in different situations. For the time being, however, a genuine interviewing of policy-makers is impossible. This means that interviews must be imaginary. . . . In short, the presumable outcome of a real interview must be forecast. [7, p. 4].

This quotation suggests that there may be considerable uncertainty about the values of parameters in policy-makers' welfare functions, even abstracting from aggregation problems and the relation of policy-makers' welfare functions to those of private citizens. Herein, for simple quadratic criterion functions, that Tinbergen has indicated may serve as useful approximations in certain instances,[1] the effects of errors in assigning target values and in assessing the cost of changing policy instruments are evaluated analytically.[2] Target values and cost of change are emphasised because it is believed that these are key considerations in Q.E.P.[3] In fact, Tinbergen points out that, 'the relevant starting point to any quantitative policy . . . is the set of target values. . . .' [5, p. 133]. Some of the issues analysed below are the following: (*a*) what are some well-defined conditions in which there may be uncertainty about the parameters of simple quadratic criterion functions? (*b*) can errors in assigning target values be offset by errors in assessing the cost of changing policy instrument variables? (*c*) do overly ambitious policy-makers who overstate target values and underestimate cost of change fare better in terms of expected utility than do more conservative policy-makers who understate target values and overestimate cost of change? These questions, and others, are considered below in connection with some problems in Q.E.P. involving control of regression processes.

2. Criterion Functions and the Control of a Simple Regression Process

In this section, an example illustrating uncertainties that can arise concerning values of a criterion function's parameters is presented. Then an analysis of the effects of such uncertainties on the solution to a one-period Q.E.P. problem is reported.

[1] See [9] for some results on the effects of departures from the quadratic form.

[2] In particular cases, sensitivity analysis can of course be performed numerically.

[3] In [8], the effects of departures from temporally independent preferences are analysed in a deterministic framework with extremely interesting findings.

Let the criterion function for individual i be the following quadratic loss function[4]

$$L_i = (y_i - a_i)^2 + c_i(x - x_0)^2 \qquad (i = 1, 2, \ldots, N) \tag{1}$$

where y_i is an endogenous variable, a_i is the ith individual's target value for y_i, x is a policy instrument or control variable that a policy-maker controls, x_0 is the known initial value for x, and c_i is a positive parameter. If we attach a weight,[5] w_i, to individual i's loss, L_i, with $0 \leq w_i$ and $\sum_{i=1}^{N} w_i = 1$, and assume that it is appropriate to sum individuals' weighted losses to obtain total loss, L'_T, we obtain

$$L'_T = (y - \bar{a})^2 - 2(y - \bar{a})\sigma_{wa} + c(x - x_0)^2 + (1/N)\sum(\delta y_i - \delta a_i)^2 + \sum \delta w_i[(\delta y_i - \delta a_i)^2 + 2\,\delta y_i(y - \bar{a})] \tag{2}$$

where summations extend from $i = 1$ to $i = N$, $y = \sum y_i/N$, $\bar{a} = \sum a_i/N$, $\delta y_i = y_i - y$, $\delta a_i = a_i - \bar{a}$, $\delta w_i = w_i - \overline{w}$, $\overline{w} = \sum w_i/N = 1/N$, $c = \sum w_i c_i$, and $\sigma_{wa} = \sum \delta w_i \delta a_i$. If we assume a simple regression connecting y_i and x, that is, $y_i = \beta x + u_i$ $(i = 1, 2, \ldots, N)$, then

$$y = \beta x + u \tag{3}$$

where $u = \sum u_i/N$. Since $\delta y_i = y_i - y = u_i - u$ does not depend on x, we can express (2) as follows

$$L'_T = \left[y - \bar{a}\left(1 + \frac{\sigma_{wa}}{\bar{a}}\right)\right]^2 + c(x - x_0)^2 + \varepsilon \tag{4}$$

where ε represents all other terms and is such that its mathematical expectation does not depend on the value of the control variable x. Thus we can write

$$L_T = L'_T - \varepsilon = (y - a)^2 + c(x - x_0)^2 \tag{5}$$

where $a = \bar{a}(1 + \sigma_{wa}/\bar{a})$ and $c = \sum w_i c_i$.

[4] The ith individual's utility, U_i, can be regarded as given by $U_i = -L_i + K_i$, where K_i is an arbitrary constant.

[5] Tinbergen writes, 'Some of the controversies between communist policies and Western policies may be expressed in terms of the weight given to the interests of various social groups constituting society. . . . [6, p. 76].

In this problem, the policy-maker's criterion function is assumed to be (5) and (3) is his simple economic model for y. In Q.E.P., the policy-maker must assign numerical values to the parameters a and c of (5). The value of a depends on the mean, a, of individuals' targets, and the covariance σ_{wa} between individuals' weights and target values. The parameter c in (5) is a weighted average of the individual c_is. Since the policy-maker generally does not know the values of the a_is and the c_is and since there is often considerable uncertainty about the appropriate w_is to employ, it is to be expected that the values assigned to a and to c in (5) will generally depart from 'true' values. To allow for such a departure, we write the loss function that the policy-maker actually uses as follows

$$L = (y - k_1 a)^2 + k_2 c(x - x_0)^2 \tag{6}$$

where the parameters k_1 and k_2 have been introduced to allow for errors in assigning values to a and c. Of course, if $k_1 = k_2 = 1$, there are no errors. In what follows, we shall assume k_1, $k_2 > 0$ and a, $c > 0$.

If a policy-maker minimises the mathematical expectation of L in (6) with respect to x, it is of interest to determine how his minimising value for x, say x^*, depends on the values of k_1 and k_2 and the extent to which it departs from the optimal value of x, say x^0, obtained with $k_1 = k_2 = 1$ in (6). Also, it is relevant to determine how $E(L_T \mid x = x^*)$, with L_T given in (5), depends on k_1 and k_2 and the extent to which it differs from minimal expected loss, namely $E(L_T \mid x = x^0)$. The analysis of these problems will be carried forward initially under the assumption that the value of β in (3) is known and positive. Then the case in which β's value is unknown will be analysed.

Analysis When Value of β is Known ($\beta > 0$)

In (3), we assume $Eu = 0$ and $Eu^2 = \sigma^2 < \infty$. Then the mathematical expectation of the loss function in (6) is

$$EL = (\beta x - k_1 a)^2 + k_2 c(x - x_0)^2 + \sigma^2 \tag{7}$$

The value of x, say x^*, that minimises expected loss in (7) is given by

$$x^* = (k_1 a/\beta + k_2 v x_0)/(1 + k_2 v) \tag{8}$$

where $v = c/\beta^2$. It is seen that x^* is a weighted average of k_1a/β and x_0 with weights 1 and k_2v, respectively. In addition, k_1a/β is the value of x that provides a minimal value to $(\beta x - k_1a)^2$, the first term on the right-hand side of (7), while x_0 is the value of x that gives a minimal value to the second term on the right-hand side of (7). Thus x^* is a weighted average of quantities, k_1a/β and x_0, that minimise individual components of expected loss.

For comparison with x^*, the optimal setting for x, say x^0, is the value of x that minimises (7) when $k_1 = k_2 = 1$. When $k_1 = k_2 = 1$, (7) is identical to (5), the true loss function. The optimal value for x is given by

$$\begin{aligned} x^0 &= (a/\beta + vx_0)/(1 + v) \\ &= x_0 - (\beta x_0 - a)/\beta(1 + v) \end{aligned} \tag{9}$$

From the first line of (9), it is seen that x^0 is a weighted average of a/β and x_0. Since x^* can differ from x^0, given $k_1, k_2 \neq 1$, use of $x = x^*$ can, of course, result in suboptimal Q.E.P., except in situations in which errors in assigning the target value and the value of the cost of change parameter happen to be offsetting (see below).

With respect to x^* in (8) and x^0 in (9), the following results are of interest.

(*a*) With $a/\beta > 0$, from (8) $\partial x^*/\partial k_1 > 0$; that is, with all other quantities held constant, x^* will be greater in value the larger is k_1.

(*b*) From (8), $\partial x^*/\partial k_2 = v(x_0 - k_1a/\beta)/(1 + k_2v)^2$. Then $\partial x^*/\partial k_2 > 0$ if $x_0 > k_1a/\beta$ and $\partial x^*/\partial k_2 < 0$ if $x_0 < k_1a/\beta$. The dependence of the algebraic sign of this derivative on x_0 and k_1a/β can be appreciated by remembering that x^* is a weighted average of x_0 and k_1a/β with weights k_2v and 1, respectively. Thus, when $x_0 > k_1a/\beta$, increasing k_2, an increase in the weight given to x_0, increases x^* while when $x_0 < k_1a/\beta$, increasing k_2 results in a decrease in x^*.

(*c*) With $k_1 = 1$, no error in the target value, overstatement of the cost of change parameter, i.e. $k_2 > 1$, results in x^* being closer to x_0 than is x^0, given $a/\beta \neq x_0$, while with having $k_2 < 1$ results in x^* being farther from x_0 than is x^0.

(*d*) With $k_2 = 1$, no error in assessing cost of change, $x^* > x^0$ if $k_1 > 1$ and $x^* < x^0$ if $k_1 < 1$.

(*e*) With $a, \beta > 0$, if $k_2/k_1 = 1$, i.e. equally proportionate over- or understatement of target value and cost of change, then $x^* > x^0$ if $k_2, k_1 > 1$ and $x^* < x^0$ if $k_1, k_2 < 1$.

(*f*) Values of k_1 and k_2, not necessarily equal to one, can be found such that $x^* = x^0$. Such values are obtained by equating (8) and (9) to yield

$$k_1 = -k_2 v(\beta x_0 - a)/a(1 + v) + \beta x^0/a \qquad (10a)$$

or

$$\delta_1 = -\delta_2 \phi \gamma \qquad (10b)$$

where

$$\delta_1 = k_1 - 1, \qquad \delta_2 = k_2 - 1,$$

$$\phi = v/(1 + v) \qquad \text{and} \qquad \gamma = (\beta x_0 - a)/a \qquad (10c)$$

Since we assumed $k_1, k_2 > 0$ and $\delta_1, \delta_2 > -1$. The relations (10a) and (10b) indicate that errors in assessing the target value and cost of change can be offsetting. With $\gamma > 0$, *an overstatement of the cost of change, $\delta_2 > 0$, must be accompanied by an understatement of the target value, $\delta_1 < 0$, for x^* to equal x^0. With $\gamma < 0$, for minimal expected loss to be experienced, i.e. $x^* = x^0$, δ_1 and δ_2 must have the same algebraic signs which means joint over- or understatement of target value and cost of change.*[6]

Having investigated several features of the dependence of x^* on the values of k_1 and k_2, we now turn to a consideration of how the expectation of the 'true' loss function in (5) depends on k_1 and k_2 when $x = x^*$ with x^* shown in (8). After some straightforward algebra, we have

$$E(L_T \mid x = x^*) = \frac{a^2\gamma^2}{1 + v}\left[\left(\frac{w + z}{1 + z}\right)^2 + v\right] + \sigma^2 \qquad (11a)$$

where $v = c/\beta^2$, $\gamma = (\beta x_0 - a)/a$, $w = \delta_1/\gamma$, $z = v\delta_2/(1 + v)$, $\delta_1 = k_1 - 1$ and $\delta_2 = k_2 - 1$. Since $w = z = 0$ when

[6] The dependence of these results on the algebraic sign of $\gamma = (\beta x_0 - a)/a$, can be appreciated if it is noted that x^0 is a weighted average of x_0 and a/β, with weights v and 1, respectively, while x^* is a weighted average of x_0 and $k_1 a/\beta$, with weights $k_2 v$ and 1, respectively. Thus, for example, if $a/\beta > x_0 (\gamma < 0)$ and $k_1 > 1$, k_2 must be less than 1 for x^0 to be equal to x^*. If $a/\beta < x_0 (\gamma > 0)$ and $k_1 > 1$, k_2 must be greater than 1 for x^0 to equal x^*.

$k_1 = k_2 = 1$ (or $\delta_1 = \delta_2 = 0$), minimal expected loss is

$$E(L_T \mid x = x^0) = a^2\gamma^2 v/(1 + v) + \sigma^2 \tag{11b}$$

A condition on w and z in (11a) sufficient to achieve minimal expected loss shown in (11b), is $w = -z$, which is the same as (10b). Further, expected loss in (11a) will be constant for values

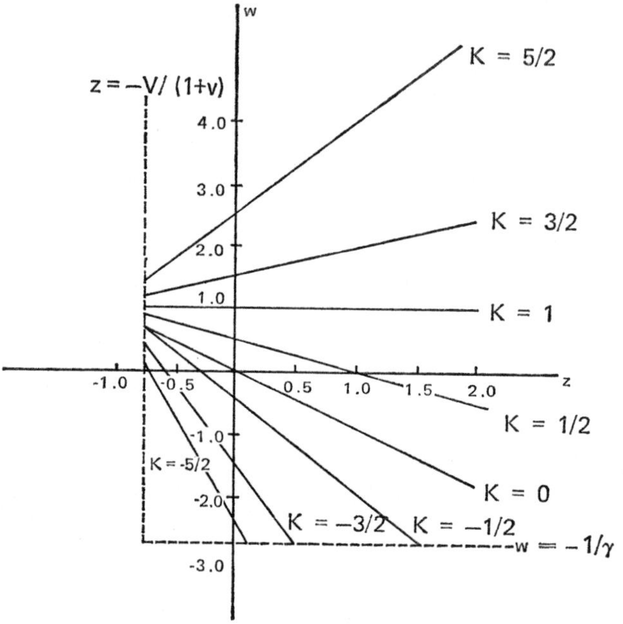

FIG. 7.1. *Contours Associated with* (11a)*

*In the figure it is assumed that $\gamma = (\beta x_o - a)/a > 0$.

of w and z satisfying $(w + z)/(1 + z) = K$, where K is a constant; that is

$$w = K + (K - 1)z \tag{12a}$$

or

$$\delta_1 = \gamma K + (K - 1)\gamma v \delta_2/(1 + v) \tag{12b}$$

with $w > -1/\gamma$ and $z > -v/(1 + v)$. The contours associated with (11a) are straight lines – see Figure 7.1. When $K = 0$, (12a) yields $w = -z$, the locus such that minimal expected loss is experienced. As K's absolute value increases, expected loss increases. Note that for $K < 1$, (12a) yields negatively sloped iso-loss lines while for $K > 1$ the slopes of these lines is positive. Thus the trade-off between z and w required to keep expected loss constant changes in nature as K goes through the value 1.

Next, we consider the behaviour of expected loss in (11a) for values of δ_1 and δ_2 such that $|\delta_1| = |\delta_2| = \delta$. Here, equal absolute proportionate errors in the target value and in the cost-of-change parameter's value are assumed. Under this condition we wish to compare expected losses for the following four cases.

Case 1 $\delta_1, \delta_2 > 0$; target and cost of change overstated, denoted (0, 0)

Case 2 $\delta_1 < 0$ and $\delta_2 > 0$; target understated and cost of change overstated, denoted (U, 0)

Case 3 $\delta_1, \delta_2 < 0$; target and cost of change understated, denoted by (U, U)

Case 4 $\delta_1 > 0$, $\delta_2 < 0$; target overstated and the cost of change understated, denoted (0, U)

For these four cases, with $|\delta_1| = |\delta_2| = \delta$, expected losses from (11a) were compared[7] with the following results for the six distinct pairwise comparisons where P = 'preferred to':

(1) Case 1 (0, 0) *v* Case 3 (U, U):	(0, 0)P(U, U)
(2) Case 2 (U, 0) *v* Case 4 (0, U):	(U, 0)P(0, U)
(3) Case 1 (0, 0) *v* Case 2 (U, 0):	(0, 0)P(U, 0) if $\gamma < 0$
	(U, 0)P(0, 0) if $\gamma > 0$
(4) Case 1 (0, 0) *v* Case 4 (0, U):	(0, 0)P(0, U) if $\gamma < \delta$
	(0, U)P(0, 0) if $\gamma > \delta$
(5) Case 2 (U, 0) *v* Case 3 (U, U):	(U, 0)P(U, U) if $\gamma > -\delta$
	(U, U)P(U, 0) if $\gamma < -\delta$
(6) Case 3 (U, U) *v* Case 4 (0, U):	(U, U)P(0, U) if $\gamma < 0$
	(0, U)P(U, U) if $\gamma > 0$

It is seen that in the first two comparisons, unqualified results are obtained. In comparison (1) equal proportionate overstatement of target and cost of change is preferred to equal

[7] This involves consideration of the quantity $(w + z)^2/(1 + z)^2$.

proportionate understatement of these two items. Heuristically, overstating the cost of change tends to prevent x from being varied, thereby saving on costs of change, and to prevent y from moving to an overstated target, thereby tending to keep closer to the true value. With equal proportionate understatement, x tends to be changed too much and y tends to be brought close to an understated target value. Excessive change in x and being away from the true target inflate expected loss.

In comparison (2), understating the target and overstating the cost of change, (U, 0), is preferred to overstating the target and understating the cost of change (0, U), when absolute proportionate errors are all equal in magnitude. Note that for (U, 0), understatement of the target and overstatement of cost of change tend to keep cost of change low. In the case of (0, U), an overstatement of the target and understatement of the cost of change, both errors tend to produce a large change in x, resulting in high costs of change, and to bring y close to a mistakenly high target, thereby raising the cost of being off target.

In four of the comparisons, (3)–(6), results depend on the initial conditions, as reflected in the value of $\gamma = (\beta x_0 - a)/a$, or the relation of the relative magnitudes of γ and δ, the absolute size of the proportionate errors. From the results in (1)–(6) above, we can make the following preference orderings.

Condition on $\gamma = (\beta x_0 - a)/a$	*Preference ordering*
$\gamma < -\delta$	(0, 0)P(U, U)P(U, 0)P(0, U)
$-\delta < \gamma < 0$	(0, 0)P(U, 0)P(U, U)P(0, U)
$0 < \gamma < \delta$	(U, 0)P(0, 0)P(0, U)P(U, U)
$\delta < \gamma$	(U, 0)P(0, U)P(0, 0)P(U, U)

We see that when $\gamma < 0$, that is $x_0 < a/\beta$, *the worst pair of errors to make is overstatement of the target and understatement of the cost of change*. When $\gamma > 0$, that is $x_0 > a/\beta$, *the worst pair of errors is understatement of the target and understatement of the cost of change*. In both these cases the error in assigning a target value involves a tendency to change the control variable too much (in the upward direction in the first instance and in the downward direction in the second). This tendency toward too much change is reinforced by the underassessment of the cost of change with the result that we end up, on average, off target and experience excessive costs of change.

For $\gamma < 0$, *the least damaging pair of errors is overstatement of the target accompanied by overstatement of the cost of change, errors that are offsetting. Similarly for* $\gamma > 0$, *that is* $x_0 > a/\beta$, *understatement of the target and overstatement of the cost of change tend to be offsetting errors and are least serious.* Note that with $\gamma > 0$, understatement of the target means adopting a target value that is farther from βx_0 than is appropriate; similarly when $\gamma < 0$ an overstated target value is farther from βx_0 than is appropriate. Both of these errors make for excessive movement of the control variable which is offset by the overstatement of the cost of change.

Analysis when Values of β and σ are Unknown

When the values of the parameters β and σ, involved in (2.3), are unknown and must be estimated, it is known that such uncertainty affects the optimal setting for the control variable x – see, for example, [1], [2], [9] and [10, ch. 11]. Assume that past sample data on y and x are available that have been generated by a simple normal regression model

$$y_t = \beta x_t + u_t \qquad (t = 1, 2, \ldots, T) \tag{13}$$

We assume that the u_ts are normally and independently distributed, each with zero mean and common standard deviation, σ. If we have little information about the values of β and σ and represent this state of ignorance by the following prior p.d.f.[8]

$$p(\beta, \sigma) \propto 1/\sigma \qquad (-\infty < \beta < \infty, 0 < \sigma < \infty) \tag{14}$$

where $\propto$ denotes proportionality, the predictive p.d.f. for $y \equiv y_{T+1}$ is well known to be in the following univariate Student t form – see, for example, [10, ch. 3]

$$p(y \mid \mathbf{y}) = \frac{\Gamma[(\nu+1)/2]}{\Gamma(\frac{1}{2})\Gamma(\nu/2)} (g/\nu)^{1/2} \{1 + (g/\nu)(y - x\hat{\beta})^2\}^{-(\nu+1)/2} \tag{15}$$

[8] In (14) β and $\log \sigma$ are assumed independently and uniformly distributed, a representation of ignorance about the values of the parameters that has been employed extensively in the literature. The analysis presented below can be readily generalised to cases in which an informative prior p.d.f. in the 'normal-gamma' form is utilised.

where $\mathbf{y}' = (y_1, y_2, \ldots, y_T)$ denotes the given sample information, $x \equiv x_{T+1}$, the control variable's value in period $T + 1$, $\nu = T - 1$, $\hat{\beta} = \sum_{t=1}^{T} x_t y_t / \sum_{t=1}^{T} x_t^2$, $g^{-1} = s^2(1 + x^2/\sum_{t=1}^{T} x_t^2)$, $\nu s^2 = \sum_{t=1}^{T} (y_t - \hat{\beta} x_t)^2$, and Γ denotes the gamma function.

The mean and variance of the p.d.f. for y in (15) exist for $\nu > 2$ and are given by

$$E(y \mid \mathbf{y}, x) = x\hat{\beta}$$

and

$$\operatorname{var}(y \mid \mathbf{y}, x) = \nu s^2 \left(1 + x^2 \bigg/ \sum_{t=1}^{T} x_t^2\right) \bigg/ (\nu - 2) \tag{16}$$

It is to be noted that both the mean and variance in (16) depend on $x \equiv x_{T+1}$.

With the above results set forth, we can now use (15) and (16) to obtain the mathematical expectation of the loss function in (6), namely

$$\begin{aligned} EL &= \operatorname{var}(y \mid \mathbf{y}, x) + (k_1 a - \hat{\beta} x)^2 + k_2 c(x - x_0)^2 \\ &= \bar{s}^2(1 + x^2/m) + (k_1 a - \hat{\beta} x)^2 + k_2 c(x - x_0)^2 \end{aligned} \tag{17}$$

where $\bar{s}^2 = \nu s^2/(\nu - 2)$, $m = \sum_{t=1}^{T} x_t^2$, and $x_0 \equiv x_T$. In the second line of (17), the first term will be minimised if $x = 0$, the second if $x = k_1 a/\hat{\beta}$ and the third if $x = x_0$. The value of x that minimises (17), say x^+, is a weighted average of these three quantities given by

$$\begin{aligned} x^+ &= [\hat{\beta}^2(k_1 a/\hat{\beta}) + k_2 c x_0]/(\hat{\beta}^2 + k_2 c + \bar{s}^2/m) \\ &= (k_1 a'/\hat{\beta} + k_2 \hat{v}' x_0)/(1 + k_2 \hat{v}') \end{aligned} \tag{18}$$

where $\hat{v}' = c/\hat{\beta}^2(1 + h^{-1})$, $a' = a/(1 + h^{-1})$ and $h^{-1} = \bar{s}^2/m\hat{\beta}^2$. $\hat{\beta}$ and $\bar{s}^2/m$ are the mean and variance, respectively, of the posterior p.d.f. for β. Thus h is the squared coefficient of variation associated with the posterior p.d.f. for β, a relative measure of the precision of estimation.[9]

On comparing (18), the setting for x and when β's and σ's values are unknown, with (8), the setting for x when β's value

[9] Note that h is of $O(T)$ and thus as T gets large $h^{-1} \to 0$.

is known, it is seen that $\hat{\beta}$ replaces β and an additional term, h^{-1}, appears in the denominator of (18). When T is large, (18) and (8) produce identical results. Also, the second line of (18) indicates that x^+ can be viewed as a weighted average of $k_1 a'/\hat{\beta}$ and x_0 with weights 1 and $k_2\hat{v}'$, respectively.

If no errors are made in assigning the target value and the cost-of-change parameter's value ($k_1 = k_2 = 1$), the optimal setting for x is, with $\hat{v} = c/\hat{\beta}^2$,

$$\begin{aligned} x^{\otimes} &= (a/\hat{\beta} + \hat{v}x_0)/(1 + \hat{v} + h^{-1}) \\ &= (a'/\hat{\beta} + \hat{v}'x_0)/(1 + \hat{v}') \end{aligned} \tag{19}$$

which is (18) with $k_1 = k_2 = 1$. Since (18) and (19) are precisely similar in form to (8) and (9), respectively, the dependence of x^+ on the values of k_1 and k_2 will be similar to that presented for x^* earlier. Also, as above, there are values of k_1 and k_2, not necessarily both equal to one, such that $x^+ = x^{\otimes}$. These are given by

$$\delta_1 = -\delta_2\hat{\phi}'\gamma' \tag{20}$$

where $\delta_1 = k_1 - 1$, $\delta_2 = k_2 - 1$, $\hat{\phi}' = \hat{v}'/(1 + \hat{v}')$ and $\gamma' = (\hat{\beta}x_0 - a')/a'$. The relation in (20) is precisely similar in form to that in (10b). Since this is the case, the analysis following (10b) can be utilised in the present case as well and thus will not be repeated.

3. Control of a Multiple Regression Process with a Mis-specified Loss Function

A scalar endogenous policy variable y is assumed to be generated by the following multiple regression process

$$y = \mathbf{x}'\boldsymbol{\beta} + u \tag{21}$$

where $\mathbf{x}' = (x_1, x_2, \ldots, x_k)$ is a $1 \times k$ vector of control variables,[10] $\boldsymbol{\beta}' = (\beta_1, \beta_2, \ldots, \beta_k)$ is a $1 \times k$ vector of regression coefficients with known values, and u is a random disturbance term with $E(u) = 0$ and $E(u^2) = \sigma^2 < \infty$. Let our loss function be

$$L_T = (y - a)^2 + (\mathbf{x} - \mathbf{x}_0)'\mathbf{C}(\mathbf{x} - \mathbf{x}_0) \tag{22}$$

[10] Here we assume that all variables in $\mathbf{x}$ can be controlled. Generalisation to the case in which a subset of the variables is under control is direct and will not be presented – see, e.g. [10, Chap. 11].

where, as above, a is a given target value for y, $\mathbf{x}_0$ is a $k \times 1$ vector of given initial values for $\mathbf{x}$ and $\mathbf{C}$ is a positive definite symmetric matrix with elements having known values. Then the mathematical expectation of L_T is

$$E(L_T) = (\mathbf{x}'\boldsymbol{\beta} - a)^2 + (\mathbf{x} - \mathbf{x}_0)'\mathbf{C}(\mathbf{x} - \mathbf{x}_0) + \sigma^2 \tag{23}$$

On differentiating (23) with respect to the elements of $\mathbf{x}$, the value of $\mathbf{x}$ that minimises expected loss, say $\mathbf{x}^0$, is given by[11]

$$\begin{aligned} \mathbf{x}^0 &= (\mathbf{C} + \boldsymbol{\beta}\boldsymbol{\beta}')^{-1}(a\boldsymbol{\beta} + \mathbf{C}\mathbf{x}_0) \\ &= \mathbf{x}_0 - (\boldsymbol{\beta}'\mathbf{x}_0 - a)\mathbf{C}^{-1}\boldsymbol{\beta}/(1 + \boldsymbol{\beta}'\mathbf{C}^{-1}\boldsymbol{\beta}) \end{aligned} \tag{24}$$

It is interesting to observe that the computed value of y with $\mathbf{x} = \mathbf{x}^0$ can be expressed as

$$\boldsymbol{\beta}'\mathbf{x}^0 = \frac{1}{1 + \boldsymbol{\beta}'\mathbf{C}^{-1}\boldsymbol{\beta}}\boldsymbol{\beta}'\mathbf{x}_0 + \frac{\boldsymbol{\beta}'\mathbf{C}^{-1}\boldsymbol{\beta}}{1 + \boldsymbol{\beta}'\mathbf{C}^{-1}\boldsymbol{\beta}}a \tag{25}$$

a weighted average of $\boldsymbol{\beta}'\mathbf{x}_0$ and a. Further, expected loss given $\mathbf{x} = \mathbf{x}^0$ is:

$$E(L_T \mid \mathbf{x} = \mathbf{x}^0) = \sigma^2 + a^2\gamma^2/(1 + \boldsymbol{\beta}'\mathbf{C}^{-1}\boldsymbol{\beta}) \tag{26}$$

where $\gamma = (\boldsymbol{\beta}'\mathbf{x}_0 - a)/a$.

If, instead of (22) we employ the following loss function

$$L = (y - k_1 a)^2 + (\mathbf{x} - \mathbf{x}_0)'\mathbf{G}(\mathbf{x} - \mathbf{x}_0) \tag{27}$$

where, just as in Section 2, k_1 is a parameter introduced to allow for possible errors in specifying the target value. Also, $\mathbf{G}$ is assumed to be a positive definite symmetric matrix. If $k_1 = 1$ and $\mathbf{G} = \mathbf{C}$, (27) is identical to (22), the true loss function.

On computing the expected value of L in (27) and solving for the value of $\mathbf{x}$, say $\mathbf{x}^*$, that minimises $E(L)$ we obtain

$$\begin{aligned} \mathbf{x}^* &= (\mathbf{G} + \boldsymbol{\beta}\boldsymbol{\beta}')^{-1}(k_1 a\boldsymbol{\beta} + \mathbf{G}\mathbf{x}_0) \\ &= \mathbf{x}_0 - (\boldsymbol{\beta}'\mathbf{x}_0 - k_1 a)\mathbf{G}^{-1}\boldsymbol{\beta}/(1 + \boldsymbol{\beta}'\mathbf{G}^{-1}\boldsymbol{\beta}) \end{aligned} \tag{28}$$

[11] Note that

$$(\mathbf{C} + \boldsymbol{\beta}\boldsymbol{\beta}')^{-1} = \mathbf{C}^{-1} - \frac{\mathbf{C}^{-1}\boldsymbol{\beta}\boldsymbol{\beta}'\mathbf{C}^{-1}}{1 + \boldsymbol{\beta}'\mathbf{C}^{-1}\boldsymbol{\beta}}.$$

which is similar to (24) except that $k_1 a$ replaces a and $\mathbf{G}$ replaces $\mathbf{C}$. From (28), we have

$$\boldsymbol{\beta}'\mathbf{x}^* = \frac{1}{1 + \boldsymbol{\beta}'\mathbf{G}^{-1}\boldsymbol{\beta}}\boldsymbol{\beta}'\mathbf{x}_0 + \frac{\boldsymbol{\beta}'\mathbf{G}^{-1}\boldsymbol{\beta}}{1 + \boldsymbol{\beta}'\mathbf{G}^{-1}\boldsymbol{\beta}}k_1 a \tag{29}$$

a weighted average of $\boldsymbol{\beta}'\mathbf{x}_0$ and $k_1 a$. On comparing (25) with (29) it is seen that there is a difference in the weights and in (29) $k_1 a$ replaces a in (25).

From (24) and (28), we can relate $\mathbf{x}^*$ and $\mathbf{x}^0$ as follows:

$$\begin{aligned}\mathbf{x}^* = \mathbf{x}^0 &+ (\boldsymbol{\beta}'\mathbf{x}_0 - a)\\ &\times \left[\frac{1}{1 + \boldsymbol{\beta}'\mathbf{C}^{-1}\boldsymbol{\beta}}\mathbf{C}^{-1} - \frac{1}{1 + \boldsymbol{\beta}'\mathbf{G}^{-1}\boldsymbol{\beta}}\mathbf{G}^{-1}\right]\boldsymbol{\beta}\\ &+ \frac{\delta_1 a \mathbf{G}^{-1}\boldsymbol{\beta}}{1 + \boldsymbol{\beta}'\mathbf{G}^{-1}\boldsymbol{\beta}}\end{aligned} \tag{30}$$

where $\delta_1 = k_1 - 1$. We see from (30) that the elements of $\mathbf{x}^*$ depend directly on the value of δ_1, the error in specifying the target value. If in (30), $\delta_1 = 0$ and $\mathbf{G} = \mathbf{C}$, then $\mathbf{x}^* = \mathbf{x}^0$; however, these are not the only conditions under which $\mathbf{x}^* = \mathbf{x}^0$. Broader sufficient conditions for $\mathbf{x}^* = \mathbf{x}^0$ are obtained by equating the last two terms on the right-hand side of (30) to zero. This yields the following sufficient condition for $\mathbf{x}^*$ to be equal to $\mathbf{x}^0$:

$$\delta_1 = -\gamma\left(\frac{\boldsymbol{\beta}'\mathbf{G}^{-1}\boldsymbol{\beta} - \boldsymbol{\beta}'\mathbf{C}^{-1}\boldsymbol{\beta}}{\boldsymbol{\beta}'\mathbf{G}^{-1}\boldsymbol{\beta}}\right)\left(\frac{1}{1 + \boldsymbol{\beta}'\mathbf{C}^{-1}\boldsymbol{\beta}}\right) \tag{31}$$

where $\delta_1 = k_1 - 1$ and $\gamma = (\boldsymbol{\beta}'\mathbf{x}_0 - a)/a$. The condition in (31) parallels that given in (30) and indicates that errors in assigning values to the true target and to the cost-of-change matrix $\mathbf{C}$ can be offsetting.

The expected loss associated with $\mathbf{x} = \mathbf{x}^*$, derived from the true loss function in (22), is

$$E(L_T \mid \mathbf{x} = \mathbf{x}^*) = \sigma^2 + (\boldsymbol{\beta}'\mathbf{x}^* - a)^2 + (\mathbf{x}^* - \mathbf{x}_0)'\mathbf{C}(\mathbf{x}^* - \mathbf{x}_0) \tag{32}$$

Using $\boldsymbol{\beta}'\mathbf{x}^* - a = \boldsymbol{\beta}'\mathbf{x}^0 - a + \boldsymbol{\beta}'(\mathbf{x}^* - \mathbf{x}^0)$ and $\mathbf{x}^* - \mathbf{x}_0 = \mathbf{x}^0 - \mathbf{x}_0 + \mathbf{x}^* - \mathbf{x}^0$, we can write (32) as

$$\begin{aligned}E(L_T \mid \mathbf{x} = \mathbf{x}^*) = {}& E(L_T \mid \mathbf{x} = \mathbf{x}^0)\\ &+ (\mathbf{x}^* - \mathbf{x}^0)'(\mathbf{C} + \boldsymbol{\beta}\boldsymbol{\beta}')(\mathbf{x}^* - \mathbf{x}^0)\\ &+ 2(\mathbf{x}^* - \mathbf{x}^0)'\{\mathbf{C}(\mathbf{x}^0 - \mathbf{x}_0) + (\boldsymbol{\beta}'\mathbf{x}_0 - a)\boldsymbol{\beta}\}\end{aligned} \tag{33}$$

where $E(L_T \mid \mathbf{x} = \mathbf{x}^0)$, expected loss associated with the optimal setting of $\mathbf{x}$, is given in (26). The last two terms on the right-hand side of (33) represent the extent to which expected loss may be inflated if $\mathbf{x}^* \neq \mathbf{x}^0$. From (33) it is the case that

$$E(L_T \mid \mathbf{x} = \mathbf{x}^*) - E(L_T \mid \mathbf{x} = \mathbf{x}^0) \geq 0.$$

With regard to (21), if the elements of $\boldsymbol{\beta}$ and σ have unknown values and if we have past data on y and $\mathbf{x}$, we can proceed as in Section 2 to derive the predictive p.d.f. for y and use it to evaluate the mathematical expectations of the loss functions in (22) and (27). With diffuse prior assumptions regarding $\boldsymbol{\beta}$ and σ,[12] it is well known that the predictive p.d.f. for y in the standard linear normal regression model is in the univariate Student t form with mean $\mathbf{x}'\hat{\boldsymbol{\beta}}$ and variance $\bar{s}^2(1 + \mathbf{x}'\mathbf{M}^{-1}\mathbf{x})$ where $\hat{\boldsymbol{\beta}} = (\mathbf{X}'\mathbf{X})^{-1}\mathbf{X}'\mathbf{y}$, the sample least squares quantity, $\mathbf{M} = \mathbf{X}'\mathbf{X}$ and $\bar{s}^2 = \nu s^2/(\nu - 2)$ with $\nu s^2 = (\mathbf{y} - \mathbf{X}\hat{\boldsymbol{\beta}})'(\mathbf{y} - \mathbf{X}\hat{\boldsymbol{\beta}})$, the residual sum of squares and $\nu = T - k$, where T is the sample size.

Using the predictive p.d.f. for y, we obtain the following expression for the expectation of L in (27)

$$E(L) = \bar{s}^2(1 + \mathbf{x}'\mathbf{M}^{-1}\mathbf{x}) + (k_1 a - \mathbf{x}'\hat{\boldsymbol{\beta}})^2 + (\mathbf{x} - \mathbf{x}_0)'\mathbf{G}(\mathbf{x} - \mathbf{x}_0) \quad (34)$$

The value of $\mathbf{x}$ that minimises (34), say $\mathbf{x}^+$, is given by

$$\begin{aligned}\mathbf{x}^+ &= (\bar{s}^2\mathbf{M}^{-1} + \mathbf{G} + \hat{\boldsymbol{\beta}}\hat{\boldsymbol{\beta}}')^{-1}(k_1 a\hat{\boldsymbol{\beta}} + \mathbf{G}\mathbf{x}_0) \\ &= \hat{\mathbf{x}}_0 + (k_1 a - \hat{\boldsymbol{\beta}}'\hat{\mathbf{x}}_0)\bar{\mathbf{G}}^{-1}\hat{\boldsymbol{\beta}}/(1 + \hat{\boldsymbol{\beta}}'\bar{\mathbf{G}}^{-1}\hat{\boldsymbol{\beta}}) \end{aligned} \quad (35)$$

with $\hat{\mathbf{x}}_0 = (\mathbf{I} - \bar{s}^2\bar{\mathbf{G}}^{-1}\mathbf{M}^{-1})\mathbf{x}_0$ and $\bar{\mathbf{G}} = \mathbf{G} + \bar{s}^2\mathbf{M}^{-1}$. When $k_1 = 1$ and $\mathbf{G} = \mathbf{C}$, (35) yields the optimal setting for $\mathbf{x}$, say $\mathbf{x}^{\otimes}$, based on the true loss function in (22), namely

$$\mathbf{x}^{\otimes} = \tilde{\mathbf{x}}_0 + (a - \hat{\boldsymbol{\beta}}'\tilde{\mathbf{x}}_0)\bar{\mathbf{C}}^{-1}\hat{\boldsymbol{\beta}}/(1 + \hat{\boldsymbol{\beta}}'\bar{\mathbf{C}}^{-1}\hat{\boldsymbol{\beta}}) \quad (36)$$

with $\tilde{\mathbf{x}}_0 = (\mathbf{I} - \bar{s}^2\bar{\mathbf{C}}^{-1}\mathbf{M}^{-1})\mathbf{x}_0$ and $\bar{\mathbf{C}} = \mathbf{C} + \bar{s}^2\mathbf{M}^{-1}$. Since (35) and (36) are in the same forms as (24) and (28), the comparison of (35) and (36) is quite similar to that for (24) and (28) and thus will not be presented.

[12] We employ a widely used diffuse prior p.d.f. for $\boldsymbol{\beta}$ and σ, namely, $p(\boldsymbol{\beta}, \sigma) \propto 1/\sigma$ with $0 < \sigma < \infty$ and $-\infty < \beta_i < \infty$ $(i = 1, 2, \ldots, k)$. Here the elements of $\boldsymbol{\beta}$ and $\log \sigma$ are assumed uniformly and independently distributed.

4. Concluding Remarks

We have examined the consequence of employing mis-specified targets and costs of changing policy instrument variables within the context of one-period control of simple and multiple regression processes. As is to be expected, errors in formulating criterion functions will generally, but not always, lead to poorer, in terms of expected loss, policy decisions. In general, both for cases in which model parameters have known or unknown values, the iso-expected loss lines for mis-specified quadratic loss functions were found to be linear. Also, it was found that in general errors in assessing target values and cost of change can be offsetting. However, this of course does not imply that errors will always be offsetting in actual problems. In each practical problem, it appears important to assess the consequences of possible errors in assigning values to parameters of a criterion function as well as the consequences of other possible errors. This conclusion is far from novel and, in fact, is reflected in much of Tinbergen's work.

References

[1] FISHER, W., 'Estimation in the Linear Decision Model', *International Economic Review*, III (January 1962) 1–29.

[2] PRESCOTT, E. C., 'Adaptive Decision Rules for Macro Economic Planning', unpublished doctoral dissertation, Graduate School of Industrial Administration, Carnegie-Mellon University, 1967.

[3] TINBERGEN, J., *Centralization and Decentralization in Economic Policy*, (Amsterdam: North-Holland Publishing Co., 1954).

[4] TINBERGEN, J., *On the Theory of Economic Policy*, 2nd ed., (Amsterdam: North-Holland Publishing Co., 1955).

[5] TINBERGEN, J., *Economic Policy: Principles and Design*, (Amsterdam: North-Holland Publishing Co., 1956).

[6] TINBERGEN, J., *Central Planning*, (New Haven/London: Yale University Press, 1964).

[7] VAN EIJK, C. J. and SANDEE, J., 'Quantitative Determination of an Optimum Economic Policy', *Econometrica*, XXVII (January 1959) 1–13.

[8] WAN, H. Y., 'Optimal Saving Programs under Intertemporally Dependent Preferences', *International Economic Review*, XI (October 1970) 521–47.

[9] ZELLNER, A. and GEISEL, M. S., 'Sensitivity of Control to Uncertainty and Form of the Criterion Function', in *The Future of Statistics*, ed. D. G. Watts (New York: Academic Press, 1968, 269–89).

[10] ZELLNER, A., *An Introduction to Bayesian Inference in Econometrics*, (New York: John Wiley and Sons, Inc., 1971).

PART II ECONOMIC THEORY AND MISCELLANEOUS

8 Acceleration Incentives and X-Efficiency

BY WILLIAM J. BAUMOL*

1. Acceleration *v*. Level-Modification Incentives

SUBSIDIES and taxes have long commended themselves as devices for the modification of incentives, both in the world of the designer of public policy and in the more abstract realm of economic analysis. The obvious arrangement for their use involves a payment, positive or negative, that varies directly with some measure of contribution. Thus, if social policy calls for the stimulation of exports, subsidy payments are proportioned to a firm's export volume, etc. In this way it is hoped to strengthen the workings of the invisible hand as an instrument of social policy, making it more nearly true that 'what is good for General Motors is good for the country'.

I shall argue in this paper that while such incentive payments do utilise the profit mechanism as a means for the achievement of public goals, the method it employs may be in at least one sense weaker than that inherent in a considerable part of the workings of the competitive market. Moreover, I shall show that this is not an unavoidable characteristic of any attempt to redirect incentives but that it is merely a consequence of the specific procedures that are utilised for the purpose.

Specifically, it will be maintained that while incentive subsidies are normally arranged to reward the decision-maker on the basis of the *level* of his contribution, the competitive market remunerates him, at least partly, on the basis of the *rate of growth* of his achievement. In symbolic terms, if a_t is the

* Princeton University and New York University. The author would like to thank the National Science Foundation which through its support facilitated considerably the completion of this paper.

index on the basis of which the subsidy payment s_t is provided, under normal incentive arrangements we have something in the order of

$$s_t = f(a_t), \qquad f' > 0 \tag{1}$$

On the other hand, if r_t is the corresponding return provided by a competitive market, the analogous relationship takes a form more nearly like

$$r_t = g\left(\frac{\mathrm{d}a_t}{\mathrm{d}t}\right), \qquad g' > 0 \tag{2}$$

or one such as

$$r_t = G\left(\frac{\mathrm{d}a_t}{a\,\mathrm{d}t}\right), \qquad G' > 0 \tag{3}$$

under which rewards grow monotonically with percentage rate of growth in achievement. Incentives of the first type I will refer to as 'level-modification incentives', while those of the second and third varieties I will call 'accelerator incentives'. The reason for this nomenclature should be obvious.[1]

Finally, I will maintain that while acceleration incentives may plausibly be held to be the more powerful of the two forms of inducement, a closer look at the matter indicates that it is rather more complicated. A number of circumstances will be described under which the level-inducement incentives may be more effective in achieving the results they are intended to obtain.

2. (Visible) Weapons Held in the Invisible Hand

If there is anything surprising in what has so far been said, it presumably resides at least in part in the assertion that the competitive market mechanism relies to a considerable extent on acceleration incentives. Yet a glance at the Schumpeterian

[1] The terminology is clearly derived by direct analogy with the 'acceleration principle'. One may quibble that the use of the term 'acceleration' is, in both cases, something of a misnomer. A true acceleration incentive might perhaps more appropriately be said to refer to a payment based on the magnitude of the *second* derivative of a_t, with payments of type (2) being called 'growth incentives'. However, language is surely established by usage, and since the term 'acceleration incentive' makes its point rather more forcefully, I will adhere to its use.

process readily confirms that this is so. It will be recalled that Schumpeter's analysis maintains that economic profits can be earned only by innovation, and that a constant stream of profits requires a steady flow of innovations. For any modification in the activities of a firm will, after some delay, be followed by a host of imitators who will soon wipe out the advantage held by the enterprise that initiated the change. Thus, with freedom of entry, profits can be maintained over longer periods only by the continued influx of innovations, which, it will be remembered, include not just changes in technology, but also the introduction of new products, and of cost-saving changes in administrative arrangements, the opening of new markets, etc.[2]

All of this obviously means that the company must constantly find more effective ways to meet the demands of the public as distilled through the market or its profits will vanish. Moreover, the more significant the innovation, i.e. the greater the *rate of change* in the efficiency with which effective demands are served, the higher will be the *level* of the profits of the firm. This surely is a clear-cut case of reward system of the sort described by (2) or by (3) – an acceleration incentive mechanism.[3]

Now let me not appear to exaggerate by implying that the competitive mechanism relies exclusively on motivators of this variety. On the contrary, in all of the static welfare analysis of perfect competition it is the level-modification incentive that plays the central role. For example, the firm is led to produce at the point of minimum cost on its long-run average cost curve by the loss of profits which result from a deviation from this point. Moreover, this profit loss will vary monotonically with

[2] See: [2, esp. p. 66 and chap. IV]. Since we are here concerned with the competitive process, we need not deal with Schumpeter's somewhat questionable attempt to utilise the capitalisation process to treat the monopolistic case in a similar manner. On this score I will remark only that if a competitive firm has demonstrated to the securities market an ability to produce a continuous supply of innovations and hence a relatively uninterrupted flow of economic profits, this too will only produce a once-for-all addition to the company's capitalised value.

[3] As a reader who is impressed by Schumpeter's volume I have always been a bit uncomfortable in trying to pin down more specifically the nature of his achievement. Perhaps the recognition of the role of incentives of the accelerator variety in the competitive process is at least an important component of that contribution.

the magnitude of the social loss which such a departure occasions. Similar remarks apply to the remainder of the decisions of the participants in a long-run competitive equilibrium.

But there is much to be said for the view that a considerable part of the vitality and the contribution of the market mechanism escapes the static welfare analysis, that it falls rather under the head of Professor Leibenstein's [1] somewhat mysterious X-efficiency, which is surely related to entrepreneurship, changing technology, increased managerial efficiency and other like matters, all of which can be driven by the Schumpeterian mechanism, and hence are subject to rewards and penalties that constitute acceleration incentives.

Note, moreover, that this mechanism does not require for its effectiveness a regime to any considerable degree resembling perfect competition. A set of vigorous and aggressive oligopolists can, at least in principle, be just as effective in competing away the fruits of innovation by imitation of successful changes in operation. Cases where this has occurred in practice should readily come to mind. All that the market structure requires for the operation of an acceleration-incentive mechanism is a freedom of entry sufficient to permit the required degree of imitation. Experience suggests that such imitations are typically not long in coming.

3. Effectiveness of the Two Sorts of Incentive

It is easy to jump to the plausible conclusion that acceleration incentives will always prove more effective than level-modification incentives in the degree of achievement of social objectives which they stimulate. And on the whole the conclusion is perhaps broadly true, but the issue is somewhat more complicated than it may at first appear.

An obvious reservation relates to the comparative magnitudes of the expenditures involved. If the amounts of money devoted to the provision of acceleration incentives are negligible, one can hardly expect substantial results. But as we will see presently, this may, at least in the long-run, prove less significant a reservation than one might expect.

An analytical complication enters when we recognise that the relative effectiveness of the two types of arrangements may well vary with the role played by profits in the objectives of the firm. If profits are the one overriding goal of management, the role of pecuniary incentives of the sort we are considering is quite different than it is in a 'satisficing' enterprise whose management is willing to rest content with some prespecified profit level that it considers viable. This, too, will presently be made more explicit.

A more specific qualification relates to the distance of the planning horizon. When the incentives are intended to achieve long-run results then the acceleration approach is in its element, while if shorter-run objectives are of higher priority the level-modification techniques may be more effective. A moment's thought will indicate why this is so. An increase in the rate of growth, in da/dt, is, as it were, an investment in the future. Only with the passage of time will it yield substantial results. Thus, if resources are to be allocated between the achievement of increases in a and in da/dt the terms of the trade-off will favour the latter if the relevant period is sufficiently long to permit its payoff to grow to significant size.[4]

[4] This and the preceding point can easily be illustrated with the aid of a simple example. Consider a profit satisficing firm which desires to obtain a flow of profits at a constant rate of p dollars and let us assume that incentive arrangements (1) and (2) are linear and unlagged, taking the respective forms

$$s_t = ba_t \tag{1a}$$

and

$$r_t = c\dot{a}_t \tag{2a}$$

where $\dot{a} = da/dt$ and b and c are constants. With incentives of type (1a), i.e. level modification incentives, to obtain a yield of $s_t = p$ we must have

$$a_t = p/b \text{ (constant).} \tag{4}$$

However, with the acceleration incentives (2a), the profit requirement is met if

$$\dot{a} = p/c$$

so that $a = k + pt/c$ where $k = a_0$ is a constant of integration. Thus, over the time interval from the initial date, $t = 0$, to the horizon date, $t = h$, even taking $a_0 = 0$, this yields an average value of a given by $\bar{a} = ph/2c$.

Comparing this with the level modification case where, by (4), $\bar{a} = p/b$ we see that for h sufficiently large the accelerator incentives will always yield the greater average (and hence the greater cumulative) results, *no matter what the relative values of b and c*, the relative incentive payment rates. Specifically, for $h > 2c/b$ we will always have $ph/2c > p/b$.

However, once we remember that future yields should be discounted in order to render them comparable with present returns, even the distant horizon does not guarantee an advantage to the acceleration incentives. For, while these will yield relatively great returns in the distant future, those are the returns that are discounted most heavily. Therefore, only if the discount rate is not too high can we be sure that the acceleration incentives are the more powerful.[5]

Another problem for the comparative evaluation of the two types of incentive arises out of the possibility of their interaction. That is, while we think of a level-modification incentive as one which acts only on the level of achievement, a, while an acceleration incentive appears to confine its effects to the time derivative, $\dot{a} = \mathrm{d}a/\mathrm{d}t$, such a clear distinction need not generally hold. The most direct source of interdependence resides in the funds out of which incentive payments are provided, because a reallocation of funds toward the promotion of the value of a

[5] Thus, consider the discounted present value of an infinite stream of yields, growing at the constant percentage rate w, so that its value at time t will be ae^{wt}. If the discount rate is i then the required present value will be

$$v = \int_0^\infty ae^{(w-i)t}\,\mathrm{d}t$$

which (provided $i > w$ so that the integral converges) is readily seen to be

$$v = a/(i-w)$$

Now let us compare what results from two incentive systems, one of which bases its reward on the percentage increase in the initial level a, and the other of which remunerates on the basis of w, the rate of increase. To compare their results we must compare the elasticity of v with respect to a to the elasticity of v with respect to w. These are, respectively,

$$\frac{\mathrm{d}v}{\mathrm{d}a} \times \frac{a}{v} = \frac{1}{i-w} \times \frac{a(i-w)}{a} = 1$$

and

$$\frac{\mathrm{d}v}{\mathrm{d}w}\frac{w}{v} = \frac{a}{(i-w)^2}\frac{w(i-w)}{a} = \frac{w}{i-w}.$$

The latter is larger than the former if, and only if, $2w > i$. That is, the acceleration incentive will produce the larger yield in terms of capitalised present value only if the discount rate i is not too large relative to the growth rate, w.

may well leave less for inducements for modification in the value of $\dot{a}$. But aside from this, unless we know precisely in what ways, other than through the incentive payments, the variables a and $\dot{a}$ enter the profit function, we cannot be sure how a change in incentive payments will affect the equilibrium values of a and $\dot{a}$. A change in the value of the parameters in, say, (1) which is designed to change the value of a may perhaps be shown by a comparative statics analysis to produce substantial consequences for $\dot{a}$.[6] In such circumstances it is even conceivable that the *indirect* effects of a level modification arrangement may make it the more efficient means for the stimulation of $\dot{a}$.

If, despite all of these reservations, one retains some belief in the greater efficacy of acceleration incentives, this must apparently be a reflection of faith rather than evidence. For we cannot be sure of the indirect effects of level increasing incentives on the value of da/dt, or the effects of acceleration incentives on the value of a; and we have no basis on which to

[6] Here the point may best be illustrated in terms of the behaviour of a profit maximising firm whose profit function can for our purposes be written as $\prod(a, \dot{a})$. To this profit function adjoin the linear incentive functions of footnote 4. Then the new returns relationship becomes

$$\prod(a, \dot{a}) + ba + c\dot{a}$$

The first-order maximum conditions are (writing $\prod_a$ for $\partial\prod/\partial a$, etc.)

$$\prod_a + b = 0, \qquad \prod_{\dot{a}} + c = 0.$$

Differentiating totally, to determine the effects of a change in b and in c, we obtain

$$\prod_{aa}da + \prod_{a\dot{a}}d\dot{a} = -db \qquad \text{and} \qquad \prod_{\dot{a}a}da + \prod_{\dot{a}\dot{a}}d\dot{a} = -dc$$

Solving (after first setting $dc = 0$ and then $db = 0$ to obtain *partial* derivatives) we have

$$\frac{\partial a}{\partial b} = -\frac{\prod_{\dot{a}\dot{a}}}{\Delta}, \quad \frac{\partial \dot{a}}{\partial b} = \frac{\prod_{\dot{a}a}}{\Delta}, \quad \frac{\partial a}{\partial c} = \frac{\prod_{a\dot{a}}}{\Delta}, \quad \frac{\partial \dot{a}}{\partial c} = -\frac{\prod_{aa}}{\Delta},$$

where Δ is the determinant of the system and where, by the second-order conditions, $\Delta > 0$, $\prod_{aa} < 0$, $\prod_{\dot{a}\dot{a}} < 0$. Thus, if the variables are independent in the sense that $\prod_{a\dot{a}} = \prod_{\dot{a}a} = 0$, then $\partial\dot{a}/\partial b = 0$, $\partial a/\partial c = 0$, while $\partial a/\partial b > 0$ and $\partial\dot{a}/\partial c > 0$. On the other hand, where the independence assumption fails we cannot, in general, rule out the possibility

$$\partial a/\partial b < \partial\dot{a}/\partial c \qquad \text{or} \qquad \partial\dot{a}/\partial c < \partial a/\partial c,$$

i.e., an incentive payment designed to enhance a may provide a greater stimulus to $\dot{a}$, and vice versa.

assume that the business planning horizon is sufficiently long or the relative discount rate sufficiently low to assure us that an increase in da/dt will yield social benefits greater than the increase in a for which it is substituted.

There is only one conclusion we can draw with any confidence – if our prime objective is to keep the economy *moving* (in whatever direction we may choose) – then acceleration incentives are, in general, the appropriate device for the purpose. For by their very nature, level incentives offer rewards even to managements which rest on their laurels, while the recipient of acceleration incentive payments must keep running if he wishes his income to remain still. The point is that, after all, acceleration incentives (or shall we say growth incentives?) are a reward to growth, and so, if growth is our goal, they are the means designed to help us promote it, particularly because they offer zero reward to those who are content with the performance they turned in yesterday.

4. Some Policy Issues

Despite the unsatisfactory state in which the preceding discussion leaves the matter it is unfortunately impossible to avoid decisions between the alternatives. They arise repeatedly in the formulation of practical policy. I close with a brief description of two such cases drawn from recent experience. The first is the investment tax credit which for several years was made available to business firms in an effort to stimulate capital formation and economic growth. While in the theoretical literature and in some of the earlier legislative discussion the possibility of acceleration incentives was considered, this form of inducement was soon abandoned for the more conventional level-modification subsidies.

The second case in which the alternative arises involves a slightly more current and continuing issue, the regulation of public utilities, where to prevent these firms from earning monopoly profits it is customary for the regulatory agencies to impose a ceiling on the rate of return on their investment. The trouble with such an arrangement, if the demand for any of the company's services is inelastic, is that by a suitable choice of rates, management can, in effect, guarantee itself the maximum return permitted by regulation. One loses thereby an important pecuniary inducement for innovation and increases in operating efficiency, for whatever its mode of operation the firm will earn the same profits (assuming inefficiencies do not become so blatant that they invite direct regulatory intervention). A number of proposals have been devised to offer alternative inducements for efficiency in such regulated enterprises. The most obvious are a number of specific level-modification incentives; for example, arrangements whereby the firm is permitted to increase its earnings monotonically with reductions in its operating or its capital costs. But a more subtle alternative has also been advocated rather widely, an arrangement generally referred to as 'regulatory lag'. Suppose utility rates are examined by the regulatory commission only periodically, every few years, and set so as to permit the firm to earn no more than its accepted rate of return. In the interexamination period the firm is not authorised to raise any of its rates (except perhaps for some special adjustments in periods of inflation) but is allowed to keep any profits it earns through cost reductions introduced in the interim. It is then automatically subjected to pressures for innovation very similar to those inherent in the Schumpeterian process. The firm must constantly introduce innovations because the special returns derived from earlier cost-reducing efforts are wiped out at the next regulatory reconsideration date. Here we have an acceleration inducement, and one which is to a considerable degree already implemented in practice, not by conscious policy decision but as a result of the delays which are a near inevitable concomitant of the regulatory process. Perhaps it is to these that we can ascribe some of the decline over the years in the real cost of supply of electric power, telephonic communication and some of the other services supplied by regulated firms.

References

[1] LEIBENSTEIN, HARVEY, 'Allocative Efficiency vs. X-Efficiency', *American Economic Review*, LIII (June 1966) 392–415.

[2] SCHUMPETER, JOSEPH, *The Theory of Economic Development* (R. Opie, trans.), (Cambridge, Mass.: Harvard University Press, 1936).

9 The Size Distribution of Labour Incomes Derived from the Distribution of Aptitudes

BY H. S. HOUTHAKKER*

THIS article owes its inspiration to one of Tinbergen's most original contributions to economic theory [9], in which he endeavours to derive the distribution of labour incomes from the choice of occupation by individuals. This is also the aim of the present paper, which, however, uses somewhat different techniques of analysis and has a more limited scope. Whereas Tinbergen relied heavily of the differential calculus, I use mostly linear inequalities and integration in order to take account of the fact that most individuals have only one job at a time and to permit analysis of what has become known as a 'continuum of traders'. Unlike Tinbergen, moreover, I shall not consider individuals' non-monetary preferences concerning different types of work.

The assumptions of the principal model explored here, which are similar to those made by Roy [8], are no doubt too simple to provide a realistic description of the labour market; nevertheless they will be shown to have fairly realistic implications concerning the size distribution of income. The purpose of this model is to demonstrate the relation between aptitude, or productive ability, and income in a fully competitive economy; in particular, it will be shown that the observable distribution of income normally has a quite different shape than the (generally unobservable) distribution of aptitudes. Much of the literature[1]

* Harvard University. Some of the results of this paper were first contained in an unpublished *Cowles Commission Discussion Paper* (Economics 2043, 2 June 1952)

[1] For a good recent survey see Lydall [4].

is, quite properly, concerned with the mathematical form of the size distribution of income. A variety of models has been constructed to yield such favourites as the lognormal or the Pareto, though often only after so many approximations and ad hoc assumptions that the economic justification of the model becomes hard to see. The model presented here does not try to establish any particular distribution as the correct one; it is quite general and apart from strong continuity assumptions does not involve approximations. Since its basic postulate is maximisation of income its economic logic should be transparent. Indeed, it is so transparent that a generalisation has been added to allow for some of the market imperfections that are obviously present in reality.

The Basic Model

Each individual is assumed to maximise his earnings by choosing among occupations according to his aptitude for each occupation. His aptitudes are summarised by a vector $(y_i, \ldots, y_n)$, where y_i is the quantity of the ith commodity that the individual could produce in a given length of time if he did nothing else. Thus if i refers to bricks then y_i is the number of bricks the individual could lay per day if he were a full-time brick-layer. The individual's working time is assumed to be fixed; the fraction of this time devoted to the ith occupation is $x_i (0 \leqslant x_i \leqslant 1)$. The market price of the ith commodity is p_i, also assumed to be given. Thus the individual's income is $\sum_i p_i x_i y_i$. In the basic model he is supposed to allocate his working time so as to maximise his income, hence

$$\max_{x_i} \sum_i p_i x_i y_i \tag{1}$$

subject to

$$\sum_i x_i = 1 \tag{2}$$

The maximum is reached by working all the time on the occupations for which the money yield $p_i y_i$ is greatest. Normally there is only one such occupation;[2] if there is more than one, the allocation of time between those is indeterminate.

This simple micro-model lends itself readily to aggregation over individuals, provided we are willing to make suitable continuity assumptions. For this purpose we shall assume that the aptitude vector $(y_i, \ldots, y_n)$ varies randomly over individuals with a continuous density function $f(y_i, \ldots, y_n)$. The distribution function $F(y_i, \ldots, y_n)$ is then also continuous, and will in fact be assumed to be twice differentiable. To eliminate the indeterminacy of the x_i mentioned in the preceding paragraph only density functions where ties (cases where $p_i y_i = p_j y_j$) have a probability of zero will be considered. Apart from these assumptions there are no restrictions on admissible density function; thus the aptitudes in different occupations may or may not be independent of each other.

From now on it will also be assumed for simplicity that all prices are equal to unity ($p_i = 1$), i.e. that all quantities are measured in 'dollar's worths'. The determination of prices in models of the kind discussed here is a separate problem to which I hope to return on another occasion. With this convention each individual's income is equal to y_k, where k now refers to the occupation he is actually engaged in. The (cumulative) distribution function for labour incomes will be called $G(z)$, and the corresponding density $g(z)$. The most important implication of the basic model for the distribution of income is then

$$G(z) = F(z, z, \ldots, z) \tag{3}$$

or in words, *the proportion of labour incomes up to an amount z equals the proportion of individuals whose productive ability in any occupation is at most z.*

This follows immediately from the fact that $z = y_k$, and that accordingly, for all $i \neq k$, $y_i \leqslant y_k$.

[2] This follows from the additive nature of the maximand. In [3] it was argued, following Adam Smith, that there is a cost in switching from one job to another. This cost, which does not appear in the present model, makes it even less likely that a person has two or more occupations. In reality working hours are often fixed by law or custom, and this probably is the main motive for 'moon-lighting' by those who wish to work more hours than is customary in any one job.

As an illustration we shall first use a bivariate exponential distribution, selected for computational convenience rather than for realism.[3] The density function of aptitudes is assumed to be

$$f(y_1, y_2) = \alpha_1\alpha_2 e^{-\alpha_1 y_1 - \alpha_2 y_2} \tag{4}$$

and the proportion of individuals with an income up to z who are in the ith occupation ($i = 1, 2$) will be called $G_i(z)$ with a density of $g_i(z)$. The distribution of income within an occupation is also of interest and will therefore be used in the derivation, even though this is not strictly necessary.

$$G_1(z) = \alpha_1\alpha_2 \int_0^z \int_0^{y_1} e^{-\alpha_1 y_1 - \alpha_2 y_2}\, dy_1\, dy_2$$

$$= \frac{\alpha_1}{\alpha_1 + \alpha_2} e^{-(\alpha_1+\alpha_2)z} - e^{-\alpha_1 z} + \frac{\alpha_2}{\alpha_1 + \alpha_2} \tag{5}$$

and similarly

$$G_2(z) = \frac{\alpha_2}{\alpha_1 + \alpha_2} e^{-(\alpha_1+\alpha_2)z} - e^{-\alpha_2 z} + \frac{\alpha_1}{\alpha_1 + \alpha_2} \tag{6}$$

Adding up we find that

$$G(z) = e^{-(\alpha_1+\alpha_2)z} - e^{-\alpha_1 z} - e^{-\alpha_2 z} + 1$$

$$= (1 - e^{-\alpha_1 z})(1 - e^{-\alpha_2 z}) \tag{7}$$

which could also have been derived directly from (3) and (4). The income density within the first occupation is

$$g_1(z) = \alpha_1 e^{-\alpha_1 z}(e^{-\alpha_2 z} - 1) \tag{8}$$

and similarly for the second occupation. The total density is

$$g(z) = \alpha_1 e^{-\alpha_1 z} + \alpha_2 e^{-\alpha_2 z} - (\alpha_1 + \alpha_2) e^{-(\alpha_1+\alpha_2)z} \tag{9}$$

As a numerical illustration we shall take the arbitrary values $\alpha_1 = 0{\cdot}01$ and $\alpha_2 = 0{\cdot}02$. These correspond to median abilities

[3] The distribution used here is the product of two univariate exponentials, and therefore does not allow for dependence. Bivariate exponential distribution with dependence have been introduced by Gumbel [2] and Marshall and Olkin [7]; see also Mardia [6]. Gumbel's distribution, however, is not a true generalisation of the univariate exponential because its margins are not exponential. The Marshall-Olkin distribution is a true generalisation, but it violates our assumption that ties have a probability of zero. Neither distribution could therefore be used here.

of 69·3 and 34·7 respectively. Although the density function of abilities is of course J-shaped for each occupation, the density of income in each looks much more like the income distributions encountered in reality (see Figure 9.1). This applies particularly to the overall distribution of incomes which is remarkably similar to the 'typical' distribution presented by

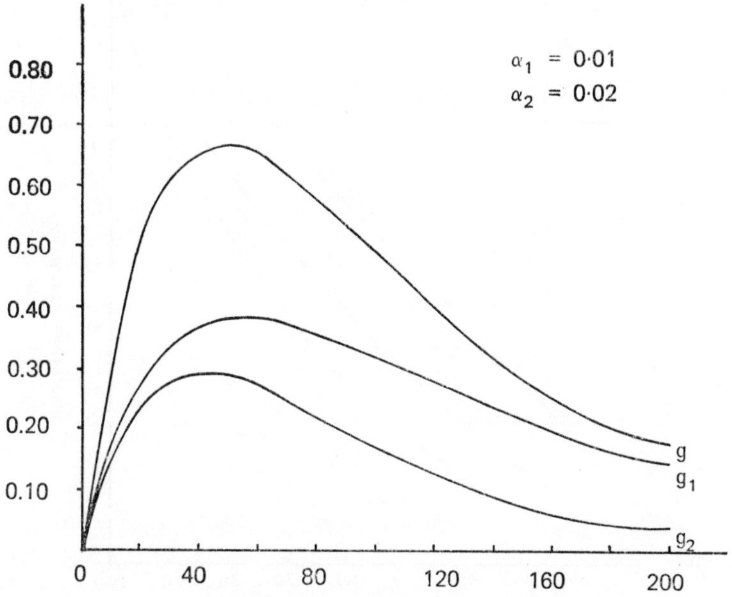

FIG. 9.1. *Bivariate exponential: Income Distributions*

Lydall [4, Figure 2.2], even though the present example was virtually chosen at random.

For somewhat more accurate evalutation of the merits of an exponential aptitude distribution it is useful to draw Lorenz curves. This is done for two different cases in Figure 9.2. In both cases the exponents α_i are equal to 0·01 for all occupations, but in one case there are two occupations, and in the other there are ten. It will be seen that increasing the number of occupations lessens the inequality, measured customarily by the area between the curve and the diagonal.[4] For ten occupations the distribution of income is not too unrealistic, with the

[4] As the number of occupations increases, however, the assumption of independence among the aptitudes becomes less plausible.

top 5 per cent of the recipients getting only 11 per cent of the income, while the bottom 50 per cent receive about 34 per cent. These figures are in reasonable agreement with those given for a number of countries by Lydall [4, Appendix 7].

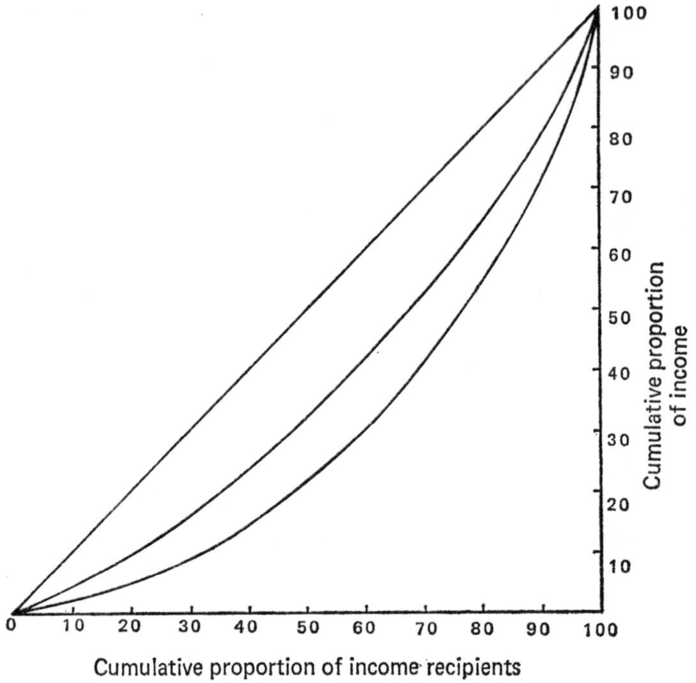

FIG. 9.2. *Bivariate exponential: Lorenz curves for* $n = 2$ (*lower curve*) *and* $n = 10$ (*upper curve*)

As another example let us nevertheless consider the Pareto distribution, which has long had pride of place in this field of research.[5]

[5] It should be noted, however, that the Pareto curve is applied here in the first instance to the distribution of aptitudes rather than the distribution of incomes. The Pareto distribution and its generalisation, the Pareto-Levy distribution have also been introduced as an ability distribution by Mandelbrot [5], but his model differs from the one considered here. Mandelbrot's very interesting model is expressed in terms of the psychological traits determining aptitudes rather than in terms of the aptitudes themselves. In this respect Mandelbrot's model recalls the approach of Boissevain [1].

This time the number of occupations will be three, in order to make the generalisation to an arbitrary number more obvious. Let the density function of the aptitudes be

$$f(y_1, y_2, y_3) = A y_1^{-\alpha_1 - 1} y_2^{-\alpha_2 - 1} y_3^{-\alpha_3 - 1} \tag{10}$$

where $\alpha_i > 1$ and $y_i > c > 0$ $(i = 1, 2, 3)$. The constant c, which in a more general model could be made to depend on the occupation, is necessary to ensure convergence at the lower end of the aptitude scale. By integrating over all the y_i from c to infinity it can easily be shown that

$$A = \alpha_1 \alpha_2 \alpha_3 c^{\alpha_1 + \alpha_2 + \alpha_3} \tag{11}$$

The proportion of persons with incomes up to Z is according to (3)

$$G(z) = -c^{\alpha_1 + \alpha_2 + \alpha_3}(z^{-\alpha_1} - c^{-\alpha_1})(z^{-\alpha_2} - c^{-\alpha_2})(z^{-\alpha_3} - c^{-\alpha_3}) \tag{12}$$

For large z, this expression, when expanded by powers of z, is increasingly dominated by the term whose exponent is smallest in absolute value; if this term involves the second occupation, for instance, it will equal $-(c/z)^{\alpha_2}$. Consequently, this income distribution approaches the Pareto curve at the right, but the approach is not very rapid. The corresponding density function is

$$\begin{aligned} g(z) = \frac{1}{z}\{&(\alpha_1 + \alpha_2 + \alpha_3)(c/z)^{\alpha_1 + \alpha_2 + \alpha_3} - (\alpha_1 + \alpha_2)(c/z)^{\alpha_1 + \alpha_2} \\ &- (\alpha_1 + \alpha_3)(c/z)^{\alpha_1 + \alpha_3} - (\alpha_2 + \alpha_3)(c/z)^{\alpha_2 + \alpha_3} \\ &+ \alpha_1 (c/z)^{\alpha_1} + \alpha_2 (c/z)^{\alpha_2} + \alpha_3 (c/z)^{\alpha_3}\} \end{aligned} \tag{13}$$

and its logarithm is plotted against $\log z$ in Figure 9.3. It will be seen that to the right of the mode the curve is visually indistinguishable from a straight line. The latters's slope does not come very close to its asymptotic value for moderate values of z, but the curvature is very slight. For Figure 9.3 it was assumed that $c = 10$, $\alpha_1 = 1{\cdot}5$, $\alpha_2 = 1{\cdot}7$, $\alpha_3 = 1{\cdot}9$. With those parameters the slope would be 2·618 for $z = 300$, appreciably above the asymptotic value of 2·5, but since the second derivative of $\log g$ with respect to $\log z$ is only 0·001 no curvature is apparent.

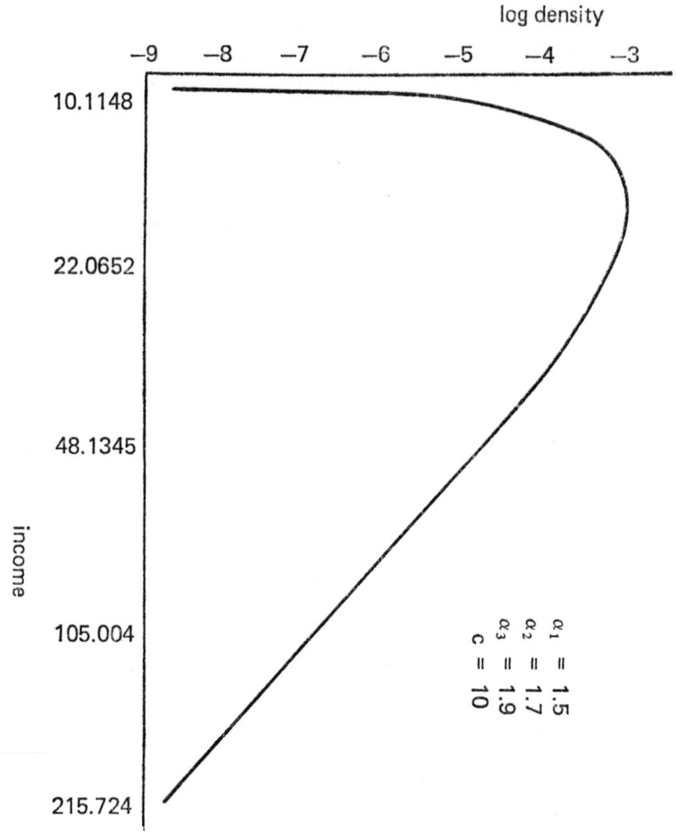

FIG. 9.3. *Bivariate Pareto: Income Distribution (on double log scale)*

The main feature of the Pareto distribution as compared to the exponential is the greater inequality of income it implies for plausible values of the α_i. For the parameter values used in Figure 9.3, for instance, it turns out that 16 per cent of the income is received by only 2 per cent of the population. At the lower end 50 per cent of the population accounts for only 29 per cent of the income, which is more reasonable. Although the Pareto model could be improved somewhat by choosing other parameter values, other models have to be considered.[6]

[6] In the Pareto model, unlike the exponential model, not a great deal can be done by increasing the number of occupations since at the upper end the income distribution is influenced primarily by the occupation(s) with the smallest α_i.

A More General Model

The many imperfections of actual labour markets also make it desirable to relax the hypothesis of income maximisation underlying the basic model. There are many conceivable ways of doing so, and the particular method used here may be of some interest in itself. This method assumes that an individual does not necessarily enter the occupation that will provide him with the highest income but that for every occupation there is a probability that he will choose it; this probability is itself determined by the individual's ability vector. Specifically, if w_i is the probability of entering the ith occupation, then we could for instance postulate that

$$w_i = \frac{e^{ky_i}}{\sum_j e^{ky_j}} \tag{14}$$

where the abilities y_i are still measured in dollar's-worths and where k is a parameter that reflects the efficiency of allocation. Thus if $k = 0$ all occupations have an equal probability of being chosen, irrespective of the individual's abilities.[7] As $k \to \infty$ the denominator tends to be dominated by the term with the largest y_i, so that $w_i \to 1$ for that occupation and $w_j \to 0$ for all other occupations. The case $k = \infty$ therefore corresponds to the basic model. For $0 < k < \infty$, ability plays some role in the choice of occupation, but it does not determine it.[8]

It is natural to combine (10) with (4); in fact that is the reason for using exponential functions in (10). Using much the

[7] This suggests that greater generality may be obtained by introducing further constants in (10), so that the probabilities for $k = 0$, while still independent of ability would not be equal. For the sake of simplicity no further constants are considered here, but the interested reader can easily put them in. It should be added that the exponential function used in (10) is just one of many that could be used for the purpose.

[8] The case $k < 0$, corresponding to counter-selection, can perhaps be seen in some totalitarian countries where intellectuals and other enemies of the regime are given the jobs to which they are least suited.

same reasoning as before we now find that

$$G(z) = \int_0^z \int_0^\infty w_1(y_1, y_2) f(y_1, y_2)\, dy_1\, dy_2$$

$$+ \int_0^\infty \int_0^z w_2(y_1, y_2) f(y_1, y_2)\, dy_1\, dy_2$$

$$= \int_0^z \int_0^\infty \frac{e^{ky_1}}{e^{ky_1} + e^{ky_2}} \alpha_1 \alpha_2 e^{-\alpha_1 y_1 - \alpha_2 y_2}\, dy_1\, dy_2$$

$$+ \int_0^\infty \int_0^z \frac{e^{ky_2}}{e^{ky_1} + e^{ky_2}} \alpha_1 \alpha_2 e^{-\alpha_1 y_1 - \alpha_2 y_2}\, dy_1\, dy_2$$

$$= \alpha_1 \alpha_2 \int_0^z \int_0^\infty \frac{e^{-\alpha_1 y_1 - \alpha_2 y_2}}{1 + e^{k(y_2 - y_1)}}\, dy_1\, dy_2$$

$$+ \alpha_1 \alpha_2 \int_0^\infty \int_0^z \frac{e^{-\alpha_1 y_1 - \alpha_2 y_2}}{1 + e^{k(y_1 - y_2)}}\, dy_1\, dy_2 \qquad (15)$$

The analysis of this formula, which appears to be related to the Beta distribution (Pearson's Type I), still presents some difficulties. So does the corresponding approach for a Pareto distribution of aptitudes, where it is natural to assume that

$$w_i = \frac{y_i^k}{\sum_i y_i^k} \qquad (16)$$

In conclusion we can say that the explanation of the size distribution of income from the distribution of aptitudes appears to hold considerable promise, but that much more work is needed before this promise is realised. This additional work will have to be both theoretical and numerical and it will have to be completed by empirical study in order to evaluate the realism of the conclusions. In this paper one of several directions suggested by Tinbergen's seminal paper has been investigated; other directions may be at least as promising.

References

[1] Boissevain, C. H. 'Distribution of Abilities Depending Upon Two or More Independent Factors' *Metron*, xv (1939) 48–58.

[2] GUMBEL, E. J., *Statistics of Extremes*, (New York: Columbia University Press, 1960).
[3] HOUTHAKKER, H. S., 'Economics and Biology: Specialization and Speciation', *Kyklos*, IX (1956) 181–7.
[4] LYDALL, H. F., *The Structure of Earnings*, (Oxford University Press, 1968).
[5] MANDELBROT, B., 'Paretian Distribution and Income Maximization', *Quarterly Journal of Economics*, LXXVI (1962) 57–85.
[6] MARDIA, K. V., *Families of Multivariate Distributions*, (London: Griffin, 1971).
[7] MARSHALL, A. W. and OLKIN, I., 'A Multivariate Exponential Distribution', *Journal of the American Statistical Association*, LXII (1967) 30–44.
[8] ROY, A. D., 'Some Thoughts on the Distribution of Earnings', *Oxford Economic Papers*, new series, III (1951) 135–46.
[9] TINBERGEN, J., 'Some Remarks on the Distribution of Labour Incomes', (original in Dutch, 1947), translated in *International Economic Papers*, I (1951) 195–207.

10 The Economic Theory of Replacement and Depreciation

BY DALE W. JORGENSON

1. Introduction

THE ECONOMIC theory of production – including the description of technology, the conditions for producer equilibrium, and the response of variables determined in the theory to changes in parameters – may be developed in a form that abstracts from specific interpretations.[1] In the intertemporal theory of production each commodity is distinguished by point of time. As an illustration, an hour of labour today and an hour of labour tomorrow are treated as distinct commodities. Given this convention the intertemporal theory of producer behaviour is formally analogous to the standard atemporal theory.[2]

The special character of the intertemporal theory of production arises from more detailed specifications of technology, permitting a more precise characterisation of producer behaviour. The most important specialisation of technology results from the introduction of durable capital as a factor of production.[3] Although the central concepts of capital theory – capital assets, capital services and investment – are inessential to the development of the intertemporal theory of production, they provide additional structure that permits a much more detailed analysis of producer behaviour.

To describe the durable goods model we begin with the relative efficiency of durable goods of different ages. At each point of time durable goods decline in efficiency, giving rise to

[1] See, for example, G. Debreu [4], J. Hicks [18] and P. A. Samuelson [26].

[2] This analogy has been developed extensively by I. Fisher [9], J. Hicks [18], E. Lindahl [22] and E. Malinvaud [23].

[3] The durable goods model was developed by L. Walras [28], G. Åkerman [1] and K. Wicksell [29].

needs for *replacement* in order to maintain productive capacity. For any given durable good the price of acquisition declines, reflecting the current decline in efficiency and the present value of future declines in efficiency; the decline in price is *depreciation* on the durable good.

The durable goods model is characterised by price-quantity duality.[4] Capital stock corresponds to the acquisition price of investment goods, acquisition of investment goods corresponds to the time rental price of capital. Replacement corresponds to depreciation. In this paper we present the economic theory of replacement and its dual, the theory of depreciation. We then consider applications of the theory to the explanation of replacement investment and capital goods prices.

2. Replacement

2.1 *Introduction*

Characterisation of the durable goods model of production begins with a description of the relative efficiency of durable goods of different ages. Replacement requirements are determined by losses in efficiency of existing durable goods as well as actual physical disappearance or retirement of capital goods. When a durable good is retired its relative efficiency drops to zero. To estimate replacement requirements we must introduce an explicit description of decline in relative efficiency.

In the durable goods model the services provided by a given durable good at different points of time are proportional to each other. The proportions describing relative efficiency at different points of time depend only on the age of the durable good and not on the time the good is acquired.[5] In our

[4] The dual to the durable goods model was developed by K. J. Arrow [2] and R. E. Hall [15], on the basis of earlier work by H. S. Hotelling [19] and T. Haavelmo [13].

[5] The assumption that relative efficiency depends only on the age of durable equipment is dropped by Hall [15]. Variations in efficiency among capital goods of the same age acquired at different times correspond to 'embodied' technical change. Variations in efficiency among capital goods of the same age used at different times correspond to 'disembodied' technical change. This terminology coincides with that of R. M. Solow [27, pp. 89–104].

description of technology we employ discrete time. In discrete time the *relative efficiency* of a durable good may be described by a sequence of non-negative numbers[6]

$$d_0, d_1, \ldots$$

We normalise initial relative efficiency at unity and assume that relative efficiency is decreasing so that:

$$d_0 = 1, \qquad d_\tau - d_{\tau-1} \leqq 0 \quad (\tau = 0, 1, \ldots)$$

We also assume that every capital good is eventually retired or scrapped so that relative efficiency declines to zero,

$$\lim_{\tau \to \infty} d_\tau = 0$$

Replacement requirements are determined by declines in efficiency of previously acquired capital goods. The proportion of a given investment to be replaced during the τth period after its acquisition is equal to the decline in relative efficiency. We may refer to the decline in relative efficiency as the *mortality distribution* of a capital good, say m_τ, where:

$$m_\tau = -(d_\tau - d_{\tau-1}) \quad (\tau = 1, 2, \ldots) \tag{1}$$

By our assumption that relative efficiency is decreasing, the mortality distribution may be represented by a sequence of non-negative numbers,

$$m_1, m_2, \ldots$$

where

$$\sum_{\tau=1}^{\infty} m_\tau = \sum_{\tau=1}^{\infty} (d_{\tau-1} - d_\tau) = d_0 = 1$$

Replacements requirements, say R_t, are a weighted average of past investments, say A_t

$$R_t = m_1 A_{t-1} + m_2 A_{t-2} + \cdots \tag{2}$$

or, where S is the lag operator,

$$R_t = (m_1 S + m_2 S^2 + \cdots) A_t = m(S) A_t$$

and $m(S)$ is a power series in the lag operator,

$$m(S) = m_1 S + m_2 S^2 + \cdots$$

[6] We assume that the proportions are non-random; for a treatment of the economic theory of replacement with random deterioration in efficiency, see [20].

Capital stock at the end of the period, say K_t, is the sum of past investments, each weighted by its relative efficiency

$$K_t = \sum_{\tau=0}^{\infty} d_\tau A_{t-\tau} \tag{3}$$

Taking the first difference of this expression, we may write

$$\begin{aligned} K_t - K_{t-1} &= A_t + \sum_{\tau=1}^{\infty} (d_\tau - d_{\tau-1})A_{t-\tau} \\ &= A_t - \sum_{\tau=1}^{\infty} m_\tau A_{t-\tau} \\ &= A_t - R_t \end{aligned} \tag{4}$$

the change in capital stock in any period is equal to the acquisition of investment goods less replacement requirements.

Finally, we may express replacement requirements in terms of present and past net investments. First, we rewrite the expression for the change in capital stock in the form

$$K_t - K_{t-1} = A_t - m(S)A.$$

so that

$$\begin{aligned} A_t &= \frac{1}{1 - m(S)} [K_t - K_{t-1}] \\ &= [1 + \delta(S)][K_t - K_{t-1}] \\ &= [K_t - K_{t-1}] + \sum_{\tau=1}^{\infty} \delta_\tau [K_{t-\tau} - K_{t-\tau-1}] \end{aligned} \tag{5}$$

where $\delta(S)$ is a power series in the lag operator. We may refer to the sequence of coefficients,

$$\delta_0, \delta_1, \ldots$$

as the *replacement distribution*. Each coefficient δ_τ is *the rate of replacement* of a stock replaced τ periods after initial acquisition. The rate of replacement includes replacement of the initial investment and subsequent replacements of each succeeding replacement.

The sequence of replacement rates $\{\delta_\tau\}$ can be computed recursively from the sequence $\{m_\tau\}$ of mortality rates. The proportion of an initial investment replaced at time ν and again at a later time $\tau > \nu$ is equal to $m_\nu \delta_{t-\nu}$. The proportion of the stock replaced at the τth period is the sum of proportions replaced first at periods 1, 2, . . . , and later at period τ; hence

$$\delta_\tau = m_1\delta_{\tau-1} + m_2\delta_{\tau-2} + \cdots + m_\tau\delta_0 \quad (\tau = 1, 2, \ldots).$$

This equation is, of course, the *renewal equation* [8, pp. 290–3].

Since replacement requirements may be expressed in the form

$$R_t = \sum_{\tau=1}^{\infty} \delta_\tau[K_{t-\tau} - K_{t-\tau-1}]$$

the *average replacement rate* for capital stock at the beginning of the period

$$\hat{\delta} = \frac{R_t}{K_{t-1}} = \sum_{\tau=1}^{\infty} \delta_\tau \frac{[K_{t-\tau} - K_{t-\tau-1}]}{K_{t-1}} \tag{6}$$

is a weighted average of replacement rates with weights given by the relative proportions of net investments of each age in beginning of period capital stock.

To illustrate these relationships we take the relative efficiency distribution to be geometric

$$d_\tau = (1 - \delta)^\tau \quad (\tau = 0, 1, \ldots)$$

Obviously, relative efficiency is initially normalised at unity, decreases and eventually declines to zero. The corresponding mortality distribution (1) is geometric since

$$m_\tau = d_{\tau-1} - d_\tau = (1 - \delta)^{\tau-1} - (1 - \delta)^\tau = \delta(1 - \delta)^{\tau-1}$$

The coefficients of the mortality distribution are non-negative and sum to unity.

Replacement requirements (2) are given by

$$R_t = \sum_{\tau=1}^{\infty} \delta(1 - \delta)^{\tau-1}A_{t-\tau}$$

Capital stock at the end of the period (3) may be expressed as a weighted sum of past net investments,

$$K_t = \sum_{\tau=0}^{\infty} (1 - \delta)^\tau A_{t-\tau}$$

so that the change in capital stock (4) may be written

$$K_t - K_{t-1} = A_t - \sum_{\tau=1}^{\infty} \delta(1 - \delta)^\tau A_{t-\tau}$$
$$= A_t - \delta K_{t-1}$$

Replacement requirements are proportional to capital at the beginning of the period

$$R_t = \delta K_{t-1}$$

Finally, the replacement distribution (5) takes the form

$$\begin{aligned} A_t &= \frac{1}{1 - m(S)}(K_t - K_{t-1}) \\ &= \frac{1}{1 - \dfrac{\delta S}{1 - (1 - \delta)S}}(K_t - K_{t-1}) \\ &= K_t - K_{t-1} + \sum_{\tau=1}^{\infty} \delta(K_{t-\tau} - K_{t-\tau-1}) \end{aligned}$$

The sequence of replacement rates $\{\delta_\tau\}$ and the average replacement rate $\hat{\delta}$ are constant and equal to δ. The average replacement rate is, of course, independent of the time path of past net investments.

A wide variety of retirement distributions have been found useful in describing the retirement or physical disappearance of capital goods.[7] Relatively little information is available on the decline in efficiency of existing capital goods.[8] In measuring capital stock net of replacement requirements, which include both retirement and decline in efficiency of existing capital goods, a smaller range of mortality distributions has been employed.[9] The geometric mortality distribution is among the distributions most commonly used in measuring capital stock.[10] A fundamental result of renewal theory is that the sequence of replacement rates $\{\delta_\tau\}$ tends to a constant value for almost any mortality distribution (1). The geometric mortality distribution, resulting in a constant rate of replacement of capital stock, may provide a useful approximation to replacement requirements for

[7] A relatively recent work on capital equipment is [24]. The classic work in the field is [21] which provides other references.

[8] See Section 4, below, for a review of the evidence.

[9] A representative study is the OBE Capital Goods Study; in this research straight line and double declining balance methods are employed [11, pp. 46–52].

[10] This distribution is imployed by Y. Grunfeld [12] for individual firms and by B. Hickman [17] for industry groups.

a broad class of mortality distributions. We turn now to estimation of replacement requirements for constant and growing (or declining) capital stock.

2.2 *Single investment, constant capital*

An initial investment generates a set of replacements distributed over time and each replacement generates a new set of subsequent replacements. This process repeats itself indefinitely. Renewal theory shows that the distribution of replacements for such an infinite stream approaches a constant fraction of capital stock for (almost) any mortality distribution and for any initial age distribution of the capital stock. The result that replacement is a constant fraction of capital stock, which holds exactly for the geometric distribution, holds asymptotically for (almost) any distribution. We verify this proposition in two stages: (*a*) considering a capital stock of fixed size; (*b*) extending the analysis to a growing (or declining) capital stock.

Consider a capital stock consisting of investments which are replaced over time according to the mortality distribution (*a*). Suppose that every investment is eventually replaced and that there is no integer greater than one such that replacements for a single investment can occur only at integral multiples of this integer. Then the proportion of capital stock replaced in any period approaches the inverse of the expected value of times to replacement as the age of the capital stock increases without limit.

The assumption that every investment is eventually replaced completely requires no loss of generality for the analysis of replacement demand. The restriction that there is no integer $\phi >$ 1 such that replacements can occur only at integral multiples of ϕ, rules out purely periodic replacements. For a single initial investment with a fixed interval between replacements (the length of the interval being some integer greater than unity), the fraction of equipment replaced in each period is unity for integral multiples of the replacement interval and zero elsewhere. However, by taking the time period to be equal to the replacement interval, the conclusion holds as stated above.

To state the fundamental theorem of renewal theory formally, it is convenient to let

$$m_0 = 0, \qquad \delta_0 = 1 \tag{7}$$

If for the sequence $\{\delta_\tau\}$ there is an integer $\theta > 1$ such that the subsequence $\delta_\theta, \delta_{2\theta}, \ldots$ may be nonzero, but all δ_τ for $\tau \neq \theta, 2\theta, \ldots$ are zero, the sequence may be said to be periodic. The greatest θ with this property is called *period* of the sequence. Obviously, $\{\delta_\tau\}$ is periodic if and only if $\{m_\tau\}$ is periodic.

Let μ represent the expected value of the time to replacement. Then

$$\mu = \sum_{\tau=0}^{\infty} \tau m_\tau \tag{8}$$

or where

$$m(\lambda) = \sum_{\tau=0}^{\infty} m_\tau \lambda^\tau$$

is the generating function of the sequence $\{m_\tau\}$

$$\mu = m'(1)$$

The main theorem may now be stated as follows. If the sequence $\{\delta_\tau\}$, representing the proportion of the total stock replaced in each period, is *not* periodic, and the sequence $\{m_\tau\}$, representing the distribution of replacements of the initial investment over time sums to unity, then

$$\delta_\tau \to \frac{1}{\mu} \tag{9}$$

as $\tau \to \infty$.[11] To cover the case of periodic replacement, this theorem may be reformulated as follows. If the sequence $\{\delta_\tau\}$ has period θ and the sequence $\{m_\tau\}$ sums to unity, then

$$\delta_{\tau\theta} \to \frac{\theta}{\mu} \tag{10}$$

for $\tau = 1, 2, \ldots$ and $\delta_\tau = 0$ otherwise.[12]

2.3 *Multiple investments, constant capital*

These theorems are easily extended to an arbitrary distribution of the initial investment over time. Let the proportion of the initial investment completed at time τ be denoted ϕ_τ. The

[11] See [8, p. 286, Theorem 3]. Proof of this theorem is given on pp. 306–7.
[12] See [8, p. 287, Theorem 4].

distribution of investments over time is described by a sequence of non-negative numbers

$$\phi_0, \phi_1, \ldots \tag{11}$$

where

$$\sum_{\tau=0}^{\infty} \phi_\tau = 1 \tag{12}$$

the entire amount of the investment is eventually completed. At this point we may drop the assumption that $\delta_0 = 1$, that is, that the entire capital stock is completed at period zero. Investment at any time is equal to new investment ϕ_τ plus replacement investment; representing the sequence of investments by $\{\delta_\tau\}$ we have the following recursive relationships

$$\begin{aligned} \delta_0 &= \phi_0 \\ \delta_1 &= \phi_1 + m_1\delta_0 \\ &\cdots\cdots\cdots\cdots\cdots\cdots \\ \delta_\tau &= \phi_\tau + m_1\delta_{\tau-1} + m_2\delta_{\tau-2} + \cdots + m_\tau\delta_0 \end{aligned} \tag{13}$$

These relationships specialise to the preceding case when $\delta_0 = \phi_0 = 1$ and $\phi_\tau = 0$ for $\tau > 0$.

If μ is defined as above (8), the main theorem can be stated as follows. If the sequence $\{\delta_\tau\}$, representing investment as a proportion of total stock in each period, is *not* periodic, if the sequence $\{m_\tau\}$, representing the distribution of replacements of the initial investment over time sums to unity, and if the sequence $\{\phi_\tau\}$, representing the distribution of the initial investment over time also sums to unity, then

$$\delta_\nu \rightarrow \frac{\sum_{\tau=0}^{\infty} \phi_\tau}{\mu} = \frac{1}{\mu} \tag{14}$$

as $\nu \rightarrow \infty$. As before, if $\{\delta_\tau\}$ has period θ and the sequence $\{m_\tau\}$ sums to unity, then

$$\delta_{\nu\theta} \rightarrow \frac{\theta}{\mu} \sum_{\tau=0}^{\infty} \phi_\tau = \frac{\theta}{\mu} \tag{15}$$

for $\nu = 1, 2, \ldots$ and $\delta_\tau = 0$ otherwise [8, p. 294]. The proportion of replacement investment in total investment approaches unity as $\tau \to \infty$, so that

$$\delta_\tau \to m_1\delta_{\tau-1} + m_2\delta_{\tau-2} + \cdots + m_\tau\delta_0$$

as $\tau \to \infty$. Hence statements (14) and (15) hold for the sequence of replacement investments.

2.4 *Single investment, changing capital*

For a growing capital stock we adopt the convenient fiction that an initial investment is the progenitor of an infinite stream of new investments leading to the expansion of capacity. As an illustration, this model would include the situation considered by Domar [5] and Eisner [6] in which gross investment grows at a fixed percentage rate. As before, we represent the distribution of replacements over time by the sequence of non-negative numbers

$$m_0, m_1, \ldots$$

It is convenient to assume

$$m_0 = 0$$

and

$$\sum_{\tau=1}^{\infty} m_\tau = 1$$

as before. We next represent the distribution of new investments by a sequence of non-negative numbers

$$\gamma_0, \gamma_1, \ldots \tag{16}$$

where it is convenient to assume

$$\gamma_0 = 0 \tag{17}$$

and, where $\gamma(\lambda)$ is the generating function of the sequence (16), that $\gamma(1)$ is finite. The sum of the sequences $\{m_\tau\}$, $\{\gamma_\tau\}$ is represented by $\{\alpha_\tau\}$, where

$$\alpha_\tau = m_\tau + \gamma_\tau \quad (\tau = 1, 2, \ldots) \tag{18}$$

For a constant capital stock the sequence representing gross investment approaches, as a limit, the sequence representing replacement investment. For a growing capital stock the difference between the two sequences does not converge to zero. Consequently, it is necessary to introduce sequences representing gross investment, replacement investment and investment for the expansion of capacity. First, we introduce a sequence representing gross investment as a proportion of initial capital stock. This sequence, denoted $\{\delta_\tau\}$, is computed recursively from the sequence $\{\alpha_\tau\}$, representing replacement and new investment as a proportion of any initial investment. The proportion of the initial capital stock invested at time ν and again at a later time $\tau > \nu$ is equal to $\alpha_\nu \delta_{\tau-\nu}$. The proportion of the initial stock invested at the τth period is the sum of the proportions invested first at periods 1, 2, . . . and later at period τ; hence

$$\delta_\tau = \alpha_1 \delta_{\tau-1} + \alpha_2 \delta_{\tau-2} + \cdots + \alpha_\tau \delta_0 \tag{19}$$

As before, it is convenient to assume

$$\delta_0 = 1$$

in particular, $\alpha_\tau = \alpha_\tau \delta_0$. Equation (19) is, of course, the renewal equation. Unless the generating function for the sequence $\{\gamma_\tau\}$, $\gamma(\lambda)$, is zero at $\lambda = 1$, the sequence diverges.

Next, we introduce sequences representing replacement investment and investment for expansion of capacity as a proportion of initial capital stock. Let $\{\beta_\tau\}$ represent the sequence of replacement investments and $\{\kappa_\tau\}$ the sequence of investments for expansion of capacity. Then

$$\begin{aligned} \beta_\tau &= m_1 \delta_{\tau-1} + m_2 \delta_{\tau-2} + \cdots + m_\tau \delta_0 \\ \kappa_\tau &= \gamma_1 \delta_{\tau-1} + \gamma_2 \delta_{\tau-2} + \cdots + \gamma_\tau \delta_0 \end{aligned} \tag{20}$$

of course

$$\delta_\tau = \beta_\tau + \kappa_\tau$$

That is, gross investment is the sum of replacement investment and investment for the expansion of capacity. Finally, we introduce a sequence representing current capital stock as a proportion of initial capital stock. Let $\{\varepsilon_\tau\}$ represent this sequence; then

$$\varepsilon_\tau = \delta_0 + \sum_{\nu=0}^{\tau-1} \kappa_\nu \tag{21}$$

But $\varepsilon_0 = \delta_0$, so that

$$\varepsilon_\tau = \varepsilon_0 + \sum_{\nu=0}^{\tau-1} (\gamma_1 \delta_{\nu-1} + \gamma_2 \delta_{\nu-2} + \cdots + \gamma_\nu \delta_0)$$

Unless $\gamma(\lambda)$ is zero for $\lambda = 1$, each of the sequences $\{\beta_\tau\}$, $\{\kappa_\tau\}$ and $\{\varepsilon_\tau\}$ diverges.

The following discussion is based on the fundamental result of renewal theory that if $\gamma(1)$ is not zero and if the sequence $\{\alpha_\tau\}$ is not periodic, there exists a unique positive root, $\xi < 1$, of the equation

$$\alpha(\xi) = m(\xi) + \gamma(\xi) = 1 \tag{22}$$

where $\alpha(\lambda)$, $m(\lambda)$ and $\gamma(\lambda)$ are the generating functions of the sequences $\{\alpha_\tau\}$, $\{m_\tau\}$ and $\{\gamma_\tau\}$, such that

$$\delta_\tau \sim \frac{1}{\alpha'(\xi)} \xi^{-\tau} \tag{23}$$

where the sign $\sim$ indicates that the ratio of the two sides approaches unity as $\tau \to \infty$. Asymptotically, the sequence of gross investment $\{\delta_\tau\}$ grows at a rate $\xi^{-1} - 1$; this rate, defined as a root of Equation (22), is non-negative since the generating functions $m(\lambda)$, $\gamma(\lambda)$ have non-negative coefficients; it is positive if and only if $\gamma(1) > 0$. The rate of growth, $\xi^{-1} - 1$, is unique since the function $\alpha(\xi)$ is monotone. We consider the sequences $\{\delta_\tau \xi^\tau\}$, $\{\alpha_\tau \xi^\tau\}$; since $\alpha(\xi) = 1$

$$\delta_\tau \xi^\tau \to \frac{1}{\alpha'(\xi)}$$

as $\tau \to \infty$, by (9) above. Hence

$$\delta_\tau \sim \frac{1}{\alpha'(\xi)} \xi^{-\tau}$$

as $\tau \to \infty$, as asserted.

As a consequence of the result (23) for the sequence of gross investments $\{\delta_\tau\}$, we have the following result for the sequence of replacement investments $\{\beta_\tau\}$

$$\beta_\tau \sim m_1 \frac{\xi^{-(\tau-1)}}{\alpha'(\xi)} + m_2 \frac{\xi^{-(\tau-2)}}{\alpha'(\xi)} + \cdots + m_\tau \frac{\xi^0}{\alpha'(\xi)}$$

$$= \frac{1}{\alpha'(\xi)} (1/\xi) \sum_{\nu=1}^{\tau} m_\tau \xi^\tau$$

so that

$$\beta_\tau \sim \frac{m(\xi)}{\alpha'(\xi)} \xi^{-\tau} \tag{24}$$

If gross investment grows at a rate $\xi^{-1} - 1$, replacement investment grows, asymptotically, at the same rate. This implies that replacement investment approaches a constant proportion of gross investment. This proportion is, of course, $m(\xi) \leq 1$.

Similarly, for the sequence of investments for the expansion of capacity $\{\kappa_\tau\}$, we have the result

$$\kappa_\tau \sim \frac{\gamma(\xi)}{\alpha'(\xi)} \xi^{-\tau} \tag{25}$$

that is, investment for expansion grows at the same rate as gross investment and replacement investment, asymptotically. Investment for expansion of capacity approaches the proportion $\gamma(\xi)$ of gross investment.

Finally, the sequence $\{\varepsilon_\tau\}$, representing capital stock, takes the form

$$\begin{aligned}\varepsilon_\tau &= \varepsilon_0 + \sum_{\nu=0}^{\tau-1} \kappa_\nu \\ &= \varepsilon_0 + \sum_{\nu=0}^{\tau-1} \frac{\gamma(\xi)}{\alpha'(\xi)} \xi^{-\nu} \\ &= \varepsilon_0 + \frac{\gamma(\xi)}{\alpha'(\xi)} \sum_{\nu=0}^{\tau-1} \xi^{-\nu} \\ &= \varepsilon_0 \frac{\gamma(\xi)}{\alpha'(\xi)} \frac{1 - \xi^\tau}{1 - \xi} \xi^{-\tau}\end{aligned}$$

Hence

$$\varepsilon_\tau \sim \frac{\xi\gamma(\xi)}{(1 - \xi)\alpha'(\xi)} \xi^{-\tau} \tag{26}$$

that is, capital stock grows at the same rate as gross investment.

We conclude that, for a growing capital stock, replacement investment approaches a constant proportion of capital stock

$$\frac{\beta_\tau}{\varepsilon_\tau} \to \frac{\dfrac{m(\xi)}{\alpha'(\xi)} \xi^{-\tau}}{\dfrac{\gamma(\xi)}{(1 - \xi)\alpha'(\xi)} \xi^{-\tau}} = \frac{(1 - \xi)m(\xi)}{\xi\gamma(\xi)} \tag{27}$$

as $\tau \to \infty$. A similar expression may be derived for the limit of the proportion of investment for the expansion of capacity to capital stock

$$\frac{\kappa_\tau}{\varepsilon_\tau} \to \frac{\dfrac{\gamma(\xi)}{\alpha'(\xi)}\,\xi^{-\tau}}{\dfrac{\xi\gamma(\xi)}{(1-\xi)\alpha'(\xi)}\,\xi^{-\tau}} = \frac{1}{\xi} - 1 \tag{28}$$

which is the rate of growth of capital stock. Since $0 < \xi \leq 1$, both the expressions (27) and (28) are non-negative.

2.5 *Multiple investments, changing capital*

These results are easily generalised to an arbitrary distribution of the initial investment over time. As before, we introduce the sequence of non-negative numbers

$$\phi_0, \phi_1, \ldots$$

where ϕ_τ represents the proportion of the initial investment put in place at time τ. Condition (12) is satisfied as follows

$$\sum_{\tau=0}^{\infty} \phi_\tau = 1$$

The recursive relations (13) hold in the form

$$\begin{aligned}
\delta_0 &= \phi_0 \\
\delta_1 &= \phi_1 + \alpha_1\delta_0 \\
&\cdots\cdots\cdots\cdots\cdots\cdots \\
\delta_\tau &= \phi_\tau + \alpha_1\delta_{\tau-1} + \alpha_2\delta_{\tau-2} + \cdots + \alpha_\tau\delta
\end{aligned}$$

The fundamental result (23) takes the form

$$\delta_\tau \sim \frac{\sum_{\nu=0}^{\infty}\phi_\nu}{\alpha'(\xi)}\,\xi^{-\tau} = \frac{1}{\alpha'(\xi)}\,\xi^{-\tau}$$

The sequence of new investments $\{\kappa_\tau\}$ is represented by

$$\kappa_\tau = \phi_\tau + \gamma_1\delta_{\tau-1} + \gamma_2\delta_{\tau-2} + \cdots + \gamma_\tau\delta_0 \tag{29}$$

Of course $\delta_0 = \phi_0$. The sequence $\{\varepsilon_\tau\}$, representing capital stock as a proportion of the initial investment, becomes

$$\varepsilon_\tau = \sum_{v=0}^{\tau-1} \phi_v + \sum_{v=0}^{\tau-1} (\gamma_1 \delta_{v-1} + \gamma_2 \delta_{v-2} + \cdots + \gamma_v \delta_0)$$

where $\sum_{v=0}^{\infty} \phi_v$ plays the role of ε_0, the remaining argument is essentially unchanged.

In conclusion, then, if the sequence $\{\alpha_\tau\}$ is periodic with period θ

$$\frac{\beta_{\theta\tau}}{\varepsilon_{\theta\tau}} \to \frac{(1 - \xi) m(\xi)}{\xi \gamma(\xi)} \tag{30}$$

as $\tau \to \infty$ and $\beta_\tau / \varepsilon_\tau = 0$ for $\tau \neq 1\theta, 2\theta, \ldots$.

For illustrative purposes we consider the special case discussed by Domar [5] and Eisner [6] in which replacement investment is equal to gross investment v periods previous and gross investment grows at a constant rate. We choose the sequence $\{m_\tau\}$, $\{\gamma_\tau\}$ and $\{\phi_\tau\}$ as follows

$$m_0 = m_1 = \cdots = m_{v-1} = m_{v+1} = \cdots = 0$$

$$\gamma_0 = \gamma_1 = \cdots = \gamma_{v-1} = \gamma_{v+1} = \cdots = 0$$

and

$$m_v = 1$$

$$\gamma_v = (1 + \gamma)^v - 1$$

where γ is the rate of growth of gross investment

$$\phi_\tau = \phi_{\tau-1}$$

for $\tau < v$ and

$$\phi_\tau = 0$$

for $\tau \geq v$. Finally

$$\phi_0 = \frac{1 + \gamma}{\sum_{\tau=1}^{v} (1 + \gamma)^\tau}$$

Then, the asymptotic result (27) becomes

$$\frac{(1-\xi)m(\xi)}{\gamma(\xi)} = \frac{\left(\frac{1}{1+\gamma}\right)^{\nu}}{\{(1+\gamma)^{\nu}-1\}\left(\frac{1}{1+\gamma}\right)^{\nu}}$$

$$= \frac{\gamma}{(1+\gamma)^{\nu}-1}$$

which holds exactly for $\tau \geq \nu$. Using methods based on renewal theory, it is a simple matter to derive replacement as a proportion of gross investment for *any* distribution of replacement over time.

3. Depreciation

3.1 *Introduction*

The durable goods model developed above is characterised by price-quantity duality. In this section we develop the depreciation model dual to the model of replacement developed in the preceding section. The price model relates the price of acquisition of investment goods to future time rental prices of capital input. It also relates changes in the acquisition price to the current time rental and current depreciation.

We begin presentation of the depreciation model by introducing an intertemporal price system. The *present price* of the ith commodity in period t, say p_{it}, is the present unit value of that commodity purchased in the present period for delivery in period t. We assume that present prices are positive and go to zero as time increases,

$$p_{it} > 0, \qquad \lim_{t\to\infty} p_{it} = 0$$

Similarly, the *future price* of the ith commodity in period t, say q_{it}, is the unit value of that commodity purchased in period t for delivery in that period.

The *rate of interest* (on money) is defined as

$$r_t = -\frac{p_t - p_{t-1}}{p_t} \tag{31}$$

where p_t is the present price of money or the price of a bond maturing in period t so that $p_0 = 1$. The present price of money may be expressed in the form

$$p_t = \prod_{s=1}^{t} \frac{1}{1 + r_s}$$

The present price of a commodity is the product of the future price and the present price of money

$$p_{i,t} = p_t q_{it} = \prod_{s=1}^{t} \frac{1}{1 + r_s} q_{it}$$

By analogy with the rate of interest on money we may define the *own-rate of interest* on the *i*th commodity as

$$r_{it} = \frac{p_{i,t-1} - p_{it}}{p_{it}} \tag{32}$$

which is equivalent to

$$q_{it} r_{it} = q_{i,t-1} r_t - (q_{it} - q_{i,t-1})$$

the future price of the ith commodity in period t multiplied by the own-rate of interest on that commodity is equal to the money rate of interest multiplied by the future price of the commodity in period $t - 1$ plus the difference between the future price in period $t - 1$ and the price in period t.

3.2 *Price-quantity duality*

Capital stock is the sum of *past* acquisitions of capital goods weighted by their current *relative efficiency* given by the sequence $\{d_\tau\}$

$$K_t = \sum_{\tau=0}^{\infty} d_\tau A_{t-\tau} \tag{33}$$

The price of acquisition of a capital good is the sum of *future* rental prices of capital services weighted by the relative efficiency of the capital good

$$p_{At} = \sum_{\tau=0}^{\infty} d_\tau p_{K,t+\tau+1} \tag{34}$$

Replacement requirements are a weighted average of *past*

investments with weights given by the *mortality distribution*

$$R_t = \sum_{t=1}^{\infty} m_\tau A_{t-\tau} \tag{35}$$

Depreciation on a capital good p_{Dt} is a weighted average of *future* rental prices of capital services with weights given by the mortality distribution:

$$p_{Dt} = \sum_{\tau=1}^{\infty} m_\tau p_{K,t+\tau} \tag{36}$$

Taking the first difference of the expression for the price of acquisition of a capital good

$$\begin{aligned} p_{At} - p_{A,t-1} &= -p_{Kt} - \sum_{\tau=1}^{\infty} (d_\tau - d_{\tau-1}) p_{K,t+\tau} \\ &= -p_{Kt} + \sum_{\tau=1}^{\infty} m_\tau p_{Kt+\tau} \\ &= -p_{Kt} + p_{Dt} \end{aligned} \tag{37}$$

The capital service price is equal to depreciation less the period-to-period change in the price of acquisition.

Finally, we may express the capital service price in terms of present and future changes in asset prices. First, we rewrite the expression for change in the asset price in the form

$$\begin{aligned} p_A - p_{A,t-1} &= -p_{Kt} + \sum_{\tau=1}^{\infty} m_\tau p_{K,t+\tau} \\ &= -p_{Kt} + \sum_{\tau=1}^{\infty} m_\tau T^\tau p_{Kt} \\ &= -p_{Kt} + m(T) p_{Kt} \end{aligned}$$

where T is the lead operator and $m(T)$ is a power series in the lead operator

$$m(T) = \sum_{\tau=1}^{\infty} m_\tau T^\tau$$

Solving for the price of capital services, we obtain

$$\begin{aligned} p_{Kt} &= -\frac{1}{1 - m(T)} [p_{At} - p_{A,t-1}] \\ &= -[1 + \delta(T)][p_{At} - p_{A,t-1}] \\ &= -[p_{At} - p_{A,t-1}] - \sum_{\tau=1}^{\infty} \delta_\tau [p_{A,t+\tau} - p_{A,t+\tau-1}] \end{aligned} \tag{38}$$

where $\delta(T)$ is a power series in the lead operator. The sequence of coefficients $\{\delta_\tau\}$ is the *replacement distribution* and can be computed from the mortality distribution by means of the renewal equation [8].

Depreciation may be expressed in the form

$$p_{Dt} = -\sum_{\tau=1}^{\infty} \delta_\tau [p_{A,t+\tau} - p_{A,t+\tau-1}]$$

so that the *average depreciation rate* on the acquisition price of the capital good,

$$\bar{\delta} = \frac{p_{Dt}}{p_{At}} \tag{39}$$

may be expressed as a weighted average of replacement rates,

$$\bar{\delta} = -\sum_{\tau=1}^{\infty} \delta_\tau \frac{[p_{A,t+\tau} - p_{A,t+\tau-1}]}{p_{At}}$$

or, alternatively,

$$= \sum_{\tau=1}^{\infty} \delta_\tau r_{A,t+\tau} \prod_{s=1}^{\tau-1} (1 - r_{A,t+s})$$

where

$$r_{At} = -\frac{p_{At} - p_{A,t-1}}{p_{A,t-1}}$$

is the own-rate of interest on the acquisition of capital goods. The weights may be expressed in terms of changes in the forward acquisition prices of capital goods $\{p_{At}\}$.

The price of capital services may be expressed in the form

$$\begin{aligned} p_{Kt} &= -[p_{At} - p_{A,t-1}] + \bar{\delta} p_{At} \\ &= p_{At}[r_{At} + \bar{\delta}] \end{aligned} \tag{40}$$

the capital service price is the product of the price of acquisition of investment goods and the sum of the current own-rate of interest on investment goods and the average depreciation rate. This expression for the capital service price is in terms of present prices. An analogous expression in terms of future prices is

$$q_{Kt} = q_{A,t-1} r_t + q_{At}\bar{\delta} - (q_{At} - q_{A,t-1})$$

where q_{Kt} is the future price of capital services, q_{At} is the future price of acquisition of investment goods and r_t is the rate of interest on money.

As before,[13] we illustrate these relationships by taking the relative efficiency distribution to be geometric,

$$d_\tau = (1 - \delta)^\tau \qquad (\tau = 0, 1, \ldots)$$

The mortality distribution is also geometric,

$$m_\tau = d_{\tau-1} - d_\tau = \delta(1 - \delta)^{\tau-1} \qquad (\tau = 1, 2, \ldots)$$

Finally, the replacement distribution is constant,

$$\delta_\tau = \delta \qquad (\tau = 1, 2, \ldots)$$

The price of acquisition of capital goods becomes

$$p_{At} = \sum_{\tau=0}^{\infty} (1 - \delta)^\tau p_{K,t+\tau+1}$$

depreciation may be expressed in the form

$$p_{Dt} = \sum_{\tau=1}^{\infty} \delta(1 - \delta)^{\tau-1} p_{K,t+\tau}$$

$$= \sum_{\tau=1}^{\infty} \delta(p_{A,t+\tau} - p_{A,t+\tau-1})$$

$$= \delta p_{A,t}$$

The average depreciation rate p_{Dt}/p_{At} is a constant.

The capital service price may be expressed as:

$$p_{Kt} = p_{At}(r_{At} + \delta)$$

The time rental of capital at any time depends only on the current price and own-rate of interest of capital goods and is independent of future prices; for arbitrarily given own-rates of interest geometric decline in efficiency is necessary and sufficient for independence of future prices. Alternatively, if the weights in the average depreciation rate are constant over time, the average rate is constant. In terms of future prices the time rental price of capital services is

$$q_{Kt} = q_{A,t-1} r_t + q_{At}\delta - (q_{At} - q_{A,t-1})$$

for geometric decline in efficiency.

[13] See Section 2.1, above.

The replacement distribution $\{\delta_\tau\}$ enters the theory of investment behaviour in two ways. First, the average rate of depreciation $\bar{\delta}$ entering the time rental price of capital services is a weighted average of replacement rates with weights determined by future own-rates of interest on investment goods.[14] Second, the average rate of replacement $\hat{\delta}$ entering the determination of replacement requirements is a weighted average of replacement rates with weights determined by past net investments as a proportion of current capital stock. For the geometric mortality distribution replacement rates are constant and

$$\bar{\delta} = \hat{\delta} = \delta$$

where δ is the constant rate of replacement.

A fundamental result of renewal theory is that the sequence of replacement rates $\{\delta_\tau\}$ tends to a constant value for almost any mortality distribution (1). For the geometric mortality distribution the average rates of replacement, $\bar{\delta}$ and $\hat{\delta}$, are independent of future own-rates of interest or investment goods and of past net investments, respectively. For almost any mortality distribution these average rates of replacement are independent own-rates of interest on investments goods in the distant future and net investments in the distant past, since the sequence of replacement rates $\{\delta_\tau\}$ tends to a constant value as τ, the time elapsed since initial acquisition of an investment good, increases. The geometric distribution may be employed as an approximation to an arbitrary mortality distribution. The quality of this approximation depends on the speed of convergence of the sequence of replacement rates $\{\delta_\tau\}$ to a constant value and on the variation of weights that determine the average depreciation rate $\bar{\delta}$ and the average replacement rate $\hat{\delta}$. Even if the weights are constant, the average rates may be constant but unequal to each other.

4. Form of the Replacement Distribution

The geometric mortality distribution is very commonly employed in the estimation of replacement requirements in econometric studies of investment behaviour. This distribution has been

[14] See formula (39), above.

employed by Grunfeld in analysing annual data on investment by individual firms and by Hickman in analysing data on investment by industry groups [12] [17]. The geometric mortality distribution has also been extensively employed in measuring capital for social accounting purposes, as in Office of Business Economics capital goods studies [11]. Although the geometric distribution may provide a useful approximation to an arbitrary mortality distribution in estimating replacement requirements, the validity of the approximation must be tested.

A direct test of the validity of the geometric approximation can be obtained from data on replacement investment and capital stock or from data on rental prices of capital goods and prices of used capital goods. Very little direct evidence is available on replacement requirements relative to the extensive evidence available on retirement of capital goods. As we have already emphasised, retirement is only part of the decline in efficiency that generates the mortality distribution. We now review the limited evidence on mortality distributions available from studies of replacement investment. Meyer and Kuh have studied the 'echo effect' in analysing data for individual firms [25, pp. 91–100]. An extreme form of the 'echo effect' is associated with a periodic mortality distribution, resulting in a periodic distribution of replacements and periodic cycles of replacement investment.[15] A weaker form of the echo effect is associated with relatively high values of the replacement distribution at particular ages. This is the form of the echo effect tested by Meyer and Kuh. The age of a firm's capital equipment is measured by accumulated depreciation reserves divided by gross fixed assets at the beginning of the period. Firms are divided into fifteen industry groups within manufacturing, corresponding roughly to two-digit industries [25, pp. 209–232.]. The dependent variable is gross investment divided by gross fixed assets on the grounds '. . . that since replacement investment is included in gross investment the net impact of the echo effect should be ascertainable even when using gross investment as the dependent variable – although perhaps not as precisely as would be desirable'. [25, p. 93].

Meyer and Kuh employ a profit model and a sales model to

[15] See Section 2.2, above.

explain gross investment. In regressions for averages of annual data over the period 1946–50 the age variable is significant in both models for only one industry group – Vehicles and Suppliers; age is significantly negative for this industry, suggesting high rates of replacement for low ages of capital goods [25, pp. 255–56]. For other industry groups the age variable is both positive and negative with small negative values predominating. Age is significantly negative for Light Chemicals in the sales model but not in the profits model. The proportion of significant results – three out of thirty regressions – is not out of line with the null hypothesis that the echo effect plays no role in the determination of investment for individual firms. It may be noted that these results hold for the immediate post-war period, when the assumption of constant weights for the average replacement rate $\hat{\delta}$, based on a constant growth rate of capital stock, is least likely to hold. The validity of the geometric approximation evidenced in these data may be attributed to relatively rapid convergence of the sequence of replacement rates $\{\delta_\tau\}$ to a constant value.[16]

As alternative test of the validity of the geometric approximation has been proposed by Feldstein and Foot [7]. If data on replacement investment and capital stock are available separately, the geometric approximation may be tested by analysing the ratio of replacement investment to capital stock. This variable is, of course, the average rate of replacement $\hat{\delta}$. The average replacement rate depends on the time path of past net investment; the geometric approximation may be tested by regressing the average replacement rate on lagged values of net investment divided by current capital stock. If the geometric approximation is appropriate, the average replacement rate is a constant and is independent of lagged values of net investment. Obviously, this test requires data on both replacement investment and capital stock; net investment can be calculated only by observing period-to-period changes in capital stock; the level of capital stock is required to compute the average replacement rate $\hat{\delta}$. Feldstein and Foot have obtained data on replacement investment from the McGraw-Hill survey. However, this survey does not provide the corresponding data on capital stock, so that a test of the geometric approximation cannot be carried out.

[16] See Section 2, above.

Feldstein and Foot compute average replacement rates using perpetual inventory estimates of capital stock for the manufacturing sector by the Department of Commerce [11]. In these estimates a fixed mortality distribution is applied to past data on gross investment. Capital stock is a weighted sum of past acquisitions of investment goods with each acquisition weighted by its relative efficiency (3). Of course, the capital stock estimates imply a set of estimates of replacement investment; replacement investment is a weighted sum of past acquisitions with weights given by the mortality distribution (2). This set of estimates of replacement investment is, of course, distinct from the estimates of Feldstein and Foot, based on the McGraw-Hill survey. It would be possible to estimate a regression of the average replacement rate $\hat{\delta}$ implicit in the Department of Commerce estimates of capital stock on past net investments as a proportion of current capital stock with past net investments also derived from the Department of Commerce estimates of capital stock. However, this would result in a set of coefficients equal to the replacement rates implicit in the mortality distribution employed in the Department of Commerce perpetual inventory estimates. Regression of this type would provide no independent evidence on the mortality or replacement distributions.

Feldstein and Foot proceed with a statistical analysis of average replacement rates computed from McGraw-Hill survey estimates of replacement investment and Department of Commerce estimates of capital stock. Their first error is to employ Department of Commerce data on gross capital stock in estimating the average replacement rate $\hat{\delta}$ [7, p. 52]. Gross capital stock is an unweighted sum of past gross investments; the average replacement rate is the ratio of replacement investment to a weighted sum of past gross investment with weights given by the relative efficiency of capital goods of different ages. Second, Feldstein and Foot regress the average replacement rate on variables such as cash flow and capacity utilisation. If the decline in efficiency of capital goods depends on cash flow and relative utilisation in each period, the perpetual inventory estimates of capital stock of the Department of Commerce are inappropriate. In the perpetual inventory method decline in relative efficiency is independent of time and also of variables that are functions of time, such as cash flow or capacity utilisation. The relative efficiency of a capital good depends only on the age of the capital good and not on time or other variables. The hypothesis that the average replacement rate depends on cash flow or capacity utilisation contradicts the assumptions underlying the Department of Commerce perpetual inventory estimates of capital stock. Either the perpetual inventory method is valid and the average replacement rate depends on the proportion of past net investments in current capital stock or the average replacement rate depends on such variables as time, cash flow and capacity utilisation and the perpetual inventory method is invalid. Feldstein and Foot use perpetual inventory estimates of capital stock in estimating the average replacement rate and regress the average replacement rate so estimated on cash flow and capacity utilisation, which is self-contradictory.

We conclude that Feldstein and Foot have not successfully avoided the necessity for direct observation of both replacement investment and capital stock in studying the validity of the geometric approximation to the replacement distribution. The use of perpetual inventory estimates of capital stock implies that the average replacement rate calculated from an internally consistent body of data, replacement investment and capital stock estimated by the perpetual inventory method, depends only on the proportions of past net investments in current capital stock. Analysis of this relationship by statistical methods is superfluous since a regression of the average replacement rate on the ratios of past net investments to current capital stock will simply generate the replacement distribution implicit in the mortality distribution employed in the perpetual inventory method. Regressions of average replacement rates on variables such as cash flow or capacity utilisation are self-contradictory. The conclusions of Feldstein and Foot, based on regressions of this type, are vitiated by this elementary error.

We have reviewed evidence on the mortality distribution from studies of replacement requirements. An alternative approach to the empirical study of mortality distributions is through the analysis of used equipment prices. Data on used equipment prices are limited to readily moveable assets. A study of price data for farm tractors is reported by Griliches [10, pp. 181–210] and studies of price data for automobiles are presented by Cagan and Wykoff [3], [30]. A much more intensive study of price data for pick-up trucks is given by Hall [14, pp. 240–71]. Used equipment prices, like prices for acquisition of new equipment, are equal to the sum of future rental prices weighted by the relative efficiency of the capital good over its remaining lifetime. For equipment of age σ at time t, the acquisition price is

$$p^{\sigma}_{At} = \sum_{\tau=0}^{\infty} d_{\tau+\sigma} p_{K,t+\tau+1} \tag{41}$$

For geometric decline in efficiency the acquisition prices decline geometrically with age, since

$$\begin{aligned} p^{\sigma}_{At} &= \sum_{\tau=0}^{\infty} (1-\delta)^{\tau+\sigma} p_{K,t+\tau+1} \\ &= (1-\delta)^{\sigma} \sum_{\tau=0}^{\infty} (1-\delta)^{\tau} p_{K,t+\tau+1} \\ &= (1-\delta)^{\sigma} p_{At} \end{aligned}$$

We now review the evidence on decline in relative efficiency from data on used equipment prices.

Studies of prices of acquisition of new and used capital goods reveal a sharp drop between the price of new equipment and the price of used equipment. The obvious explanation is that prices of new equipment are 'list' prices paid by relatively few purchases. The actual prices paid vary over a model year, declining as a new model year approaches; this variation is omitted from the observed list prices. The prices of used equipment are based on actual transactions and vary over the year.[17] From an examination of prices of used farm tractors ages one to thirteen for ten different points of time during the years 1937–58, Griliches concludes: 'The data point to a declining balance [geometric] depreciation model, with a rate somewhat higher in the 1930s than in the 1950s' [10, p. 198]. Wykoff's findings for used automobiles ages one to seven for five different points of time during the years 1950–68, are similar: 'After the first year cars do appear to decay exponentially [geometrically]' [30, pp. 171–2]. Cagan also finds that geometric depreciation provides a satisfactory approximation [3, pp. 225–6].

[17] This argument is developed by Griliches [10, p. 198, fn. 32].

Hall's study of pick-up trucks includes an estimate of the mortality distribution in a statistical model that also provides estimates of the time pattern of the price of acquisition of new capital goods, and an index of embodied technical change. The data are prices for secondhand pick-up trucks ages one to six for the years 1961–7. Two makes of pick-up trucks, Ford and Chevrolet, are included in the study. Hall first fits a model of used equipment prices separately to data for both makes. He then tests the hypothesis that the two makes are perfect substitutes in the sense that prices of acquisition of new capital goods move in fixed proportion to each other. This hypothesis is accepted at a level of significance of 0·05. He then imposes this hypothesis and tests the hypothesis that the mortality distribution is the same for both makes. This hypothesis is also accepted at a level of significance of 0·05. He imposes these two hypotheses and tests the hypothesis that the index of embodied technical change is the same for both makes; again the hypothesis is accepted. Finally, he imposes the hypotheses that the prices of acquisition of the two makes are proportional, that the mortality distribution is the same for the two makes, and that the index of embodied technical change is the same for both makes, and tests the hypothesis that the mortality distribution is geometric. The critical value of F at a level of significance of 0·05 is 2·57; the compound value of F is 3·59. Hall also tests the hypothesis that the index of embodied technical change is geometric.

The statistical design employed by Hall is not the most natural one for the sequence of tests he carries out. Five hypotheses are tested on the same data, used equipment prices for Fords and Chevrolets, 1961–7. A 'nested' structure for all five would be: (*a*) the two makes are perfect substitutes, (*b*) the mortality distribution is the same for both makes, (*c*) the index of embodied technical change is the same for both makes, (*d*) the mortality distribution is geometric, (*e*) the index of embodied technical change is geometric. The level of significance for all five tests is, approximately, the sum of levels of significance at each stage. Controlling the overall level of significance, the probability of rejecting at least one hypothesis when it is true, at 0·05, the level of significance at each stage would be 0·01. Hall's statistical design differs in two respects from this proposed design. First, the hypothesis that the index of embodied technical change is geometric is tested out of sequence so that the associated test statistic is not distributed independently of test statistics for the other hypotheses. Second, a level of significance of 0·05 is used for each hypothesis, so that the overall length of significance is close to 0·25. Employing the nested design we obtain the results in Table 10.1. Test statistics for each

TABLE 10.1 *Test Statistics for Hall's Study of Pick-up Trucks**

Calculated *F*-statistics		Critical values 0·05	0·01
Full *F*-tests			
Same p:	$F(7, 40) = 0{\cdot}86$	2·25	3·12
Same D:	$F(5, 40) = 0{\cdot}00$	2·45	3·51
Same b:	$F(10, 40) = 1{\cdot}00$	2·07	2·80
Geom. D:	$F(8, 40) = 1{\cdot}71$	2·18	2·99
Geom. b:	$F(20, 40) = 6{\cdot}35$	1·84	2·37
Nested *F*-tests			
Same p:	$F(7, 40) = 0{\cdot}86$	2·25	3·12
Same D:	$F(5, 47) = 0{\cdot}50$	2·41	3·43
Same b:	$F(10, 52) = 0{\cdot}79$	2·01	2·68
Geom. D:	$F(4, 62) = 3{\cdot}66$	2·51	3·64
Geom. b:	$F(10, 66) = 13{\cdot}73$	1·98	2·61

* The hypotheses tested are:
Same p: The two makes are perfect substitutes.
Same D: The mortality distribution is the same for both makes.
Same b: The index of embodied technical change is the same for both makes.
Geom. D: The mortality distribution is geometric.
Geom. b: The index of embodied technical change is geometric.

of the hypotheses and critical values for these statistics are given in the first part of this table.[18] Test statistics for the nested sequence of hypotheses outlined above are given in the second part of the table.

A second problem with Hall's test procedure arises from the assumption that errors for the two makes of pick-up trucks have the same variance and that these errors are distributed

[18] The empirical study reported in Tables 10.1 and 10.2 was carried out by Rafael Weston.

independently in each period. The residual variance for Chevrolets is 0·0006133; the variance for Fords is 0·0002991 or less than half that for Chevrolets. The covariance between error for the two makes is 0·0003315, so that the correlation is 0·774. Hall's assumption of equal variances and zero covariance for the two makes is clearly inconsistent with the evidence. Test statistics for each of the hypotheses and critical values for these statistics are given in Table 10.2;[19] the format of this table is the same

TABLE 10.2 *Test Statistics for Hall's Study of Pick-up Trucks, Estimated Variance-Covariance Matrix**

Calculated F-statistics	Critical values 0·05	0·01
Full F-tests		
Same p: $F(7, 40) = 2{\cdot}92$	2·25	3·12
Same D: $F(5, 40) = 0{\cdot}84$	2·45	3·51
Same b: $F(10, 40) = 3{\cdot}34$	2·07	2·80
Geom. D: $F(8, 40) = 1{\cdot}00$	2·18	2·99
Geom. b: $F(20, 40) = 4{\cdot}66$	1·84	2·37
Nested F-tests		
Same p: $F(7, 40) = 2{\cdot}92$	2·25	3·12
Same D: $F(5, 47) = 1{\cdot}30$	2·41	3·43
Same b: $F(10, 52) = 1{\cdot}99$	2·01	2·68
Geom. D: $F(4, 62) = 0{\cdot}92$	2·51	3·64
Geom. b: $F(10, 66) = 4{\cdot}78$	1·98	2·61

* The hypotheses tested are the same as those in Table 10.1. The test statistics are distributed asymptotically as F-ratios.

as that for Table 10.1. The results differ substantially from those of Hall. First, at levels of significance of 0·01 for each stage the only hypothesis rejected is that the index of embodied technical change is geometric. At levels of significance of 0·05 or an overall level of significance of 0·25 for all five stages, the hypotheses that the makes are perfect substitutes would be rejected. Hall's conclusion is that '... the geometric [mortality distribution] function is probably a reasonable approximation for many purposes. Certainly, there are no grounds for believing that any very serious error has been committed by using a geometric deterioration function in calculating capital stock'

[19] See Note 11, above.

[14]. The fitted relative efficiency sequence, normalising on the value of the function at age one year is $d_1 = 1{\cdot}000$, $d_2 = 0{\cdot}828$, $d_3 = 0{\cdot}693$, $d_4 = 0{\cdot}581$, $d_5 = 0{\cdot}475$, $d_6 = 0{\cdot}381$ [14]. We conclude that Hall's data on the mortality distribution for pick-up trucks supports the conclusions of Cagan, Griliches and Wykoff for automobiles and farm tractors. The geometric mortality distribution explains the behaviour of used equipment prices for all three types of capital goods.

5. Summary and Conclusion

In this paper we have presented the economic theory of replacement and its dual, the economic theory of depreciation. This theory is based on the durable goods model of capital, relating capital stock to past acquisitions of capital goods and changes in capital stock to current acquisitions and current replacement requirements. Replacement requirements are determined by losses in efficiency of existing capital goods as well as by retirements. Retirement represents the point at which efficiency declines to zero. A large body of evidence exists on the age of retirement of capital goods, but relatively little evidence is available on losses in efficiency of existing capital goods.

A fundamental result of renewal theory is that the replacement distribution corresponding to almost any morality distribution converges to a constant value. This result suggests the possibility of approximating replacement requirements and the time rental value of capital services by means of a geometric mortality distribution with constant replacement rate δ. For this approximation the average replacement rate determining replacement requirements $\hat{\delta}$ is constant and equal to the replacement rate δ. The usefulness of the geometric approximation depends on the speed of convergence of the replacement distribution to its constant asymptotic value and in variation in the weights that determine the average replacement rate $\hat{\delta}$.

The geometric mortality distribution has been employed for estimating replacement requirements in national wealth accounting and in econometric studies of investment behaviour. Direct tests of the validity of this approximation have been made by Meyer and Kuh in analysing replacement requirements. They find that replacement requirements as a proportion of capital stock are independent of the age of capital stock, an implication of the geometric mortality distribution.

The durable goods model that underlies our theory of replacement is characterised by price-quantity duality. The level of acquisition of capital goods is dual to the rental price of capital services. Capital stock is dual to the acquisition price of capital goods. Replacement requirements, a component of investment expenditures, are dual to depreciation, a component of the rental price of capital services. Beginning with the expression of the acquisition price of a capital good as the value of future capital services we derive a model of the time rental price of capital input. This model provides the basis for further empirical investigation of the form of the mortality distribution through analysis of data on used equipment prices.

The empirical evidence from studies of used equipment prices supports the findings of Meyer and Kuh from an analysis of replacement requirements.[20] The empirical evidence on the decline in efficiency of capital goods is limited to assets for which a secondhand market exists and to overall replacement requirements. This evidence is consistent with the geometric mortality distribution. The use of this distribution in econometric studies of investment behaviour may also be justified as an approximation to an arbitrary mortality distribution.

References

[1] ÅKERMAN, G., *Realkapital und Kapitalzins*, (Stockholm, 1924).

[2] ARROW, K. J., 'Optimal Capital Policy, the Cost of Capital, and Myopic Decision Rules', *Annals of the Institute of Statistical Mathematics*, XVI (1964).

[3] CAGAN, P., 'Measuring Quality Changes and the Purchasing Power of Money: An Exploratory Study of Automobiles', *National Banking Review*, III (December 1965) 217–36.

[4] DEBREU, G., *The Theory of Value*, (New York: John Wiley and Sons, 1959).

[5] DOMAR, E. D., 'Depreciation, Replacement and Growth', *Economic Journal*, LXIII (March 1953) 1–32.

[6] EISNER, R., 'Depreciation Allowances, Replacement

Requirements and Growth', *American Economic Review*, XLII (December 1952) 820–31.

[7] FELDSTEIN, M. S. and FOOT, D. K., 'The Other Half of Gross Investment: Replacement and Modernization Expenditures', *Review of Economics and Statistics*, LIII (February 1971) 49–58.

[8] FELLER, W., *An Introduction to Probability Theory and its Applications*, vol. I, 2nd ed. (New York: J. Wiley and Sons, 1957).

[9] FISHER, I., *The Theory of Interest*, (New York: A. M. Kelley, 1961).

[10] GRILICHES, Z., 'The Demand for a Durable Input: U.S. Farm Tractors, 1921–1957', in *The Demand for Durable Goods*, ed. A. C. Harberger, (Chicago: University of Chicago Press, 1960), 181–210.

[11] GROSE, L., ROTTENBERG, S. and WASSON, R., 'New Estimates of Fixed Business Capital in the United States', *Survey of Current Business*, XLIX (February 1969) 46–52.

[12] GRUNFELD, Y., 'The Determinants of Corporate Investments', in *The Demand for Durable Goods*, ed. A. C. Harberger (Chicago: University of Chicago Press, 1960), 211–66.

[13] HAAVELMO, T., *A Study in the Theory of Investment*, (Chicago: The University of Chicago Press, 1960).

[14] HALL, R. E., 'The Measurement of Quality Changes from Vintage Price Data', in Z. Griliches (ed.), *Price Indexes and Quality Change*, (Cambridge: Harvard University Press, 1971, 240–71).

[15] HALL, R. E., 'Technical Change and Capital from the Point of View of the Dual', *Review of Economic Studies*, XXXV (January 1968) 35–46.

[16] HARBERGER, A. C. (ed.), *The Demand for Durable Goods*, (Chicago: The University of Chicago Press, 1960).

[17] HICKMAN, B., *Investment Demand and U.S. Economic Growth*, (Washington: The Brookings Institution, 1965).

[18] HICKS, J., *Value and Capital*, 2nd ed. (Oxford: Oxford University Press, 1946).

[19] HOTELLING, H. S., 'A General Mathematical Theory of Depreciation', *Journal of the American Statistical Association*, XX (September 1925) 340–53.

[20] JORGENSON, D. W., MCCALL, J. J. and RADNER, R., *Optimal Replacement Policy*, (Amsterdam: North-Holland Publishing Company, 1967).

[21] KURTZ, E. B., *Life Expectancy of Physical Property based on Mortality Laws*, (New York: Ronald Press, 1930).

[22] LINDAHL, E., 'The Place of Capital in the Theory of Prices', in E. Lindahl, *Studies in the Theory of Money and Capital*, (London: Allen and Unwin, 1939).

[23] MALINVAUD, E., 'Capital Accumulation and the Efficient Allocation of Resources', *Econometrica*, XXI (April 1953) 233–68.

[24] MARSTON, A., WINFREY, R. and HEMPSTEAD, J. C., *Engineering Evaluation and Depreciation*, 2nd ed. (New York: McGraw-Hill, 1953).

[25] MEYER, J. and KUH, E., *The Investment Decision*, (Cambridge: Harvard University Press, 1957).

[26] SAMUELSON, P. A., *Foundations of Economic Analysis*, (Cambridge: Harvard University Press, 1947).

[27] SOLOW, R. M., 'Investment and Technical Progress', in *Mathematical Methods in the Social Sciences, 1959*. ed. K. J. Arrow, S. Karlin and P. Suppes (Stanford: Stanford University Press, 1960).

[28] WALRAS, L., *Elements of Pure Economics*, Translated by W. Jaffé, (Homewood, Illinois: R. D. Irwin, 1954).

[29] WICKSELL, K., 'A Mathematical Analysis of Dr. Åkerman's Problem', in *Lectures on Political Economy*, vol. I. Translated by E. Classen, (London: G. Routledge and Sons, 1934, 274–99).

[30] WYKOFF, F., 'Capital Depreciation in the Postwar Period: Automibles', *Review of Economics and Statistics*, LII (May 1970) 168–72.

11 Demographic Aspects of the Distribution of Income among Families: Recent Trends in the United States

BY SIMON KUZNETS*

FAMILY income is the dominant component of the size distribution of income among a country's population. As of March 1970, families accounted for 185 million out of a total population of the United States of 205 million – the rest being unattached persons and the institutional population.[1] And if the family is defined, as it is in the basic source used here, as 'a group of two or more persons related by blood, marriage or adoption and residing together' [see S-III, p. 8], it is the unit that makes most decisions relating to employment, other sources of income and the disposition of income received – and is therefore the relevant recipient unit in the analysis of the size distribution of income. But this means that differences and changes in the structure of family units have direct bearing upon the income distribution.

This paper deals with changes in a few demographic characteristics of family units and their effect on the distribution of money income among families in the United States since 1947. To this end we used the results of an annual survey of family income, which contains demographic data for March of the year following that for which income is given. Although deficient in that it excludes non-money income (the two important types are farm products retained for own consumption and income from owner-occupied dwellings) and its coverage of money income is incomplete, the survey provides considerable information on the demographic and labour force characteristics of

* Harvard University.

[1] The total number of persons in families is from [5, Table 18, p. 42] (referred to below as S-III). Total population (average of estimates for 1 March and 1 April, 1970) is from [3, Table 2, p. 5].

family heads and other members of the families.[2] For our purpose – to illustrate the increasing importance within the family income distribution of certain distinctive demographic groups among the families – the data, despite their shortcomings, are adequate.

1. The Three Selected Family Subgroups

Three groups among families distinguished by the age and sex of their heads are of particular interest here: those with relatively young heads; those with relatively old heads; and those with female heads. The more specific definitions (dictated by the available data) are: all families with heads under the age of 25 (listed in the data as 14 through 24); all families with heads aged 65 and over; families with female heads aged 25 through 64. This leaves a residual fourth category, families with male heads aged 25 through 64. Table 11.1 summarises the characteristics of these family subgroups that are easily derived from the data. These characteristics suggest why this particular classification has bearing on the income distribution among families (and hence on the total size distribution of income).

By definition, a family can have only one head. And while the

[2] The total money income of the family, as defined in the surveys, is the sum of money wages and salaries, net income from self-employment, and income other than earnings, of all income recipients in the family. The amounts cover gross income before deductions for personal taxes, Social Security and the like. Income other than earnings includes not only the usual property income (dividends, interest, net rental income, royalties, income from trusts and estates), but also public assistance and welfare payments, unemployment compensation, government pensions and veterans' payments, private pensions, annuities, alimony, regular contributions from persons not living in the household, and a variety of transfers. The only receipts resembling income that are excluded are gifts and tax refunds, and receipts and gains from sale of property (unless the recipient is engaged in the business, in which case they are recorded under net income from self-employment).

> It is estimated that the income surveys conducted by the Bureau of the Census during the past few years have obtained about 89 per cent of the comparable total money income aggregates and about 97 per cent of the comparable money wage or salary aggregates included in the personal income series prepared by the OBE. [S-III, p. 12]

More detailed appraisals of the data are given in [8], referred to below as S-I; in [4], referred to below as S-II; in S-III; and in [9, chap. III, Section B, pp. 58–72].

sources define head as 'the person regarded as the head by members of the family' [S-III, p. 9] the term for the most part relates to the person who makes the major contribution to family income, regardless of the weight he or she carries in decisions on uses of income. One should note also that 'women are not classified as heads if their husbands are resident members of the family at the time of the survey' and that 'married couples related to the head of a family (and living with the family) are included in the head's family and are not classified as separate families' (ibid., p. 9). The implication that the head is the main contributor to family income warrants the grouping in Table 11.1. Some of the associated characteristics may now be noted.

First, the three groups, those with young heads, old heads, and female heads aged 25–64, accounted for well over a quarter of the total number of families (line 1). As expected, the income per family in 1968–69 for each of these groups was lower than the countrywide average – ranging from about 36 per cent below the average for the group with old heads to over 40 per cent below for the group with female heads, either aged 25–64 or of all ages (line 3). Obviously, the lower income of families with young heads at the beginning of the life cycle of earnings, of those with old heads past the phase of full engagement, and of those with the distinct disadvantage of female heads as the main income providers (in families without male heads), contribute significantly to income inequality among families in the customary size distribution.

Second, the large proportion of Negroes in the group with female heads – about a quarter compared with the countrywide ratio of Negro heads of about 9 per cent (lines 4–5) – points to the greater prevalence of 'broken' family units among Negroes than among whites. It also contributes to the lower per family income for families with female heads, although the average income of families with *white* female heads is also distinctly below the countrywide average. The arithmetic mean income for families with white female heads aged 25–64 is \$6·44 thousand in 1968–69; for families with white female heads, all ages, \$6·30 thousand [see S-II, Table 12, pp. 28–34 and S-III, Table 17, pp. 35–42].

Third, not only are the three groups subaverage with respect to income per family, they are also subaverage in size of family,

Table 11.1 *Selected Demographic Characteristics of Families, United States, Average of March 1969 and March 1970 (unless otherwise indicated)*

		Age and sex of head				
	Total (1)	All, age below 25 (2)	All, age 65+ (3)	Female, age 25–64 (4)	Male, age 25–64 (5)	All female (6)
Number and income						
1. Number of families (total in million) and per cent shares	50·9	6·7	13·9	7·9	71·5	10·8
2. Families with female heads, per cent in line 1	10·8	11·0	15·9	100	0	100
3. Money income per family, arithmetic mean ($1000)	10·12	6·64	6·46	5·84	11·64	5·73
Race (per cent shares)						
4. White	89·9	87·6	92·1	72·7	91·5	74·8
5. Negro	9·3	11·8	7·3	26·3	7·5	24·3
Size-of-family groups (per cent shares)						
6. 2 persons	34·4	44·9	77·7	37·7	24·7	45·5
7. 3 persons	20·9	34·6	14·5	24·8	20·3	23·3
8. 4 and more persons	44·7	20·5	7·8	37·5	55·0	31·2
9. Average number of persons per family	3·63	3·00	2·39	3·44	3·95	3·22
10. Money income per person, ($1000) (line 3/line 9)	2·79	2·21	2·70	1·70	2·95	1·78
With own children under 18 (per cent)						
11. Proportion of families	55·9	58·6	3·1	64·0	65·0	52·6

Non-farm and farm families, March 1963–5, by age and sex of head (per cent shares)

		Age and sex of head		
	Total (millions) (1)	All, age below 25 (2)	All, age 65+ (3)	All, female head (4)
12. Non-farm	44·3	6·0	13·9	10·6
13. Farm	3·13	2·7	19·6	5·7

Labour force participation rates (per cent), male

	1950 (1)	1960 (2)	1960 (3)	1965 (4)	1969 (5)
14. Aged 20–24	81·9	86·1	88·9	86·2	85·3
15. Aged 65 and over	41·4	30·5	32·2	26·9	26·2

Demographic data in the surveys are for March of the year following that for which income is given. Entries in lines 1–2, 4–9, and 11 are, therefore, arithmetic averages although those with female heads are fairly close to the average (line 9). The families with young heads have about three persons per family, about a fifth below the countrywide average; and those with heads 65 years of age or more have only 2·4 persons. There are similar differentials in the proportion of families with own children under 18, particularly distinctive for families with heads 65 years of age or more (line 11). While it is not entirely justifiable to divide the average income per family by the average number of persons per family, if only because all persons are not of the same weight as consuming units (and because of size of family variance within each family group), the results in line 10 suggest that the three groups are also characterised by lower than average income per person – although that for the families with heads aged 65 and over is only slightly lower than the countrywide average.

Fourth, families with young or female heads are far less common among the farm than among the non-farm families (lines 12–13). On the other hand, the proportion of families with heads aged 65 and over is distinctly higher among the farm than among the non-farm families (about 20 and 14 per cent respectively). And yet even here the weight of this group with subaverage income is reduced by the finding that in 1962–64 the average family income for farm families with heads aged 65 and over was as high as 77 per cent of the average family income for all farm families, whereas the average income of the same age group among the non-farm families was less than 70 per cent of that for all non-farm families (for 1959–61 the

---

of the estimates for March 1969 and March 1970. Entries in line 3 (and line 10) are arithmetic averages of income in 1968 and 1969.
Lines 1–3: calculated from S-II, Table 15, pp. 42–43 and S-III, Table 20, pp. 49–50.
Lines 4–5: calculated from S-II, Table 12, pp. 30–34 and S-III, Table 17, pp. 35–41. The shares do not add to 100 because other non-white races are not shown.
Lines 6–8: column 1 calculated from S-II, Table 13, p. 35 and S-III, Table 18, p. 42. Columns 2–6 calculated from S-II, Table 15, pp. 42–43 and S-III, Table 20, pp. 50–51.
Line 9: entries in lines 6–8 multiplied by the number of persons per family. For families with four or more persons, the average number was derived from S-II, Table 13, p. 35 and S-III, Table 18, p. 42 (5·20 and 5·15 respectively) and the average, 5·175, was was applied to line 8, columns 2–6.
Line 11: calculated from S-II, Table 16, pp. 44–5 and S-III, Table 21, pp. 51–2.
Lines 12–13: calculated from S-I, Tables 2 and 3, pp. 51–62. The shares were calculated from arithmetic means of the number of families for March 1963–65.
Lines 14–15: columns 1–2 are from [6, p. 71] and [7, p. 13] and are for the United States excluding Hawaii and Alaska. Columns 3–5 are from [3, Table 317, p. 214], and are for the United States including Hawaii and Alaska.

corresponding relatives were 87 per cent for farm families and 70 per cent for non-farm families [see S-I, Table 25, pp. 182–87].

Fifth, participation in the labour force must differ between male and female heads of families; and among males, between the young and old heads, on the one hand, and those aged 25–64, on the other. Although complete data are lacking, some approximations can be made for male heads. The labour force participation rates shown in lines 14–15 cannot be applied directly to male heads of families, since all males within a given age class cannot be presumed to be heads of families. However, if we assume that almost all male heads of families in the young group are 20–24 years old, the ratio of heads among the latter for 1969 is roughly 39 per cent; whereas the ratio of family heads aged 65 and over to all males aged 65 and over is roughly 72 per cent.[3] These figures suggest that the high labour force participation rates among all males aged 20–24, between 80 and 90 per cent, would tend to be true also of the young male heads of families; and that the relatively low labour force participation rates among all males aged 65 and over, between 41 and 26 per cent, and rapidly declining, would tend to be true also of the old heads of families.

2. Trends in Shares of Selected Family Groups within Ordinal Divisions of the Family Distribution by Money Income

(a) *The findings*

Have the changes in the three selected subaverage income family groups, with the characteristics noted for 1969–70, had any effect on the total family distribution (and hence on the total size-of-income distribution)? In other words, have the *trends* in the shares of these groups affected trends in income inequality, as shown by the size distribution of money income among all families?

[3] The percentages are derived by comparing the number of male heads aged just below 25 in March 1969 with the number of all males aged 20–24 in July of the same year; and by the same procedure for males aged 65 and over. The data on male heads of families by age are from S-II, Table 15, pp. 42–43; those on all males by age for mid-1969 are from [3, Table 8, p. 10].

Table 11.2 summarises the data on the shares of the three subgroups within the ordinal divisions in the distribution of all families by money income, for some two decades extending from 1947–69. We also give the shares, within ordinal divisions of family heads who were not members of the labour force, and of the average number of persons per family – because of the close association between these characteristics, the low level of labour force participation among the family heads aged 65 and over and probably also among female heads of families, and the relatively small size of families among those with young heads or heads aged 65 and over.

The first major finding suggested by Table 11.2 is that over the twenty-two years, covering most of the period since the Second World War, the shares of all three selected family subgroups in the total number of families rose: the share of families with young heads rose from 5 to over 6·5 per cent of all families; that of families with heads aged 65 and over, from 12 to 14 per cent or slightly less; and that of families with female heads aged 25–64, from 7 to almost 8 per cent (column 7, lines 1 and 5, 6 and 10, 11 and 15). For the three subgroups combined, the share rose from about 24·2 to 28·5 per cent, a substantial rise over a relatively short period (column 7, lines 16 and 20).

Perhaps the rise in the proportions of families with heads aged 65 and over with female heads and the decline in the labour force participation rate among the old family heads (indicated in Table 11.1, line 15), contributed to the marked rise in the proportion, in the total of all families, of those with heads not in the labour force – from less than 13·5 per cent in 1948–51 to 19 per cent in 1968–69 (column 7, lines 21 and 25). Since only 1·2 million members of the armed forces were included in the survey for March 1970, and not all of them were heads of families, and this subgroup covers almost 9·8 million families, any increase in the armed forces component could not have contributed much to the rise in the share of families with heads not in the labour force [see S-III, p. 6 and Table 30, p. 68].

The increase in the proportions of families with young and old heads, all other conditions being equal, should have made for a *decline* in the average number of persons per family – since these two subgroups are characterised by a lower than average size of family (see Table 11.1, line 9). But Table 11.2 shows that

TABLE 11.2 *Selected Aspects of Family Structure, within Ordinal Divisions in the Distribution of Family Money Income, United States, 1947–69 (columns 1–7 for March of the following year)*

		Ordinal divisions						All families	Income per family relative
		Lowest fifth	Second fifth	Middle fifth	Fourth fifth	Top 80 to 95 per cent	Top 5 per cent		
		(1)	(2)	(3)	(4)	(5)	(6)	(7)	(8)
Families, head aged below 25, per cent shares									
1.	1947–52	6·2	8·1	5·7	4·0	1·9	0·3	5·1	0·725
2.	1953–58	6·5	8·3	5·5	3·4	1·7	0·3	5·0	0·717
3.	1959–61	7·8	8·9	5·7	3·5	1·4	0·3	5·4	0·674
4.	1962–64	8·9	9·2	6·4	3·6	1·2	0·2	5·8	0·657
5.	1968–69	10·7	10·8	7·1	3·8	1·2	0·6	6·7	0·656
Families, head aged 65+, per cent shares									
6.	1947–52	27·7	11·8	7·1	6·1	6·9	10·6	12·1	0·748
7.	1953–58	31·2	13·5	7·3	5·7	6·6	8·9	13·0	0·694
8.	1959–61	32·4	15·3	7·4	6·1	5·8	10·0	13·6	0·700
9.	1962–64	34·1	16·2	7·9	6·2	6·4	9·7	14·3	0·694
10.	1968–69	35·5	15·1	7·8	5·4	5·2	6·7	13·9	0·639
Families, female head aged 25–64, per cent shares (lines 11–14 estimated)									
11.	1947–52	14·2	7·9	5·0	3·9	4·3	2·9	7·0	0·694
12.	1953–58	15·5	8·3	4·7	3·5	3·3	2·4	7·0	0·642
13.	1959–61	16·6	9·0	4·6	3·4	2·6	1·6	7·2	0·592
14.	1962–64	17·3	9·4	4·8	3·2	2·8	2·3	7·5	0·596
15.	1968–69	19·4	9·8	4·8	3·3	2·2	1·6	7·9	0·567
Total of the three family groups above, per cent shares									
16.	1947–52	48·1	27·8	17·8	14·0	13·1	13·8	24·2	0·728
17.	1953–58	53·2	30·1	17·5	12·6	11·6	11·6	25·0	0·684
18.	1959–61	56·8	33·2	17·7	13·0	9·8	11·9	26·2	0·665
19.	1962–64	60·3	34·8	19·1	13·0	10·4	12·2	27·6	0·660
20.	1968–69	65·6	35·7	19·7	12·5	8·6	8·9	28·5	0·623
Families, head not in labour force, per cent shares (including members of Armed Forces, living on post or with their families off post)									
21.	1948–51	31·4	13·6	8·2	7·0	7·3	5·9	13·3	0·661
22.	1953–58	40·2	16·8	9·1	6·6	6·6	6·4	15·8	0·615
23.	1959–61	43·8	20·0	9·6	6·8	6·6	7·0	17·3	0·609
24.	1962–64	46·7	21·2	9·9	7·2	6·8	6·9	18·3	0·603
25.	1968–69	46·0	23·0	11·5	9·1	5·5	5·7	19·0	0·574
Average number of persons per family (column 8 shows sum of absolute deviations, signs disregarded, of the average within each ordinal division, properly weighted, from the average of all families)									
26.	1947–52	3·23	3·51	3·59	3·62	3·82	4·02	3·56	0·156
27.	1955–58	3·31	3·62	3·79	3·78	3·76	3·96	3·66	0·158
28.	1959–61	3·25	3·62	3·83	3·83	3·86	3·95	3·68	0·198
29.	1962–64	3·25	3·64	3·85	3·93	3·90	4·02	3·72	0·220
30.	1968–69	3·06	3·52	3·71	3·86	3·96	4·09	3·63	0·270
Number of persons per family, estimate based on the averages for the four family sub-groups in 1968–9 (column headings as for lines 26–30)									
31.	1947–52	3·39	3·65	3·76	3·80	3·80	3·77	3·68	0·126
32.	1968–69	3·20	3·56	3·74	3·81	3·85	3·83	3·63	0·201

Lines 1–4, 6–9, 16–19, and 21–24, columns 1–7: taken directly or calculated from S-I, Tables A and C, pp. 3–14 and 20–31. These tables contain annual series (for March of the following year), 1947–64, showing the shares of family groups distinguished by age of head, or by sex of head, or by non-participation of head in labour force

(excluding 1947 and 1952), in the total and within each ordinal division. The entries are arithmetic means of these shares for the periods shown in the stub. The shares for the top 80–95 per cent group were derived from those given for the top fifth and the top 5 per cent.

Lines 11–14, columns 1–7: since S-I does not provide a breakdown of families with female heads by age of head, we used the relation for March 1969–March 1970 of female heads, aged 25–64, to female heads of all ages, within each ordinal division, to approximate the entries in lines 11–14, column 1–6 (these ratios were 0·70, 0·77, 0·755, 0·755, 0·715 and 0·67, for columns 1–6 respectively). The combined share in column 7 was then derived from the shares within the ordinal divisions properly weighted (to allow for the differences in weight between columns 1–4 and 5–6).

Lines 1–4, 6–9, 11–14, 16–19 and *21–24, column 8:* taken directly or calculated from S-I, Tables 24, 25 and 29, pp. 176–187 and 200–204. These tables show the annual arithmetic mean income per family for groups of families distinguished by age of head, by sex of head, and by the head's non-participation in the labour force. These incomes, in current prices, were then averaged (logarithmically) for the periods indicated in the stub, and converted to ratios to the average family income for all families.

For families with female heads aged 25–64 we assumed an average income per family identical with that of all families with female heads (the only relevant average available). This assumption seemed justified since for 1968–69 the two were less than 2 per cent apart (see Table 11.1, line 3, columns 4 and 6).

Lines 16–20, column 8: calculated from lines 1–15, column 8, by weighting the income relative for each group by its share in the total of all families shown in column 7 and dividing by the sum of these shares.

Lines 5, 10, 15 and 25: the entries in columns 7 and 8 calculated from S-II, Table 15, pp. 42–43 and S-III, Table 20, pp. 49–50. Since shares *within* ordinal divisions (columns 1–6) were not shown in S-II and S-III, estimates had to be made. These were based on the distributions of families by eighteen family money income brackets, shown for all families, and for families distinguished by age, sex, and labour force status of the head [in S-II, Table 15, pp. 42–43 and in S-III Table 20, pp. 49–50, for age and sex of head groups; and in S-II, Table 23, p. 59 and S-III, Table 30, p. 68, for families with head not in labour force]. From these frequency distributions, the shares of the selected subgroups were calculated, *corresponding* to the ordinal divisions within the total family distribution (by arithmetic interpolation in order for the sum of the shares to equal hundred).

Lines 26–29, columns 1–7: calculated from S-I, Tables A and C. These tables show the shares of families with two, three and up to seven and over persons, within each ordinal division and for all families, annually, for 1947–52 and 1955–64. Arithmetic means of these shares, for the ordinal divisions and for the total of all families, were calculated for the periods shown in the stub; and the average number of persons for each ordinal division was computed, setting the average for the group of seven persons and over at 8·28 persons [the average of 8·34 derived from S-II, Table 13, p. 85 and 8·21 derived from S-III, Table 18, p. 42]. Column 7 was derived as a weighted mean of the averages in columns 1–6.

Line 30, columns 1–7: here, as for all estimates for 1968–69, the shares within the ordinal divisions had to be calculated from the tables showing the distribution by eighteen income brackets and the grouping of families by size corresponding to each income bracket [given in S-II, Table 13, p. 35 and S-III, Table 18, p. 42]. Column 7, the weighted mean of the averages in columns 1–6 agrees with the arithmetic mean size of family, given in the sources.

Lines 26–30, column 8: the sum, disregarding signs, of absolute deviations of the averages within the ordinal divisions (columns 1–6) from the average for all families (column 7), the deviations weighted to allow for the lower weights of the ordinal divisions in columns 5 and 6.

Lines 31–32: the averages in columns 1–6 were obtained by weighting the averages for the four subgroups (young, old, female heads aged 25–64, and male heads aged 25–64) in line 9 of Table 11.1 (for 1968–69) by the shares in lines 1, 5, 6, 10, 11, 15 and the complement of lines 16 and 20 above. The average in column 7 was derived from the averages in columns 1–6, properly weighted. The average deviation in column 8 was calculated like that in lines 26–30.

the average number of persons per family rose, at least through 1962–64; and while declining slightly thereafter, was still above the 1947–52 average in 1968–69 (see column 7, lines 26–30). Apparently other conditions changed; and the higher birth rate that marked the period, reaching its peak in the late 1950s, must have contributed to the slight rise in the average size of the family unit.

We can now turn to the movements, more significant for our purposes, in the shares *within* the ordinal divisions. And here there is a marked similarity in the trends for all three subgroups: the shares of the families with young heads, or old heads, or female heads aged 25–64 (and also female heads of all ages), *within the lower* ordinal divisions rose much more than their shares in the total of all families; whereas the shares within the upper ordinal divisions either declined or rose much less. Thus, the share of families with young heads within the lowest fifth rose from 6·2 per cent in 1947–52 to 10·7 per cent in 1968–69, a rise of over seven-tenths; their share in all families rose from 5·1 to 6·7 per cent, a rise of less than a third. Similar comparisons can be made for the shares of families with old or female heads.

Since families with young, old, and female heads drifted downward within the family income distribution, i.e. toward the lower ordinal divisions, the average income per family within these three subgroups, while below the average for all families throughout the period, declined in proportion to that average. Column 8, lines 1–5, 6–10 and 11–15, reveals that income per family, relative to that for all families, declined over the period from 1947–52 to 1968–69: for families with young heads, from about 73 per cent to about 66 per cent; for families with old heads, from 75 per cent to 64 per cent; and for families with female heads, from 69 per cent to 57 per cent. For the three groups combined, the family income relative dropped from 73 per cent to 62 per cent (lines 16–20, column 8).

The downward drift within the income distribution of the families with heads aged 65 and over, and with female heads, presumably contributed heavily to the similar trends for families with heads not in the labour force (lines 21–25). The rise in the share of this group within the two lower fifths was particularly striking, compared with their significant decline within the top 80 to 95 and the top 5 per cent. And correspondingly, the income relative for this group dropped from 66 per cent in 1948–51 to 57 per cent in 1968–69.

We noted that the average number of persons per family did not decline over the period, despite the rise in the share of families with young and old heads. But even here the downward drift of these two family subgroups meant that, after a while, the average size of the family in the low ordinal divisions tended to drop whereas that in the higher ordinal divisions tended to rise. This difference in trends in family size among ordinal divisions, which emerged after 1955–58, can be observed in columns 1 and 2 and columns 4–6 of lines 26–30. As a result, the disparity in size of family among the ordinal divisions, shown in column 8, increased from 0·16 in 1955–58 to 0·27 in 1968–69.

Lines 31–32 show that differences among the four family subgroups distinguished by age and sex of head in their shares within ordinal divisions contributed heavily to differences in average size of family between the lower and upper ordinal divisions. In 1947–52 the estimate reflecting inter-family subgroup differences in family size and in shares within the several fifths accounts for 0·38 points out of 0·79, or about one half, of the total range of differences in family size among the ordinal divisions in the family distribution; and in 1968–69 it accounts for 0·63 points out of 1·03, or six-tenths (the differences between columns 6 and 1 in lines 31 and 26; and those between the same columns in lines 32 and 30). This effect of the differences among the four family subgroups in their shares and family size is particularly conspicuous in the movement from the lower to the middle fifth. Of even greater interest is the fact that the downward drift of the three selected family subgroups contributed markedly to the widening divergence among the ordinal divisions with respect to average family size: of the 0·114 points of rise in the average deviation in the total distribution between 1947–52 and 1968–69, the shifting weight of the three family subgroups contributed 0·075 points, or almost seven-tenths (see column 8, lines 26 and 30 and lines 31 and 32).

(b) *Explanatory suggestions*

Why did the proportions of families with young, old and female heads rise, and why did their income relative to that of all families decline? No tested answers can be provided within the limits of this paper; but some exploration, with the help of data easily at hand, permits us to glimpse the more general implications of the effects of these trends upon inequality within the total family distribution as usually measured.

The rise in the proportion of families with heads 65 years of age and over and partly also of those with young heads, appears to have been associated with similar trends in the proportions of these age groups in the country's adult male population. Thus, the proportion of males aged 65 and over within the total population of males aged 20 and over (we exclude the population under 20 for comparability with heads of families) rose from slightly under 12 per cent in 1950 to about 14 per cent in 1960 and then tended to remain at this level to 1969; similar proportions for females were slightly less than 13 per cent in 1950, 16 per cent in 1960 and 17 per cent in 1969.[4] Table 11.2 shows that the proportion of families with heads aged 65 and over was 12 per cent in 1947–52, 13·6 per cent in 1959–61 and 13·9 per cent in 1968–69. The trend in these shares is thus a reflection of the rise in the proportion of the group aged 65 and over within the total adult population, particularly male – and this rise in turn must have been associated with the decline in the birth rate in early decades, and the longer life associated with death rates at advanced ages possibly declining more than those for the younger adults.

There is a rough parallel also between the proportion of families with heads aged below 25 and the proportion of males 20–24 in the total of all adult males (i.e. all males aged 20 or over). The latter proportion was about 11·5 per cent in 1950, declined to about 10 per cent in 1960 and then rose again to 12·9 per cent in 1969. The share of this subgroup among all families in Table 11.2 moved from 5·1 per cent in 1947–52 to 5·4 per cent in 1959–61 and 6·7 per cent in 1968–69. The rise in the proportion of young family heads is more consistent and relatively more substantial than that in the share of males aged 20–24 among all male adults. The implication is that the marriage rate and separate family formation must have risen – and some corroboration is provided by the median age of the group at

[4] These rates are from [6], [7] and [3], all cited in earlier footnotes and in the notes to the tables. Only additional sources will be indicated in this subsection.

first marriage, which declined from over 23 years in the early 1950s to below 23 in the late 1950s and the middle (but not late) 1960s.

The trend in the proportion of families with female heads aged 25–64, shown in Table 11.2, *cannot* be explained by movements in the proportion of all females of these ages within the total of all adult females. This subgroup of families reflects the incidence of broken family units, deprived of a male head by death, desertion, separation, or divorce. And the rise in the share of such units, estimated from the relationship to families with female heads of all ages in 1968–69, from 7 per cent in the early 1950s to 8 per cent in the late 1960s, probably reflects a greater incidence of divorce or other types of separation (with some effect of the widening differential in longevity between males and females, in favour of the latter). Part of the explanation may lie in the greater weight of urban population in the later years, since non-farm families show greater incidence of female headship (see Table 11.1, lines 12 and 13); and there is enough evidence of an increasing divorce rate to suggest why the share of families with female heads should have risen.

When we ask why these three family subgroups drifted downward within the ordinal divisions of the total family distribution, i.e. why their average income relative to that of all families should have declined, the available demographic data are not helpful. And in considering this decline in relative income it must be recognised that, over the period covered, per family and per person income in constant prices, based on the sample data, rose substantially. Table 11.3 shows that per family money income in 1964 dollars rose from 4·9 thousand in 1947–52 to 8·8 thousand in 1968–69, or some 80 per cent. Thus, even though income per family of each of the three subgroups did not grow as much, it still grew 62 per cent for the group with heads aged below 25, 52 per cent for the group with heads aged 65 and over, and 46 per cent for the group with female heads aged 25–64 – all rather substantial growth rates; and they would be about the same on a per person basis.

The lower growth rate of per family or per person income in the three family subgroups may reflect several demographic and economic variables. In the subgroup with older heads, the average age of heads 65 or over may have risen gradually, since within the total male population 65 or over the proportion of males aged 65–74 declined from 70 per cent in 1950 to 64 per cent in 1969, and that of those aged 75 and over rose from 30 to 36 per cent.[5] And in so far as pensions and other fixed types of income formed an increasing proportion of the incomes of heads aged 65 and over, rising inflation might have limited the growth of their real income. It may also have been increasingly difficult to remain in the labour force, with the continuing shift from self-employment to employee status and the trend toward compulsory retirement at ages below 70.

The lower growth rate of income of families with young heads may have been due to an increase in relative importance of occupations with a wider range within the life cycle of earnings – in which the younger entrants would be receiving incomes much lower than the occupational lifetime average. If this is true of professional workers and salaried managers and executives, the greater concentration of young entrants in these occupations might, despite their generally higher compensation levels, make for a lag in the growth of their per family income. Sources S-I and S-III show that the proportions of professional workers and of salaried managers in the total (including heads not in the labour force but excluding the unemployed) rose from about 11 per cent in 1948–52 to 21 per cent in 1969. And some contribution to the trend might have been made by young family heads who were still in training, even if in advanced stages, with rather limited income.

For the families with female heads one would have to consider the possibility that the proportion of Negro heads increased over the period, with the substantial shift of the Negro population to the cities, where the incidence of female headship is much greater than in the countryside. A rise in the proportion of Negroes among all female heads aged 25–64 would retard the growth rate of income per family for that subgroup – which could also be affected by fixed income components (such as pensions or relief payments) that do not respond adequately to increasing consumer prices.

The above suggestions are clearly ad hoc, and could be pursued with greater effort to assemble and probe into the

[5] The data are from [2, Table A-2, p. 139].

relevant data. But within the limits of this paper, we can only suggest some of the demographic and economic variables that might help to explain the downward drift in the relative income position of the three selected family subgroups.

3. Effects on the Income Distribution

The trends illustrated and noted in the preceding section have, obviously, widened inequality within the distribution of money income among families. The rise in the proportions of families with young, old and female heads would have contributed to widened inequality even if the income per family, within each subgroup or for the three combined, relative to average income of all families, had remained the same. However, their relative incomes did not remain constant but declined, thus contributing even more to widening income inequality.

Having found that the three selected family subgroups have contributed to generally wider inequality, we now ask whether inequality in the money income distribution among other families has also widened. In other words, what happens when, from the money income distribution among all families, we subtract the numbers and income of these special family subgroups, whose income could be expected to be lower than the average, given the characteristics of the head? A tentative answer is provided in Table 11.3.

Panel A shows the income shares of the ordinal divisions distinguished in the sources, with slight adjustments of the shares in 1968 and 1969 for greater comparability with earlier years. This distribution, for all families, seems to have been relatively stable during the 1950s: the shares are about the same in 1959–61 as in 1947–52. Thus, while per family income grew by over a third, relative inequality remained about the same. It was only in the 1960s that inequality narrowed somewhat, with the share of the lowest fifth rising from 4·9 to 5·6 per cent and that of the top 5 per cent division dropping from 16·8 to 14·8 per cent. But these movements toward equality were minor.

Panel B shows the effect of the exclusion of the three family subgroups, with the shares of the standard ordinal divisions in the distribution recalculated. The details of the procedure are described in the notes to the table and need not be repeated here.

TABLE 11.3 *Average Family Income and Shares of Income Received by Ordinal Divisions, Distributions of Families by Money Income, Original, Omitting Three Selected Family Subgroups, or Allowing for Size of Family among Ordinal Divisions, 1947–69*

		Ordinal divisions						Average income per family, 1964$ (000s)
		Lowest fifth (1)	Second fifth (2)	Middle fifth (3)	Fourth fifth (4)	Top 80 to 95 per cent (5)	Top 5 per cent (6)	(7)
A. *Shares (per cent) and average income, original distribution*								
1.	1947–52	4·8	12·1	17·2	23·4	25·3	17·2	4·93
2(*a*).	1953–58	4·8	12·3	17·8	23·8	25·1	16·2	5·83
2(*b*).	1955–58	5·0	12·4	17·9	23·6	24·9	16·2	6·02
3.	1959–61	4·9	11·9	17·6	23·5	25·3	16·8	6·69
4.	1962–64	5·1	12·1	17·5	23·8	25·6	15·9	7·21
5.	1968–69	5·6	12·2	17·6	23·6	26·2	14·8	8·80
B. *Shares (per cent) and average income, distribution excluding families with young) old, and female heads* (col. 7 shows relative of income per family to that in lines 1–5,								
6.	1947–52	5·8	13·0	17·5	23·1	24·6	16·0	1·09
7.	1953–58	6·1	13·5	18·1	23·3	24·2	14·8	1·10
8.	1959–61	6·3	13·2	17·9	23·1	24·3	15·2	1·12
9.	1962–64	6·6	13·4	17·9	23·4	24·4	14·3	1·13
10.	1968–69	7·0	13·8	17·9	23·4	24·8	13·1	1·15
C. *Shares (per cent) and average income, distribution adjusted for differences in size of family among ordinal divisions* (col. 7 shows average income per person, in thousands of 1964$)								
11.	1947–52	5·7	12·8	17·7	23·8	24·6	15·4	1·38
12.	1955–58	5·9	13·1	17·8	23·3	24·9	15·0	1·64
13.	1959–61	6·0	12·8	17·5	23·2	24·8	15·7	1·82
14.	1968–69	6·3	13·1	17·6	23·2	23·0	14·8	1·94
15.	1968–69	7·2	13·4	18·1	23·2	24·8	13·3	2·42

D. *Aggregative measures of inequality*

	Periods						Per cent change, col. 1 to col. 6
	1947–52 (1)	1953–58 (2)	1955–58 (3)	1959–61 (4)	1962–64 (5)	1968–69 (6)	(7)
16. Average Gini ratio, distributions in lines 1–5	0·373	0·360	0·356	0·370	0·359	na	na
17. Sum of deviations in lines 1–5	51·8	50·2	49·4	51·2	50·6	49·2	−5·0
18. Sum of deviations in lines 6–10	47·4	44·6	nc	45·2	44·2	42·6	−10·1
19. Sum of deviations in lines 11–15	47·6	na	46·4	47·4	46·0	42·6	−10·5

TABLE 11.3 (*continued*)

E. *Range: ratio of share of top fifth to that of lowest fifth*

	Periods						Per cent change, col. 1 to col. 6
	1947–52	1953–58	1955–58	1959–61	1962–64	1968–69	
20. Distributions in lines 1–5	8·86	8·60	8·22	8·59	8·14	7·32	−17·4
21. Distributions in lines 6–10	7·00	6·39	nc	6·27	5·86	5·41	−22·7
22. Distributions in lines 11–15	7·02	na	6·76	6·75	6·32	5·29	−24·6

nc—not calculated.
na—not available.

Lines 1–4, columns 1–6: calculated from S-I, Table 25, pp. 182–87. This table shows annual shares of the five fifths and of the top 5 per cent group; and the entries here are arithmetic means of these shares for the periods shown in the stub. The share of the top 80–95 per cent division was calculated from those of the top fifth and the top 5 per cent.
Lines 1–4, column 7: arithmetic mean income per family in current prices is shown annually in the table cited for lines 1–4, columns 1–6. Current price figures were converted to 1964 prices by the consumer price index shown in S-I, p. 33. The averages for the periods are logarithmic means.
Line 5: derived from S-II, Table 8, p. 22 and S-III, Table 11, p. 26 (shares in income of ordinal divisions) and Table A of both surveys, p. 1 (which show income for 1947 in current and 1968 or 1969 dollars, permitting us to shift the price base to 1964). Since the sampling procedure was revised in 1966, the income shares of identical ordinal divisions shown in the surveys are not strictly comparable with those for the earlier years. However, an overlap, given for 1966 in S-II, permitted us to adjust the 1968 and 1969 income shares for comparability.
Lines 6–10, columns 1–6: the underlying calculations assume that within each ordinal division, average income per family is the same for the three subgroups as for the rest of the division. This assumption is corroborated when we compare the arithmetic mean income relative, derived by multiplying the shares in columns 1–6, lines 16–20 of Table 11.2 by the per family income relative given in columns 1–6, lines 1–5 above, with the average income relative directly calculated (in column 7, lines 16–20 of Table 11.2). The two sets of relatives for the successive periods are: 0·731 and 0·728; 0·686 and 0·684; 0·663 and 0·665; 0·664 and 0·660; 0·634 and 0·623. Since the discrepancy is so slight, the error in the shares of the three omitted subgroups must be negligible.

Given the above assumption, we subtracted both the number and income of the omitted subgroups from the total number and income of each ordinal division; recumulated the arrays of shares in the remaining number and income; and interpolated a new set of partition lines (based on the logarithms of the cumulated shares).
Lines 6–10, column 7: derived from lines 1–5 and from data underlying columns 1–6.
Lines 11–15, columns 1–6: lines 26–30, columns 1–7 of Table 11.2 show the average number of persons per family, within each ordinal division and for the total distribution. Multiplying by the shares of the ordinal divisions within the total of families gave us the proportion of all *persons* (in families) in the lowest fifth of all families, in the second fifth, and so on. Having these shares in total persons, and the shares in total income (both limited to families), the latter shown in columns 1–6, lines 1–5 above, we recumulated the shares in number and income, and interpolated new partition values (again based on logarithms of the cumulated shares).

Although the procedure is approximate, a more thorough recalculation would have had an only slightly greater effect. First, we find that the per family income of the new distribution (column 7, lines 6–10) is, as should be expected, larger than that of the original wider distribution, by a percentage that rises steadily from nine in the earliest period to fifteen in 1968–69. Second, the shares of the lowest fifth, and to a lesser extent of the second fifth, are perceptibly higher, while that of the top 5 per cent division is lower, narrowing inequality significantly. Third, and most important, the adjusted distribution shows a steady narrowing of inequality: the share of the lowest fifth rises steadily from 5·8 to 7·0 per cent; that of the second fifth, less steadily and slightly, from 13·0 to 13·8 per cent; while that of the top 5 per cent drops from 16·0 to 13·1 per cent. In short, while the income distribution among all families is relatively stable with only slight movement toward equality in the 1960s (Panel A), the distribution among families with male heads aged 25–64 (what might be called 'standard' family units) showed a sustained movement of some magnitude toward equality through almost the whole period (Panel B).

Largely as a result of the trends in the proportion and relative distribution of the three selected family subgroups, there were movements in the difference in number of persons per family among the ordinal divisions. The adjustment, in Panel C, allows only for the changing differences in *average* number of persons per family among the six ordinal divisions. It does *not* represent a conversion of the original distribution among families to a distribution among persons. To approximate a distribution among persons, each size group of families within each income class (if not each individual family) would have to be reduced to a per person basis, and the resulting cells would have to be recumulated, and new partition lines drawn. Depending upon the assumptions used, the conversion might produce a different range of income inequalities, if not a

---

Lines 11–15, column 7: calculated from the average income per family, column 7, lines 1–5 above; and the average number of persons per family, column 7, lines 26–30 of Table 11.2.

Line 16: the Gini ratios are given annually in S-I, Table 25, pp. 182–87. The entries are arithmetic means (logarithmic means would be almost the same).

Lines 17–19, columns 1–6: sum of deviations, signs disregarded, of shares in income from shares in number.

different trend over time. The adjustment in Panel C is far more limited, only allowing for differences among wide ordinal divisions in average size of family, differences largely associated with the shares and family size of the four family subgroups distinguished. In short, the adjustment is primarily for family size as *affected by* and *associated with* distinctive age and sex characteristics of family heads.

Given the nature of the adjustment, it is not surprising that the differences between Panels C and A are similar to those between Panels B and A. Here also the adjustment reduces perceptibly the range between income shares of the lower and upper fifths, and reveals a sustained narrowing of inequality over the period.

Panels D and E provide crude measures of inequality. Panel D concentrates on the sum of differences, signs disregarded, between shares in number and in income of the six ordinal divisions. This measure is closely connected with the Gini ratio, which is based on the differences between *cumulated* shares in number and income. The sum of deviations in lines 17–19 is the sum of differences in *uncumulated* shares (the two arrays being the same as those for the Gini ratio); and the similarity of the movements of entries in lines 16 and 17 reveals this close association. As might have been expected from Panels A–C, the sum of deviations shows a much more substantial reduction of inequality in the adjusted than in the original distribution. And the reduction is significant: since equality means a sum of deviations equal to zero, a reduction of over a tenth toward zero is a substantial step toward complete equality. Whether equality of income is a warranted goal is not considered here.

Panel E provides a measure of the range, which has narrowed relatively more than the sum of deviations, i.e. the average weighted deviation from equality. And here again the reduction of inequality was significantly greater in Panels B and C than in Panel A.

4. Summary and Implications

Our findings can be summarised briefly.

First, the family units with young, old, and female heads, which in 1968–69 accounted for 28·5 per cent of all families, are concentrated in the lower income brackets; and, in fact, formed almost two-thirds of the lowest fifth. Two-thirds of the lowest quintile thus comprise young, old, and 'broken' families.[6]

Second, since the late 1940s, the combined proportion of the number of families in these three subgroups in the total number rose from 24·2 to 28·5 per cent; and, more important, these groups drifted downwards within the total distribution, their per family income relative to average income of all families, declining over the period. Thus, their share within the lowest fifth was less than 50 per cent in 1947–52, two-thirds in 1968–69; and their combined family income relative to that of all families declined from 0·73 to 0·62.

Third, if we exclude these three subgroups, and limit the family income distribution to those with male heads aged 25–64 (what might be called 'standard' units), the new income distribution shows appreciably narrower inequality. It is particularly interesting that inequality in this new distribution narrowed more, and more consistently over the period, than the inequality in the original distribution. The latter remained about the same during the 1950s and narrowed slightly in the 1960s.

Fourth, a similar result is found if we recognise that families with young and old family heads are much smaller than the average. Since they contribute greatly to differences in the average size of family among the wide ordinal divisions in the total family distribution, making for a smaller size in the lower income brackets, adjustment for these differences also yields an income distribution with a more sustained and large movement toward equality over the period.

Although the discussion above dealt only with a few aspects of the family income distribution – some age and sex characteristics of the head and associated size of family – the findings suggest broader implications. A rather wide variety of demographic and non-economic aspects of family structure may affect the family income distribution; and their effects on the *meaning* of income inequality may be far-reaching. In concluding this paper, I comment briefly on these possible implications.

To begin with, trends in the proportions like those illustrated in Table 11.2, namely, the rising shares of family units with

[6] A similar finding, based on the series through 1959, was reported in my earlier paper [1, pp. 34–35].

young, old, and female heads, are likely to be found in other developed countries. The movements of their birth, death and marriage rates, and increasing urbanisation with progressively easier divorce and separation, may have had similar effects. By the same token, the proportions of these three family subgroups may be expected to differ between the developed, urbanised economies, with their nuclear families, and the less developed, agricultural, more traditional economies that may still retain many larger extended families. Also, in any given period (say over the last two decades), the trends in the proportions and relative income positions of special family subgroups like those distinguished here may have been different in the less developed from those in the developed countries. And, as a result, the income distributions adjusted for these special groups may have moved differently in the former than in the latter, even if the changes in the unadjusted distributions were similar.

Furthermore, demographic aspects of family structure other than those emphasised here, may also have considerable effect on the income distribution among families. Two illustrations may suffice.

The first relates to the number of children under 18, or under any age taken to signify readiness for active participation in the labour force. While we observed that only a very small proportion of families with heads aged 65 and over have children under 18, the differences in number of young children among other families must still be quite wide, and would therefore affect the income position of families, particularly when reduced to a per person basis. Variation in this characteristic of family structure is clearly dependent upon the general level of birth rates and the extent of the differentials in the birth rate among the various economic and social groups within the population caused by the transition from high to low rates associated with long-term economic growth.

The second illustration is directly connected with the first. The rates of natural increase may differ substantially between lower and upper income bracket families, particularly in the developed countries, because birth rates differ substantially and the higher birth rate among the lower income groups more than compensates for any excess in their death rates. Thus the next generation of the lower income groups accounts for a larger share of total population, and probably of family units, than the original lower income groups. What is the effect on the ordinal shares in the distributions for the two successive generations? And would a similar effect be found in less developed countries where such differences in the rate of natural increase, negatively associated with income level, may not prevail, or may be of smaller amplitude?

Finally, one may ask what is the nature of income inequality contributed by the present lower income of family units with young and old heads. One could argue that from the standpoints of productivity, equity, and welfare, the incomes of these units, on a per person basis, should be lower than those of the 'standard' family units. After all, young family heads are in their training period and may look forward to much higher returns that would compensate them later. Moreover, no equity or welfare considerations warrant claiming a per person return for them as high as that which they will secure later, if the current returns are at least minimally adequate. Nor does the contribution of old family heads, largely in their retirement period, warrant an income equal to that of prime members of the labour force. Also, they do not need income for investment, either to improve their efficiency or to provide for the future, or for the purchase of 'new' products – given their limited time prospects and their lesser receptivity to new products than that of younger family units. It is thus permissible to argue that the young and old heads, despite their low incomes, do not contribute to *unwarranted* earnings differentials (unwarranted by differential productivity) or to *undesirable* welfare differentials. If these arguments hold, the demographic trends that raise the proportions of family units with young and old heads, or even those that make for a decline in their standing within the income distribution, contribute to a wider measured income inequality that has none of the analytical meaning often attributed to it. A similar argument may be made for all demographic and other non-economic differences which may affect the measured income distribution, and, in fact, represent life cycle and other near-biological differences that have a warranted reflection in income differentials and inequalities. The very meaning of income inequality in the customary distributions, and of trends in such inequality, is obscure unless the income effects of these non-economic institutional differences, and of their movements, are recognised.

References

[1] KUZNETS, SIMON, 'Income Distribution and Changes in Consumption', in *The Changing American Population*, ed. Hoke S. Simpson. (New York: Institute of Life Insurance, 1962).

[2] SHELDON, HENRY D., *The Older Population of the United States*, a census monograph. (New York: Social Science Research Council and Bureau of the Census, 1958).

[3] *Statistical Abstract of the United States, 1970*. (Washington, D.C., 1970).

[4] U.S. Bureau of the Census, 'Income in 1968 of Families and Persons in the United States', *Current Population Reports, Series P-60, no. 66*. (Washington, D.C., 1969).

[5] U.S. Bureau of the Census, 'Income in 1969 of Families and Persons in the United States', *Current Population Reports, Series P-60, no. 75*. (Washington, D.C., 1970).

[6] U.S.Bureau of the Census, *Historical Statistics of the United States*, (Washington, D.C., 1960).

[7] U.S. Bureau of the Census, *Historical Statistics of the United States, Continuation to 1962 and Revisions*. (Washington, D.C., 1965.).

[8] U.S. Bureau of the Census, 'Trends in the Income of Families and Persons in the United States, 1947–1964', *Technical Paper no. 17*, by Mary P. Henson (Washington, D.C., 1967).

[9] U.S. Congress, *The Distribution of Personal Income*, Joint Committee Print, 88th Congress, 2nd Session, (Prepared for the Subcommittee on Economic Statistics of the Joint Economic Committee). (Washington, D.C., 1965).

12 Money, Debt and Wealth

BY ABBA P. LERNER*

1.

OVER many years, like most economists, I have taught that the national debt differs from personal debt. Since it is owed only to ourselves, it is not a burden to the nation to be subtracted from our assets in measuring our national wealth, by analogy with the necessity of subtracting personal debt in figuring personal wealth. The false analogy has recently surfaced again, though presented as a burden not on ourselves but on future generations, in apparent justification of President Eisenhower's frowning on the immorality of imposing this burden on our grandchildren. The results of the ensuing debate may be summarised as follows.

It is possible for the present generation to reduce the wealth of future generations, but this can be done only by increasing the national debt and letting future generations pay it off. They would only be paying it to themselves – to the same future generations. The national debt cannot transport resources over time, taking them from some future period and making them available for people to consume in the present. It is no more a burden on future generations than on the present generation.

If one defines 'different generations' not as people living at different times but as people of different age living at the same time, one can say that when a government borrows money from the 'generation' of people over thirty instead of taxing them, and taxes more heavily the 'generation' of people under thirty to raise the money with which to repay the loan, it is shifting a burden from one 'generation' to another.[1] But this is not what President Eisenhower meant.

* I am indebted to my colleague, Professor John Letiche, for improvements in formulation and for the elimination of some mistakes.

[1] See the discussion on 'The Burden of Debt', [5], [4].

Professor Franco Modigliani provided a different argument. He pointed out that government bonds (of which the national debt consists) make their owners feel richer. They will therefore consume more and leave less resources available for investment in capital goods for future generations to inherit. The national debt, he argued, therefore *does* constitute a burden on future generations.[2]

I found this argument unacceptable because I could not distinguish between *feeling* rich and *being* rich. I could see no good reason for leaving out the satisfaction people get from owning government bonds when counting the total satisfaction that people get from their wealth.

It is true that future generations will be poorer in that they will inherit smaller quantities of machinery and buildings because of the smaller physical investment. But on the other hand they will be richer in that they will inherit the government bonds. And that will *more* than offset the diminished inheritance of physical capital. This is because the increased consumption (which is responsible for the decreased investment) can be only a fraction of the increased (feeling of) wealth from the ownership of the national debt. Future generations will therefore be not poorer but *richer* as a result of the increase of the national debt in the present generation.

It is true that continued lower investment may in time decrease the stock of future wealth by as much as the initial increase in the national debt. If that happens some future generation will be neither richer nor poorer than if there had been no increase in the national debt. But this is just as true if we begin with an increase in physical capital instead of in national debt.

Professor Modigliani's argument was based on not counting the national debt as 'genuine' wealth. But to refuse to count government bonds as wealth is just as arbitrary as to refuse to count any other item. Suppose we decided that buildings of

[2] See the discussion in [2]. Of course to the degree that people are made unhappy by concern about the national debt – perhaps counting some part of it as their own personal burden so that they feel poorer – they may consume *less*. There would then be exactly the opposite effect. By consuming less they leave *more* resources for investment in physical capital for further generations to inherit. But there can be little doubt that very few people feel as much impoverished by the existence of the National Debt as they feel enriched by their ownership of the government bonds.

more than ten stories, like the Tower of Babel, were sinful, and therefore should not be counted in the national wealth. Skyscrapers, though sinful, would still be useful and would reduce the need for smaller buildings so that less of these (which *are* counted in the national wealth) will be built. We would then have to say that the building of skyscrapers diminishes the wealth of future generations.

2.

At this point in the discussion I discovered that I had changed my basic position on the national debt. Over the years, I had been saying that the national debt, since we owe it to ourselves, cancels out – that it does not make us (or future generations) either poorer or richer. Now I found myself saying that the National Debt does not cancel out but is a *positive* item in the national wealth.

An identical analysis applies to 'inside money' which does not come from outside the economy – unlike 'outside money' (such as gold which is dug up from the ground) – but is created *within* the economy. The inside money consists essentially of bank deposits created by the banks. From the point of view of the banks they are obligations – I.O.U.s or debts. Parallel to the argument that because we owe the national debt to ourselves it cancels out, is the argument that the debts of the banks offset the wealth of the owners of the bank deposits, so that they cancel out, the sum of the two adding to zero.[3]

[3] This analysis was apparently first put forward by Michal Kalecki [3] on which Modigliani's argument rests. The Pigou effect is the argument that with flexible wages and prices unemployment causes deflation of prices. This increases the value of the money stock and makes people wealthier so that they increase their consumption. Thus there is an automatic cure for depression even if the economy is caught in a liquidity trap. To the extent that the money is inside money, the increase in the value of the money stock is cancelled out by the increased debt of the banks, and to this extent the Pigou effect is weakened. Professor Morris A. Copeland [1] has shown that *fixed charges* consisting of tax liabilities and depreciation allowances respond in their real value and in their effect on consumption in the opposite direction to the fixed claims of the Pigou effect; and that they could more than offset the Pigou effect, rendering the economy macroeconomically *un*stable. In situations where this is the case, the Pigou effect would not merely be weakened, as by Kalecki's argument, but

On this the position has been taken by Pesek and Saving[4] that inside money constitutes wealth just as much as outside money because its owners feel richer and behave richer in just the same way as owners of outside money. I find myself in agreement with this position and see it as identical to my view of the national debt (though Pesek and Saving are apparently unready to apply their inside money analysis to the national debt).

The obligations of the banks to their depositors do not have to be subtracted from the assets in figuring national wealth because it is not expected that these debts will be paid off. It is true that every bank must be ready to repay every one of its deposits in cash. But this is no different from the government having to repay every bond on its due date. Just as the national debt continues because the government can depend on being able to borrow again (possibly even from the very same person), so does the volume of bank money continue because the banking system can depend on the money being redeposited by somebody as long as the economy continues to function.

Resistance to this analysis can take the form of asking 'How is it possible to create wealth merely by writing an I.O.U.?', (since a bank deposit is in the nature of a bank's I.O.U.). Or it may be asked, 'When is a debt not a debt?' The answer to these questions is: 'Writing an I.O.U. creates wealth if the writer has such good credit that the I.O.U. has general acceptance and is never presented for payment but remains in circulation as money', or, 'A debt is not a debt when it is a credit'. If I lend $10 to Rothschild it is indeed only an exchange of $10 for an I.O.U. But everybody knows that Rothschild will honour his I.O.U., so nobody need present it for redemption. He can use it instead to buy something from somebody else. Everybody will accept it as a money payment. The I.O.U. is as good as money (if not as good as gold). Rothschild and I now have between us the equivalent of $20. Rothschild credit has turned his I.O.U. from a debt into money and the banks are just like Rothschild.

---

reversed; and policies relying on the Pigou effect for the automatic correction of inflation and depression (*not* put forward by Pigou himself) would lose all of any validity they may have had.

[4] See also [7].

3.

Professor Don Patinkin, in a review of Pesek and Saving's book [7], accepts (for the sake of argument only) their proposition that bank debts (i.e. the bank deposits) are not expected to be paid off in any relevant future. But he substitutes another reason why we should count them as negative items in national wealth so that inside money will still cancel out or add up to zero. His argument is that the value of the liquidity services enjoyed by the owners of the money is equal to what the money could have earned if loaned out at interest and which is forgone for the sake of enjoying the liquidity services. This value is in turn equal to the gross income or gross revenue of the banks, the interest on the loans they have made, which loans have in turn become the deposits we have just considered. If there is freedom of entry into the banking business, the costs incurred by the banks will be just equal to their gross revenues. This is because as long as the revenues exceed the costs, the difference is excess profit which will attract more and more banks into the banking business, increasing their total costs, until the total costs become just equal to the total revenue. The costs represent the resources used up in producing the liquidity services. They must therefore be subtracted from the value of the liquidity services in measuring the G.N.P. Since the total costs are just equal to the gross revenue of the banks and these are just equal to the interest forgone by the holders of the deposits, and this is just equal to the value of the liquidity services, the subtraction of the costs from the benefits, i.e. from the value of the liquidity services, leaves us with a zero contribution to the G.N.P.

The expected continuing flows of costs and benefits over the future can be capitalised to show present values and their contribution to national *wealth*. Since the expected future costs are just equal to the expected future benefits, the two present values must also be equal and must exactly cancel each other. The present value of the expected future liquidity services is simply the value of the money stock. This is equal to the present value of the expected future bank costs so that when the latter is subtracted from the former, nothing is left. With freedom of entry into the banking business, the contribution of inside money to the national wealth also comes to just zero.

4.

I would argue that all this is irrelevant to our problem. With the invention of paper money, the creation of money became a practically zero cost industry. When money was made of gold, a great deal of hard work and physical danger was involved in its production as well as enormous monetary investment and great financial risk. Although every gold producer would extend his rate of production up to the point where his marginal cost was equal to its price (of $35 an ounce), the average cost was often considerably less than the price so that there were great profits to be made by the lucky discoverers and developers of low cost gold mines. The profit lay in the excess of the price or marginal cost over the average cost.

This difference between marginal and average cost is what economists call *rent* or *surplus*. It constitutes 'pure gravy' which can be appropriated by the government in taxes, by anybody who controls an element that is essential for the production (or for that matter by gangsters as 'protection money') without disturbing the production. How such 'gravy' is shared among the various claimants depends on military, legal, traditional and other power categories and is strictly irrelevant for the production of the gold.

The same thing is more obvious in the case of oil. Where the average cost is much less than the marginal cost or the world price, as in the Middle East, there is an enormous surplus available. There are no objective principles as to how the gravy should be divided and we can see before our eyes the squabbles over it between the oil companies and the Middle East governments.

In the case of paper money, the cost of production is practically zero. One consequence of this is that *the whole* of the revenue is rent, whereas in gold or in oil only *a part* of the revenue is rent. Another consequence is that while the value of gold is not in danger of being greatly lowered by massive increases in production – it is protected by the rising marginal cost curve – the value of money has no such 'natural' protection. Complete freedom of entry into the money producing industry would result in the output of money increasing up to the point where the value of money, its purchasing power, was no greater than the marginal cost, that is to say no greater than the value of the paper and ink needed to make it. There would be such an inflation of prices that the money would become useless. There therefore has to be some other way of limiting the total quantity of money produced if it is to continue to be used as money.

The way the total quantity of money is limited by the government authorities (via the central bank) imposing on the banks required reserve ratios of government-produced money and limiting the quantity of the government-produced money. For the banking system as a whole, the supply curve or marginal cost curve of bank money is at zero marginal cost up to that quantity of money which utilises all the available reserves. At this point the curve becomes a vertical line, and the value of money (the inverse of the price level) settles at the height at which the quantity of money satisfies the demand for money to hold at the current rate of interest. The area between the marginal cost curve and the horizontal price line, as we have seen in the examples of gold and oil, represents the rent. In the case of money, this includes the whole rectangle: *all the revenue is rent.*

Historically, the surplus provided by the excess of the value of money over its cost of production has generally been appropriated by kings and princes as 'seignorage' and by representative governments as a natural source of income for national purposes. But by an historical accident, the surplus from bank-created money has been left as a kind of absent-minded gift in the hands of the banks. It amounts to the total value of all the bank money that has been issued by the banks – the bank deposits – minus the quantity of government money that they keep as reserve. In the United States this gift has built up to some $150 billion of checking account deposits.

The banks, of course, deny that they have been given any such enormous gift but one cannot pay too much attention to such denials. We all remember how the banks used to deny that they were able to create any money at all.

5.

The first reason for the failure to see this enormous 'gift' is that the banks were not free simply to spend it. They had to lend it out if they were to continue to be banks and continue to reap the gradually growing gift as the quantity of money (in real terms) that could be absorbed by the economy grew as the economy grew. The banks could therefore enjoy only the *income* from the money they created – the interest on the loans they made. At five or six per cent interest, this has now reached the sum of $7½ to $9 billion a year (its capitalised present value, however, is the $150 billion mentioned above).

The second and much more important reason is that with freedom of entry into the banking business, bank costs would indeed be equal to bank revenue as pointed out by Professor Patinkin. But this is only because *freedom of entry destroys the surplus* made available by the manufacture of money out of paper or by book-keeping instead of out of gold. The costs are incurred not in producing the money but in competing for the customers. The resources are used up by the banks in trying to tempt customers from each other – on devices for inducing people to patronise one bank rather than another. These consist of expenditure on beautiful buildings, on pretty tellers, on ancillary services, on advertisements and on prizes to new depositors and to people who persuade their friends to become new depositors. The banks compete for the deposits because without them they are not permitted to make the loans which yield the revenues.

Freedom of entry is generally considered to be 'a good thing' but that is because it generally refers to freedom of entry into an industry to *increase production*. But here this is not possible. The total amount of money is limited by the quantity of government money available and the reserve ratio of government money required of the banks by law. Freedom of entry here means only freedom *to get a share* of a fixed total production by reducing the share of the others. Such freedom of entry only increases costs – not costs of production but costs of *shifting* production of some of the money from one bank to another and costs of *resisting* such shifts. With *complete* freedom of entry the costs would rise until none of the rent or surplus is left. It is the incompleteness in the freedom of entry into the banking system that is responsible for a substantial part of the rent still remaining.

6.

Wasteful freedom of entry such as this is no stranger to economic theory. We have Professor Pigou's parable of the wide but long road and the short but narrow road connecting two cities. Freedom of entry to the short but narrow road so crowds it that the social gain from its existence is completely destroyed.

We also know about the kibbutz with equal sharing and freedom of entry as ideological principles. If, as a result of many years of hard work, the kibbutz has built up its capital and its skills, the shared average product will be way above the marginal product of labour and therefore above the wage earned outside the kibbutz. Many people will therefore want to join the kibbutz. This, of course, will keep on lowering the average product. But as long as the average product remains greater than the wage outside, still more people will want to join even if their marginal product in the kibbutz has fallen to zero and even if it has become negative. The movement will stop only when the average product has fallen to what prospective members can earn outside. In other words, freedom of entry (to share in the high average product) will have completely destroyed the fruit of all the past investments in the kibbutz.

The kibbutz may seem an esoteric and even theoretical example (it managed to escape this fate). Similar in principle and much more important both in scale and in realism, is the extended family of poor countries like India. Members of the family stay on in the village, even though their marginal product is very small if not negative, because they still get their share of the family income – the average income per member of the extended family. More recently, the same phenomenon has appeared in the cities where people from the village join their relatives in the cities, even though they cannot obtain work there, because they share the income of the working members of the extended family. Here, of course, their unemployment is not 'disguised', and the waste of their time and even of their lives, is much more conspicuous.

The classical treatment of wasteful free entry is of course the analysis, by Joan Robinson and Edward Chamberlin, of imperfect or monopolistic competition. This analysis shows how free entry makes the price equal to the average cost and destroys the potential monopoly profit, even though the monopolistic restriction of ouput remains in force.

7.

The waste from free entry into banking is, however, somewhat obscured because the devices used by banks in their competition for customers consist partly of activities that are of use to the customers. Thus my bank clears my cheques and does some of my book-keeping for me, charging me less than the full cost of providing these services. But this does not nullify the 'free entry' waste.

If customers were charged the full cost of the useful services provided, this would increase the profits of banking by as much as their costs. The gross profits would still be equal to the interest earned by the banks on the loans they had made in the course of creating the bank money. With free entry, potential bankers would still try to 'muscle in' on this 'gravy' until it was all dissipated in the other competitive activities for which the customers could not be charged. Since customers are generally charged less than the cost of providing the services (often not charged at all), there is less gravy to be dissipated by the freedom of entry; but there arises instead the waste due to the customers using too much of these services. They use them beyond the point where the marginal benefit (equal to the charge) is *below* the marginal social cost.

8.

It should be noted that although the 'gravy' passed on to the customers in this way is not all rescued from the waste, it is *mitigated* by the consumers' surplus enjoyed from the cheap or free services. Such benefits do not find proper recognition in the available measures of income and wealth. Nor is this the only place where these measures fail us.

Current concern with pollution has made us more aware than before of the inadequacies of our measures of income and wealth as indicators of human welfare. For rich countries like the United States an increase in G.N.P., unless it is accompanied by an improvement in distribution or allocation, or is due to an increase in employment, does not really mean that the people are any happier (except perhaps for those at the very bottom whose increased ability to satisfy basic needs is not negated by an equal increase in what are considered basic needs). Perhaps the most important effect of an increase in G.N.P. is that it uses up our natural resources more rapidly.

On the other hand, 'inside money' and the national debt are traditionally not counted in the national wealth; and the continuing benefits of the liquidity service of the inside money, which actually *sets free* natural resources rather than using up any, and the continuing 'pure wealth' enjoyment of ownership of both these – the satisfaction obtained by the owners from *knowing*, and being able to show, that they could use up this wealth if necessary – are traditionally not counted in the G.N.P. Why then should we be concerned as to whether money (or National Debt) is or is not wealth? What does this analysis yield in the direction of hints for policy?

9.

In the first place the recognition that the costs of the banks are incurred not in producing the inside money, but in wasteful competition of unproductive freedom of entry, and that the benefits from ownership of inside money and national debt involve no social cost, could lead to a reform of the system which would avoid the waste while retaining the benefits.

Further, it provides an additional argument for holding down the population. With a smaller population, or with a smaller rate of growth of population, there will be a lower schedule of the marginal efficiency of investment, a lower equilibrium rate of interest and therefore a higher valuation of the physical capital, of long-term government bonds and of the land. There will therefore be a greater pure wealth enjoyment from both the physical capital, including the land and the national debt.

This analysis also gives some support to a related and extremely classical proposition; namely, that thrift – the desire to save – is a good thing. A stronger desire to save will, via a lowering of the rate of interest, raise the value of capital goods and government bonds, increasing the enjoyment of these by their owners. (Unless the authorities invite a depression by failing to bring about the lower rate of interest needed to induce the increase in investment required to maintain the level of employment). This is related to the previous point because a greater increase in population involves a greater need (potential demand) for saving, while greater thrift provides a greater (potential) supply of saving. Finally, this analysis more directly supports proposed policies which would allow us to make fuller use of the invention of costless liquidity.

10.

The marginal social cost of producing money is zero. (The marginal *private* cost of producing money is of course not zero, but it is really the cost of obtaining the reserves legally required for *the right* to produce money at zero cost.) The general principle of social efficiency, namely that the price paid for enjoying anything should be equal to the marginal social cost of producing it, tells us that the price paid for the enjoyment of liquidity – the interest forgone in holding money – should be zero. But the marginal efficiency of investment is positive; a given sacrifice of current output enables us to increase future output by a larger amount. This means that future goods have a lower marginal cost than present goods. They should therefore be cheaper than present goods and this seems to suggest that we should have a falling price level.

A falling price level is, to say the least, extremely inconvenient. A positive rate of interest, however, makes it unnecessary. Future goods, discounted at the positive rate of interest, are in fact cheaper than present goods (in terms of present value) even if we have a constant price level. But then we would seem to have to give up the social efficiency of having the price of liquidity equal to the zero marginal social cost of providing it.

The problem can be solved by the payment of interest on holdings of money. The rate of interest can then be equal to the positive marginal efficiency of investment, while the price of liquidity is reduced by the interest earned on money held. If the rate of interest paid on money held is equal to the marginal efficiency of investment, then the cost of holding money is reduced to zero. This would make possible the (larger) optimum holdings of money, which would reduce the marginal utility of liquidity to zero, and avoid the waste of using up resources in measures for economising in the quantity held of the costless money.

A practical and important step towards that would be simply to remove the prohibitions or limitations on banks' paying interest on deposits. This would mean that the competition of the banks with each other would take the form of monetary or *price* competition: interest paid on deposits. This does not *use up* resources. It only *transfers* command over resources. It distributes the 'gravy' among the depositors for them to enjoy, instead of having it used up in the wasteful 'non-price' competition.

References

[1] COPELAND, MORRIS A., 'On Unemployment and Over-employment assuming Wage and Price Flexibility', *Journal of Economic Issues*. (June–September 1970) 40–59.

[2] JOHNSON, H. G., 'Objectives, Monetary Standards, and Potentialities', *Review of Economics and Statistics*, XLV (February 1963), Comment by A. P. Lerner, pp. 144–6.

[3] KALECKI, MICHAL, 'Professor Pigou on the "Classical Stationary State"—A Comment', *Economic Journal*, LIV (1944) 131–2.

[4] LERNER, ABBA P., 'The Burden of Debt', *Review of Economics and Statistics*, XLIII (May 1961) 139–41.

[5] MEADE, J. E., 'The Public Debt Reconsidered: A Reply', *Review of Economics and Statistics*, XLII (September 1960) 325–6.

[6] PATINKIN, DON, 'Money and Wealth: A Review Article', *Journal of Economic Literature*, VII (December 1969) 1140–60.

[7] PESEK, B. P. and SAVING, T., *Money, Wealth and Economic Theory*. (New York: Macmillan, 1967).

13 Demand Conditions under Multidimensional Pricing

BY LAWRENCE H. OFFICER*

1. Introduction

THE unidimensional nature of microeconomic analysis has been subjected recently to long-overdue criticism, on the grounds of its distance from reality.[1] It is stressed by critics that a product should be defined not in terms of a one-dimensional unit of measurement but rather in terms of its *attributes*, *aspects* or *characteristics*, which generally are multidimensional. Nevertheless, this 'abstract-product' approach, to use Baumol's terminology, remains in a primitive state. Advances have been most noteworthy in the theory of consumer demand. Yet even the most elegant studies in this field – those of Baumol [1] and Lancaster [3] – suffer from oversimplified models. Thus Baumol [1, p. 682] must resort to artificial devices to cope with his assumption of completely inelastic demand for any one consumer, and Lancaster makes the strong assumption that the characteristics of a product are identical for all consumers. Quite apart from unrealistic assumptions, however, their models suffer a fundamental deficiency: pricing according to attributes, i.e. *multidimensional pricing*, is not considered.

In the present paper, in contrast, I make quite general assumptions regarding the consumers of a product. Their individual demand functions are downward-sloping. Also, consumers do not behave as one – not only may their demand functions differ but the attributes that each derives from a product may differ. Most important of all, in focusing on *pricing* as

* Michigan State University. The author is grateful to Roger Sherman for comments on an earlier draft of this paper.

[1] See Baumol [1], Lancaster [3], Simmonds [5] and the references cited therein.

a multidimensional phenomenon, I am able to study thoroughly the properties of the demand for a product *expressed in terms of the demand for its attributes*. While for geometrical convenience I consider the two-dimensional case, the results are readily extendible to an arbitrary number of dimensions.

In pricing according to the attributes received by a consumer, it turns out that the price of the product is not uniform over all consumers. Thus it might be objected that I am dealing with a case of discriminatory pricing. However, the variation in price according to the receipt of attributes is *not* genuine discrimination; for the attributes of the product that I consider are measurable and known to the producer as well as the consumer.

One set of situations that fit into my model is covered by the peak-load problem. Provision of public utility services (such as electricity) with peak-time and off-peak-time use as the attributes is the standard example. Another situation is the provision of transportation services, in which the volume and weight specifications of a commodity are the relevant attributes. Still another set of circumstances to which the model applies involves the use of time as an attribute in addition to the conventional dimension of a product. Thus the delivery date or time of performance of service would involve a charge quite in addition to the price of the product itself, with an earlier date presumably having a higher rate. To venture a prediction, I suggest that multidimensional pricing will come to constitute the normal form of pricing in the future, as technological developments at once make products more complicated and facilitate the measurement of their attributes.

2. Assumptions of the Model

I consider the market for a certain product, say x, the price of which faced by consumer i is denoted by p_i. Letting x_i represent the number of units of x demanded by consumer i, his individual demand function is

$$x_i = f_{1i}(p_i) \tag{1}$$

I assume that this demand function is downward-sloping between the axes, that it involves satiety, i.e. $f_{1i}(0)$ is finite, and that a sufficiently high price, say $\tilde{p}_i$ cuts off all demand, i.e. $f_{1i}(p_i) = 0$ for $p_i \geq \tilde{p}_i$.

Product x may be defined in terms of its attributes, say a and b. The number of units of each of these attributes that consumer i obtains per unit of product x is a_i and b_i, respectively. These magnitudes are fixed irrespective of the value of x_i.[2] Define $T_i = b_i/a_i$, the 'trade-off' between the attributes on the part of individual i.

There are a total of n consumers. Thus $i = 1, \ldots, n$. It is assumed that $i \neq j \Rightarrow T_i \neq T_j$. This does not mean that individuals cannot have the same trade-offs. One simply redefines an 'individual' or 'consumer' as the set of all consumers with the same trade-off. The corresponding 'individual' demand function (1) is obtained by adding the basic individual demand functions 'horizontally' (i.e. with price as the parameter) in the usual fashion.

Now, the producers of x follow a multidimensional pricing policy. Let r and q represent the rates per unit of attribute a and b, respectively. Thus the price of product x faced by consumer i is

$$p_i = ra_i + qb_i \tag{2}$$

Though the price of product x varies according to the consumer, the pricing is non-discriminatory *when considered as the pricing of attributes*. Varying the rates r and q according to the consumer would represent genuine discriminatory pricing.

For convenience, I follow the convention that

$$r, q \geq 0 \tag{3}$$

The case of 'dis-attributes' is covered; for if a is a dis-attribute, with, therefore, a negative price r, one redefines a_i as its negative and r switches to a positive sign.

3. The Functions to be Studied

Combining (1) and (2), we may rewrite the demand function (1) of consumer i as

$$x_i = f_{1i}(ra_i + qb_i) \tag{4}$$

[2] 'Constant coefficients' of attributes are also assumed by Baumol [1] and Lancaster [3].

Since a_i and b_i are fixed irrespective of the number of units of x demanded, the function (4) may be re-expressed with the two-dimensional price vector as the independent variable:

$$x_i = f_{2i}(r, q) \tag{5}$$

Proceeding in step, we now alter the dependent variable so that it refers to the *demand for attributes.* With attributes two-dimensional, the dependent variable also is a two-dimensional vector. Letting A_i and B_i denote the demand for attributes a and b on the part of consumer i, his demand function becomes

$$(A_i, B_i) = f_{3i}(r, q) \tag{6}$$

where

$$\left.\begin{aligned} A_i &= a_i f_{2i}(r, q) \\ B_i &= b_i f_{2i}(r, q) \end{aligned}\right\} \tag{7}$$

Letting A and B denote the total demand, i.e. the demand on the part of all n consumers, for attributes a and b, respectively, the market demand function is

$$(A, B) = f_3(r, q) \tag{8}$$

obtained by vectoral addition for each value of (r, q):

$$\begin{aligned} (A, B) &= (\sum A_i, \sum B_i) = \sum (A_i, B_i) \\ &= \sum f_{3i}(r, q) = f_3(r, q) \end{aligned}$$

The summing of function (6) is analogous to the conventional addition of individual demand curves. The difference is that both demand and price are two-dimensional rather than uni-dimensional.

The market demand function (8) *is single valued.* To every value of (r, q) corresponds a unique value of (A, B). This is because (8) is obtained by applying addition and scalar multiplication to a set of single-valued functions (5) and the set of all single-valued functions is closed with respect to these operations.

Consider the inverse of the market demand function:

$$(r, q) = f_3^{-1}(A, B) \tag{9}$$

Although (8) is defined for all non-negative values of (r, q), (9) is defined only for those values of (A, B) which satisfy (8). Thus, the domain of (8), hence the range of (9), is the set of all two-dimensional vectors whose elements are non-negative real numbers. However, as will be shown subsequently, the range of (8), hence the domain of (9), is only a subset of this set.

While, as shown above, (8) is a single valued function, (9) is not single valued. In precise terms, (8) is single valued for all points in its domain while (9) is single valued only in part of its domain. However, it will be demonstrated that (9) is 'effectively' single valued in the sense that to each point in its domain corresponds a unique total expenditure, R, on product x. Thus the total-expenditure function

$$R = f_4(A, B) \tag{10}$$

defined as follows:

$$R = rA + qB, \qquad \text{subject to (9)}$$

is single valued, as demonstrated finally in Section 6.

4. The Case of One Consumer

The case of one consumer ($n = 1$) is important not only because it is a first step in the examination of the n-consumer case but also because it represents fully the situation in which the trade-off of the attributes is identical for all consumers, i.e. $T_i = T$ for all i. In the latter situation we can collapse the n consumers to only one, so that the 'individual' demand function *is* the market demand function, as discussed in Section 2 above.

In this section we develop graphical representations of the individual demand function and its inverse. In addition, we show that the expenditure function for the individual consumer, say i, is single valued.

Suppose a given price, say $\bar{p}_i$, is faced by the consumer. According to (1) this produces a unique quantity of product x demanded, say $\bar{x}_i$. To $\bar{x}_i$, in turn, corresponds a unique value of (A_i, B_i), say $(\bar{A}_i, \bar{B}_i)$, given by

$$(\bar{A}_i, \bar{B}_i) = (a_i\bar{x}_i, b_i\bar{x}_i)$$

Now, there exists a set of values of (r, q), say $\{(\bar{r}, \bar{q})\}$, each element of which satisfies both (3) and (from (2))

$$\bar{p}_i = ra_i + qb_i \tag{11}$$

a straight line, which may be rewritten as

$$r = \bar{p}_i/a_i - T_i q \tag{12}$$

The plotted inner straight line in Figure 13.1 is the graph of (12) in the first quadrant, and its set of co-ordinates (including the end-points) is $\{(\bar{r}, \bar{q})\}$. The line is labelled with the unique value of (A_i, B_i) to which it pertains. As the given value of p_i

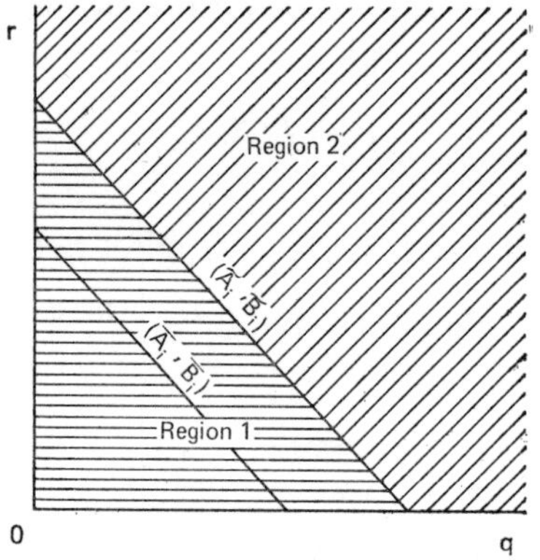

FIG. 13.1

increases, x_i decreases (via (1)) and hence (A_i, B_i) also decreases. Simultaneously, the line (12) moves outward with greater intercepts but the same slope, T_i. Figure 13.1 is everywhere dense with lines of Equation (12) plotted for all non-negative values of p_i.

Two limiting cases may be noted. $p_i = 0$ implies that $r = q = 0$, i.e. $\{(r, q)\} = (0, 0)$, and (12) shrinks to the origin. At that point the maximum x_i and (A_i, B_i) are reached. There is also a limit point in the other direction. For p_i at and above $\tilde{p}_i$ a zero value of x_i, hence of (A_i, B_i), is obtained. Thus for all $p_i \geq \tilde{p}_i$ $(A_i, B_i) = 0$, while for any $p_i < \tilde{p}_i$ the value of (A_i, B_i) is unique and positive.

Let $(\tilde{A}_i, \tilde{B}_i)$ be the value of (A_i, B_i) corresponding to $\tilde{p}_i$. Then for $p_i = \tilde{p}_i$ (12) divides the first quadrant into two regions, as shown in Figure 13.1. Region 1 consists of all points (r, q) below this line and region 2 of all points on or above the line. Given a value of (r, q) in region 1, the corresponding value of (A_i, B_i) is uniquely determined by the line (12) which passes through the given point and (A_i, B_i) is positive. Given any value of (r, q) in region 2, the corresponding (A_i, B_i) is zero. Thus the individual demand function (6) is portrayed in Figure 13.1.

Any (A_i, B_i) in the range of (6) satisfies $B_i/A_i = T_i$. Figure 13.2 represents the range of (6) as a segment $0I$, of the straight line passing through the origin with slope T_i. Any given point, say $(\bar{A}_i, \bar{B}_i)$, on $0I$ may be labelled with the set of (r, q) which satisfies

$$(r, q) = f_{3i}^{-1}(A_i, B_i) \tag{13}$$

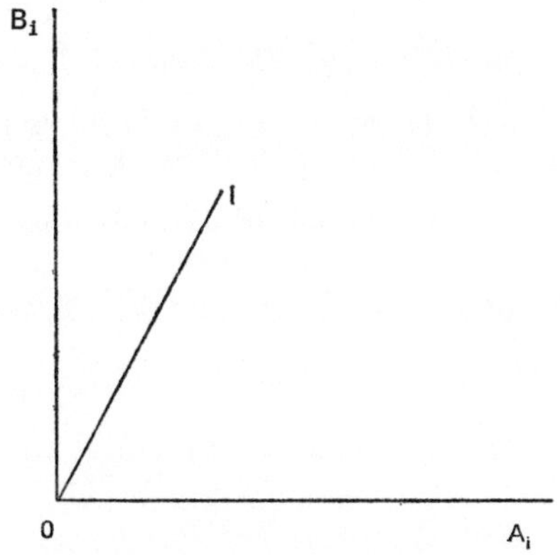

FIG. 13.2

and this set is $\{(\bar{r}, \bar{q})\}$. The two limiting points are noteworthy. For $(A_i, B_i) = (0, 0)$, $\{(r, q)\}$ = region 2. For the maximum value of (A_i, B_i), namely, the point I, $\{(r, q)\} = (0, 0)$. This is the only point for which $\{(r, q)\}$ is unary.

Consider any point, say $(\hat{A}_i, \hat{B}_i)$, not in the range of (6), that is, not on $0I$. Then $\{(r, q)\}$ = the empty set. Therefore $(\hat{A}_i, \hat{B}_i)$ is not a feasible point, a fact rooted either in the consumer's trade-off among the attributes (if $(\hat{A}_i, \hat{B}_i)$ is not on the straight line passing through the origin with slope T_i) or in the fact that demand is satiable (if $(\hat{A}_i, \hat{B}_i)$ is on that line).

Thus, Figure 13.2 portrays the inverse of the individual demand function (13). The domain of (13) is $0I$ and there is only one point, namely I, for which (13) is single valued.

A given point, say $(\bar{A}_i, \bar{B}_i)$, in the domain of (13) corresponds to a set $\{(\bar{r}, \bar{q})\}$, but each element in that set satisfies (11), where $\bar{p}_i$ is unique. Moreover, $(\bar{A}_i, \bar{B}_i)$ corresponds to a unique value of x_i, say $\bar{x}_i$, given by

$$\bar{x}_i = \bar{A}_i/a_i = \bar{B}_i/b_i$$

Therefore, $\bar{R}_i = \bar{p}_i\bar{x}_i$, the consumer's total expenditure on the product, is also unique. Thus, it has been demonstrated that *the individual consumer's expenditure function*

$$R_i = f_{4i}(A_i, B_i) \tag{14}$$

is single valued.

5. Graphical Representation of the Market Demand Function

We now move directly from the case of one consumer to the most general situation: n consumers. In this section we derive a graphical representation of the market demand function (8). This is done for the purpose of delineating the multi-valued properties of the inverse market demand function (9) in Section 6.

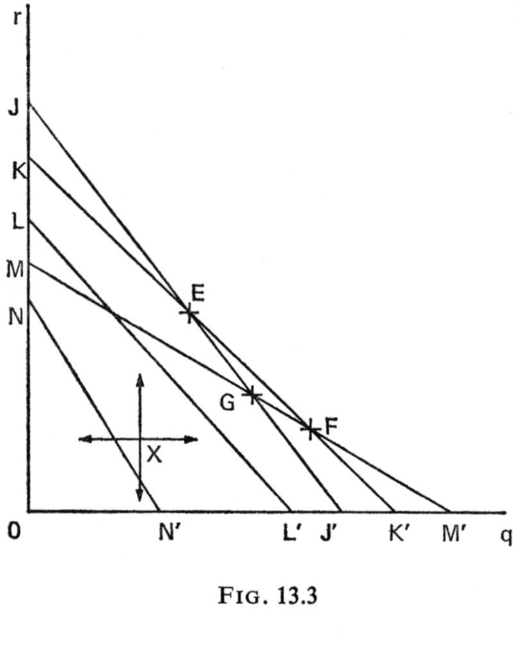

FIG. 13.3

Consider Figure 13.1 again. Such a portrayal of the individual demand function may be performed for every consumer, and the representations may take place on a single diagram, as in Figure 13.3. For each consumer (a typical one denoted as i), Figure 13.3 is everywhere dense with graphs of Equation (12). Since $(A_i, B_i) = 0$ for any point in region 2, (12) need be plotted and appropriately labelled (with the corresponding value of (A_i, B_i)) only for region 1 and the boundary between the two regions. Only one line (12) is actually drawn for a given consumer, the line (part of region 2) constituting the boundary between regions 1 and 2. This line is JJ' for consumer j, KK' for consumer k, etc.

Analogous to the case of one consumer, considered in Section 4 above, two regions can be defined with the joined line-segments $JEFM'$ as the boundary between them. For any (r, q) on or 'above' $JEFM'$, which is a short-hand way of saying 'for any (r, q) on $JEFM'$ or to the northeast of *any* point on $JEFM'$' or 'for any (r, q) *not* in the polygon $OJEFM'$ exclusive of the outer part, $JEFM'$, of its perimeter,' (A, B) is zero. This is because (A_i, B_i) equals zero for every i. The complement of the closed set $OJEFM'$, together with the boundary $JEFM'$, is denoted as region II. Thus (A, B) is zero in region II.

The set $OJEFM'$ exclusive of the boundary $JEFM'$ is called region I. Any (r, q), say $(\bar{r}, \bar{q})$, in region I corresponds to a unique positive value of (A, B), say $(\bar{A}, \bar{B})$. The value is unique because the point $(\bar{r}, \bar{q})$ is on at most one line (12) for each consumer, and $(\bar{A}, \bar{B})$ is determined as $(\sum \bar{A}_i, \sum \bar{B}_i)$, where $(\bar{A}_i, \bar{B}_i)$ is the corresponding value of (A_i, B_i), namely, that value associated with Equation (12) which is satisfied by $(\bar{r}, \bar{q})$ or, geometrically, with the line (12) on which $(\bar{r}, \bar{q})$ is a point. As noted in Section 3, $(\bar{A}_i, \bar{B}_i)$ is unique for a given consumer i. The value of $(\bar{A}, \bar{B})$ corresponding to $(\bar{r}, \bar{q})$ in region I is positive because, by definition of region I, $(\bar{A}_i, \bar{B}_i)$ is positive for at least one i. If for a particular consumer i there is no line (12) on which $(\bar{r}, \bar{q})$ is a point, then $(\bar{A}_i, \bar{B}_i) = 0$. This assumes the convention of not considering (12) for a given consumer i as drawn in region 2 for that consumer. On the other hand, suppose (12) *were* plotted in region 2. Then if the line (12) satisfied by $(\bar{r}, \bar{q})$ is in region 2, that line is labelled as $(A_i, B_i) = (0, 0)$.

Thus every point (r, q) in the first quadrant of Figure 13.3 is labelled with the unique value of (A, B) corresponding to it. Hence, Figure 13.3 is a complete diagrammatic representation of the market demand function (8). Furthermore, it has been demonstrated anew that this function is single valued.

6. Multi-valued Properties of the Inverse of the Market Demand Function

We wish to examine the single- cum multi-valued properties of (9), the *inverse* of the market demand function (8). This, too, will be done with the aid of Figure 13.3.

There are three regions to be considered, namely:

I_s = the set of (r, q) for which there is positive demand on the part of two or more consumers
I_m = the set of (r, q) for which there is positive demand on the part of one and only one consumer
II_m = the set of (r, q) for which there is positive demand on the part of no consumer

Referring to Figure 13.3, the polygon *OKEGFK'*, exclusive of the *KEGFK'* part of its perimeter, constitutes I_s; the triangles *JKE*, *EGF* and *FK'M'*, including *KEGFK'* but excluding the outer part of the perimeter of the polygon *OJEFM'*, namely, *JEFM'*, constitutes I_m, and region II constitutes II_m. To examine the properties of (9), we compare the label (i.e. value of (A, B)) attached to a given point in each of the regions I_s, I_m, II_m in turn, with that attached to any other point over all three regions.

6.1 *The Region* I_s

Consider a given point $X = (r_X, q_x)$ in I_s. To this point corresponds a unique value of (A, B), say (A_X, B_X). We wish to compare (A_X, B_X) with the value of (A, B), say (A_W, B_W), associated with any other point, say $W = (r_W, q_W)$ domain of (r, q), i.e. in the first quadrant. Clearly, the latter point is on one (and only one) vector (with a given direction) protruding from X as the origin. Define all such vectors to be exclusive of the origin (the point X itself). There are four vectors of importance in delineating cases, namely, those due north, due south, due east and due west.

Case (i) w on the due west, due south, or any intermediate vector (A_W, B_W) is unambiguously greater than (A_X, B_X). The proof is as follows. If W is on the due west vector, $q_W < q_X$ while $r_W = r_X$; if on the due south vector, $r_W < r_X$ while $q_W = q_X$; if on an intermediate vector, $r_W < r_X$ and $q_W < q_X$. In all three situations P_{w_i} is unambiguously less than p_{X_i} for every consumer i. Therefore $(A_{W_i}, B_{W_i}) \geq (A_{X_i}, B_{X_i})$ for every i. However, since $(A_{X_i}, B_{X_i}) > 0$ for at least one i (in fact, for at least two i), it must be that for these $i\,(A_{W_i}, B_{W_i}) > (A_{X_i}, B_{X_i})$. It follows that $(A_W, B_W) > (A_X, B_X)$.

If X is on both the r and q axes, i.e. at the origin, then none of the vectors considered is defined. Such situations do not affect the demonstration, since, irrespective of the location of X, any other point in the domain of (r, q) is on a defined vector.

Case (ii) W on the due north, due east, or any intermediate vector
An argument precisely analogous to that used for case (i) demonstrates that $(A_W, B_W) < (A_X, B_X)$. This holds irrespective of whether W is in I_s, I_m or II_m. The important facts in the demonstration are that $p_{W_i} > p_{X_i}$ for all i and $(A_{X_i}, B_{X_i}) > 0$ for at least one i.

Case (iii) W northwest or southeast of X
The only remaining situations to consider are W in any vector intermediate between due north and due west or due south and due east. Associated with any such vector, considered as a straight line in the first quadrant, is its slope, the absolute value of which is denoted as T_{W^*}, the subscript W indicating correspondence to that point. A value of T_{W^*} corresponds to two vectors, one northwest, the other southeast of X, where the designations 'northwest' and 'southeast' exclude the due north, due west and due south, due east vectors, respectively. The following statements hold for all i. If W is northwest of X, $T_i > T_{W^*} \Rightarrow p_{W_i} < p_{X_i}$ and $T_i < T_{W^*} \Rightarrow p_{W_i} > p_{X_i}$. If W is southeast of $X, T_i > T_{W^*} \Rightarrow p_{W_i} > p_{X_i}$ and $T_i < T_{W^*} \Rightarrow p_{W_i} < p_{X_i}$. In either case $T_i = T_{W^*} \Rightarrow p_{W_i} = p_{X_i}$. We recall that

$$p_{W_i} < p_{X_i} \Rightarrow (A_{W_i}, B_{W_i}) \geq (A_{X_i}, B_{X_i})$$

$$p_{W_i} > p_{X_i} \Rightarrow (A_{W_i}, B_{W_i}) \leq (A_{X_i}, B_{X_i})$$

$$p_{W_i} = p_X \Rightarrow (A_{W_i}, B_{W_i}) = (A_{X_i}, B_{X_i})$$

In Case (iii) $(A_W, B_W) \neq (A_X, B_X)$. This will be proved by contradiction. Let W be northwest of X. If $(A_W, B_W) = (A_X, B_X)$ then, in particular, $A_W = A_X$ and $B_W = B_X$. Assume $A_W = A_X$. It will be shown that this implies $B_W \neq B_X$.

For every consumer i $B_i = T_i A_i$, irrespective of the value of A_i. Define $\Delta A = A_W - A_X$, $\Delta B = B_W - B_X$, $\Delta A_i = A_{W_i} - A_{X_i}$, and $\Delta B_i = B_{W_i} - B_{X_i}$. For ease in notation let p_* range over the set of i for which $\Delta A_i > 0$ and n_* range over the set of i for which $\Delta A_i < 0$. Now $\Delta A = \sum_{p_*} \Delta A_i + \sum_{n_*} \Delta A_i = 0$ by hypothesis. We want to prove that $\Delta B = \sum_{p_*} \Delta B_i + \sum_{n_*} \Delta B_i = \sum_{p_*} T_i \Delta A_i + \sum_{n_*} T_i \Delta A_i \neq 0$, i.e. that $\sum_{p_*} T_i \Delta A_i \neq -\sum_{n_*} T_i \Delta A_i$. For any i in the subset ranged over by p_*, $T_i > T_{W^*}$; for any i in the subset ranged over by n_*, $T_i < T_{W^*}$. By transitivity T_i for any i in the set ranged over by p_* exceeds T_i for any i in the set ranged over by n_*. By hypothesis $\sum_{p_*} \Delta A_i = -\sum_{n_*} \Delta A_i$. Therefore $\sum_{p_*} T_i \Delta A_i > -\sum_{n_*} T_i \Delta A_i$, providing only that both the set of i ranged over by p_* and the set of i ranged over by n_* are not empty. If both sets are empty, then $\sum_{p_*} T_i \Delta A_i = -\sum_{n_*} T_i \Delta A_i = 0$. However, the fact that X is in I_s eliminates the possibility that both sets are empty. There is positive demand at X on the part of at least two consumers. It is true that $T_i = T_{W^*} \Rightarrow \Delta A_i = 0$. However, by assumption $i \neq j \Rightarrow T_i \neq T_j$; therefore there cannot be more than one consumer for whom $T_i = T_{W^*}$. Hence, for at least one consumer i, $\Delta A_i \neq 0$. This fact combined with the hypothesis $\Delta A = 0$ implies that $\sum_{p_*} \Delta A_i$, $\sum_{n_*} \Delta A_i \neq 0$, that is, neither of the subsets of i can be empty. Thus it has been demonstrated that $A_W = A_X \Rightarrow B_W > B_X$ and, in particular, $B_W \neq B_X$. An analogous proof applies for W southeast of X.

In summary, for any given point (r, q) in I_s the corresponding value of (A, B) differs from that of any other point in the domain of (r, q).

6.2 *The region* I_m

Consider a given point $Y = (r_Y, q_Y)$ in I_m. The unique value of (A, B), say (A_Y, B_Y), corresponding to this point is to be compared with that corresponding to any other point, say W, in the domain of (r, q). The latter point is on one (and only one) vector having Y as its origin. If W is on either (i), the due west, due south, or any intermediate vector or, (ii), the due north, due east, or any intermediate vector, then the proofs and results associated with X in I_s are directly applicable, with X replaced by Y. After all, these demonstrations were dependent only on $(A_{X_i}, B_{X_i}) > 0$ for at least one consumer i, a condition fulfilled in I_m.

Let k be the consumer the demand of whom is positive at Y, that is, $(A_{Y_k}, B_{Y_k}) = (A_Y, B_Y)$. If W is northwest or southeast of Y, two cases must be examined: $T_{W*} \neq T_k$ and $T_{W*} = T_k$.

Case (i) $T_{W*} \neq T_k$

In this case $(A_W, B_W) \neq (A_Y, B_Y)$. The proof is similar to that used for X in I_s and that demonstration will be followed. Let W be northwest of Y. Assume $A_W = A_Y$. It will be shown that this implies $B_W \neq B_Y$. In the definition of the Δ variables replace X by Y. It need only be checked that both the set of i ranged over by p_* and the set of i ranged over by n_* are not empty. Recall that $(A_{Y_i}, B_{Y_i}) > 0$ for $i = k$ and $= 0$ for $i \neq k$. $\Delta A_k = 0 \Rightarrow T_{W*} = T_k$, but the latter relationship is excluded by hypothesis. Therefore $\Delta A_k \gtrless 0$. Then the hypothesis $\Delta A = 0$ implies that $\Delta A_i \lesseqgtr 0$ for at least one other i. Hence $\sum_{p_*} \Delta A_i$, $\sum_{n_*} \Delta A_i \neq 0$. Thus it has been proved that $B_W \neq B_Y$. A similar argument applies for W southeast of Y.

Case (ii) $T_{W*} = T_k$

If $T_{W*} = T_k$, then $\Delta A_k = 0$. Providing W is sufficiently close to Y, for all $i \neq k$ $(A_{W_i}, B_{W_i}) = (A_{Y_i}, B_{Y_i}) = (0, 0)$ (with the latter equation true by hypothesis), hence $\Delta A_i = 0$ and $(A_W, B_W) = (A_Y, B_Y)$. The meaning of 'sufficiently close' is that W lies not merely in I_m but in that part of I_m in which k is the consumer with positive demand ('the applicable subregion'), which is obviously that subregion in which Y is situated. Actually the designation of the appropriate subregion is superfluous under the hypothesis $T_{W*} = T_k$. This is because (A_k, B_k) is constant along the vector of slope T_k passing through W and has a positive value of (A_{Y_k}, B_{Y_k}). W can be neither in II_m nor in any part of I_m in which k is not the consumer with positive demand; for these locations imply $(A_{W_k}, B_{W_k}) = 0$. Thus it suffices to say that W lies in I_m, providing the condition $T_{W*} = T_k$ is understood. For example, considering Figure 13.3, assume $k = J$. Then the applicable subregion is the triangle JKE inclusive of the side KE but exclusive of the side JE. If W is outside the applicable subregion and $T_{W*} = T_k$, then W must be in I_s (as is apparent from Figure 13.3). Then $(A_W, B_W) > (A_Y, B_Y)$, since $(A_Y, B_Y) = (A_{Y_k}, B_{Y_k})$, $\Delta A_k = 0$ and $(A_{W_i}, B_{W_i}) > 0$ for at least one $i \neq k$. Of course, the statement has already been proved in examination of the region I_s. (Notationally, transform W into X and X into W.)

In summary, for any given point (r, q) in I_m the corresponding value of (A, B) differs from that of any other point in the domain of (r, q), with the exception of all points in the applicable subregion of I_m that are on the line (12) that passes through the given point and pertains to the consumer with positive demand at that point.

6.3 *The region* II_m

By definition any point in II_m corresponds to $(A_i, B_i) = 0$ for all i, hence to $(A, B) = 0$. On the other hand, since for any point in I_s or I_m the corresponding $(A_i, B_i) > 0$ for at least one i, the (A, B) $(= (0, 0))$ associated with any point in II_m differs from the (A, B) $(> (0, 0))$ associated with any point in I_s or I_m.

Summary of multi-valued properties of (9)

Define the following regions in the A–B plane:

I_s^{-1} = the set of (A, B) given by (8) restricted to I_s
I_m^{-1} = the set of (A, B) given by (8) restricted to I_m
II_m^{-1} = the set of (A, B) given by (8) restricted to II_m

Recalling that $(A, B) = (\sum A_i, \sum B_i)$, equivalent definitions are:

I_s^{-1} = the set of (A, B) for which at least two of the n components (A_i, B_i), $(i = 1, \ldots, n)$ are positive
I_m^{-1} = the set of (A, B) for which one of the n components (A_i, B_i) is positive
II_m^{-1} = the set of (A, B) for which none of the n components (A_i, B_i) is positive, i.e. $II_m^{-1} = (0, 0)$

I_s^{-1}, I_m^{-1}, and II_m^{-1} are disjoint regions that exhaust the range of (8); but the range of (8) is the domain of (9). Therefore the above analysis provides a complete description of the single-valued cum multi-valued properties of (9), summarised as follows.

(1) Given any (A, B) in I_s^{-1}, the corresponding value of (r, q) is unique. Thus (9) restricted to I_s^{-1} is single valued and (8) restricted to I_s is one-to-one.

(2) Given any (A, B) in I_m^{-1}, there is a corresponding *set* of (r, q) (that is, a set given by (9)) each element of which satisfies

$$\bar{p}_k = ra_k + qb_k$$

where k is the consumer with positive demand at the given value of (A, B) and $\bar{p}_k$ is a particular value of p_k.

(3) Corresponding to $(A, B) = (0, 0)$ (the sole value of (A, B) in II_m) is the set of (r, q) each element of which satisfies

$$p_i = ra_i + qb_i \qquad (i = 1, \ldots, n)$$

where $p_i \geqslant \tilde{p}_i$ and $\tilde{p}_i$ is the value of p_i beyond which $(A_i, B_i) = (0, 0)$.

The total-expenditure function

Clearly, the multi-valued nature of (9) in regions I_m^{-1} and II_m^{-1} is analogous to that of (13) in regions 1 and 2 of its range, respectively. Then one would expect that *the total-expenditure function (10) is single valued*, which is true and proved as follows.

For a given value of (A, B) in I_s^{-1}, (9) yields a unique value of (r, q). Then the value of R corresponding to (A, B) is also unique, because $R = rA + qB$ and each variable on the right-hand side has a unique value.

Corresponding to a given value of (A, B), say $(\bar{A}, \bar{B})$, in I_m^{-1} is a unique value of p_k, say $\bar{p}_k$, where k is the consumer with positive demand at $(\bar{A}, \bar{B})$, that is, $(\bar{A}, \bar{B}) = (\bar{A}_k, \bar{B}_k) > 0$. The given point also determines unique values of p_i, say $\bar{p}_i$, for all $i \neq k$. However, by hypothesis, (1) yields $0 = \bar{x}_i = f_{1i}(\bar{p}_i)$, all $i \neq k$, and $x_i = 0 \Leftrightarrow (A_i, B_i) = 0$. Therefore R_k is uniquely given by $\bar{p}_k\bar{x}_k$ or, equivalently, by

$$R = R_k = f_{4k}(\bar{A}_k, \bar{B}_k)$$

Corresponding to (A, B) in II_m^{-1}, that is, to $(A, B) = (0, 0)$, $R = 0$ and is therefore unique.

7. Graphical Representation of the Inverse of the Market Demand Function

Just as Figure 13.3 is a portrayal of (8), so it is desired to achieve diagrammatic representation of the inverse function (9). In principle the task is as straightforward as the derivation of Figure 13.2 given in Figure 13.1. In fact, it logically begins with a representation of (13) for each i as in Figure 13.2 but on a unique diagram. The problem is to convert the A_i–B_i plane to the A–B plane. This is done as follows. For a given value of (r, q) the corresponding (unique) values of (A_i, B_i), $(i = 1, \ldots\ n)$ are found on the diagram. Apply vector addition to these values of (A_i, B_i); the result is (A, B), and this point is labelled by the given value of (r, q). This may be performed for all values of (r, q); the result is a geometric representation of (9). Of course, some values of (A_i, B_i) will be associated with multiple values of (r, q). A unique labelling is obtained by converting the diagram to a representation of (10). In that case the domain (A, B) remains unchanged; but each point is identified by the total expenditure R pertaining to it.

While the above analysis is correct, it is too general to answer certain questions of importance in examining market equilibrium. For example, can a sufficiently small neighbourhood be drawn around any given point in the domain of (9) such that no other point in the domain is within that neighbourhood? In other words, is the domain a set of points all disconnected? Or, to take another extreme, is the domain a convex set? The general problem is, clearly, to determine the form of the set of points constituting the domain. This requires a detailed performance of the procedure outlined above. We begin with the case of two consumers ($n = 2$), and then extend the analysis to an arbitrary number of consumers.

7.1 *The case of two consumers*

Even for $n = 2$ we consider two sub-cases. First, we assume that neither (A_j, B_j) nor (A_k, B_k) is zero everywhere in region I_m. Later we remove this assumption.

Case (i) Neither (A_j, B_j) nor (A_k, B_k) zero everywhere in I_m

As in Figure 13.3, (12) is plotted for region 1 and the boundary between regions 1 and 2 for each consumer j and k. In Figure

13.4 representative lines (12) are drawn from the boundaries to the origin. It is assumed that $T_j > T_k$. Hence the steeper set of lines pertains to consumer *j*. As in Figure 13.2, (13) is represented for $i = j, k$ as *OJ* and *OK*, respectively, in Figure 13.5.

The maximum values of (A_j, B_j) and (A_k, B_k), namely, those for $(r, q) = (0, 0)$, are represented by the points *J* and *K* in Figure 13.5. Applying (vectoral) addition to these points, the

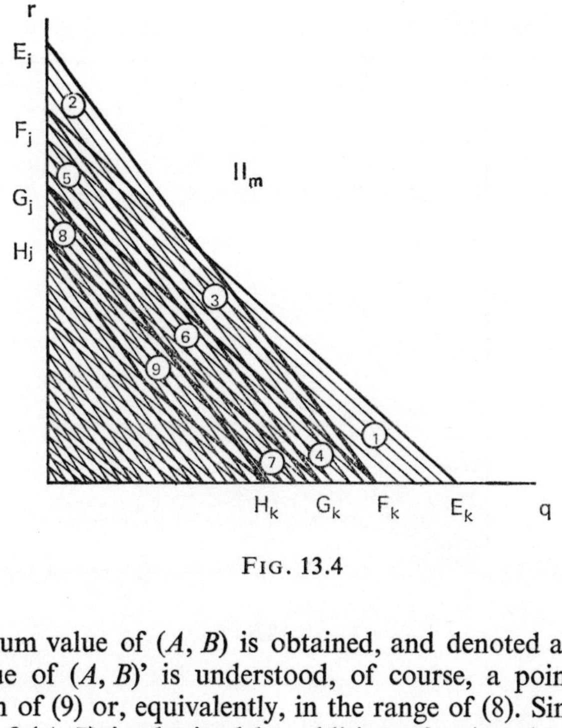

FIG. 13.4

maximum value of (A, B) is obtained, and denoted as *M*. By a 'value of (A, B)' is understood, of course, a point in the domain of (9) or, equivalently, in the range of (8). Since every value of (A, B) is obtained by addition of points (A_j, B_j) and (A_k, B_k), and the latter points are on the lines $0J$ and $0K$, respectively, the domain of (9) is covered by the parallelogram *OJMK*. The latter object is the set of all sums $((A_j, B_j) + (A_k, B_k))$ such that (A_j, B_j) is a point on $0J$ and (A_k, B_k) a point on $0K$. Viewing Figure 13.4, it is clear that it is not true that every line (12) for consumer *j* intersects every line for consumer *k*. In fact, no line for either consumer intersects *every* line of the other consumer. Hence the domain of (9) is not the entire parallelogram *OJMK* but only part of it. The maximum value of (A, B) is M; the minimum value is the origin (0) and applies for (r, q) in region 2 of both consumers. To discover the other points in the domain, a detailed analysis of Figure 13.5 is required.

The dark lines in Figure 13.4 separate I_s and I_m into subregions. These subregions are either triangles or parallelograms and are identified by a number. Also, II_m is demarcated by

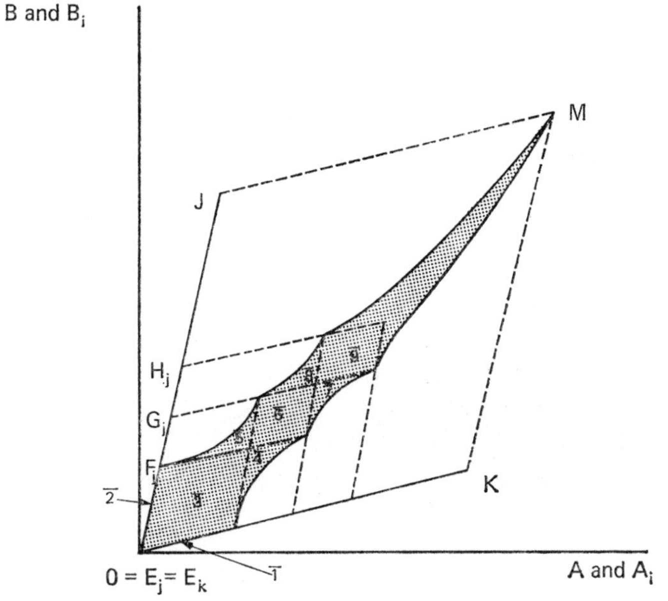

FIG. 13.5

these lines. Each of the dark lines corresponds to a particular value of (A_j, B_j) or (A_k, B_k), as the case may be. These values are represented by appropriately subscripted capital letters which, for convenience, are printed along the vertical axis for consumer j and the horizontal one for consumer k. They are also indicated along the lines $0J$ and $0K$ in Figure 13.5. In this plane E_j and E_k coincide with the origin. The procedure is to map each region or subregion in the r–q plane (Figure 13.4) into the A–B plane (Figure 13.5). The corresponding regions in Figure 13.5 are indicated by the same numbers as in Figure 13.4, but with a bar above. Corresponding to 1 and 2 are the segments E_kF_k and E_jF_j, respectively, in Figure 13.5. Region 3 involves every line (12) corresponding to (A_j, B_j) between E_j and F_j, inclusive, intersecting every line corresponding to (A_k, B_k) between E_k and F_k, inclusive. Thus $\bar{3}$ is the set of all points (including the perimeter) in the parallelogram determined by 0, F_j and F_k. Region 4 consists of intersections of lines E_j to F_j with lines F_k to G_k. However, not all lines E_j to F_j intersect all lines F_k to G_k. F_j alone does that; E_j, on the other hand, intersects only F_k. There is a continuous increase in the lines (A_k, B_k) intersected as (A_j, B_j) moves from E_j to F_j. (Actually, the intersections of F_k with the E_j to F_j lines have already been counted in $\bar{3}$; but it clearly is irrelevant whether or not the parallelogram $\bar{3}$ is considered net of the outer half of its perimeter or, in general, to what regions boundary (dark) lines are assigned.) Addition of the appropriate points, thus determined, on $0J$ and $0K$ produces region $\bar{4}$. Region $\bar{5}$ is obtained analogously. Region $\bar{6}$ is the intersection of all lines F_j to G_j with all lines F_k to G_k. In Figure 13.5 this corresponds to the parallelogram with vertices $(F_j + F_k)$, $(G_j + F_k)$, $(G_j + G_k)$ and $(F_j + G_k)$. Regions $\bar{7}$, $\bar{8}$ and $\bar{9}$ are determined precisely analogously to regions $\bar{4}$, $\bar{5}$ and $\bar{6}$, respectively; in the above description the intervals F_j to G_j and F_k to G_k are replaced by G_j to H_j and G_k to H_k, respectively. The procedure of mapping triangles and parallelograms in the r–q plane into semi-triangles (that is, three-sided objects, at least two sides of which are straight lines) and parallelograms, respectively, in the A–B plane may be continued indefinitely. Point M will be reached as a limit. Thus the domain of (9) is the shaded area in Figure 13.5. Concerning the semi-triangles, a comment should be made about the side opposite the joint vertex of two parallelograms (called the 'third side'). In the diagram this side is drawn as a curved line convex to the vertex. Alternatively, the side may be a curve concave to the vertex or even a straight line. However, it must be downward-sloping with respect to that vertex (as already demonstrated), and the precise form is one of the three outlined and is identical for all semi-triangles. The latter circumstances are reflections of the fact that all triangular regions in the r–q plane are essentially of the same nature as regards the set of intersections of the j and k lines.

In summary, the domain of (9) is entirely within the parallelogram *OJMK*, includes the points 0 and *M*, and consists of a set of points that is closed and everywhere dense within (and on) its boundary. There are no discontinuities or gaps in the set constituting the domain. It is a connected set with minimum and maximum values of 0 and *M*, respectively. However, it is not necessarily a convex set.

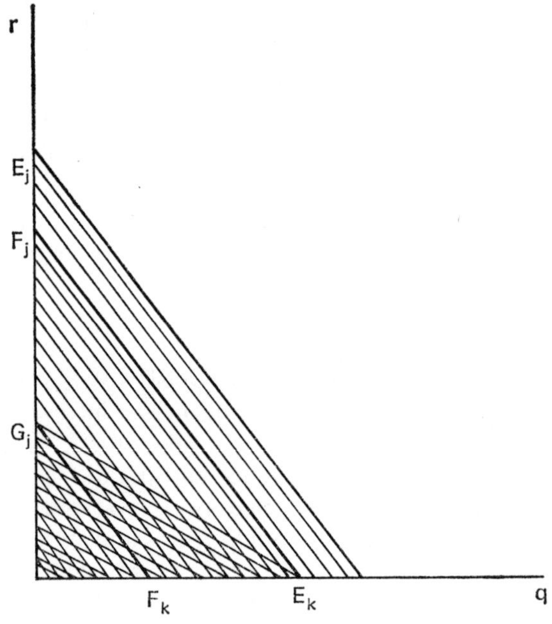

FIG. 13.6

Case (*ii*) (A_j, B_j) *and* (A_k, B_k) *arbitrary in* I_m

The assumption that both (A_j, B_j) and (A_k, B_k) have positive values in I_m may now be dropped. Suppose, for example, that (A_k, B_k) is zero everywhere in I_m. Then Figure 13.6 replaces Figure 13.4. The mapping from the *r–q* plane to the *A–B* plane may be performed in a manner similar to that outlined in detail above, that is, as a transformation of parallelograms and triangles into parallelograms and semi-triangles. Alternatively, the domain of (9) may be obtained by viewing it as the resultant of the intersection of successive individual *j* lines with successive *sets* of *k* lines. In the *A–B* plane (Figure 13.7) this corresponds to marking off points along each line parallel to $0K$ in the parallelogram *OJMK*. The only points on the lines from 0 to F_j constitute the segment $0F_j$ ($= E_jF_j$) itself. Then the relevant points on the parallel lines are intervals rather than single points until *M* is reached. The point set constituting the domain is the shaded area in Figure 13.7. It remains true that the domain is a

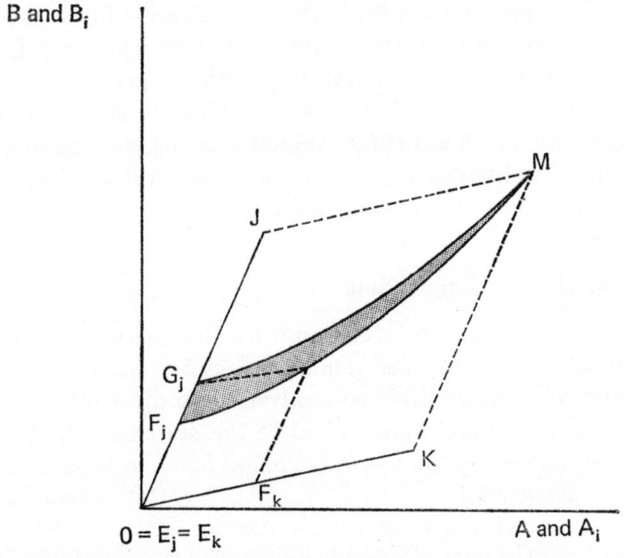

FIG. 13.7

connected set with minimum and maximum values of 0 and *M*, respectively. However, it includes no point (apart from 0) on the line $0K$.

7.2 *The case of n consumers*

The deductions regarding the shape of the mapping on the *A–B* plane remain valid for an arbitrary number of consumers. *The minimum value of the point set constituting the domain of the inverse of the market demand function is the origin (0); the maximum value (M) is calculated as the sum of all vectors 0I, I varying with i. A connected set joins the minimum and maximum points. This set is everywhere dense within (and on) its boundary. It contains no discontinuities or gaps.* The basic reason for these properties is that the individual demand functions (1), hence (6), are themselves continuous. In particular, they are continuous in the positive neighbourhood of $x_i = 0$ (or $(A_i, B_i) = (0, 0)$). It is this property which preserves the connectedness of the domain as (r, q) is altered to induce, on the part of a particular consumer, demand that is positive for the first time.

This completes the detailed description of the representation of the inverse demand function (9) in the A–B plane. Although the discussion has centred on the shape of the *domain* of (9), it should be recalled that every point on the domain is labelled by the corresponding set of values of (r, q). This set is not unary for all points, i.e. (9) is not single valued everywhere. However, if the labelling is changed to the corresponding value of R, the total-expenditure function (10) is obtained, and it is single valued.

8. Determination of Equilibrium

Multi-dimensional pricing according to the attributes of a product results in a market demand function that is well-behaved and quite susceptible to analysis. The most important results of this paper are summarised in the statement that *the domain of the inverse of the market demand function is an everywhere-dense connected set with a unique total expenditure corresponding to any given point in the domain.* These properties give rise to the existence of equilibrium under the usual market structures.

The cost conditions for the suppliers of the product may involve individual costs per unit of production of each attribute (costs which may be zero) and joint (non-separable) costs of producing the attributes 'together'. If the attributes are produced in unvarying proportions, the 'supply curve' (i.e. the industry total-cost curve) is represented by a straight line through the origin with slope equal to the 'production trade-off' of the attributes. This line may be plotted in Figures 13.2, 13.5, or 13.7 above.

Then two cases may be distinguished. The 'supply curve' may or may not intersect the inverse of the market demand function. If this intersection occurs, the determination of the equilibrium output (A, B) and price (r, q) becomes a simple matter. Under pure competition, for example, the *maximum* (A, B) in the intersection constitutes the point of supply, unless such a point involves a negative profit for the marginal supplier. In the latter circumstances, the equilibrium point is the maximum among those points in the intersection for which this profit is non-negative. Under pure monopoly, in contrast, the supplier selects as the amount of his output that point (A, B) in the intersection which maximises his profit.

What happens in the case of a null intersection of the 'supply curve' and the inverse of the market demand function? Then one of the attributes is redundant, and under pure competition its price falls to zero. We recall that M is the point of maximum (A, B) in the domain of the inverse of the market demand function. If M yields a non-negative profit for the marginal supplier, it is the equilibrium point. If a negative profit is obtained, then supply is given by the point in the domain which involves maximum output, subject to non-negative profit for the marginal supplier. Under *either* equilibrium, suppliers obtain revenue from only the non-redundant attribute, its price given by the applicable element in the range of the inverse of the market demand function.

A null intersection under monopoly also gives a determinate solution. We are assuming that the monopolist throws onto the market the entirety of his production, resulting now in a zero price for the redundant attribute. Then he selects that point in the domain which maximises his profit, all of which emanates from the non-redundant attribute. The monopolist would be able to obtain a greater profit, however, by hoarding part of his output of the redundant attribute, so that he obtains a positive price for it. Yet he might refrain from doing so to avoid a loss in goodwill.

Thus far we have assumed that there is a fixed 'production trade-off' of the attributes. If this assumption is relaxed, the above analysis still holds. The 'supply curve' is represented no longer by a straight line but rather by a greater expanse. If the attributes can be produced in any combination at all, then the intersection of the 'supply curve' and the inverse of the market demand function becomes that inverse itself, and the analysis then proceeds as above.

Indivisibilities in production would give rise to further complications. Nevertheless, points of equilibrium would exist under both purely-competitive and monopolistic market structures.[3]

References

[1] BAUMOL, WILLIAM J., 'Calculation of Optimal Product and Retailer Characteristics: The Abstract Product Approach', *Journal of Political Economy*, LXXV (5) (October 1967) 674–85.

[2] CREW, MICHAEL A., 'The Optimality of Pure Competition in the Capacity Problem: Further Comment', *Quarterly Journal of Economics*, LXXXIII (2) (May 1969) 341–3.

[3] LANCASTER, KELVIN J., 'A New Approach to Consumer Theory', *Journal of Political Economy*, LXXIV (2) (April 1966) 132–57.

[4] OFFICER, LAWRENCE H., 'The Optimality of Pure Competition in the Capacity Problem', *Quarterly Journal of Economics*, LXXX (4) (November 1966) 647–51.

[5] SIMMONDS, KENNETH, 'Making Micro-Economics Multi-Dimensional', *Journal of Industrial Economics*, XVII (1) (November 1968) 18–28.

[3] For consideration of production indivisibilities in the case where the *domain* of the inverse of the market demand function can be treated as one-dimensional (i.e. $A = B$, in the terminology of the present paper), see Crew [2] and Officer [4].

Appendix: Bibliography of Jan Tinbergen

MANY of Jan Tinbergen's articles were published in Dutch, German, Danish, French and other languages. The selected bibliography in this Festschrift covers only Tinbergen's work originally published in English and some translations from other languages into English. This means that a large number of his important publications will not be listed. The reader can find an extensive bibliography of Jan Tinbergen in his *Selected Papers*, edited by L. H. Klaassen, L. M. Koyck and H. J. Witteveen (Amsterdam: North-Holland Publishing Co., 1959). A short supplement to that bibliography was published in *De Economist*, CVII (1959) 798–9, written by J. B. D. Derksen. Finally, J. P. Pronk wrote the most up-to-date bibliography of Jan Tinbergen, covering the period 1959–69 in *De Economist*, CXVIII (1970) 156–73. The selected bibliography presented here is ordered chronologically and includes the following areas: international trade and finance, long-term economic development and planning, econometrics and economic theory. The section on economic theory also includes publications on the theory of economic policy and miscellaneous topics in economics.

1. International Trade

[1] *International Economic Co-operation*, (Amsterdam: Elsevier Economische Bibliotheek, 1945). Translated into English by P. H. Breitenstein and E. Inglis Arkell.

[2] *Some Remarks on the Problem of Dollar Scarcity*, (Washington: Congress Econometric Society, 1946).

[3] 'Unstable Equilibria in the Balance of Payments', in: *Economic Research and the Development of Economic Science and Public Policy*, (New York, 1946).

[4] International Economic Co-operation, *Erasmus Speculum Scientiarum*, Aarau, Switzerland, I, 1 (1947).

[5] 'The Equalization of Factor Prices between Free-Trade Areas', *Metroeconomica*, I, (April 1949) 38–47.

[6] 'Long-Term Foreign Trade Elasticities', *Metroeconomica*, I, (December 1949) 174–85.

[7] 'Some Remarks on the Problem of Dollar Scarcity', *Econometrica*, XVII, (July 1949) Supplement 73–97.

[8] 'The Possibility of Price and Exchange Adaptation', in: *Tracing a New International Balance*, (Leiden: Stenfert Kroese, 1950).

[9] 'On the Theory of Economic Integration', *Les Cahiers de Bruges*, 4 (1952) 292–303.

[10] 'The Relation between Internal Inflation and the Balance of Payments', *Banca Nazionale del Lavoro Quarterly Review*, V, (1952) 187–94.

[11] TINBERGEN, J. and VAN DER WERFF, H. M. A. 'Four Alternative Policies to Restore the Balance of Payments Equilibrium: A Comment and an Extension', *Econometrica*, XXI, (February 1953) 332–5.

[12] 'Customs Unions: Influence of Their Size on Their Effect,' *Zeitschrift für die Gesamte Staatswissenschaft*, CXIII, (1957) 404–14.

[13] 'An International Economic Policy', *Indian Journal of Economics*, XXXVIII, (1957) 11–16.

[14] 'Heavy Industry in the Latin American Common Market', *Economic Bulletin for Latin America*, V, (January 1960) 1–5.

[15] 'The Impact of the European Economic Community on Third Countries', in: *Sciences Humaines et Intégration Européenne*, (Leiden: A. W. Sythoff, 1960), 386–98.

[16] TINBERGEN, J., RIJKEN VAN OLST, H., HARTOG, F. *et al.*, *Shaping the World Economy: Suggestions for an International Economic Policy*, (New York: The Twentieth Century Fund, 1962).

[17] 'The European Economic Community: Conservative or Progressive?', in *Wicksell Lectures 1963*. (Stockholm/Gøteborg/Uppsala: Almqvist and Wiksell, 1963), 38ff.

[18] *Lessons from the Past*, (Amsterdam: Elsevier, 1963).

[19] TINBERGEN, J., HART, A. G. and KALDOR, N. *The Case for an International Commodity Reserve Currency;* A memorandum submitted to the United Nations Conference on Trade and Development, 1964.

[20] 'The Evolution in Communist Views on International Trade', *World Justice*, VI, (January 1964) 5–8.

[21] *International Economic Integration*, 2nd revised edition, (Amsterdam/New York: Elsevier, 1965).

[22] 'International, National Regional and Local Industries', in *Trade, Growth and the Balance of Payments; Essays in Honor of Gottfried Haberler on the Occasion of his 65th Birthday*, ed. by R. E. Caves, H. G. Johnson and P. B. Kenen, (Amsterdam: North-Holland, 1965), 116–25.

[23] 'Trade between Western and Communist Countries', *Cronache Economiche della CCIA di Torino*, (1965) 266–7.

[24] TINBERGEN, J. *et al. Terms of Trade and the Concept of Import Purchasing Power of the Exports of Developing Countries;* UNCTAD, Trade and Development Board, Permanent Subcommittee on Commodities, First Session (TB/BIC 1/PSC/5), Geneva, 1966.

[25] 'Balance of Payments and Project Appraisal', *Development Planning Problems and Techniques Series*, No. 1, African Institute for Economic Development and Planning, 1967, 5–10.

[26] 'Shaping the World Economy', in: *World Peace Through World Economy*, Youth and Student Division of the World Association of World Federalists, 6th International Study Conference, (Assen, Netherlands: Van Gorcum, 1968).

2. Long-Term Economic Development and Economic Planning

[1] 'Central Planning in the Netherlands', *Review of Economic Studies*, XV, (1947/48) 70–7.

[2] 'The Netherlands' Central Economic Plan for 1947' *Revue Suisse d'Economie Politique et de Statistique*, LXXXIII (January 1947) 19–29.

[3] 'Problems of Central Economic Planning in the Netherlands', *National Økonomisk Tidskrift*, LXXXV, (1947) 96ff.

[4] 'Government Budget and Central Economic Plan', *Public Finance: Openbare Financiën*, XLII, (March 1949) 195–205.

[5] 'Planning for Viability', *The Way Ahead*, II (1949) 38–61.

[6] 'Capital Formation and the Five-Year Plan', *Indian Economic Journal*, I (January 1953) 1–5.

[7] 'Problems Concerning India's Second Five-Year Plan', *Public Finance: Openbare Financiën*, XI, (February 1956) 103–10.

[8] The appraisal of Road Construction, two Calculation Schemes', *Review of Economics and Statistics*, xxxix, (August 1957) 241–9.

[9] 'The Optimum Choice of Technology', *Pakistan Economic Journal*, vii, (February 1957) 1–7.

[10] 'The Use of a Short-Term Econometric Model for Indian Economic Policy', *Sankhyā; The Indian Journal of Statistics*, xvii, (April 1957) 337–44.

[11] 'Choice of Technology in Industrial Planning', *Industrialization and Productivity; Bulletin of the United Nations*, i, (January 1958) 24–33.

[12] 'International Co-ordination of Stabilization and Development Policies', *Kyklos*, xii, (March 1959) 283–9.

[13] 'Problems of Planning Economic Policy', *UNESCO International Social Science Journal*, xi, (March 1959) 351–60.

[14] 'Fundamental and Derived Aims of Economic Development', *The Punjab University Economist*, i, (February 1960) 1–6.

[15] *Programming Techniques for Economic Development*, (Co-author) (Bangkok: U.N. Economic Commission for Asia and the Far East, 1960).

[16] 'The Appraisal of Investment Projects: the Semi-Input-Output Method', *Industrial India*, 1961, 25–6.

[17] 'Development Theory, and Econometrist's View', in: *Money, Growth and Methodology, and Other Essays in Economics in Honor of Johan Åkerman*, ed. by H. Hegeland, (Lund: Gleerup, 1961, 49–58).

[18] Tinbergen, J. and Bos, H. C. 'The Global Demand for Higher and Secondary Education in the Underdeveloped Countries in the Next Decade', *Policy Conference on Economic Growth and Investment Education;* Washington, D.C., (O.E.C.D., 1961), Vol. iii.

[19] 'The Spatial Dispersion of Production: A Hypothesis', *Schweizerische Zeitschrift für Volkswirtschaft und Statistik*, xcvii, (April 1961) 1–8.

[20] 'Again – The Development Issue', *The Ecumenical Review*, xix, (February 1962) 226–8.

[21] 'Planning in Stages', *Statsøkonomisk Tidskrift*, (January 1962) 1–20.

[22] TINBERGEN, J. and CORREA, H. 'Quantitative Adaptation of Education to Accelerated Growth' *Kyklos*, xv, (April 1962) 768–86.

[23] TINBERGEN, J. and BOS, H. C. 'The Financing of Higher Education in Africa', *The Development of Higher Education in Africa*, Report of the Conference on the Development of Higher Education in Africa, Tananarive, 3–12 September 1962. (Paris: UNESCO, 1963, 155–212).

[24] 'Project Criteria', in: *Economic Planning*, ed. by L. J. Zimmerman, (The Hague: Mouten, 1963, 7–19).

[25] 'Projections of Economic Data in Development Planning' *Planning for Economic Development in the Caribbean*, (Caribbean Organization, Hato Rey, Puerto Rico, 1963), 26–51.

[26] 'A World Development Policy', *World, Nations and Groups in Development*, (The Hague: Mouten, 1963), 39–55.

[27] *Central Planning*, (New Haven/London: Yale University Press 1964), 1964.

[28] *Development Planning*, (New York, Toronto: McGraw-Hill, 1966).

[29] *Development Planning: The Sector Phase, with Different Gestation Periods* (Nederlands Economisch Instituut, Publication 26/64, Rotterdam, 1964).

[30] 'Educational Assessments', *Economic and Social Aspect of Educational Planning*, (UNESCO, Paris, 1964, 165–222).

[31] *Essays in Regional and World Planning*, (New Delhi: National Council of Applied Economic Research, 1964).

[32] TINBERGEN, J. and BOS, H. C. 'A Planning Model for the Educational Requirements of Economic Development', *The Residual Factor and Economic Growth*, (Paris: O.E.C.D., 1964, 147–69).

[33] 'Possibilities for Application of Operational Research to Problems of Development', *Management Science*, x, (February 1963) 193–6.

[34] 'Project Appraisal: A Traditional Approach', *Essays on Econometrics and Planning, Presented to Professor P. C. Mahalanobis on the Occasion of his 70th Birthday*. (Calcutta: Pergamon, 1964), 295–300.

[35] 'Reply', to T. Balogh, 'Education and Economic Growth', *Kyklos*, xvii, (February 1964) 261–75.

[36] 'Discussion on the Organization of Coexistence', *Review of International Affairs*, XVI, (October 1965) 13–14.

[37] 'Economic Development and Investment Indivisibilities', *Problems of Economic Dynamics and Planning; Essays in Honor of Michal Kalecki*, ed. T. Kowalik, (Warsaw: P.W.N. Polish Scientific, 1965), 455–67.

[38] 'The Economic Framework of Regional Planning', *Semaine d'Etude sur le Rôle de l'Analyse Econométrique dans la Formulation de Plans de Développement*, Pontificiae Academiae Scientarium, Scripta Varia, No. 28, (Rome, 1965), 1233–64.

[39] 'Ideologies and Scientific Development: The Optimal Order', *Review of International Affairs*, XVI, (October 1965) 6–7.

[40] 'Improving International Development Policies', *Review of International Affairs*, XVI, (September 1965) 10–12.

[41] 'Simple Devices for Development Planning', in: *Problems in Economic Development*, ed. by E. A. G. Robinson. (London/New York: Macmillan, 1965).

[42] *Some Principles of Regional Planning*, (Rotterdam: Nederlands Economisch Instituut, Publication 29/65), 1965.

[43] 'The Concept of Unbalanced Growth', in: *Economic Development: Issues and Policies*, Dr P. S. Lokanathan 72nd Birthday, Commemoration Volume, ed. P. H. Butani and P. Singh. (Bombay 1966) 14–17.

[44] 'Economic Growth Plans and Their Impact on Business Management', *United Malayan Banking Corporation Economic Review*, XI, (February 1966) 20–6.

[45] 'International Economic Planning', *Daedalus Journal of the American Academy of Arts and Sciences*, 1966 issue: 'Conditions of World Order', 530–57.

[46] 'Some Refinements of the Semi-Input-Output Method', *Pakistan Development Review*, VI, (February 1966) 243–247.

[47] 'Concluding Remarks', in: *Towards a Strategy for Development Co-operation*, ed. H. B. Chenery *et al.* (Rotterdam: Rotterdam University Press, 1967), 93–101.

[48] 'The Hierarchy Model of the Size Distribution of Centers', *Regional Science Association: Papers*, XX, (1967) 65–68.

[49] 'Links between National Planning and Town and Country Planning', paper presented at the *Symposium on Urbanization of the International Union of Local Authorities*, (The Hague, 1967).
[50] 'Planning in the Common Market', *Sosialøkonomen*, XXI, (June 1967) 14–16.
[51] 'Chenery: Efficient Development Research', *Economisch Statistische Berichten*, LIII, (November 1968) 1013–14.
[52] 'Myrdal's Asian Drama', *Pakistan Development Review*, VIII, (April 1968) 618–25.
[53] 'The Optimal International Division of Labour', *Acta Oeconomica Academiae Scientarium Hungaricae*, III, (March 1968) 257–82.
[54] 'Optimalization – of What?' *Co-Existence*, V, (1968) 1–5.
[55] TINBERGEN, J. and BOUWMEESTER, J. 'The Role of Social Security as Seen by the Development Planner', in: *The Role of Social Security in Economic Development*, ed. E. M. Kassalow. (Washington, 1968), 39–50.
[56] 'The Significance of Science for the Developing Countries', *Higher Education and Research in the Netherlands*, XII, (March 1968) 24–9.
[57] 'Similarities and Differences between the Social Problem and the Development Problem', *Mens en Maatschappij*, XLIII, (January 1968) 120–7.
[58] 'Wanted: A World Development Plan', *International Organization*, XXII, (January 1968) 417–31.
[59] *Gunnar Myrdal on Planning Models*, U.N. Asian Institute for Economic Development and Planning, Institute Monograph No. 11, (Bangkok, 1969), 13ff.

3. Econometrics

[1] *An Econometric Approach to Business Cycles Problems*, (Paris: Hermann and Cie, 1937).
[2] 'Statistical Evidence on the Acceleration Principle', *Economica*, New Series v (1938) 164–76.
[3] *Business Cycles in the United States of America, 1919–1932*, (Geneva: League of Nations, 1939).
[4] 'Econometric Business Cycle Research', *Review of Economic Studies*, (1939/40) 73–90.

[5] *A Method and its Application to Investment Activity*, (Geneva: League of Nations, 1939).

[6] TINBERGEN, J. and DE WOLFF, P. 'A Simplified model of the Causation of Technological Unemployment', *Econometrica*, VII, (July 1939) 193–207.

[7] 'An Acceleration Principle for Commodity Stockholding and a Short Cycle Resulting from It', in: *Studies in Mathematical Economics and Econometrics*, ed. by Lange *et al.*, (Chicago: University of Chicago Press, 1942), 255–267.

[8] 'Some Measurements of Elasticities of Substitution', *Review of Economics and Statistics*, XXVIII, (August 1946) 109–16.

[9] 'The Use of Correlation Analysis in Economic Research', *Ekonomisk Tidskrift*, XLIX, (March 1947) 173–92.

[10] TINBERGEN, J. and DERKSEN, J. B. D. 'Recent Experiments in Social Accounting: Flexible and Dynamic Budgets', in: The Econometric Society Meeting, September 1947, Washington, 1949.

[11] *Business Cycles in the United Kingdom, 1870–1914*, (Amsterdam: North-Holland, 1951).

[12] 'Schumpeter and Quantitative Research in Economics', *Review of Economics and Statistics*, XXXIII, (May 1951) 111–19.

[13] 'Some Neglected Points in Demand Research', *Metroeconomica*, III, (February 1951) 49–54.

[14] 'Comments' on: ORCUTT, GUY H. 'Toward Partial Redirection of Econometrics', *Review of Economics and Statistics*, XXXIV, (March 1952) 205ff.

[15] 'Import and Export Elasticities: Some Remarks', *International Statistical Institute, Bulletin*, XXXIII, (1953) 215–26.

[16] 'The Functions of Mathematical Treatment: Mathematics in Economics, Discussion of Mr. Novicks' Article', *Review of Economics and Statistics*, XXXVI, (November 1954) 365–9.

[17] 'Quantitative Economics in the Netherlands Model Building for Economic Policy', *Higher Education and Research in the Netherlands*, II, (March 1958) 3–7.

4. Economic Theory (and Miscellaneous)

[1] 'Annual Survey of Significant Developments in General Economic Theory', *Econometrica*, II, (1934) 13–36.
[2] 'On the Theory of Business Cycle Control', *Econometrica*, VI, (January 1938) 22–39.
[3] 'The Dynamics of Share-Price Formation', *Review of Economics and Statistics*, XXI, (November 1939) 153–60.
[4] 'On a Method of Statistical Business Cycle Research: A Reply', *The Economic Journal*, L, (March 1940) 141–54.
[5] 'Unstable and Indifferent Equilibria in Economic Systems', *Revue de l'Institut International de Statistique*, IX, (1941) 36–50.
[6] 'Critical Remarks on Some Business Cycle Theories', *Econometrica*, X, (April 1942) 129–46.
[7] 'Does Consumption Lag Behind Incomes?', *Review of Economics and Statistics*, XXIV, (February 1942) 1–8.
[8] 'Professor Douglas' Production Function', *Revue de l'Institut International de Statistique*, X, (1942) 37–48.
[9] 'Some Problems in the Explanation of Interest Rates', *Quarterly Journal of Economics*, LXI, (1947) 397–438.
[10] 'The Reformulation of Current Business Cycle Theories as Refutable Hypotheses', in: *Conference on Business Cycles*, National Bureau of Economic Research, 1949.
[11] 'Economic Policy in the Netherlands', *Statsøkonomisk Tidsskrift*, LXIV, (1950) 70–80.
[12] *On the Theory of Economic Policy*, (Amsterdam: North-Holland, 1952).
[13] 'The Influence of Productivity on Economic Welfare', *The Economic Journal*, LXII, (1952) 68–86.
[14] 'Financing Social Insurance out of Premiums or out of Income Tax', *Archive of Economic and Social Sciences*, XXXII, (1952) 71–7.
[15] 'Efficiency and Future of Economic Research', *Kyklos*, V, (April 1952) 309–19.
[16] *Centralization and Decentralization in Economic Policy*, (Amsterdam: North-Holland, 1954).
[17] *Economic Policy: Principles and Design*, (Amsterdam: North-Holland, 1956).

[18] 'On the Theory of Income Distribution', *Weltwirtschaftliches Archiv*, LXXVII, (January 1956) 10–31.
[19] 'The Optimum Rate of Savings', *The Economic Journal*, LXVI, (1956) 603–9.
[20] TINBERGEN, J. *et al.* 'Comments on the Economics of Governor Stevenson's Program Paper: Where is the Money Coming From?', *Review of Economics and Statistics*, (May 1957) 134–42.
[21] 'Welfare Economics and Income Distribution', *American Economic Review, Papers and Proceedings*, XLVII, (February 1957) 490–503.
[22] 'The Economic Principles for an Optimum Use of Space', *Les Cahiers de Bruges*, XI, (1958) 15–18.
[23] 'Should the Income Tax be Among the Means of Economic Policy?', *Festskrift til Frederick Zeuthen*, (København, 1958), 351–62.
[24] *Selected Papers*, (Amsterdam: North-Holland, 1959).
[25] 'The Theory of the Optimum Regime', *Selected Papers*, (Amsterdam: North Holland, 1959, 264–304).
[26] 'Economic Models of the Explanation of Inflation', in: *Stabile Preise in Wachsender Wirtschaft. Erich Schneider zum 60 Geburtstag*, ed. by G. Bomback, (Tübingen: J. C. B. Mohr, 1960, 115–24).
[27] 'Optimum Savings and Utility Maximization over Time', *Econometrica*, XXVIII, (February 1960) 481–90.
[28] TINBERGEN, J. and BOS, H. C. *Mathematical Models of Economic Growth*, (New York: McGraw-Hill, 1962).
[29] 'Do Communist and Free Societies Show a Converging Pattern?', *Soviet Studies*, XII, (April 1961) 333–41.
[30] 'The Significance of Welfare Economics for Socialism', *On Political Economy and Econometrics, Essays in Honour of Oskar Lange*, (Warsaw: P.W.N. Polish Scientific Publishers, 1965).
[31] 'On the Optimal Social Order and a World Economic Policy', (A discussion with Professor L. Leontiev), *Oost-West*, V, (October 1966) 242–4.
[32] TINBERGEN, J. and BOS, H. C. 'A Planning Model for the Educational Requirements of Economic Development', *The Residual Factor and Economic Growth*, (Paris: O.E.C.D., 1964, 147–69).

[33] 'A Model for a Flow of Funds Analysis of an Open Country', in *Essays in Honour of Marco Fano*, (Padova, 1966), 688–92.

[34] 'Some Suggestions on a Modern Theory of the Optimum Regime', in *Socialism, Capitalism and Economic Growth, Essays Presented to Maurice Dobb*, ed. by C. H. Feinstein, (London: Cambridge University Press, 1967), 125–32.

[35] TINBERGEN, J., LINNEMANN, H. and PRONK, J. P. 'Convergence of Economic Systems in East and West', in *Disarmament and World Economic Interdependence*, ed. by E. Benoit, (Oslo: Universitestsforlaget, 1967), 246–60.

[36] 'A Few Comments on Professor Lev Leontiev's Answer', *Oost-West*, VI, (May 1967) 49ff.

[37] 'Development Strategy and Welfare Economics', *Co-Existence*, VI, (July 1969) 119–26.

[38] 'Future Relations Between the Countries of Eastern and Western Europe', *Oost-West*, VIII, (May 1969) 165–6.

[39] 'Ideology and Coexistence', *Review of International Affairs*, XX, (1969) 1–2.

Index